Cultivating Critical Language Awareness in the Writing Classroom

This book introduces Critical Language Awareness (CLA) Pedagogy as a robust and research-grounded framework to engage and support students in critical examinations of language, identity, privilege, and power.

Starting with an accessible introduction to CLA, chapters cover key topics—including World Englishes, linguistic prejudice, news media literacy, inclusive language practices, and more—in an inviting and thought-provoking way to promote reflection and analysis. Part I provides an overview of the foundations of CLA pedagogy, while Part II highlights four instructional pathways for CLA pedagogy: Sociolinguistics, Critical Academic Literacies, Media/Discourse Analysis, and Communicating Across Difference. Each chapter is structured around Essential Questions and Transferrable Skills, and includes three thematic learning sequences. Part III offers tools and guidance for tailoring CLA pedagogy to the reader's own teaching context and to students' individual needs.

The volume's wealth of resources and activities are a pedagogical toolkit for supporting and embracing linguistic diversity in the classroom. The cohesive framework, concrete strategies, engaging activities, and guiding questions in this volume allow readers to come away with not only a deeper understanding of CLA, but also a clear roadmap for implementing CLA in the classroom.

Synthesizing relevant research from educational linguistics and writing studies, this book is ideal for courses in English/literacy education, college composition, L2 writing instruction, and educational linguistics.

Shawna Shapiro is Associate Professor of Writing and Linguistics at Middlebury College, USA.

Support Material

Some of the tools discussed and displayed in this book are also available for download on the Routledge website.

You can access these downloads by visiting www.routledge.com/ 9780367767402. Click on the tab that says "Support Material" and select the files to view or download to your computer.

The resources from the book that are also available online include:

- Access to an external online Hub (http://clacollective.org/), with additional classroom materials and other resources
- Examples of syllabi from courses referenced in the book
- A selection of activities, tasks, and assignments from each chapter
- Samples of student work

Cultivating Critical Language Awareness in the Writing Classroom

Shawna Shapiro

Routledge
Taylor & Francis Group

NEW YORK AND LONDON

Cover image: © Getty Images

First published 2022
by Routledge
605 Third Avenue, New York, NY 10158

and by Routledge
2 Park Square, Milton Park, Abingdon, Oxon, OX14 4RN

Routledge is an imprint of the Taylor & Francis Group, an informa business

© 2022 Shawna Shapiro

The right of Shawna Shapiro to be identified as author of this work has been asserted in accordance with sections 77 and 78 of the Copyright, Designs and Patents Act 1988.

Library of Congress Cataloging-in-Publication Data
A catalog record for this book has been requested

ISBN: 978-0-367-77520-9 (hbk)
ISBN: 978-0-367-76740-2 (pbk)
ISBN: 978-1-003-17175-1 (ebk)

DOI: 10.4324/9781003171751

Typeset in Goudy
by Apex CoVantage, LLC

Access the Support Material: www.routledge.com/9780367767402

For Garrett, Daniel, and Michael, whose love of words and language play is just one of the many delights they bring to my life each day.

Table of Contents

List of Figures

List of Tables

Author Biography

Shawna Shapiro is an associate professor of writing and linguistics at Middlebury College who also teaches courses in teacher education. Prior to her work in higher education, she taught ESOL, English language arts, and social studies to middle and high school students, including through a Spanish immersion program. Shapiro's current research focuses on the transition to higher education for immigrant and refugee students, and on innovative approaches to working with multilingual/L2 writers. Her work has appeared in many peer-reviewed journals, including *Research in the Teaching of English*, *Equity & Excellence in Education*, *TESOL Quarterly*, *Composition Studies*, and *Journal of Language, Identity & Education*. Her first co-authored book was entitled *Fostering International Student Success in Higher Education* (2014). Her second book, a co-edited collection entitled *Educating Refugee-background Students: Critical Issues and Dynamic Contexts*, was published in 2018. She has also written for public audiences, including pieces with *Inside Higher Ed* and *The Conversation*, and has contributed to a number of initiatives aimed at improving educational equity for English Learners in her local school district.

Acknowledgements

This book is the result of more than a decade's worth of teaching, research, and reflection, much of which would have been impossible without the inspiration and support from others.

First, I would like to thank the students at Middlebury College I have had the privilege of working with over the past 12 years. Your passion for learning and vibrant curiosity about language have fueled my teaching and scholarship, bringing so much joy to my professional life! I am particularly grateful to the students who have allowed me to share excerpts from their work here and online. Your voices enrich this book in so many ways! I also want to thank the students at Lake Champlain Waldorf School, who gave me the opportunity to adapt some of the material in this book for middle and high school levels. Y'all impressed me so much!

I would also like to thank my colleagues at Middlebury College—in particular, those in the Writing & Rhetoric Program, who have encouraged my pedagogical experimentation with CLA Pedagogy. Thank you, Genie Giaimo, James Chase Sanchez, Hector Vila, and Catharine Wright, for all your encouragement along the way. I also appreciate the learning and mentorship I received from my two emeritus colleagues Mary Ellen Bertolini and Kathy Skubikowski. My colleagues in the Linguistics Program have also supported this work in many ways, including by being open to and encouraging of CLA-oriented courses and events. I wish to recognize Sayaka Abe in particular, who helped to shape my thinking on intersections between CLA, linguistics research, and global citizenship.

I am also incredibly grateful to the members of my CLA reading group, who provided thoughtful feedback and brilliant suggestions on drafts, and expanded my knowledge about pedagogical applications by sharing their own examples and resources. This volume is so much richer as a result of our conversations! Thank you DaMonique Ballou, Jessica Bannon, Kristen di Gennaro, Allison Ellsworth, Whitney Gegg-Harrison, Erika I-Tremblay, Joanna Johnson, Kathleen Turner Ledgerwood, Andrea Lunsford, Leah Metzger, Greer Murphy, Jay Peters, Josie Rose Portz, Malavika Shetty, Stella Wang, and Maria Zlateva. I would not have connected with this group of people without attending an online dialogue event between Asao Inoue and Erec Smith, coordinated by Matthew Abraham, so—thanks, guys!

A number of other people provided feedback on chapter drafts from this manuscript, including folks with K-12 and/or TESOL experience, who helped to ensure that the chapters are inclusive of teachers working in those contexts. These include Anna Bradshaw Kelsey DeCamillis, Kate Donley, James Dyer, Michelle Medved, and Amie Van Horn-Gabel. There are many other people whose enthusiasm and expertise shaped this project in its early phases, including Karen Batten, Raichle Farrelly, Eunjeong Lee, Lisa Leopold, Brooke Schreiber, Megan Siczek, Emily Suh, Zuzana Tomaš, and Missy Watson. The feedback from the anonymous proposal reviewers for this book was also extremely helpful in the early phases of this project, as were my email exchanges with Hilary Janks, who provided some valuable historical context for CLA Pedagogy as an educational movement.

I also have received so much valuable feedback and guidance from Karen Adler at Routledge/Taylor & Francis. Thank you, Karen, for answering my many questions and providing words of reassurance when my confidence wavered. Bethany White and the rest of the editorial team have also been wonderful to work with!

Finally, I am so grateful to my family. My parents Steve and Sheilah helped to instill in me a love of learning and a respect for educators early on. My siblings Stephanie and Shad are among my biggest fans. And my husband Garrett, stepson Daniel, and son Michael have helped me stay grounded in this process. Your playful, loving, and impactful words reveal the power of language to me every day. And your brilliant humor reminds me not to take myself too seriously. ;-) Thank you for enriching my life in so many beautiful ways! Garrett, I could not have asked for a more loving and supportive partner. I am so grateful to have you as my spouse—and as my occasional co-teacher!

Part I

Foundations of CLA Pedagogy

1
Introduction

Why Do We Need CLA Pedagogy?

It seems that everywhere one looks these days within writing/literacy education, teachers are talking about language difference. Whether we are referring to English Learners with immigrant and refugee backgrounds, students of color who use multiple dialects, international students who are multilingual/L2[1] writers, or millennials engaging with social media, conversations about the writing classroom and curriculum are infused with a growing awareness of linguistic complexity. Now, more than ever, educators are eager for instructional strategies that celebrate and build on students' linguistic resources. We do not just want to affirm the value of linguistic diversity, however; we also want to promote our students' *rhetorical agency*—to empower them to use language for a variety of academic, professional, civic, and personal purposes.

Yet many teachers struggle to enact this two-pronged vision of linguistic affirmation and rhetorical agency. On the one hand, we tend to be pragmatists: Most of us believe that practical, relevant writing instruction can expand students' access to power and increase their opportunities at school, at work, and in their local and global (and even digital) communities. We want our students to come away from our classes with an expanded set of rhetorical knowledge and strategies—a linguistic "utility belt" that is fuller than it was when they entered our classrooms.

On the other hand, many educators are becoming more aware of the dangers of a purely "utilitarian" approach to writing instruction. We know—or are learning—that education often (re)creates an uneven linguistic playing field, where some forms of speaking and writing are valued more than others. We want to level that playing field wherever possible. We know that writing instruction has traditionally upheld the linguistic status quo, which is disempowering to particular groups of students, including many multilingual and multidialectal writers. Under the guise of "basic skills" and "standards," we

DOI: 10.4324/9781003171751-2

have seen—and still see—practices that are ineffective and unethical—from remedial curricula that aim to "fix" student writers (Rose, 1985; Shapiro, 2011) to tests and other assessments that are punitive and/or discriminatory (Inoue, 2015; Poe & Elliot, 2019). Thus, in attempting to prepare students to write for the world that is, we may miss opportunities to co-create the world as we want it to be—a place where language difference is seen and treated as an asset, rather than a liability.

This tension between **pragmatism** (i.e., what students need for today) and **progressivism** (i.e., what the world needs for a more just tomorrow) puts many educators in an ideological bind. Again and again, I have heard both pre-service and practicing teachers ask some version of the following question: *How can we teach writing in a way that reflects our commitment to linguistic diversity and social justice, while also preparing student writers for success in school and beyond?*

This book is designed to answer that very question. Or, more precisely, this book provides many answers to that question, all of which are undergirded by a common theoretical framework: Critical Language Awareness (CLA). There are a number of ways to define CLA and the pedagogies that are informed by this theoretical framework, as we will discuss in Chapters 2 and 3. But for the sake of this introductory chapter, here is a working definition:

> **CLA Pedagogy** is an approach to language and literacy education that focuses on the intersections of language, identity, power, and privilege, with the goal of promoting self-reflection, social justice, and rhetorical agency among student writers.

To help illustrate why we need CLA pedagogy, I present three common scenarios:

1   Instructor A teaches a required writing course for first-years at her university. When she surveys her incoming students about their goals as writers, she encounters a wide range of answers: Some want to be able to write for their intended programs of study, which include everything from art history to zoology. Others want to be prepared to communicate for professional purposes. A few are engaged in local activism and hope to use writing to increase the visibility and impact of that work. What can this instructor realistically offer to students with so many different literacy goals—particularly when her own background is in English literature?

2   Instructors B and C co-teach an Advanced Placement (or International Baccalaureate) English class at a highly tracked secondary

school. After attending a workshop on inclusive pedagogy, they are committed to redesigning their course to increase representation from minority groups, including students who use English as an additional language (EAL) and students of color, as well as students from lower-income households. Their first step was to revise their reading list to include more writers from diverse cultural and linguistic backgrounds. But where might they go from there? And how can they ensure that students from underrepresented groups feel that they truly belong in this class?

3   Instructor D teaches a developmental/transitional writing class that has a mix of international and domestic students, most of whom learned English as an additional language. Many of his students seem resentful and unmotivated—in part because they were required to take his course based on standardized test scores rather than choosing the course for themselves. After attending a workshop on translingual writing, Instructor D added a "code-meshing" assignment that invites students to include other languages or dialects in their academic writing. But student responses to the assignment range from mild interest to apathy to anxiety. How can this instructor set up and scaffold this assignment, so that students see it as valuable? What can he offer to those who do not see themselves as multilingual or multidialectal (i.e., who do not think they have multiple "codes"[2] to begin with)? And how else might he make his course engaging and relevant to students from so many different backgrounds?

All of these hypothetical instructors are committed to student-centered teaching that responds to the needs, goals, and interests of a diverse student population. All of them want to promote rhetorical agency through their writing curricula and instruction. All of them seek an approach to writing pedagogy that is pragmatic but also progressive.

Is Pragmatism the Problem?

Yet much of the recent scholarship in writing/literacy studies—particularly around language difference—seems to suggest that pragmatism is itself a problem. Often, teachers are given the impression that their desire to meet students' immediate, practical needs is somehow in conflict with their commitment to promoting more socially and linguistically just schools and societies. One place we can observe this perceived tension is in a 2019 address given at the Conference for College Communication and Composition

(CCCC)—the largest annual gathering of postsecondary writing teachers in the United States. The speaker was Asao Inoue, an advocate of anti-racist pedagogy and policy, who was that year's conference chair.[3] Inoue's talk discussed how writing instructors—White instructors, in particular—have been teaching and assessing writing in ways that perpetuate "White language supremacy"—i.e., a linguistic status quo that advantages students already familiar with dominant (traditionally White) norms and standards. This dynamic, Inoue explained, causes real harm to students from less privileged backgrounds, including many students of color. Responding to the pragmatic argument that teaching standardized[4] English is "just about preparation for the future, just about good critical thinking and communicating," he says:

> We must stop justifying White standards of writing as a necessary evil. Evil in any form is never necessary. We must stop saying that we have to teach this dominant English because it's what students need to succeed tomorrow. They only need it because we keep teaching it!

Though Inoue does not rule out the possibility of including standardized English somewhere within an anti-racist writing curriculum, he does make clear that evaluating students on conformity with "White standards of writing" perpetuates racial inequality. And since most teachers consider it best practice to assess students on what they learn in class, rather than on what they already know and can do, it seems that Inoue is calling for, at minimum, a marked decrease in emphasis on standardized English.[5]

Inoue's address was intentionally provocative. And provocation is valuable—we all need to be shaken up once in a while! But some attendees, myself included, felt that the talk set up an overly simplistic binary in which practicality is at odds with the aims of social justice. And indeed, if pragmatism is interpreted as a complete acceptance of the status quo, then it does seem logical that a purely pragmatic orientation is problematic. After all, one of the fundamental tenets of anti-racism is that if we—White folks, in particular—are not working to dismantle systems of racial inequality, then we are in effect maintaining and even strengthening those systems (e.g., Kendi, 2019; see also the work of Angela Davis).[6]

Clearly, Inoue is pushing us to ask ourselves: *Do we want to be part of the problem or part of the solution to racial inequality?* This question is also at the heart of a CCCC document released in July 2020 entitled "This Ain't Another Statement! This is a DEMAND for Black Linguistic Justice!"[7] which is the latest among the organization's position statements on "language issues" (I'll say more on these statements later in this chapter). The statement calls on teachers to "acknowledge and celebrate Black students' use of Black Language in all its linguistic and cultural glory." It also exhorts teachers to "stop using academic language and standard English as the accepted communicative norm!" and to "STOP telling Black students that they have to 'learn standard English to be successful because that's just the way it is in the real world.'"

Both Inoue's talk and the "Black Linguistic Justice" statement argue persuasively that simply teaching for the linguistic status quo is not the answer to racial inequality in education. But this leaves many writing teachers wondering: *What do we do, instead?* How do we prepare student writers for the world of today while working to promote a better, more just world for tomorrow?

A Pedagogical Conundrum

Thus, as many teachers commit to being part of the solution to racism and other forms of oppression, we receive the message that a focus on academic norms and/or standardized English—particularly in terms of assessment—is antithetical to that aim. This leaves us in a pedagogical conundrum that goes something like this:

> If academic/standardized language[8] perpetuates White supremacy, then should I avoid teaching it altogether?
>
> If I do not focus on academic/standardized language in my writing classes, then what should I be teaching instead? Is my main goal simply to validate what students already know and do as language users?
>
> And if that is my goal, how do I justify it to my students, who have been told that my class is designed to help them write for academic or professional purposes? Was that false advertising?
>
> Also, how does a shift away from academic/standardized language *inside* my classroom actually change things in the world, including the academic world, *outside*?
>
> Maybe I'm in the wrong profession?! I really want to do what is best for students—particularly for those from less privileged backgrounds. But I'm not even sure what that is anymore!

The actual conversations, of course, are more lengthy and nuanced. But I hope this line of reasoning illustrates the *very real tension* many educators are facing as they wrestle with what it means to teach writing in both pragmatic and progressive ways. This tension has only grown stronger in recent years, as public conversations about racial and economic justice have increased in so many of our communities (e.g., Associated Press, 2020).

Looking for Both/And

Most anti-racist writing/literacy scholars will—when pressed—admit that the norms of academic/standardized language still hold power, and that ignoring them completely would be unhelpful to students. Inoue, for example, has said in other venues (e.g., Flaherty, 2019) that his classes do include some attention to dominant norms and standards—if nothing else, as a point of contrast with the linguistic norms and practices that are already familiar to many of his students. And of course, many of the scholars calling for resistance to academic norms and linguistic standards are doing so in writing that seems to conform quite closely to those norms and standards—although to be fair, there are some exceptions to this trend (e.g., Smitherman, 1986; Villanueva, 1993; Young, 2010).[9]

Clearly, discussions of linguistic and racial justice in writing/literacy studies must be centered not on *whether* to be pragmatic or progressive, but on *how* to integrate the two into our curricula and instruction. The trouble is that by the time we get to this point in the conversation (or presentation, or article, or workshop), there is usually little time or space left for discussing what this integration looks like in practice. One scholar who has argued for and exemplified approaches that are both pragmatic and progressive is Lisa Delpit. Delpit (1988, 2006) argues that students from less privileged backgrounds—in particular, working-class, multidialectal students of color—need both linguistic affirmation *and* explicit instruction in academic/standardized language, or what she calls the "codes of power":

> I am certain that if we are truly to effect societal change, we cannot do so from the bottom up, but we must push and agitate from the top down. And in the meantime, we must take the responsibility to *teach*, to provide for students who do not already possess them, the additional codes of power.

(p. 40)

Yet despite this nuanced stance, Delpit has been criticized by some scholars (e.g., Canagarajah, 2013b; Flores & Rosa, 2015; Young, 2014) for emphasizing linguistic "appropriateness," an assimilationist stance, over linguistic affirmation and justice. Canagarajah (2013b) writes that scholars like Delpit embody a "pragmatist position" because they "acknowledge the power differences in the language of academic writing but don't argue for change" (p. 110). While I do believe some of Delpit's work could be enriched with a more critical view of language difference and variation, I mention her here as an illustration of how pervasive this perceived tension is between pragmatism and progressivism, among scholars talking about language difference and academic literacy.

We see this same tension as well within scholarship promoting a translingual orientation to literacy, which has dominated much of the discussion about multilingual/L2 writers over the past decade among U.S. composition scholars. Some brief historical context, for those new to this area of scholarship: Although the label "translingual" has been used for decades to refer to authors who write in multiple language and/or codes (e.g., Kellman, 2005), it was taken up in the early 2010s among writing studies scholars—particularly among compositionists working in U.S. postsecondary education.

Translingualism as a theory about language tends to highlight hybridity, multiplicity, and porousness, as well as intercultural and transnational aspects of language (e.g., Canagarajah, 2013a; Lu & Horner, 2016). Translingual scholars contrast this rich, multi-faceted conception of language with the "monolingual ideology" prevalent in most writing classrooms and curricula, where teachers often try to "fix" language—i.e., to treat it as static, as well as to "remediate" language that is deemed inappropriate for school settings. (For an excellent overview of the strands within monolingual ideology, see Watson & Shapiro, 2018).

A translingual approach, similar to a CLA approach, treats **language difference as an asset** (Britton & Lorimer Leonard, 2020; Guerra, 2016)[10]—a theoretical orientation central to other frameworks as well, such as linguistically responsive instruction (e.g., Lucas et al., 2008) and teaching for linguistic justice (e.g., Baker-Bell, 2020; Schreiber et al., forthcoming). One pedagogical strategy translingual scholars have put forward as a way of enacting this asset orientation is to incorporate course materials and/or assignments that use "code-meshing"—i.e., that integrate multiple languages and/or codes within a single piece of writing (e.g., Young & Martinez, 2011).[11] Although the meaning of the term "translingual pedagogy" has evolved—or rather, expanded—significantly since early usage (see, for example, Horner et al., 2011 vs. Lu & Horner, 2013, 2016), code-meshing still dominates many of the case studies of translingual pedagogy. And indeed, as I will explain in later chapters of this volume, using texts and assignments that mix codes and styles is one of the many ways we can cultivate CLA in our writing classrooms!

Yet code-meshing alone feels to some teachers more like a minor pedagogical tweak than a transformation. Many of us conclude that this strategy is *necessary but not sufficient* in preparing student writers to achieve their academic, professional, and civic goals, especially since most of their readers—including most instructors in other disciplines—will not have been exposed to translingual theories about language. Moreover, despite its commitment to seeing language in complex, nuanced ways, translingual scholarship tends to say little about how to work with academic norms and linguistic standards in the classroom, beyond recognizing that those norms and standards are often leveraged punitively against students. Thus, conversations about translingual approaches to writing often end up in the same pedagogical conundrum outlined earlier—with teachers wondering *how* to be both pragmatic and progressive in their work with student writers from a variety of linguistic backgrounds.[12]

One way some translingual scholars have tried to resolve this tension is by focusing on *student agency*. Watson and Shapiro (2018), for example, suggest that teachers committed to linguistic diversity need to "contextualize[e] the oppressive aspects of [Standardized English] so that students are armed, just as we are, with the knowledge needed to **make decisions about how, whether, and when to push against standardized norms**" (p. 11 of pdf, emphasis mine). Similarly, Schreiber and Watson (2018) propose that our job as writing teachers must be to "help[] students master grammatical and genre conventions even as we critique them" (p. 96). Without both elements (mastery and critique), they point out, agency is impossible, since students "who don't yet understand the social and racial hierarchies that inform language standards" (p. 96) cannot make informed rhetorical choices.

With this focus on informed decision-making, translingual scholarship begins to echo earlier scholarship on "rhetorical grammar" (e.g., Kolln & Gray, 2013; Micciche, 2004), which tends to emphasize writerly decision-making—rather than linguistic absolutes—when it comes to academic/standardized language (See also Lu & Horner, 2013; Guerra, 2016; Lee, 2016; Shapiro et al., 2016). If students *want* to be able to write in ways that conform to academic norms and linguistic standards, then it would seem that part of our job as progressive, student-centered writing teachers is to create opportunities for them to do so.

Thus, we begin to see a pattern: A scholarly conversation that promotes radical thinking about language often becomes much more pragmatic when it turns to questions about writing pedagogy (See Cox & Watson, 2020; Gere et al., 2021; Ruecker & Shapiro, 2020 for more on this dynamic). And sadly, most of these discussions leave unanswered the most important question: What do we need to teach—and how—in order to prepare students to make these agentive choices as writers, and to do so in keeping with our progressive orientation to language difference?

Looking Back

It may be comforting (or perhaps disheartening) to realize that U.S. writing teachers have been wrestling with this question for decades. Perhaps the most prominent example of this is in the ongoing conversation about Students' Right to Their Own Language (SRTOL), which has become its own line of scholarship (e.g., Perryman-Clarke et al., 2014), and which I am only discussing briefly here for historical context. The first SRTOL resolution,[13] approved by members of the (U.S.-based) National Council of Teachers of English (NCTE)[14] in 1974, articulates a familiar argument: It opens by denouncing the predominantly negative attitude toward "nonstandard dialects" and "the prejudicial labeling of students that resulted from this view." It goes on to affirm "students' right to their own language—to the dialect that expresses their family and community identity, the idiolect that expresses their unique personal identity." Yet a few lines down, the resolution also affirms that teachers have a responsibility to "provide the opportunity for students to learn the conventions of what has been called written edited American English." Once again, the key question is not *whether* to teach "written edited American English" but *how* to do so in a linguistically affirming way. Unfortunately, this resolution leaves that "how" question, well, unresolved.[15]

This same line of argument is evident in a number of other NCTE/CCCC position statements[16]: The 1988 "Guideline on the National Language Policy," responding to public debates about "official English" and English-only policies, affirms the linguistic reality that the United States is and has been a "multilingual society." But it also recognizes "the historical reality that . . . English has become the language of wider communication," and therefore advocates for writing/literacy instruction that reflects both realities. The 1998 "Statement on Ebonics," responding to the controversial debate about whether and how to integrate use of Black, vernacular English (sometimes called "Ebonics") into literacy instruction for African American students, calls for "training to provide . . . adequate knowledge about Ebonics" among teachers and other professionals. But it also says educators need to "build on existing knowledge about Ebonics to help students to expand their command of the Language of Wider Communication ('standard English')."

Likewise, the "Statement on Second Language Writing and Multilingual Writers," first approved in 2001, aims to "make visible otherwise underutilized linguistic and literacy resources that enrich academic life and should be valued and supported" and to "promote social justice for all multilingual members of the academic community." But there is little in the statement that would suggest shifting focus away from English altogether—or away from an emphasis on academic/standardized language within the writing curriculum.[17]

All of these statements—and these are just a sampling!—reaffirm the value of linguistic diversity and call for professional training that furthers our understanding of the linguistic resources students bring with them to the writing classroom. All of them also suggest that there is a place for academic/standardized language within a curriculum that is both progressive and pragmatic. But none of them offers much guidance on how to enact this "both/and" approach in practice.[18]

Moving Forward: CLA as "Both/And" Pedagogy

Of course, ideological binaries and theory-practice gaps are almost cliché in educational research, including in writing/literacy studies. Many scholars have themselves called for a richer, more nuanced pedagogical conversation around language difference, suggesting we should be building alliances rather than drawing ideological lines (e.g., Cox & Watson, 2020; Howell et al., 2020; Silva & Wang, 2020; Tardy, 2017). As Schreiber and Watson (2018) argue, teachers need room to "experiment" with linguistically affirming pedagogies "without fear of being labeled as uninformed and uncritical" (p. 96).

But this fear is real and understandable: Teachers have been told that the stakes for this work are high—that linguistic injustice and other forms of oppression have a tangible, material impact on our students. We want to be part of the solution, and we certainly don't want to contribute to the problem. Thus, one concern about the lack of guidance and frameworks for "both/and" writing pedagogy is that it can cause *pedagogical paralysis*. Moreover, it can lead to pendulum swings in curriculum and instruction, as has happened with other issues, such as the "reading wars" debate around best practices for early literacy (Lemann, 1997; Pearson, 2004) which has been flaring up again in recent years (Hood, 2019).

But the biggest danger, in my view, is that teachers may *give up altogether* on reforming their pedagogies. They may simply revert back to what they already know. Or, more likely, teachers may tinker at the edges of their curriculum without truly changing the core of what they do. Instructor A (from the scenarios above) will likely design her course around literary analysis, as this is her area of expertise. She may add a new assignment—a blog post, perhaps, or a multimodal project—and will hope that this addition is a meaningful gesture toward relevance and inclusion. Instructors B and C, though proud about their newly diversified reading list, will probably re-use most of the same activities and assignments that work with their more privileged students. But they may not adapt their instruction in ways that are supportive and affirming of students from multilingual and multidialectal backgrounds, and as a result, those students may question whether they belong in the course—and they may not be prepared for the high-stakes exam at the end of the term. Instructor D will enjoy reading a new batch of "code-meshed" essays, but may wonder: Are the students simply performing for me? Is this just a new version of "Please the Teacher," with a multilingual twist? He may not see much of a change in student affect and motivation, either.

All of these instructors will continue to ask themselves whether they are in fact promoting *rhetorical agency* among their students—especially among those from less privileged backgrounds. Moreover, all of them will also probably continue evaluating writing as they always have, which may not be in line with their values of equity and inclusion. In Chapter 9, we will consider how CLA can shape our feedback and evaluation practices, by the way!

I have moved very quickly here in mapping out the central issues and questions at the core of this book. I will return to many of these topics later, and I will also suggest readings and other media that can allow readers to take a deeper dive. But what I hope I have demonstrated is that the perceived tension between pragmatism and progressivism in the teaching of writing—particularly in regard to academic norms and standardized English—is **not new and has never been resolved**.

And yet it **cannot be ignored**. As writing teachers, we must find ways to work creatively with this tension, in order to enact our commitment to linguistic diversity, social justice, and rhetorical effectiveness, for and with all of the students in our classrooms. Critical Language Awareness (CLA) is the best framework I have found for doing just that. To this end, I offer below an expanded version of the definition of CLA Pedagogy provided earlier:

> CLA pedagogy is an approach to language and literacy education that focuses on the intersections of language, identity, power, and privilege, with the goal of promoting self-reflection, social justice, and rhetorical agency. A CLA approach to writing instruction aims to promote a more

just future, while also preparing students for the (often unjust) present. CLA pedagogy does not ignore the power of academic norms and other linguistic standards (i.e., the status quo), but aims to demystify, critique, and—at times—resist those norms and standards.

CLA Pedagogy is grounded theoretically in what applied linguist Alistair Pennycook (1997) calls **critical pragmatism**.[19] In contrast with "vulgar pragmatism," which claims to be politically neutral and prioritizes efficiency and utilitarianism, critical pragmatism remains open to the possibility of changing the status quo, while still taking seriously students' needs and expectations for using language/literacy within that status quo. Although the term "critical pragmatism" was never taken up widely in linguistics or writing/literacy studies, there have been other scholarly attempts to reconcile criticality and pragmatism—particularly among practitioners working with multilingual/L2 writers. The most notable of these is Critical English for Academic Purposes (e.g., Benesch, 1996, 2001), which I view as an early iteration of CLA pedagogy (for more on critical pragmatism in relation to writing pedagogy, see Ruecker & Shapiro, 2020).

A CLA approach to writing and literacy instruction engages students from a variety of language backgrounds in rich conversations about how language shapes them and how they can shape language (e.g., Clark et al., 1990, 1991; Fairclough, 1992/2014). CLA Pedagogy can include some of the strategies mentioned here, such as incorporating readings or other media from multilingual or multidialectal writers, or inviting students to "mesh" multiple languages/codes in their own writing. But it can involve so much more: Investigating the many varieties of English around the world, analyzing the language of news media, studying how linguistic prejudice plays out in cartoons and courtrooms, and even debating the role that academic/standardized language plays—or should play—in our own programs and institutions.

CLA is informed by cutting-edge research in linguistics, education, rhetoric/composition, and literacy studies. Even prior to the emergence of CLA in the early 1990s, which we will trace in Chapter 2, applied linguistics research demonstrated that language awareness (LA), defined as "explicit knowledge about language, and conscious perception and sensitivity in language learning, language teaching and language use" (ALA, n.d.), has a positive impact on students' engagement, growth, and confidence as readers, writers, and orators (e.g., Cots, 2013; Hawkins, 1999; James & Garrett, 1992). Likewise, teachers who receive LA training as part of their professional development report feeling more prepared to teach about language and literacy in ways that are pedagogically effective (Andrews, 2007; Bunch, 2013; Wright & Bolitho, 1993).

When LA instruction includes links to identity, power, and privilege—i.e., a CLA approach—teachers tend to come away with a heightened curiosity about language in society, greater appreciation for cultural and linguistic diversity, and a deeper understanding of how their work as language/literacy teachers is tied to social justice (e.g., Endo, 2015; Godley et al., 2015; Metz, 2018a; Shi & Rolstad, 2020). These outcomes, in turn, reinvigorate many teachers' sense of efficacy, so that they are better prepared to promote equity and inclusion through their curricula and classroom practices (e.g., Baker-Bell, 2020; Bunch, 2013; Haddix, 2008). When it comes to academic language/literacy, CLA opens up conversations that neither deny the social power of linguistic standards nor overlook the real harm that is often done in the name of upholding those standards (Gere et al., 2021; Godley & Reaser, 2018; Weaver, 2019).

Student responses to CLA Pedagogy are equally promising: After engaging with a CLA-oriented curriculum—in particular, one that focuses on linguistic variation, as we will explore in Chapter 4—students from linguistic minority backgrounds (i.e., who use a language or dialect other than standardized English at home) report a greater sense of linguistic and cultural pride (e.g., Baker-Bell, 2020; Metz, 2018b; Reaser et al., 2017). Students from more privileged backgrounds, moreover, deepen their understanding of how their attitudes and actions can contribute to social (in)justice (e.g., Abe & Shapiro, 2021; Devereaux & Palmer, 2019; Weaver, 2019).

Although many of the recent case studies of CLA Pedagogy in the U.S. have come from English language arts or writing/composition classrooms, as well as English teacher education programs, CLA has also informed the work of many ESOL/English Learner and world/heritage language teachers (see Achugar, 2015; Devereaux & Palmer, 2019; Fairclough, 1992/2014, for a representative sampling). Courses built around CLA may focus primarily on academic literacy (or literacies—see Chapter 5), but CLA can also be integrated into professional or technical writing courses, writing for public/civic audiences, and creative or expressivist writing curricula. CLA Pedagogy has been taken up among educators in a wide variety of other disciplines, too, including literary studies, film and media studies, history, theater, psychology, business, political science, environmental studies, and medicine! (I am currently developing some bibliographies of this research, which will be available with the e-resources to this volume). Moreover, this approach has been adapted for *all levels of instruction*, from primary grades through graduate school and community-based education programs.

Perhaps what excites me most about CLA pedagogy, though, is its transformative potential.

A CLA approach does not simply try to *add on* to our already crammed curricula. Rather, it invites us to *open up* our hearts and minds, our course materials and assignments, our conversations with students, and even our feedback and assessment practices. When we foreground issues of language, identity, privilege, and power in both the content and the delivery of our curriculum, we begin to see and do our work differently. This includes working with and through the tensions around linguistic norms and standards—not just in academia, but everywhere. (If you don't believe that linguistic norms exist outside of education, ask a typical teenager about whether to end a text message with a period. You will likely get an earful!). As we will explore in future chapters, the tendency to prescribe what people should do with language is present in every linguistic community. Why? Because we define our relationships, our communities, and our very identities through language. Is it any wonder, then, that discussions about linguistic norms and standards become so fraught?

Looking Ahead

To conclude this chapter—and to pique your interest in the rest of the book—I wish to return once more to the three teaching scenarios mentioned near the beginning. Instructor A, who is overwhelmed by the variety of goals and needs expressed by her first-year college students—including intended majors that range, literally, from A to Z!—has several options. Rather than reverting back to literary analysis as the default or trying to choose a few disciplines to focus on, she could design her course, or a unit of her course, around the theme of "academic disciplines as linguistic communities" (see Chapter 5). Her students could learn about Writing in the Disciplines (WID) research, and even use empirical methods themselves (e.g., ethnographic observation, instructor or student interviews) to investigate the language norms within particular disciplines or programs of study. Ultimately, each student would become an academic "cultural informant" for their peers, building and sharing valuable institutional and rhetorical knowledge (see Benesch, 2001; Johns, 1997; Shapiro, 2009, for more on how to scaffold these kinds of investigations). Alternatively, or in addition, Instructor A's class could focus on linguistic analysis of news media (see Chapter 6), which students could apply to coverage of social issues they care deeply about.

Instructors B and C, who want to diversify and support the students in their AP/IB course, might decide to rebuild their curriculum around sociolinguistics themes (e.g., Baker-Bell, 2020; Devereaux & Palmer, 2019; Reaser et al., 2017). Students could document linguistic diversity at their school and in the local community by conducting peer-to-peer surveys, using linguistic atlases and other online resources, and even analyzing spoken or written exchanges on social media (see Chapters 4, 6, and 7). Their students could also use sociolinguistics concepts as a lens to analyze film or other media, including multidialectal literature (also Chapter 4). They may even organize a school "teach-in" or other event about resisting linguistic prejudice, in which students from marginalized groups would have the opportunity to lead, rather than follow. Critical news media literacy (Chapter 6) may also work well with these students.

Instructor D, whose developmental writing students seem resentful and unmotivated, may keep the code-meshing assignment. But he could make it one option in a unit using "writing-as-(re)design" (see Chapter 7), in which students write for a variety of audiences, using their close analysis skills to make informed rhetorical decisions. He may also incorporate an "academic informant" project similar to Instructor A, and/or engage the topic of "linguistic pluralism in the academy" (see Chapter 5), in order to open up critical conversations about the impact of his program/institution's policies on students (see also Chapter 10). Students could even be invited to research, write, and/or speak about their experiences, sharing their work—if they choose—with key stakeholders and advocating for more equitable alternatives, drawing on anti-racist, translingual, and second language writing scholarship (e.g., Benesch, 2001; Inoue, 2015; Fahim et al., 2020).

These curricular changes would, of course, not be quick or easy to implement. Each instructor would likely need to start small, perhaps with one new or revised unit or assignment, and build up to a larger transformation of their courses. But the result would be well worth it. Why? Because when they engage with literacy through a CLA lens, students learn to pay closer and more meaningful attention to language—what it looks like, what role it plays in our lives and work, and how we might use it in powerful and agentive ways. I can't think of a more relevant and energizing vision for our work as teachers of writing! I hope you, dear reader, are ready to explore this vision with me! Below is a description of each of the remaining chapters of the book, so you can map out your journey.

Chapter 2 offers a historical and conceptual overview of CLA as a movement within linguistics and literacy studies. We discuss how CLA was shaped by two phenomena: The "Knowledge about Language" movement in the United Kingdom—particularly in relation to the U.K.'s National Curriculum in 1988—and the "critical turn" in academia. We see through this story of CLA that this approach to writing/literacy education can be both versatile and subversive! I then describe how CLA Pedagogy has been taken up in some other educational settings since the early 1990s, and I consider some possible reasons for why it has been less prominent in the U.S. The chapter concludes with an overview of some key terms that are central to CLA and will be used throughout the subsequent chapters.

Chapter 3 delves further into how and why CLA works as an approach to writing/literacy pedagogy. We first unpack the definition of CLA, focusing on how CLA pedagogy promotes three overarching and interrelated goals for student writers: **self-reflection, social justice,** and **rhetorical agency.** I explain how foregrounding these three goals can help to bridge the perceived divide between pragmatism and progressivism, as we discussed earlier. I then present six core principles for CLA Pedagogy, curated from my review of educational scholarship, as well as my own teaching practice:

CLA Pedagogy

1   Includes students from all language backgrounds
2   Uses language as a bridge into social justice learning
3   Engages minds, hearts, and bodies
4   Links awareness to action
5   Works with tensions around linguistic norms and standards
6   Builds on best practices for writing/literacy instruction

In Part II (Chapters 4–7), I present four pathways for CLA pedagogy: **Sociolinguistics, Critical Academic Literacies, Media/Discourse Analysis,** and **Communicating Across Difference.** Each pathway chapter begins with an introduction to the topic, followed by a list of Essential Questions and Transferrable Skills applicable to that pathway and a paragraph summary of each of the three units in each pathway (See Figure 1.1). The highlights from each unit are also summarized in an "At-a-Glance" chart near the beginning of each chapter.

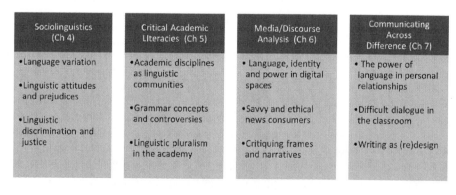

Sociolinguistics (Ch 4)	Critical Academic Literacies (Ch 5)	Media/Discourse Analysis (Ch 6)	Communicating Across Difference (Ch 7)
•Language variation	•Academic disciplines as linguistic communities	• Language, identity and power in digital spaces	• The power of language in personal relationships
•Linguistic attitudes and prejudices	•Grammar concepts and controversies	•Savvy and ethical news consumers	•Difficult dialogue in the classroom
•Linguistic discrimination and justice	•Linguistic pluralism in the academy	•Critiquing frames and narratives	•Writing as (re)design

Figure 1.1 Overview of the Four Pathways Chapters

The presentation of each unit has been structured as a **learning sequence** that includes ideas for various aspects of instruction: Tapping into students' prior knowledge and experiences, exploring the topic at hand, deepening and/or personalizing learning, and demonstrating learning. Links to online readings and other media (e.g., news articles, blog posts, TED talks) are woven throughout the sequences, as are instructions and handouts from many of my favorite activities and assignments! These learning sequences are intended to be pedagogical **menus, rather than recipes.** In other words, educators can and probably should make adaptations to the sequence, to make it a good fit with their own pedagogical goals and constraints.

Part III (Chapters 8–10) offers guidance to support educators in that adaptation. Chapter 8 discusses how teachers can design CLA-oriented units and courses tailored to their pedagogical goals and contexts. We talk through strategies for needs assessment as part of curriculum design, and I describe how I have used those strategies in creating four CLA-oriented courses that have distinct goals, student populations, and other features.[20] We then consider briefly how CLA overlaps with two sets of standards used widely among U.S. writing teachers: the Common Core Standards for English/Language Arts (CCSS ELA)[21] and the Framework for Success in Postsecondary Writing (FSPW).[22] We also consider ways to ensure that our courses and units are accessible and inclusive, drawing on Universal Design for Learning (UDL). The chapter concludes with a discussion of how I took these elements into account in the "Language and Social Justice" unit I co-taught for 7th through 10th-graders.

Chapter 9 examines how we can infuse CLA throughout our classroom instruction—no matter what topics we are including in our curricula! We address common questions such as:

- How can we implement CLA Pedagogy in teaching situations with constrained curricula or regressive policies?
- How might CLA inform how we structure and scaffold class discussion, and how we manage the difficult dynamics that can emerge when we talk about controversial or sensitive issues?
- What does a CLA approach suggest for how we structure and support academic reading, oral presentations, and peer review?
- How might CLA shape our feedback, assessment, and evaluation practices—including how we attend to issues of language and style?

This chapter also draws on some of my other research into student conceptions of inclusivity (e.g., Shapiro, 2020).

Chapter 10 considers how we can apply CLA to our educational work beyond the classroom, as well as our personal and civic lives. We briefly review research on how to assess students' development of CLA, beyond their growth as writers. We then discuss how CLA can inform our curricular and co-curricular offerings, our faculty development work, and our institutional work in relation to diversity, equity, and inclusion (DEI). The final section of the chapter—"CLA for Life!"—highlights some of the ways CLA might be relevant to our lives beyond our professional work. Throughout the chapter, I highlight topics that can be explored in greater depth, including through online gatherings and discussions at the Hub.

As we explore CLA pedagogy together, I hope you will enjoy both the journey and the destination!

Notes

1 Applied linguists use the shorthand "L2" to refer to the use of an additional language. It is important to note that for many students, English may be a third, fourth, etc. language—or they might have grown up in a bilingual household with two or more "L1s." As you will see throughout this book, linguistic labels and categories are almost always complicated! ☺

2 The term "code" is used in linguistics as a neutral way to refer to a consistent pattern of variation. A set of "codes" could refer to a group of languages, a group of dialects within the same language, or a set of context-based patterns (e.g., styles, registers, genres) within a language or dialect. Again (see footnote 1), linguistic boundaries are always complicated—and often political. We'll learn more about this in Chapters 2 and 4.

3 The full text of Inoue's (2019) address can be found at https://library.ncte.org/journals/CCC/issues/v71-2/30427. It was also published in *College Composition and Communication, 71*(2), 352–369.

4 I use the word "standardized" rather than "standard" throughout this chapter, as a way of reminding readers that standardization is something we do *to language*, including in and through literacy education (e.g., Godley et al., 2015). Standardized language, in other words, has quite a different origin story from most other types of linguistic variation. I'll discuss this a bit more in Chapter 2.

5 Inoue (2019) has in fact argued persuasively for "labor-based grading" as a more equitable alternative to standards-based assessment. I will discuss how this approach fits within CLA Pedagogy in Chapter 9.

6 The online Hub for this volume—a link to which is available at the e-resources for this volume—includes links to other resources that explain anti-racism and anti-racist pedagogy, for those newer to these topics.

7 The statement can be accessed at https://cccc.ncte.org/cccc/demand-for-black-linguistic-justice

8 In this chapter, I sometimes juxtapose "academic" and "standardized" not because the two are synonymous, but because they are often perceived as such and used interchangeably. Other terms referencing the same general idea include "Language of Wider Communication" (Smitherman, 1995), "Standard American English" (Lippi-Green, 2012), or "written, edited English" as it is framed in the NCTE resolution on SRTOL discussed elsewhere in this chapter. I will unpack this further in Chapters 2 and 3.

9 The authors of the "Black Linguistic Justice" statement do this somewhat as well, explaining that they "intentionally created a fluid text from our multiple voices rather than a singularly voiced, standardized, white document."

10 It is also worth noting that discussions about translingual scholarship have at times been contentious: Translingual scholars tend to frame their work as more progressive than that of second-language writing scholars; the latter, in return, tend to accuse translingual scholars of being vague about pedagogical implications and overly idealistic in their approach to language difference. This debate will start to sound quite familiar as we move through this chapter. See Silva and Wang (2020) for more.

11 The term "code-meshing" has itself been a bit controversial: Many translingual scholars suggest that code-meshing is distinct from "code-switching," which they often (mis)characterize as the use of separate codes for distinct situations—what Guerra (2016) and others call "code segregation." The controversy stems from the fact that linguists have traditionally defined code-switching as the mixing of codes in a single communicative situation—i.e., what translingual scholars call "code-meshing." If nothing else, I hope this example helps to illustrate once again that language matters—in particular, to scholars!

12 It is important to note that many scholars identify as *both* anti-racist and translingual (e.g., Howell et al., 2020; Condon & Young, 2017). I do not mean to suggest here that they are completely separate lines of inquiry.

13 This statement and accompanying material can be accessed at https://ncte.org/statement/righttoownlanguage/.

14 NCTE is the professional organization with which CCCC is affiliated. A CCCC Executive Committee had adopted an earlier version of the SRTOL statement in 1972, but it took two years for the larger NCTE umbrella organization to agree on a statement. For more on the rationale and history of the statement, visit https://cdn.ncte.org/nctefiles/groups/cccc/newsrtol.pdf

15 For more on how the conversation has evolved since the 1970s, see the most recent version of the SRTOL statement from CCCC (note above), which includes an excellent annotated bibliography.

16 These and a list of other statements focused on "language issues" can be found at https://cccc.ncte.org/cccc/resources/positions.

17 As is often the case in these statements, this one also calls for increased "awareness" about language and language acquisition, including "understanding the evolution of English—its fluidity and its global variation" (i.e., World Englishes).

18 U.S. teachers are not alone, of course, in trying to reconcile progressive values with pragmatic approaches. This tension has informed much of the scholarship

on critical approaches to literacy in other countries as well (e.g., Cope & Kalantzis, 2000; Janks, 2000; Lillis, 2003).

19 Pennycook did not invent these terms, but rather, borrowed them from the political scientist and teacher educator Cleo Cherryholmes. However, Pennycook brought the term into discussions of language/literacy education specifically. See Ruecker and Shapiro (2020) for more on the history and applications of this term.

20 Course descriptions and past syllabi for all of my Middlebury classes can be found at http://sites.middlebury.edu/shapiro/teaching-2/

21 www.corestandards.org.

22 http://wpacouncil.org/aws/CWPA/pt/sd/news_article/242845/_PARENT/layout_details/false.

References

Abe, S., & Shapiro, S. (2021). Sociolinguistics as a pathway to global citizenship: Critically observing 'self' and 'other'. *Language Awareness*, 30(4), 355–370.

Achugar, M. (2015). Theme: Critical language awareness approaches in the Americas: Theoretical principles, pedagogical practices and distribution of intellectual labor. *Linguistics and Education*, 32, 1–4. https://doi.org/10.1016/j.linged.2015.07.003

Andrews, S. (2007). *Teacher language awareness*. Cambridge University Press.

Associated Press (2020, June 8). *Huge crowds worldwide in name of social justice.* https://apnews.com/fe71828fb6c97178315d79987f04711b

Association for Language Awareness (ALA). (n.d.). *About.* www.languageawareness.org/

Baker-Bell, A. (2020). Dismantling anti-black linguistic racism in English language arts classrooms: Toward an anti-racist black language pedagogy. *Theory into Practice*, 59(1), 8–21. https://doi.org/10.1080/00405841.2019.1665415

Benesch, S. (1996). Needs analysis and curriculum development in EAP: An example of a critical approach. *TESOL Quarterly*, 30(4), 723–738.

Benesch, S. (2001). *Critical English for academic purposes: Theory, politics, and practice.* Routledge.

Britton, E. R., & Lorimer Leonard, R. (2020). The social justice potential of critical reflection and critical language awareness pedagogies for L2 writers. *Journal of Second Language Writing*, 50, 100776. https://doi.org/10.1016/j.jslw.2020.100776

Bunch, G. C. (2013). Pedagogical language knowledge: Preparing mainstream teachers for English learners in the new standards era. *Review of Research in Education*, 37(1), 298–341. https://doi.org/10.3102/0091732X12461772

Canagarajah, A. S. (Ed.). (2013a). *Literacy as translingual practice: Between communities and classrooms.* Routledge.

Canagarajah, A. S. (2013b). *Translingual practice: Global Englishes and cosmopolitan relations.* Routledge.

Clark, R., Fairclough, N., Ivanič, R., & Martin-Jones, M. (1990). Critical language awareness part I: A critical review of three current approaches to language awareness. *Language and Education, 4*(4), 249–260. https://doi.org/10.1080/09500 789009541291

Clark, R., Fairclough, N., Ivanič, R., & Martin-Jones, M. (1991). Critical language awareness part II: Towards critical alternatives. *Language and Education, 5*(1), 41–54. https://doi.org/10.1080/09500789109541298

Condon, F., & Young, V. A. (Eds.). (2017). *Performing antiracist pedagogy in rhetoric, writing, and communication.* WAC Clearinghouse/University Press of Colorado.

Cope, B., & Kalantzis, M. (2000). *Multiliteracies: Literacy learning and the design of social futures.* Routledge.

Cots, J. M. (2013). Language awareness. In C. Chapelle (Ed.), *The encyclopedia of applied linguistics* (pp. 1–7). Blackwell Publishing. https://doi.org/10.1002/9781405198431.wbeal0608

Cox, M., & Watson, M. (2020). A translingual scholar and second language writing scholar talk it out: Steps toward reconciliation. In T. Silva & Z. Wang (Eds.), *Reconciling translingualism and second language writing* (pp. 117–129). Routledge.

Delpit, L. (1988). The silenced dialogue: Power and pedagogy in educating other people's children. *Harvard Educational Review, 58*(3), 280–299.

Delpit, L. (2006). *Other people's children: Cultural conflict in the classroom.* The New Press.

Devereaux, M. D., & Palmer, C. C. (Eds.). (2019). *Teaching language variation in the classroom: Strategies and models from teachers and linguists.* Routledge.

Endo, R. (2015). From unconscious deficit views to affirmation of linguistic varieties in the classroom: White preservice teachers on building critical self-awareness about linguicism's causes and consequences. *Multicultural Perspectives, 17*(4), 207–214.

Fahim, N., Johnson, J., Lee, E., & Schreiber, B. (Eds.). (2020). Promoting social justice for multilingual writers on college campuses. Special issue of *Composition Forum, 44*. https://compositionforum.com/issue/44/

Fairclough, N. (1992/2014). *Critical language awareness.* Routledge.

Flaherty, C. (2019, March 28). More than hateful words. *Inside Higher Ed.* https://www.insidehighered.com/news/2019/03/28/racist-writing-instructors-listserv-post-prompts-debate-about-future-field-and-how

Flores, N., & Rosa, J. (2015). Undoing appropriateness: Raciolinguistic ideologies and language diversity in education. *Harvard Educational Review, 85*(2), 149–171.

Gere, A., Curzan, A., Hammond, J. W., Hughes, S., Li, R., Moos, A., Smith, K., Van Zanen, K., Wheeler, K. L., & Zanders, C. J. (2021). Communal justicing: Writing assessment, disciplinary infrastructure, and the case for critical language awareness. *College Composition and Communication, 72*(3), 384–412.

Godley, A. J., & Reaser, J. (2018). *Critical language pedagogy: Interrogating language, dialects, and power in teacher education.* Peter Lang.

Godley, A. J., Reaser, J., & Moore, K. G. (2015). Pre-service English language arts teachers' development of critical language awareness for teaching. *Linguistics and Education, 32*, 41–54. https://doi.org/10.1016/j.linged.2015.03.015

Guerra, J. C. (2016). *Language, culture, identity and citizenship in college classrooms and communities*. Routledge.

Haddix, M. (2008). Beyond sociolinguistics: Towards a critical approach to cultural and linguistic diversity in teacher education. *Language and Education, 22*(5), 254–270.

Hawkins, E. W. (1999). Foreign language study and language awareness. *Language Awareness, 8*(3–4), 124–142.

Hood, M. (2019, September 19). What the new reading wars get wrong. *Education Week*. www.edweek.org/ew/articles/2019/09/11/what-the-new-reading-wars-get-wrong.html

Horner, B., Lu, M. Z., Royster, J. J., & Trimbur, J. (2011). Language difference in writing: Toward a translingual approach. *College English, 73*(3), 303–321.

Howell, N. G., Navickas, K., Shapiro, R., Shapiro, S., & Watson, M. (2020). The perpetual "but" in raciolinguistic justice work: When idealism meets practice. *Composition Forum, 44*. https://compositionforum.com/issue/44/embracing.php

Inoue, A. B. (2015). *Antiracist writing assessment ecologies: Teaching and assessing writing for a socially just future*. WAC Clearinghouse. https://wac.colostate.edu/books/perspectives/inoue/

Inoue, A. (2019, March). *How do we language so people stop killing each other, or what do we do about white language supremacy?* Presentation at the Conference for College Composition and Communication.

James, C., & Garrett, P. (Eds.). (1992). *Language awareness in the classroom*. Longman.

Janks, H. (2000). Domination, access, diversity and design: A synthesis for critical literacy education. *Educational Review, 52*(2), 175–186.

Johns, A. (1997). *Text, role, and context: Developing academic literacies*. Cambridge University Press.

Kellman, S. G. (Ed.). (2005). *Switching languages: Translingual writers reflect on their craft*. University of Nebraska Press.

Kendi, I. (2019). *How to be an antiracist*. Penguin, Random House.

Kolln, M., & Gray, L. (2013). *Rhetorical grammar: Grammatical choices, rhetorical effects* (7th ed.). Pearson.

Lee, J. W. (2016). Beyond translingual writing. *College English, 79*(2), 174–195.

Lemann, N. (1997). The reading wars. *The Atlantic, 11*. www.theatlantic.com/magazine/archive/1997/11/the-reading-wars/376990/

Lillis, T. (2003). Student writing as academic literacies: Drawing on Bakhtin to move from critique to design. *Language and Education, 17*(3), 192–207.

Lippi-Green, R. (2012). *English with an accent* (2nd ed.). Routledge.

Lu, M. Z., & Horner, B. (2013). Translingual literacy, language difference, and matters of agency. *College English, 75*(6), 582–607.

Lu, M. Z., & Horner, B. (2016). Introduction: Translingual work. *College English, 78*(3), 207–218 [Special issue on Translingual Work in Composition].

Lucas, T., Villegas, A. M., & Freedson-Gonzalez, M. (2008). Linguistically responsive teacher education: Preparing classroom teachers to teach English language learners. *Journal of Teacher Education, 59*(4), 361–373.

Metz, M. (2018a). Challenges of confronting dominant language ideologies in the high school English classroom. *Research in the Teaching of English, 52*, 23.

Metz, M. (2018b). Exploring the complexity of high school students' beliefs about language variation. *Linguistics and Education, 45*, 10–19. https://doi.org/10.1016/j.linged.2018.02.003

Micciche, L. R. (2004). Making a case for rhetorical grammar. *College Composition and Communication, 55*(4), 716–737.

Pearson, P. D. (2004). The reading wars. *Educational Policy, 18*(1), 216–252.

Pennycook, A. (1997). Vulgar pragmatism, critical pragmatism, and EAP. *English for Specific Purposes, 16*(4), 253–269.

Perryman-Clarke, S., Kirkland, D., & Jackson, A. (2014). *Students' rights to their own language: A critical sourcebook.* St. Martins.

Poe, M., & Elliot, N. (2019). Evidence of fairness: Twenty-five years of research in assessing writing. *Assessing Writing, 42*, 100418.

Reaser, J., Adger, C. T., Wolfram, W., & Christian, D. (2017). *Dialects at school: Educating linguistically diverse students.* Routledge.

Rose, M. (1985). The language of exclusion: Writing instruction at the university. *College English, 47*(4), 341–359.

Ruecker, T., & Shapiro, S. (2020). Critical pragmatism as a middle ground in discussions of linguistic diversity. In T. Silva & Z. Wang (Eds.), *Reconciling translingualism and second language writing* (pp. 139–149). Routledge.

Schreiber, B. R., Fahim, N., Johnson, E., & Lee, E. (Eds.). (forthcoming). *Linguistic justice on campus: Theory, pedagogy, and advocacy for multilingual writers.* Multilingual Matters.

Schreiber, B. R., & Watson, M. (2018). Translingualism≠ code-meshing: A response to Gevers' "Translingualism revisited" (2018). *Journal of Second Language Writing, 42*, 94–97.

Shapiro, S. (2009). Two birds, one stone: Using academic experiences as content for EAP courses. In S. Barduhn & J. Nordmeyer (Eds.), *Integrating language and content* (pp. 75–87). TESOL.

Shapiro, S. (2011). Stuck in the remedial rut: Confronting resistance to ESL curriculum reform. *Journal of Basic Writing, 30*(2), 24–52.

Shapiro, S. (2020). Inclusive pedagogy in the academic writing classroom: Cultivating communities of belonging. *Journal of Academic Writing, 10*(1), 154–164. https://publications.coventry.ac.uk/index.php/joaw/article/view/607

Shapiro, S., Cox, M., Shuck, G., & Simnitt, E. (2016). Teaching for agency: From appreciating linguistic diversity to empowering multilingual matters. *Composition Studies, 44*(1), 31–52.

Shi, L., & Rolstad, K. (2020). "A good start": A new approach to gauging preservice teachers' critical language awareness. *Journal of Language, Identity & Education,* 1–15. https://doi.org/10.1080/15348458.2020.1810045 [online only for now]

Silva, T., & Wang, Z. (2020). *Reconciling translingualism and second language writing.* Routledge.

Smitherman, G. (1986). *Talkin and testifyin: The language of Black America*. Wayne State University Press.

Smitherman, G. (1995). "Students' right to their own language": A retrospective. *The English Journal, 84*(1), 21–27.

Tardy, C. M. (2017). Crossing, or creating, divides? A plea for transdisciplinary scholarship. In B. Horner & L. Tetrault (Eds.), *Crossing divides: Exploring translingual writing pedagogies and programs* (pp. 181–189). University Press of Colorado.

Villanueva, Jr., V. (1993). *Bootstraps: From an American academic of color*. National Council of Teachers of English.

Watson, M., & Shapiro, R. (2018). Clarifying the multiple dimensions of monolingualism: Keeping our sights on language politics. *Composition Forum, 38*.

Weaver, M. M. (2019). "I still think there's a need for proper, academic, standard English": Examining a teacher's negotiation of multiple language ideologies. *Linguistics and Education, 49*, 41–51. https://doi.org/10.1016/j.linged.2018.12.005

Wright, T., & Bolitho, R. (1993). Language awareness: A missing link in language teacher education? *ELT Journal, 47*(4), 292–304.

Young, V. A. (2010). Should writers use they own English? *Iowa Journal of Cultural Studies, 12*(1), 110–117.

Young, V. A. (2014). Coda: The power of language. In V. A. Young, R. Barrett, Y. Young-Rivera, & K. B. Lovejoy (Eds.), *Other people's English: Code-meshing, code-switching, and African American literacy* (pp. 153–156). Teachers College Press.

Young, V. A., & Martinez, A. (Eds.). (2011). *Code-meshing as world English: Policy, pedagogy, and performance*. National Council of Teachers of English.

2
What is CLA?

History and Concepts

Introduction

This chapter provides a short history of Critical Language Awareness (CLA) as a scholarly and educational movement. It also serves as an introduction to some concepts that are central to CLA as a theoretical framework. These two pieces help to build a solid understanding of how and why CLA pedagogy works as an approach to teaching writing.

Before we delve in, I want to recognize that some eager, action-oriented teachers may be tempted to skip over this foundation piece and progress straight to the chapters on pedagogical practice. Believe me, I get it: So often, educational scholarship focuses way more on the *why* than on the *how* of a particular pedagogical approach, which can be frustrating for teachers who are thinking, "I'm convinced, already—now please show me how to apply this stuff in my classroom!"

We'll get to teaching applications soon—I promise! But I believe the history and concepts presented here comprise a crucial foundation for two reasons: First, although CLA began as a movement in the United Kingdom, it was a response to social and political dynamics that are likely familiar to many educators in the United States, including:

- The politicization of English/literacy curricula
- Gaps between theory and practice in the application of linguistics and literacy research to classroom pedagogy
- Ongoing tensions among educators and policymakers around academic norms and linguistic standards, which we began discussing in Chapter 1

Engaging the story of CLA allows U.S. teachers to see how our colleagues in other geographic and political contexts have faced questions and challenges

DOI: 10.4324/9781003171751-3

similar to ours. It also may help us to recognize our ethnocentrist "blind spots" (Donahue, 2009) and think more transnationally about the work we do.

A second reason this chapter is important is that if we are *truly committed* to the work of empowering students as critics and users of language, we need a base of understanding on which to build that work. In order to achieve our three goals for CLA Pedagogy—**self-reflection, social justice,** and **rhetorical agency**— we need deep, research-based knowledge about how language and power are interconnected. Otherwise, we may implement this approach in a superficial way, tweaking rather than transforming what we do. History and theory are not everything, but they are useful tools in crafting a vision for what the writing classroom can be and do. That said, I have tried to be as concise and accessible as possible in laying out each piece of the puzzle. I always have in mind the fact that teachers—not theorists or historians—are my primary audience!

Are you convinced to stick with me here? I hope so!

Here is a sketch of the remainder of this chapter: First, we will trace the history of CLA, showing how it emerged from a confluence of two factors— one specific to the U.K. and the other more general across academia. As we follow the story, we will see how CLA has been informed by other areas of scholarship, including critical linguistics and critical literacy. We will also consider some reasons why CLA Pedagogy was not, until more recently, taken up widely by teachers and teacher educators in the United States. Each of these points could be an article or even book in itself, of course, so I will say up front: If you want a more detailed account, please visit the online Hub for additional readings on CLA history and theory.

In the second half of this chapter, we review concepts that are central to CLA as an approach to language and literacy. I have woven many of these concepts into the first half of the chapter, by the way, putting them in **bold.** Many readers will be familiar with some or all of these concepts—particularly if they have had prior coursework or other professional learning in linguistics. But by including my own definitions of these terms, I hope to level the playing field in terms of metalinguistic knowledge—i.e., language for talking about language. Even if none of this conceptual information is new, I hope that my newbie-friendly definitions and examples model how we can present some of these concepts to students.

CLA Origin Story

CLA as a framework for language/literacy education was the result of two trends: (1) the "Knowledge about Language" movement in the United

Kingdom and (2) the broader "critical turn" in academia, including in linguistics and education. The convergence of these two trends was what gave rise to CLA in late 1980s and early 1990s and made it appealing to many scholars and practitioners in the decades that followed.

The "Knowledge about Language" Movement: Language Study 2.0

The 1960s and 1970s were a time of great turmoil in public education, in both the U.S. and the U.K. There are important differences between the two contexts, of course, but for the sake of brevity, let's focus on similarities: There was a growing realization at the time that English/literacy[1] curricula had largely left behind something that had been a core feature decades prior: **language study** (Hudson & Walmsley, 2005; Kolln & Hancock, 2005).

What "language study" usually referred to was a curriculum "typified by atomistic analysis of language, and reinforced by narrowly formalistic methodologies, such as grammar translation, drills, and pattern practice" (Carter, 2003, p. 64). In other words, the study of language usually meant learning and conforming to **prescriptivist** rules for grammar and mechanics, rather than exploring linguistic choices and impacts—i.e., a "**rhetorical grammar**" approach, which we will learn more about in Chapters 5 and 9. Given this reductive focus, it is perhaps unsurprising that many teachers had largely abandoned this type of instruction in favor of other foci, such as literary analysis and process-focused writing (Hudson & Walmsley, 2005).

Yet by the late 1960s, as both the U.S. and the U.K. were experiencing rapid social change, many politicians and constituents became concerned about a perceived "literacy crisis" in public schools (Graff, 2010; Williams, 2007). The reality, of course, was increased racial and socioeconomic integration in public schools brought to light educational inequities that had been overlooked for decades (Berliner & Biddle, 1995; Williams, 2007). But as is often the case, the focus was on symptoms rather than the root causes, causing many calls for a "back to basics" approach—including a return to the old-school, skill-and-drill version of language study, also known as the "grammar grind" (Hudson & Walmsley, 2005; James, 1999).

Around the same time, scholarly understandings about language/literacy development were increasing rapidly (Grabe, 2010). One of the burgeoning areas of inquiry among European linguists was **language awareness,** defined as "explicit knowledge about language,[2] and conscious perception and sensitivity in language learning, language teaching and language use" (Association for Language Awareness [ALA]). Research showed that this **metalinguistic understanding** could enhance students' learning of both spoken and written language (van Essen, 2008).

Although most of the initial language awareness research focused on learning of second/additional languages (L2s), some linguists and educators in the United Kingdom and other European countries saw implications for L1 ("mother tongue") literacy instruction as well, and they began to push for the inclusion of "Knowledge about Language" (KAL) within the broader primary and secondary school curriculum for *all students* (Hawkins, 1992). KAL, they argued, could be a means of re-integrating language study into the English/literacy classroom, but in a more engaging and effective way, with greater attention to real-world language use and deeper metalinguistic understanding (Mitchell et al., 1994). In other words, KAL was an opportunity for Language Study, version 2.0.

The first attempt at promoting KAL within the U.K. curriculum was a program called "Language in Use" (see Doughty et al., 1971). These materials were developed in collaboration with linguists, including Michael Halliday, whose Systemic Functional Linguistics (SFL) approach emphasized the social and interpersonal aspects of language—i.e., language as a tool for meaning-making and relationship-building. This approach offered a rationale and framework for a literacy curriculum focusing on linguistic possibilities, rather than universals (see also Fowler et al., 1979/2018). Unfortunately, these materials were taken up by only a small number of teachers, in part because they were supplemental to the core curriculum. Many teachers simply felt there was no room for this type of language study in an already crowded English curriculum with literature as a primary focus (van Essen, 2008).

However, in the 1980s, after several disconcerting public reports on the state of English/literacy instruction, U.K. educators and policymakers began developing their first mandatory national curriculum. The English section of the curriculum was the most "problematic" (Hudson & Walmsley, 2005, p. 613)—which is unsurprising, given the tensions discussed above. However, when the National Curriculum was released in 1988, it did include "a requirement that pupils demonstrate knowledge about language" (Carter, 1994, p. 247). Hooray!

However, as any veteran teacher knows about major curriculum reforms, the devil is in the details. What did "knowledge about language" mean? What knowledge, specifically? How should it be demonstrated? And how were teachers expected to build that knowledge for themselves, when their own "grammar grind" experiences with language study had been so unengaging and ineffective—or they had received no language instruction whatsoever?

It soon became clear that there was a need for more pedagogical guidance on teaching and assessing KAL. The existing scholarship at the time was often pedagogically unhelpful: A 1990 edited collection, for example, summarized the learning goals of KAL as "Knowing things about language. Being interested in and informed about language" (Carter, 1990, cited in van Essen, 2008, p. 9). Other iterations seemed to equate KAL with the same old-school approach it was supposed to replace. A relatively recent edition of the *Oxford Dictionary of Education* defines KAL narrowly as "an understanding of, and ability to employ correctly, the rules which govern language, such as phonetic rules, spelling, syntax, and grammar" (Wallace, 2014, p. 160). Most educators thus either ignored the KAL mandate or saw it as a call to return to earlier approaches to language study (Clark & Ivanic, 1999). Ironically, a movement that was intended to be an alternative to the "grammar grind" was in danger of becoming just that! (Fairclough, 1992)

Some linguists and literacy specialists, though, had a more ambitious vision for what KAL could be. They wanted to make the "social and ideological nature of language" (Clark & Ivanic, 1999, p. 65) a central focus, in order to cultivate students' awareness of the relationship between language and power. In essence, these scholars wanted to link KAL to another movement taking place across academia: the "critical turn."

Shaking Things Up: A "Critical Turn" in Academia

Most U.S. educators encounter the word "critical" so often—critical thinking, critical literacy, critical pedagogy—that it almost seems devoid of meaning (Luke, 2012; Pennycook, 2010). But the "critical turn" in education has a traceable history, and critical theory has had a notable impact in many other disciplines. Most intellectual historians (i.e., uber-geeks!) trace "critical theory" back to the 1920s and 1930s, when thinkers in many fields—perhaps most notably those in the Frankfurt School—began to consider how Marxism and other theories about social inequality might inform their work (e.g., Slater, 2020). At the core of critical theory was an explicit commitment to *questioning the status quo*, with the ultimate goal of "decreasing domination and increasing freedom" for those who have been oppressed or marginalized in society (Bohman, 2005, para. 1).

Many scholars wanted to do more than simply describe the world as it is. They began asking questions like: *How did it become this way? And how might it be different?* As Bohman (2005) summarizes it, critical theory aimed to "explain what is wrong with current social reality, identify the actors to change it, and provide both clear norms for criticism and achievable practical goals for social transformation" (para. 3).

While these goals had always been a central priority for social reformers and community activists, they had not been as prominent within "the academy," where scholars were—and often still are—expected to be relatively disinterested in the practical or political implications for their work. The 1960s and 1970s were when the "critical turn" really began to revolutionize many disciplines. The many applications of critical theory are difficult to capture in generalities, and it is tricky to parse out which shifts trace back to Marxism vs. other philosophical movements such as poststructuralism and postmodernism (Agger, 1991). However, if we think about criticality as a *direction*, rather than an *end goal*, we can see that a "critical turn" in scholarship often entailed one or more of the following:

- Examining issues of power and oppression, at both micro and macro levels
- Complicating dominant assumptions about the nature of knowledge (e.g., rationalism, positivism, objectivity)
- Crossing—and sometimes contesting—disciplinary boundaries
- Engaging in ongoing self-critique, including of the scholar's own biases and assumptions
- Considering how scholarly inquiry might inform collective action aimed at promoting social, political, and/or economic freedom ("emancipation") for oppressed groups

The critical turn shaped not only *what* scholars were studying, but also *how* they approached their topics of study. Historians, for example, began to talk more openly about the documentation of historical narratives—i.e., "historiography"—as a political process that is shaped by the identities, biases, and lived experiences of the historian, as well as by the views of people in positions of power (Bann, 1981; LaCapra, 2004). This led to new approaches such as "microhistory," aimed at including the perspectives and counter-narratives of communities that have traditionally been left out of the story (Breisach, 2003). For psychologists, the "critical turn" meant a shift away from cognitive universals and toward more nuanced, context-specific understandings of mental health (Fox et al., 2009). As a result, many practitioners shifted toward more "culturally adapted" models for diagnosis and treatment (e.g., Griner & Smith, 2006; O'Reilly & Lester, 2017).

Even within the "hard sciences"—a phrase that itself is has been the focus of some critical examination (e.g., VanLandingham, 2014)—critical theory has had an influence. Scholars in STEM (Science, Technology, Engineering, and Mathematics) began asking questions that had largely been ignored, at least in the upper echelons: What are our ethical obligations to the individuals and communities who participate in our research? What sorts of cultural assumptions are "baked in" to our understandings of objectivity, positionality, and intellectual rigor? Why is some research read—and funded—while other work of equal merit gets ignored? (See Sengupta et al. [2019] for more on critical approaches to STEM. We'll talk more about some of these issues in Chapter 5.)

The Linguists' Turn

In the field of linguistics, the critical turn meant more attention to how language shapes and is shaped by social and political dynamics (Pennycook, 2001; Wodak, 2011). Critical linguists argue that by studying **discourse**—i.e., language as it is used in real-life situations—we can better understand how power functions in the world. We may choose to use language differently in order to empower—or at least create space for—groups that have traditionally been oppressed or marginalized. This way of approaching discourse as a social artifact and a tool for social change is known as Critical Discourse Analysis (CDA), and it is one of the most widely used methodologies in critical linguistics (Fairclough & Wodak, 1997).

CDA has since been taken up by many non-linguists as well, as a way to understand and critique academic, political, and institutional discourse, including in schools and public media (Fairclough & Wodak, 1997). In fact, some scholars have suggested that one of the most profound influences of critical theory in many disciplines was a "linguistic turn"—a shift toward discourse as a focal point for scholarly dialogue, research, and analysis (e.g., Steinberg, 1998; Surkis, 2012). We will return to some of these ideas in Chapters 5 and 6.

Education's Turn

Within the field of English/literacy education, the critical turn manifests in a number of ways—the most notable being a surge of interest in "critical pedagogy," drawing in particular on the work of Paulo Freire, author of *Pedagogy of the Oppressed* (1970). Freire argued that literacy education aimed at social consciousness-raising can be a force for emancipation from oppression. Freire's approach, which was centered around people's everyday experiences of social inequality, inspired many English/writing teachers and teacher educators to begin asking what they could do to bring critical perspectives in their own curricula. The term **critical literacy**, which is sometimes used in conjunction or alternatively with CLA (more on this in Chapter 3), can refer to many different foci and practices (e.g., Luke, 2012; Pennycook, 2001), but most approaches emphasize one or more of the following:

- Raising awareness about issues of inequality and oppression through the selection of topics and texts
- Validating and building on what students already know and can do as language users
- Broadening the range of skills and genres included in the literacy curriculum—i.e., what Cope and Kalantzis (2000) call "multiliteracies"
- Focusing more on rhetorical choices than on linguistic "correctness" in the teaching and assessment of writing (see Chapter 9 for more)

Since the 1980s, critical literacy has gained traction among many English/writing teachers and became prominent within many teacher education programs. However, many approaches to critical literacy in the U.S.—both then and now—devote strikingly little attention to *language*. This is probably because language study continues to be associated with prescriptivist, skill-and-drill instruction and is therefore seen by many educators as incompatible with a socially and politically relevant approach to literacy (Kolln & Hancock, 2005; Luke, 2012).

CLA = KAL + Critical Turn (+ Sedition?)

To pull together the threads laid out thus far, here was the situation with English/literacy education in late 1980s, when CLA was first proposed by a group of U.K. scholars:

- The U.K.'s new National Curriculum had instantiated a requirement that English teachers address KAL. Yet for many teachers, this was either ignored or misinterpreted as a call for a return to earlier, prescriptivist approaches. There was a need for more pedagogical resources to equip educators to integrate KAL in a way that was more engaging and effective.
- Meanwhile, in academia, many linguists and education scholars were invested in enacting a "critical turn" in their work. Many English teachers and teacher educators were seeking more progressive and socially relevant approaches to writing/literacy instruction.

The convergence of these factors created what rhetoricians call a "kairotic moment"—a bit of serendipity in which Critical Language Awareness was in the right place at the right time: Teachers and teacher educators were looking for a more engaging and relevant approach to KAL, and many scholars were eager to infuse critical approaches into the English/literacy curriculum. A golden opportunity!

Well, sort of.

Here's a rough sketch of what happened: In 1989, a year after the release of the National Curriculum, the U.K. government convened a group of linguists and literacy experts to create a professional development program entitled "Language in the National Curriculum" (LINC), to support the new English standards, including the KAL requirement. Most policymakers expected that the materials would focus heavily on the rules and patterns of "standard English." After all, the assumption among many—particularly among conservatives, who held a great deal of political power at the time—was that teachers needed linguistic knowledge and strategies in order to "fix" students' languaging.[3] Put another way, most government officials expected Grammar Grind 2.0—a highly prescriptivist, "back to basics" program, perhaps with slightly more appealing packaging.

That is not what they got. The LINC materials they received for review in 1991 focused more on "function" of language than on "form" (Carter, 1994). They did not ignore grammar by any means—in fact, Carter (1997) points out that there was a "more detailed description of the grammar of English there than in any mother tongue English curriculum materials anywhere in the world" (p. 41). But the materials were largely **descriptivist** in nature: they focused on how people *actually* use language in the real world, rather than on how they *should* use language.

Instead of introducing artificial models of "correct" usage, the LINC group chose to include excerpts of real speech and writing by children from a variety of ethnic and socioeconomic backgrounds (Carter, 1997). When it came to "standard English," the LINC creators tried to present a "balanced and moderate position" (ibid, p. 41), through which they taught the importance and features of standard English, both spoken and written, while *also* recognizing other linguistic varieties that many children use outside of school.[4] In essence, the LINC materials were trying to bridge pragmatism and progressivism—to enact the "both/and" approach we discussed in Chapter 1.

Moreover, many of the topics addressed in the materials were clearly political in nature. There were sections on valuing language diversity, challenging linguistic prejudices, and analyzing texts and other media through a critical lens. In other words, they tended to focus not on "deficiencies" in students' use of language, but instead on the problematic institutions and structures that label some language users as "deficient" in the first place! (James, 1999).

This was *not at all* what most policy-makers had in mind. Where were the drills? The diagrams? The worksheets? How could this curriculum help to solve the literacy crisis, if it was not focused on "fixing" students' writing? And their speech, by the way: Elocution had historically been a central feature of many English curricula in the U.K., as well as in many former British colonies (Robinson, 2019). Speaking instruction almost always prioritized "Received Pronunciation," a prestige variety of British English that is named as such because it is "received" at school—ideally at a posh boarding school—rather than learned at home.[5]

The lawmakers who had convened the LINC group decided *not* to publish or disseminate the materials—quite a remarkable decision, given the time and money that had been invested by that point! Furthermore, they refused to allow the materials to be distributed commercially, despite expressed interest from a number of publishers (Carter, 1997). The concerns that underlay this wholesale rejection of the LINC materials were ideological—not just instructional. As James (1999) explains,

> [I]t was their political ideology that made these materials unacceptable. In emphasizing the variability of language, and defending the objective linguistic equivalence of standard and nonstandard variants, the LINC materials were seen as seditious

> (p. 96)

Seditious!?

The creators of the LINC materials stood their ground. They doubled down, in fact. A group of scholars at Lancaster University, some of whom were connected to the LINC project, had begun calling their approach "Critical Language Awareness," to draw a distinction between their vision for KAL and the prescriptivist, "grammar grind" version that was more familiar to teachers and the general public (Clark et al., 1990). As van Essen (2008) explains, the "critical" in "Critical Language Awareness" was added to signal the intent of:

> being more explicitly informed about the sources of attitudes to language, about its social uses and misuses, about how language is used to manipulate, [which] can empower learners to see through language to the ideologies that particular stylistic choices embody.

> (p. 9)

In response to criticisms that their work was too "political" in nature, CLA scholars such as Romy Clark, Norman Fairclough, and Roz Ivanič argued that *all* literacy education is political, because *language* is always linked to *power*. This, of course, is why English/literacy curricula are so contentious in the first place!

Ironically, the LINC group's failure to get official sanction for their work created another kairotic moment: Once the LINC materials were considered "banned books," educators and administrators became quite eager to get ahold of them! (Carter, 1997). These materials, with their (seditious!) attention to social and political aspects of language, became the catalyst for a grassroots educational movement. In years that followed, they were photocopied and distributed widely among educators. And this was no easy task, in those days when the internet and social media were not yet widely available!

The U.K.'s National Curriculum has been revised multiple times since the 1980s, and the discussion of KAL has been expanded with each iteration. While "standard" conventions still dominate, there is some acknowledgement of other language varieties. The latest "Curriculum Framework" document from 2014, for example, recommends that students in stages 3 and 4 (ages 11–16) "start to learn about some of the differences between Standard English and non-Standard English and begin to apply what they have learnt [for example, in writing dialogue for characters]" (p. 41, brackets original). Despite this nod to a descriptivist approach, most CLA proponents would argue that KAL never went as far in the "critical" direction that they were hoping—particularly when it comes to the treatment of linguistic norms and standards (Hawkins, 1999; Murakami, 2013).

However, CLA's reach has extended well beyond the United Kingdom. The LINC materials were adapted by teachers working in a variety of contexts, for use with both L1 and L2 learners (Taylor et al., 2018). Units or courses on CLA are included in many training programs for English/writing teachers around the world. A review by Hawkins and Norton (2009), for instance, cites examples from Australia, Canada, and Hong Kong, among others. Interest in CLA has grown as well among teachers of other (world/foreign) languages (e.g., Beaudrie et al., 2019; Blyth & Dalola, 2016; Quan, 2020; Wallace, 1998). Today, there are pockets of practitioners using CLA pedagogy around the globe, including in **Africa** (e.g., Ezeifeka, 2013; Janks, 1996; Rubagumya, 1994), **Central and South America** (e.g., Achugar, 2015; Farias, 2005; Taylor et al., 2018), the **Middle East** (e.g., Abbadi, 2014; Parsaiyan, 2019) and **Asia** (e.g., Crookes, 2017; Huang, 2013; Weninger & Kan, 2013).

Some of these "CLA ambassadors" have been able to go further than their U.K. counterparts in tailoring the approach to their local contexts: Hilary Janks, a researcher and teacher educator in South Africa, used what she learned from her doctoral studies at Lancaster University, along with her earlier work with sociolinguistics and critical literacy, to create a six-volume, post-apartheid literacy curriculum (Janks, 1993) that was subversive enough that it at first had to be distributed "underground" (2018). The curriculum included topics ranging from multilingualism to media criticism to peer communication—all focused on valuing diversity, promoting inclusion, and resisting oppression.[6] Janks and her colleagues have continued updating and expanding this work over the decades in response to emergent social and political issues (e.g., Janks, 2010; Janks et al., 2014). Their latest iterations focus heavily on critical media literacy, using CDA methods to facilitate critical conversation and analysis on topics such as "alternative facts," "fake news," and media ethics (Janks, 2018; Turner & Griffin, 2019)—topics we will explore in Chapter 6. Janks has also articulated some important critiques of CLA approaches (e.g., 2010, 2018), which we will be touching on in future chapters.

What About US?

Why wasn't CLA to taken up more widely in the United States? This is a question I have been pondering for quite some time. First, it is important to acknowledge that there are many U.S.-based practitioners who have taken up CLA pedagogy in their work with teachers and students. This list includes English Language Arts teacher educators such as H. Samy Alim, April Baker-Bell, Amanda Godley, Mike Metz, Jeffrey Reaser, Rachel Swords, Rebecca Wheeler, and Walt Wolfram. CLA has also been taken up by some U.S.-based TESOL/applied linguistics specialists, including Mariana Achugar, Graham Crookes, Jason Moore, Brian Morgan, Mary Schleppegrell, and Catherine Wallace. We will be referencing some of these folks' work in future chapters.

However, CLA is largely absent from U.S.-based English/writing and ESOL curricula, and it appears only rarely in conference programs. To be honest, even though I have been using this approach for many years in my writing classes, I only became aware of the term "Critical Language Awareness" relatively recently. I've been hooked ever since!

Why has CLA received less attention from U.S. scholars and practitioners? The answer is certainly *not* that U.S. teachers are uninterested in critical approaches to their work. As alluded to earlier, "critical" has been a buzzword for decades within all levels of education in the U.S. So why hasn't the "language awareness" piece had more uptake? My best summation is that just as CLA was in the right place at the right time for U.K. educators, it seems to have been in the *wrong place at the wrong time* for U.S. teachers and scholars.

Several factors play into this. Perhaps the most salient is that the U.S.'s decentralized approach to public education makes it difficult for *any* nation-wide curricular movement to take hold (Kolln & Hancock, 2005). And if there had been no National Curriculum in the U.K. that codified Knowledge about Language as a curricular priority, there would have been less of an impetus, and probably little if any funding or infrastructure, to develop the LINC materials, which in turn would have limited the need and visibility for CLA.

The United States, unlike most developed countries, has never had a national curriculum. In fact, in 1965, it explicitly *forbade* the establishment of such a curriculum, as part of the Elementary and Secondary Education Act. The Common Core State Standards (CCSS) are the closest the U.S. has ever come to a national curriculum, and although those standards have been adopted by 41 states,[7] each state has a high degree of discretion in terms of implementation and assessment. And even with this flexibility, there has been significant pushback against CCSS since they were first developed (ASCD, 2013). A quick note to readers working in schools/districts that do use CCSS: We will discuss some points of overlap with CLA pedagogy in Chapter 8 (see also Godley et al., 2015).

Another factor preventing the widespread uptake of CLA is that U.S. teachers, including teacher educators, still place much more emphasis on literature than they do on other aspects of English/literacy instruction—which is a bit ironic, I'd say, given that the term "Language Arts" is used much more frequently in the U.S. than in other countries! Literature has remained dominant in part because it is a central feature of **multicultural education**—another movement that has been particularly influential in U.S. K-12 schools and was gaining traction in 1980s and 1990s, at the same time that CLA Pedagogy was becoming more widespread elsewhere (Banks & Banks, 2019; Gorski, 2010).

Many U.S. teachers today still see multicultural literature—i.e., literature that represents a diverse array of identities, communities, and cultural perspectives[8]—as the best (or only) way to promote diversity and inclusion within the English language arts curriculum (e.g., Goo, 2018; Kolln & Hancock, 2005). This loyalty to literature may have caused U.S. teachers to overlook the need for CLA, since they were already attending to social and political issues, at least to some extent, in conversations about literature. One central premise of this book, by the way, is that teachers *do not have to choose* between CLA and multicultural literature. The two complement one another quite well, in fact, as we will explore in Chapter 4 (see also Jalali & Ansaripour, 2014; Wissman, 2018).

The U.S. also led the way in promoting a process approach to writing, which tends to focus more heavily on students' growth and confidence as writers, rather than on the written product (Pritchard & Honeycutt, 2006). Some of the early thinking about this approach was articulated, coincidentally, at a now-infamous 1966 conference called the "Dartmouth Seminar," which brought together teachers from the U.S. and the U.K. to discuss the status and future of (L1) English education (Goodwyn et al., 2018; Vee, 2020[9]). The most heated discussions at that conference—and there were quite a few, according to attendees—had to do with the place of language and linguistics in writing curricula (Vee, 2020).

Though some scholars have claimed that the field is now "post-process" (e.g., Matsuda, 2003; Trimbur, 1994), a process orientation is still widespread in many classrooms and most writing centers (e.g., Boquet, & Lerner, 2008; North, 1984). And although a process approach to writing is quite compatible with CLA Pedagogy, as I will explain in Chapters 3 and 9, focusing more generally on process over product—including more recently with labor-based approaches to assessment (Inoue, 2019)—tends to deflect attention away from some of the thornier questions about linguistic norms and standards that would have drawn U.S. writing teachers to CLA in the first place.

A related factor that may have prevented more uptake of CLA pedagogy among U.S. scholars and practitioners is the lack of dialogue and collaboration between scholars in composition/writing studies and linguistics (Gere et al., 2021; Matsuda, 1999). The two fields are further apart in the U.S. than in many other countries, in part because the dominant approaches to linguistics in the U.S. have been theoretical and/or cognitive, focusing on universals about the nature of language rather than on variations in language use across social contexts (Kolln & Hancock, 2005). One of the most prominent U.S. linguists, Noam Chomsky, explicitly cautioned *against* trying to draw pedagogical implications from his work (Hudson & Walmsley, 2005).[10] In an interesting twist, a number of U.S. teacher educators have begun using the Hallidayan SFL approach in recent years—and have even taught it to students as part of CLA-oriented curricula! (e.g., O'Hallaron et al., 2015; Sembiante & Tian, 2021).

I suspect that there are other factors that made CLA less visible or appealing to U.S. teachers. One is the nature of the "culture wars" in the U.S., in which most any controversial educational issue comes to be thought of as two-sided battle (Dill & Hunter, 2010): There were the "reading wars" between whole language and phonics proponents (e.g., Pearson, 2004), the laws against—and later for—bilingual education in California (Mora, 2000), the ban on ethnic studies programs in Arizona (Romero, 2010), and most recently, executive orders and state-level legislation regarding Critical Race Theory and anti-racism education (Gabriel & Goldstein, 2021[11]).

It is perhaps unsurprising that similarly bellicose language—"grammar wars"—is used to refer to scholarly debates about whether and how to attend to language within the English language arts curriculum (cf., Algeo, 2019; Locke, 2010). This binary thinking can cause huge pendulum swings in educational practice, creating confusion and exhaustion for many U.S. teachers, as we touched on in Chapter 1 (see also Weisberg, 2014). Is it any wonder that they might be skeptical about new approaches to English/literacy education—particularly when those approaches are overtly political to begin with, as was the case with CLA?

One final factor worth noting is that the particular brand of individualism that remains dominant in U.S. education—one that emphasizes individual identity and attributes success in life to one's individual efforts, rather than social or political structures (e.g., DiAngelo, 2010)—may make an approach like CLA undesirable. After all, talking about language and power often means talking about how some groups are systemically disempowered, regardless of how hard individuals from those groups struggle to overcome those barriers. How depressing![12] Of course, the same can be said of any approach to multiculturalism and/or social justice education, if that approach aims to go beyond "celebrating diversity" and to engage issues of inclusion and equity (Michaels, 2016; Ngo, 2010). As we will explore in later chapters, though, conversations about oppression can be quite fun—and empowering!

The Conceptual Core of CLA

Within the story of CLA I laid out above, I have tried to integrate most of the foundational linguistics concepts that underlie this approach. I do this in part because we know from applied linguistics research that to learn new vocabulary words, we need to be exposed to them many times and in a variety of contexts. Below is a review and elaboration on many of the concepts that have been introduced thus far, plus a few additional ones that will recur throughout this book. Please note that I am explaining them here with a goal of *accessibility* rather than thoroughness. The language and examples below are what I *actually use* with my students and colleagues, in contrast to the disciplinary discourse I might use when talking with other linguists. In essence, I am trying to model a commitment to inclusion in how I explain these concepts, so that all readers—no matter what their background with language/linguistics—feel confident in applying these concepts to their lives and teaching practices.

- **Language Awareness** is awareness of how language works—in spoken and written texts, in education, and in the world more broadly. This can include knowledge about specific linguistic structures and patterns (e.g., How do we form passive voice? When might a writer use this passive construction?), but it can also be much broader in scope (e.g., What are the community values that scientists aim to convey when they write about their research using passive voice? How does this change when they are writing for the general public? We'll explore more questions like this in Chapter 5). As mentioned in a footnote earlier, Language Awareness (LA) is sometimes used interchangeably with Knowledge about Language (KAL), although some linguists have tried to draw distinctions between the two (Murakami, 2013; van Essen, 2008).
- **Discourse** is language as it is being used in the real world, as opposed to general theories about language or universal "rules" taught in grammar books and style guides. We can analyze discourse at multiple levels: We may focus on the use of a single word or phrase—i.e., a "close reading" or "unpacking" of the text. (**"Text,"** by the way, can include spoken or even multimodal discourse.) Or we might look more broadly at the structure, content, tone, or other rhetorical elements. Analyzing discourse tells us something not just about how the text works, but about why it works—or doesn't. We can consider the goals of the author/speaker, the expectations of the audience, sometimes called the "discourse community," and trends in society more broadly (e.g., is this a **kairotic moment** for this topic/argument?). There is a great deal of common ground between discourse analysis and rhetorical analysis, as will become evident in Chapters 5 and 6, but they tend to use different sets of terms because of their distinct disciplinary grounding in linguistics vs. rhetoric/communication.
- **Critical Discourse Analysis, or CDA,** which is informed by the broader field of critical linguistics, focuses more heavily on power dynamics in and around texts, compared with other approaches to discourse analysis

or language study. In addition to examining how and why a text works on multiple levels, CDA scholars ask critical questions such as: What assumptions does this text make about the audience? About the topic? About the world? Who is likely to feel included by this text? (i.e., who is the "us"?). Who is likely to feel excluded? (i.e., who is the "them"?). Ultimately, CDA helps us consider how the way we use and interpret language might empower some people and disempower others.

- **Power:** I have been using this term throughout this chapter but have not yet explained what it means in the context of CLA. Entire books have been written on the nature of power. Unfortunately, very few of them define the concept in a clear and concise way. The most useful definition I have seen comes from scholar and activist Brené Brown, who derives her definition from a 1968 speech by Dr. Martin Luther King, Jr.: Power is "the ability to achieve purpose and effect change" (Brown, 2018).[13] As we will explore in many of the chapters to come, language attitudes, policies, and practices may help or hinder us in our ability to do what we want to do—and be who we want to be—in the world.

- **Prescriptivism** is an approach to language focused on what people *should* do. Prescriptivists usually see linguistic rules as universal, rather than context-specific. They see "standard" language not just as one possible choice, but as the "correct" choice. In public discourse—which is rife with prescriptivism, as we will discuss in several chapters—prescriptivists are often called "sticklers," "language pundits," or even "grammar police."[14] One excellent example of a public prescriptivist is Lynn Truss, the author of *Eats, Shoots & Leaves: The Zero Tolerance Approach to Punctuation*, which became an international bestseller in both the U.K. and the U.S. (I hope the phrase "zero tolerance" caught your attention there! We'll talk more about Truss and prescriptivism in Chapter 5). Prescriptivist educators often prioritize linguistic norms and standards in their curricula, with the rationale that standard(ized) language, explained in a separate entry below, is not only different but better—at least in academic, professional, and other public settings.

- **Descriptivism** is an approach to language focused on what people *actually do* with language. Most linguists see themselves as descriptivists: They study what language is and how people use it, rather than prescribing how people *should* use language, as discussed above. Descriptivists do not ignore the presence of—and need for—linguistic norms and standards. However, they recognize and celebrate the existence of all linguistic varieties (i.e., dialects, languages, or styles). Descriptivists tend to critique prescriptivists for having a "my way or the highway" attitude about language, while prescriptivists critique them for acting as if "anything goes" when it comes to language use. Each of these is an over-generalization, of course, which is why the "both/and" approach of CLA is so important!

- **Variety** is a term linguists use as an alternative to "dialect," because the latter is often pejoratively to reference the colloquial (everyday) language used within marginalized communities (e.g., "She spoke in dialect," vs. "She spoke in Black/African American Vernacular English"). Another reason linguists use the term "variety" is that for political reasons, two varieties that are mutually incomprehensible may be referred to as "dialects" of a single language. For example, Chinese government officials may refer to Mandarin and Cantonese as "dialects of Chinese," in order to reinforce a nationalist or "unity" narrative about China. And the reverse happens, too, where two or more varieties that are remarkably similar to one another—such as Bosnian, Croatian, and Serbian—are referred to officially as "languages," in order to emphasize national identity and to justify ethnic and political borders. As a witticism publicized by the sociolinguist Max Weinreich puts it, "A language is a dialect with an army and a navy" (e.g., McWhorter, 2016). "Variety" can also refer to a distinct style or register within a dialect or language—for example, to distinguish between the language used in a campaign speech vs. a spoken word performance.

- **Standard(ized) language** is the linguistic variety, or collection of varieties, usually given preference in schools, workplaces, and public life. Many linguists (e.g., Godley et al., 2015) prefer to use the word "standardized" rather than "standard," because the former reminds us that standardization is what *powerful people do* to language. Linguistic standards do not appear from on high on stone tablets. They are the result of an intentional process by which someone with authority decides whose language variety should be privileged over others. Usually (surprise, surprise!), the variety selected to be the "standard"—sometimes called a "prestige variety"—is one used by communities that already have economic, cultural, and political power. That prestige variety is then taught in schools and expected in job interviews, court testimonies, and other high-stakes situations. Thus, the process of standardization *often exacerbates power imbalances in society.* That is why discussions of "standard language" often become so fraught, as we saw earlier in this chapter and in Chapter 1. It is also important to distinguish between "standardized English" and **academic English.** While both are usually expected in school, the latter often uses more abstract vocabulary and complex sentence structures—particularly when it comes to academic writing.[15]

- **Language ideology** refers to the beliefs about language and language users that we are steeped in every day. Language ideologies are replicated in schools, media and within many families and communities. Identifying, unpacking, and at times resisting these beliefs is a central feature of CLA Pedagogy. One way I like to work with the concept of language ideology with students is by tracing accent patterns in animation films for children. When they examine some of their favorite movies from childhood (e.g., *The Lion King, Shrek, Mulan, Madagascar*) through a CLA lens, students notice that the "silly sidekick" character often has features of African American Vernacular English (AAVE) or another stigmatized variety, while the protagonist often uses the prestige variety, which is **unmarked**—i.e., considered to be "neutral" or the "norm." This pattern thus reinforces stereotypes that users of stigmatized varieties are less intelligent and/or capable than users of other varieties. In Chapter 4, we will delve much more deeply into accent stereotypes and marked vs. unmarked speech. Warning: If you haven't already noticed them, you will start to see these concerning patterns everywhere—and not just in children's media![16]

In the chapters that follow, I will be introducing additional concepts that are particularly relevant to a specific Pathway or unit. But what we have covered here is enough of a foundation, I hope, for you to engage the principles of CLA Pedagogy, and to begin applying those principles to your own writing curriculum and instruction. These principles, and the broader question of *how CLA Pedagogy works*, are the focus for Chapter 3. See you there!

Notes

1 I use "English literacy" here to refer to English language arts education (ELA), or L1 (first language or mother tongue) instruction for mostly native speakers of English. This is in contrast with "English to Speakers of Other Languages" (ESOL) which refers to the teaching of English as an additional language, or L2. Of course, the two are not mutually exclusive, but there has traditionally been a "division of labor" between ELA and ESOL specialists, in both secondary and postsecondary settings (Matsuda, 1999).

2 It is worth noting that although "Knowledge about Language" (KAL) is included as one component of "language awareness" (LA) in the ALA's definition, some scholars frame KAL and LA as separate but interrelated domains: Some scholars have suggested that KAL is implicit, while LA is explicit or conscious knowledge (Murakami, 2013; van Essen, 2008). One of the few things scholars do seem to agree on is that KAL is used more frequently in reference to L1 (English/literacy) learners, while LA is used more in discussions of L2 (ESOL, EAL) learning. (See

Murakami, 2013, for more on the various characterizations of the relationship between KAL and LA.)

3 The term "languaging" is used by many linguists and literacy scholars as a way to highlight the fact that language-in-use is a dynamic process, rather than a static product (e.g., Sembiante & Tian, 2021; Swain, 2006). We'll talk more about this in Chapter 3.

4 Carter (1997) points out that "97 per cent of the examples in LINC materials are of pupils speaking, reading, and writing in standard English" (p. 41).

5 Although elocution has faded somewhat over the decades, oral communication is still a central focus of the U.K. national curriculum, which was revised most recently in 2014. Through linguistic diversity has increased in many parts of the United Kingdom, elocution instruction is still prevalent, and demand for pre-scriptivist speech instruction has in fact increased in recent years (Tickle, 2016).

6 Janks's original (1993) "Critical Language Awareness Series" has been scanned and made available freely online at: http://wiredspace.wits.ac.za/handle/10539/18069

7 www.corestandards.org/standards-in-your-state/

8 I provide my own definition here because I have discovered within the literature (pun intended!) that even the definition of "multilingual literature" has been hotly contested (e.g., Cai, 2002).

9 For a fascinating retrospective on what happened at "Dartmouth '66" and why it matters, check out the following online exhibit: https://wac.colostate.edu/resources/research/dartmouth/

10 When the work of Chomsky and other theoretical linguists has been referenced within the context of English/literacy education, it has often been misrepresented. Perhaps the most egregious example is that some teachers used his theory of Universal Grammar (UG)—i.e., the idea that humans have a "mental grammar" that allows them to acquire any human language as children, given the right circumstances—to suggest that explicit teaching of grammar was unnecessary or even harmful (Hudson & Walmsley, 2005).

11 www.nytimes.com/2021/06/01/us/politics/critical-race-theory.html

12 I'm of course being facetious here, but only a bit: One of the concerns raised about CLA has been that it is too "cynical" in its view of society. See Janks (1996) for a response to this concern from the South African perspective. Similar concerns have been raised (and ably responded to) in discussions of anti-racism and other social justice approaches (e.g., hooks, 2003; Zembylas, 2020).

13 In her work with leaders, Brown also distinguishes between "power over," which she says is motivated by fear, and "power with/to/within," which is motivated by love of self and others. For more, visit https://brenebrown.com/wp-content/uploads/2020/10/Brene-Brown-on-Power-and-Leadership.pdf

14 I could add "grammar Nazi" here, but I have mixed feelings about "Nazi" as a joke, particularly when neo-Nazism is on the rise in many parts of the world. I mention this in part to highlight that even descriptivist linguists can be prescriptive about some things—see Cameron (2012) and Chapter 5 of this volume, for more.

15 The "Three-Tiers Framework" from Beck et al. (2013) provides a helpful heuristic for distinguishing between conversational, academic, and disciplinary language. A helpful summary can be found here: www.bep.education/wp-content/uploads/2018/09/Bringing-Words-to-Life-Booklet.pdf

16 When my students complain that their CLA learning "ruined Disney" for them, I usually respond with the tongue-in-cheek apology I have seen all over social media: "Sorry not sorry!" I then say, "If a gender studies class hasn't done that for you already, then it was high time someone did!" I do continue to watch animated films with my children, though—and as we'll discuss in Chapter 4, more recent films have been getting better at resisting linguistic, racial, and cultural stereotypes.

References

Abbadi, S. O. (2014). Teaching Arabic post 9/11: Humor and the potential for critical language awareness. *Dirasat, Human and Social Sciences, 41*(1), 322–334.

Achugar, M. (2015). Theme: Critical language awareness approaches in the Americas: Theoretical principles, pedagogical practices and distribution of intellectual labor. *Linguistics and Education, 32*, 1–4. https://doi.org/10.1016/j.linged.2015.07.003

Agger, B. (1991). Critical theory, poststructuralism, postmodernism: Their sociological relevance. *Annual Review of Sociology, 17*(1), 105–131.

Algeo, J. (2019). Grammar wars: The United States. In C. Nelson, Z. Proshina, & D. Davis (Eds.), *The handbook of world Englishes* (2nd ed., pp. 495–506). Wiley.

Association for Supervision and Curriculum Development (ASCD). (2013, February 25). *Political pushback on the common core.* www.ascd.org/common-core/core-connection/02-25-13-political-pushback-on-the-common-core.aspx

Banks, J. A., & Banks, C. A. M. (Eds.). (2019). *Multicultural education: Issues and perspectives.* John Wiley & Sons.

Bann, S. (1981). Towards a critical historiography: Recent work in philosophy of history. *Philosophy, 56*(217), 365–385.

Beaudrie, S., Amezcua, A., & Loza, S. (2019). Critical language awareness for the heritage context: Development and validation of a measurement questionnaire. *Language Testing, 36*(4), 573–594. https://doi.org/10.1177/0265532219844293

Beck, I. L., McKeown, M. G., & Kucan, L. (2013). *Bringing words to life: Robust vocabulary instruction.* Guilford Press.

Berliner, B., & Biddle, D. (1995). *The manufactured crisis: Myths, fraud, and the attack on America's public schools.* Basic Books.

Blyth, C., & Dalola, A. (2016). Translingualism as an open educational language practice: Raising critical language awareness on Facebook. *Alsic. Apprentissage Des Langues et Systèmes d'Information et de Communication, 19*(1). https://journals.openedition.org/alsic/2962

Bohman, J. (2005). Critical theory. *Stanford Encyclopedia of Philosophy.* https://plato.stanford.edu/entries/critical-theory/

Boquet, E. H., & Lerner, N. (2008). After "the idea of a writing center". *College English, 71*(2), 170–189.

Breisach, E. (2003). *On the future of history: The postmodernist challenge and its aftermath.* University of Chicago Press.

Brown, B. (2018). *Dare to lead: Brave work. Tough conversations. Whole hearts.* Penguin Random House.

Cai, M. (2002). *Multicultural literature for children and young adults: Reflections on critical issues.* ABC-CLIO.

Cameron, D. (2012). *Verbal hygiene.* Routledge.

Carter, R. (Ed.). (1990). *Knowledge about language and the curriculum: The LINC reader.* Hodder.

Carter, R. (1994). Knowledge about language in the curriculum. In S. Brindley (Ed.), *Teaching English* (pp. 246–258). Routledge.

Carter, R. (1997). *Investigating English discourse: Language, literacy and literature (Ch 3: Politics and knowledge about language: The LINC project).* Routledge.

Carter, R. (2003). Language awareness (key concepts in ELT). *ELT Journal, 57*(1).

Clark, R., Fairclough, N., Ivanič, R., & Martin-Jones, M. (1990). Critical language awareness part I: A critical review of three current approaches to language awareness. *Language and Education, 4*(4), 249–260. https://doi.org/10.1080/09500789009541291

Clark, R., & Ivanic, R. (1999). Editorial: Raising critical awareness of language: A curriculum aim for the new millennium. *Language Awareness, 8*(2), 63–70. https://doi.org/10.1080/09658419908667118

Cope, B., & Kalantzis, M. (2000). *Multiliteracies: Literacy learning and the design of social futures.* Routledge.

Crookes, G. (2017). Critical language pedagogy given the English divide in Korea: A suite of practices, critique, and the role of the intellectual. *English Teaching, 72*(4), 3–21. https://doi.org/10.15858/engtea.72.4.201712.3

Department of Education. (2014, July 16). *National curriculum.* https://www.gov.uk/government/collections/national-curriculum

DiAngelo, R. J. (2010). Why can't we all just be individuals?: Countering the discourse of individualism in anti-racist education. *InterActions: UCLA Journal of Education and Information Studies, 6*(1).

Dill, J. S., & Hunter, J. D. (2010). Education and the culture wars: Morality and conflict in American schools. In S. Hitlin & S. Vaisey (Eds.), *Handbook of the sociology of morality* (pp. 275–291). Springer.

Donahue, C. (2009). "Internationalization" and composition studies: Reorienting the discourse. *College Composition and Communication,* 212–243.

Doughty, P., Pearce, J., & Thornton, G. (1971). *Language in use.* Arnold.

Ezeifeka, C. R. (2013). Strategic use of metaphor in Nigerian newspaper reports: A critical perspective. *Critical Approaches to Discourse Analysis across Disciplines, 6*(2), 174–192.

Fairclough, N. (1992/2014). *Critical language awareness.* Routledge.

Fairclough, N., & Wodak, R. (1997). Critical discourse analysis. In N. Fairclough, J. Mulderrig, & R. Wodak (Eds.), *Discourse studies: A multidisciplinary introduction* (pp. 357–378). Sage.

Farias, M. (2005). Critical language awareness in foreign language learning. *Literatura y Lingüística, 16*, 211–222 [online]. http://doi.org/10.4067/S0716-58112005000100012

Fowler, R., Hodge, B., Kress, G., & Trew, T. (1979/2018). *Language and control.* Routledge.

Fox, D., Prilleltensky, I., & Austin, S. (Eds.). (2009). *Critical psychology: An introduction.* Sage.

Freire, P. (1970). *Pedagogy of the oppressed.* New York: Continuum.

Gabriel, T., & Goldstein, D. (2021, June 1). Disputing racism's reach, Republicans rattle American schools. *New York Times.* www.nytimes.com/2021/06/01/us/politics/critical-race-theory.html

Gere, A., Curzan, A., Hammond, J. W., Hughes, S., Li, R., Moos, A., Smith, K., Van Zanen, K., Wheeler, K. L., & Zanders, C. J. (2021). Communal justicing: Writing assessment, disciplinary infrastructure, and the case for critical language awareness. *College Composition and Communication, 72*(3), 384–412.

Godley, A. J., Reaser, J., & Moore, K. G. (2015). Pre-service English language arts teachers' development of critical language awareness for teaching. *Linguistics and Education, 32*, 41–54. https://doi.org/10.1016/j.linged.2015.03.015

Goo, Y. (2018). Multicultural literature education: A story of failure? *Society, 55*(4), 323–328.

Goodwyn, A., Durrant, C., Sawyer, W., Scherff, L., & Zancanella, D. (Eds.). (2018). *The future of English teaching worldwide: Celebrating 50 years from the Dartmouth conference.* Routledge/Taylor & Francis.

Gorski, P. C. (2010). The scholarship informing the practice: Multicultural teacher education philosophy and practice in the US. *International Journal of Multicultural Education, 12*(2). http://doi.org/10.18251/ijme.v12i2.352

Grabe, W. (2010). Applied linguistics: A twenty-first-century discipline. In R. Kaplan (Ed.), *The Oxford handbook of applied linguistics* (2nd ed.). Oxford University Press. https://doi.org/10.1093/oxfordhb/9780195384253.013.0002

Graff, H. J. (2010). The literacy myth at thirty. *Journal of Social History*, 635–661.

Griner, D., & Smith, T. B. (2006). Culturally adapted mental health intervention: A meta-analytic review. *Psychotherapy: Theory, Research, Practice, Training, 43*(4), 531–548.

Hawkins, E. (1992). Awareness of language/knowledge about language in the curriculum in England and Wales: An historical note on twenty years of curricular debate. *Language Awareness, 1*(1), 5–17.

Hawkins, E. W. (1999). Foreign language study and language awareness. *Language Awareness, 8*(3–4), 124–142.

Hawkins, M., & Norton, B. (2009). Critical language teacher education. In A. Burns (Ed.), *Cambridge guide to second language teacher education* (pp. 30–39). Cambridge University Press.

hooks, B. (2003). *Teaching community: A pedagogy of hope* (Vol. 36). Routledge.

Huang, S. Y. (2013). Revising identities as writers and readers through critical language awareness. *English Teaching: Practice & Critique, 12*(3), 65–86. http://education.waikato.ac.nz/research/files/etpc/files/2013v12n3art4.pdf

Hudson, R., & Walmsley, J. (2005). The English patient: English grammar and teaching in the twentieth century. *Journal of Linguistics, 41*(3), 593–622.

Inoue, A. B. (2019). *Labor-based grading contracts: Building equity and inclusion in the compassionate writing classroom.* WAC Clearinghouse. https://wac.colostate.edu/books/perspectives/labor/

Jalali, M., & Ansaripour, E. (2014). Post-colonialism and critical language awareness (Chinua Achebe, L2, and identity). *Procedia—Social and Behavioral Sciences, 98,* 713–718. https://doi.org/10.1016/j.sbspro.2014.03.472

James, C. (1999). Language awareness: Implications for the language curriculum. *Language, Culture and Curriculum, 12*(1), 94–115. https://doi.org/10.1080/07908319908666571

Janks, H. (1993). *Critical language awareness series.* Witwatersrand University Press and Hodder & Stoughton Educational.

Janks, H. (1996). Why we still need critical language awareness in South Africa. *Stellenbosch Papers in Linguistics Plus, 29,* 172–190.

Janks, H. (2010). *Literacy and power.* Routledge.

Janks, H. (2018). Texts, identities, and ethics: Critical literacy in a post-truth world. *Journal of Adolescent & Adult Literacy, 62*(1), 95–99. https://doi.org/10.1002/jaal.761

Janks, H., Dixon, K., Ferreira, A., Granville, S., & Newfield, D. (2014). *Doing critical literacy: Texts and activities for students and teachers.* Routledge.

Kolln, M., & Hancock, C. (2005). The story of English grammar in United States schools. *English Teaching: Practice and Critique, 4*(3), 11–31.

LaCapra, D. (2004). *History in transit: Experience, identity, critical theory.* Cornell University Press.

Locke, T. (Ed.). (2010). *Beyond the grammar wars: A resource for teachers and students on developing language knowledge in the English/literacy classroom.* Routledge.

Luke, A. (2012). Critical literacy: Foundational notes. *Theory into Practice, 51*(1), 4–11.

Matsuda, P. K. (1999). Composition studies and ESL writing: A disciplinary division of labor. *College Composition and Communication, 50*(4), 699–721.

Matsuda, P. K. (2003). Process and post-process: A discursive history. *Journal of Second Language Writing, 12*(1), 65–83.

McWhorter, J. (2016, January 19). What's a language, anyway? *The Atlantic Magazine.* www.theatlantic.com/international/archive/2016/01/difference-between-language-dialect/424704/

Michaels, W. B. (2016). *The trouble with diversity: How we learned to love identity and ignore inequality.* Macmillan.

Mitchell, R., Brumfit, C., & Hooper, J. (1994). "Knowledge about language": Policy, rationales and practices. *Research Papers in Education, 9*(2), 183–205.

Mora, J. K. (2000, September). Policy shifts in language-minority education: A mismatch between politics and pedagogy. In *The educational forum* (Vol. 64, no. 3, pp. 204–214). Taylor & Francis Group.

Murakami, C. (2013). *Language awareness & knowledge about language: A history of a curriculum reform movement under the conservatives, 1979–1997* [Unpublished doctoral dissertation, University of Exeter].

Ngo, B. (2010). Doing "diversity" at dynamic high: Problems and possibilities of multicultural education in practice. *Education and Urban Society, 42*(4), 473–495.

North, S. M. (1984). The idea of a writing center. *College English, 46*(5), 433–446.

O'Hallaron, C. L., Palincsar, A. S., & Schleppegrell, M. J. (2015). Reading science: Using systemic functional linguistics to support critical language awareness. *Linguistics and Education, 32*, 55–67.

O'Reilly, M., & Lester, J. N. (2017). The critical turn to language in the field of mental health. In M. O'Reilly & J. N. Lester (Eds.), *Examining mental health through social constructionism: The language of mental health* (pp. 1–29). Springer.

Parsaiyan, S. F. (2019). "This Is a food ad but it is presenting gender stereotypes!": Practicing critical language awareness in an Iranian EFL context. *Journal of English Language Teaching and Learning, 11*(24), 227–259.

Pearson, P. D. (2004). The reading wars. *Educational Policy, 18*(1), 216–252.

Pennycook, A. (2001). *Critical applied linguistics: A critical introduction.* Routledge.

Pennycook, A. (2010). Critical and alternative directions in applied linguistics. *Australian Review of Applied Linguistics, 33*(2), 16.1–16.16. https://doi.org/10.2104/aral1016

Pritchard, R. J., & Honeycutt, R. L. (2006). The process approach to writing instruction: Examining its effectiveness. In C. MacArthur, S. Graham, & J. Fitzgerald (Eds.), *Handbook of writing research* (pp. 275–290). Guilford.

Quan, T. (2020). Critical language awareness and L2 learners of Spanish: An action-research study. *Foreign Language Annals*, 1–23. https://doi.org/10.1111/flan.12497

Robinson, J. (2019, April 25). Received pronunciation. *British Library: British Accents and Dialects.* www.bl.uk/british-accents-and-dialects/articles/received-pronunciation#

Romero, A. F. (2010). At war with the state in order to save the lives of our children: The battle to save ethnic studies in Arizona. *The Black Scholar, 40*(4), 7–15.

Rubagumya, C. (1994). Epilogue: Towards critical language awareness in Africa. *Teaching and Researching Language in African Classrooms, 98*, 155, Ch 12.

Sembiante, S. F., & Tian, Z. (2021). Culturally sustaining approaches to academic languaging through systemic functional linguistics. *Language and Education, 35*(2), 101–105. https://doi.org/10.1080/09500782.2021.189653

Sengupta, P., Shanahan, M. C., & Kim, B. (Eds.). (2019). *Critical, transdisciplinary and embodied approaches in STEM education.* Springer.

Slater, P. (2020). *Origin and significance of the Frankfurt school: A Marxist perspective.* Routledge.

Steinberg, M. W. (1998). Tilting the frame: Considerations on collective action framing from a discursive turn. *Theory and Society, 27*(6), 845–872.

Surkis, J. (2012). When was the linguistic turn? A genealogy. *The American Historical Review, 117*(3), 700–722.

Swain, M. (2006). Languaging, agency and collaboration in advanced second language proficiency. In H. Byrnes (Ed.), *Advanced language learning: The contribution of Halliday and Vygotsky* (pp. 95–108). Continuum.

Taylor, S. K., Despagne, C., & Faez, F. (2018). Critical language awareness. In *The TESOL encyclopedia of English language teaching* (pp. 1–14). John Wiley & Sons. https://doi.org/10.1002/9781118784235.eelt0660

Tickle, L. (2016, October 14). Accent snobbery boosts demand for elocution lessons. *The Guardian.* www.theguardian.com/small-business-network/2016/oct/14/accent-snobbery-boosts-demand-elocution-lessons

Trimbur, J. (1994). Review: Taking the social turn: Teaching writing post-process. *College Composition and Communication, 45*(1), 108–118.

Turner, J. D., & Griffin, A. A. (2019). Power, language, and social change: A dialogue with Hilary Janks about critical literacy in a "post-truth" world. *Language Arts, 96*(5), 318–324.

van Essen, A. (2008). Language awareness and knowledge about language: A historical overview. In J. Cenoz & N. H. Hornberger (Eds.), *Encyclopedia of language and education: Knowledge about language* (Vol. 6, 2nd ed., pp. 3–14). Springer.

VanLandingham, M. (2014). On the hard and soft sciences in public health. *Public Health Reports, 129*(2), 124–126.

Vee, A. (2020). *Introduction: What was the Dartmouth seminar?* WAC Clearinghouse https://wac.colostate.edu/resources/research/dartmouth/introduction-what-was-the-dartmouth-seminar/

Wallace, C. (1998). *Critical language awareness in the foreign language classroom* [Doctoral dissertation, Institute of Education, University of London].

Wallace, S. W. (Ed.). (2014). Knowledge about language. In *A dictionary of education.* Oxford University Press.

Weisberg, A. (2014, March 11). Watching the pendulum swing. *Huffington Post* www.huffpost.com/entry/watching-the-pendulum-swi_b_4932273

Weninger, C., & Kan, K. H. Y. (2013). (Critical) language awareness in business communication. *English for Specific Purposes, 32*(2), 59–71. https://doi.org/10.1016/j.esp.2012.09.002

Williams, B. T. (2007). Why Johnny can never, ever read: The perpetual literacy crisis and student identity. *Journal of Adolescent & Adult Literacy, 51*(2), 178–182.

Wissman, K. K. (2018). Teaching global literature to "disturb the waters": A case study. *English Education, 55*(1), 17–48.

Wodak, R. (2011). Critical linguistics and critical discourse analysis. In J. Zienkowski (Ed.), *Discursive pragmatics* (pp. 50–69). John Benjamins.

Zembylas, M. (2020). (Un) happiness and social justice education: Ethical, political and pedagogic lessons. *Ethics and Education, 15*(1), 18–32.

3
How and Why Does CLA Pedagogy Work?

Principles and Best Practices

Introduction

In Chapter 2, we learned about the history of CLA, tracing its origin to the convergence of the "Knowledge About Language" movement in the U.K. and the "critical turn" in academia. We also reviewed some core concepts that are central to CLA. This chapter is where we delve more deeply into the principles and features of a CLA approach to pedagogy, particularly as it pertains to the teaching of writing.

A few notes, before we begin:

First, as I discussed in Chapters 1 and 2, CLA has been around for several decades, and some aspects of this approach were in use even prior to the introduction of "CLA" as a new term (e.g., Doughty et al., 1971; Fowler et al., 1979/2018). This long history presents both an opportunity and a challenge for a book aimed at making the concept relevant to teachers from a wide variety of backgrounds: The opportunity is that there is a rich, diverse body of scholarship to draw from. The challenge is that it is impossible to synthesize that scholarship thoroughly while keeping the book reader-friendly.

I therefore want to state *up front*: This is not a literature review or a meta-analysis of research on CLA Pedagogy. I will inevitably leave out many people, places, and practices in my attempt to make this approach accessible and appealing to a practitioner audience. Critics may argue that I over-simplify, over-generalize, and/or cast too wide a net, in laying out what CLA Pedagogy entails and how it works.

But I care less here about comprehensiveness than I do about usefulness: I want you, dear reader, to feel that you have enough of an understanding of CLA Pedagogy that you can make it your own. I hope that you will

DOI: 10.4324/9781003171751-4

start to examine what you *already do* and think, "Wow! I was using CLA Pedagogy already—I just didn't have a label for it!" I also hope that you will start to envision ways that you could adapt or build on what you already do, to further your commitment to cultivating CLA among student writers.

What I do *not* want is for readers to come away from this book thinking, "Egads! I have to abandon everything I already do in my writing classroom and start from scratch!" Please, let that *not* be the message. I say this in part because over my many years working as a middle-school, high-school, and college-level writing teacher—as well as a teacher educator—I have encountered many "new" approaches that do not seem to build on what teachers already know and do—which is a bit ironic, considering that *building on prior knowledge* is one of those basic pedagogical principles we are taught early on in our professional training, no? Just as we want to build our students' agency as readers and writers, I want to build your own agency as an educator. I hope learning about CLA increases your confidence, piques your imagination, and adds to your teacher "toolbox," so that you feel excited and empowered to share this learning with students—and maybe with your colleagues as well!

A final reminder: This chapter presents CLA broadly as a pedagogical approach. Although I provide some a few specifics as part of the explanation, most of the curricular and instructional examples, along with other "nuts-and-bolts" type guidance, are in the chapters that follow. Readers may be tempted to skip ahead (I cautioned against this in Chapter 2, by the way, in case you skipped ahead!), but I urge you not to, for this reason: If we don't understand how and why CLA works, we may integrate something new into our classes—a topic, text, activity, or assignment—with an incomplete understanding of what we are trying to accomplish. (Remember the minor "tweaks" by instructors A through E in Chapter 1?). We may miss opportunities to "go deep" in promoting self-awareness, social justice, and rhetorical agency. In other words, a solid grounding in principles and best practices allows us to make the most of what CLA Pedagogy has to offer.

Unpacking Our Definition of CLA Pedagogy

In Chapter 2, we touched on the idea of "unpacking" language as part of Critical Discourse Analysis (CDA), an approach from critical linguistics that has been applied in many academic disciplines. To help build an understanding

of how and why CLA Pedagogy works, let's do a bit of unpacking of our initial definition of CLA Pedagogy from Chapter 1:

> CLA Pedagogy is an approach to language/literacy education that fo-
> cuses on the intersections of language, identity, power, and privilege,
> with the goal of promoting self-reflection, social justice, and rhetorical
> agency.

What does it mean to say that CLA Pedagogy is an **approach**, rather than
a "theory" or a "method"? My goal in using the word "approach" is to signal
two things: First, as is the case with other approaches (Richards & Rodgers, 1982), CLA Pedagogy has both conceptual and practical elements. Second, the use of CLA is intended to be pedagogically generative rather than
prescriptive. In other words, CLA Pedagogy is a way of viewing and doing—i.e., "approaching"—our work, informed by particular understandings
of language, literacy, and education, rather than a set of specific mandates or
procedures. Embracing CLA Pedagogy does not require teaching any specific
topic, text, skill, or assignment. However, it does require a willingness to
see your teaching, and language itself, in complex and critical ways—and as
inherently connected to identity, power, and privilege.

Why do I refer to "**language/literacy education**" and not just "**writing**"?
While this book is targeted toward writing teachers specifically, I wanted
my definition to remind readers that CLA is used in other subject areas
as well. As we talked about in Chapter 2, CLA is informed by linguistic
concepts that are applicable to both L1 ("mother tongue") and L2 (ESOL,
EAL) English/literacy instruction, as well as to instruction in languages
other than English. One of the reasons I am so passionate about CLA is
that I believe it can build and strengthen bridges among specialists in applied linguistics, English/literacy studies, composition/writing, and world
languages—fields that are often institutionally siloed in the United States.
I would love to see this bridging work happening on a local level as well:
Wouldn't it be exciting if we had teachers of English Language Arts, ESOL/
EAL, world languages, and other subjects—e.g., social studies, STEM, the
arts, etc.—engaging in dialogue and curricular collaboration around language, identity, power, and privilege? In Chapter 10, and at the online Hub,
I explore some ways we can make this happen!

The other reason I use "language/literacy" in the definition is that I want
writing teachers to embrace fully their role as teachers, users, and analysts
of language. I find it strange, to be honest, that the phrase "language arts"
is used so widely in primary and middle grades education, but is dropped in

many high schools and nearly absent altogether at the college level. Aren't we all teaching language *all the time*? Why do we talk so little about language, even though it is clearly at the heart of what we do?

This is a question on which many scholars—such as Gutiérrez et al. (1997), Kolln and Hancock (2005), and Macdonald (2007)—have a lot to say. But to recap one of the answers we discussed in Chapter 2, many English/writing teachers in the U.S. hear "language" as synonymous with the "grammar grind"—i.e., a prescriptivist, skill-and-drill approach to language to that is characterized by inaccessible jargon, boring worksheets, useless drills, and student papers covered in red ink. What teachers would consciously choose to do that to students—or to themselves?!

Of course, as we'll explore more in Chapters 5 and 6, grammar instruction does not have to be any of that. When informed by CLA, the goal is to equip students to make informed rhetorical choices, rather than to shame or punish them for using "incorrect" forms. But this linking of grammar to rhetorical agency—not to mention to social justice—is something few U.S. English/writing teachers have experienced for themselves. In other words, a CLA approach invites us to redefine what it means to work with language in the writing classroom, including teaching grammar rhetorically, rather than prescriptively.

OK, back to unpacking our definition of CLA!

Why does this definition of CLA emphasize "**language, identity, power, and privilege**"? Identity tends to be a favorite theme for U.S. English/writing teachers. Many of us invite students to explore this theme in personal essays or projects, and we often support students' analysis of identities in literature or other texts. Many U.S. teachers believe strongly in the importance of each student writer's individual "voice"[1]—i.e., their unique written identity.

Critical linguistics (and critical theory more broadly) tends to talk about identity a bit differently—as something dynamic, performative, and multi-faceted. Identities are not inherent or biological; rather, they are developed and performed through social interactions. Readers who have studied Critical Race Theory or other anti-racism frameworks may hear echoes here of the idea that identity is socially constructed and intersectional (e.g., Crenshaw, 2017). We point to our various identities within our social interactions—a phenomenon sociolinguists call "**indexicality**" (a helpful mnemonic for this is that your index finger is your "pointer" finger).

In writing this book, for instance, I am pointing to my identity as a *teacher* by using accessible language and familiar examples. But I must also maintain my credibility as an *expert*, by drawing links to disciplinary concepts and citing relevant secondary literature. I use "e.g." in many of my in-text citations, to signal to readers that I recognize there are many additional scholars I could have cited. In other words, I am constantly balancing my two identities of practitioner and scholar in my rhetorical choices—including my language use—in this book.

But the written identity I am performing in this book is a bit different from how I write about my empirical research, in which I am often using more discipline-specific language (and most certainly fewer parentheticals), in keeping with the genre and audience expectations. And those two writerly identities are distinct from the one I performed when giving a eulogy for my grandmother, who passed away last year at the ripe age of 96, because my rhetorical goal there was to convey respect and affection for someone I love. In other words, we "index" many different identities through our writing and speech, because we all "contain multitudes," as Walt Whitman famously put it.

But it gets even more complicated when we realize that others might "read into" our language use in ways we do not intend or want. This is where **power** comes into the picture. Our opportunity to "achieve purpose and effect change" (Brown's [2018] definition of power, presented in Chapter 2) may be impacted by the assumptions others make about us based on their interpretations of our languaging practices.[2] If you had met me when I was younger, you might have heard my Oklahoma twang—an accent I began suppressing in middle school because I was concerned that it sounded "uneducated"—and come to all sorts of conclusions about my background and beliefs. If you are a snobbish reader who associates intelligence with use of big words (ahem—I mean sophisticated diction), then you might question my expertise as a writer. In both cases, you might miss *what I am saying* because you have made assumptions about me based on *how I speak or write*. These linguistic judgments might cause you to tune me out or even shut me out from a job or other opportunity. This sequence of assumption, judgment, and action based on language is called **linguistic profiling,** and is one of the central themes in Chapters 4 and 5.

I am using my own experience here as an example of how language, identity, and power are interconnected. But we can also learn something here about the role of **privilege**. Although I might worry occasionally about how my speech or writing will be judged by others, I am relatively protected from un-fair treatment as a result of those judgments, because I am privileged in many ways: My race, socioeconomic class, citizenship status, and professional cre-dentials all insulate me somewhat from the impact of linguistic profiling. Yet for individuals from Black, Indigenous, and People of Color (BIPOC) communities, low-income families, and/or groups that are systemically mar-ginalized for other reasons, linguistic profiling can be a barrier to education, employment, housing, and even physical safety. The stakes of our linguistic judgments are high—sometimes literally life or death—a point we will re-turn to in Chapter 4.

Committing to CLA Pedagogy means being willing to engage these sorts of topics with students. This does not mean that we must talk about linguistic profiling or language-based discrimination in all of our classes. However, we do need to recognize that when we use language, we are performing identi-ties, and this identity work is shaped by power dynamics in our classrooms and communities. Moreover, the forms of privilege we carry may make those power dynamics more fraught for some individuals and groups than others. As the Facebook cliché goes: It's complicated!

But it's also fascinating! One of the reasons humans love to argue about lan-guage—*Which rules should be the standard? What counts as correct? Why can't kids these days write/speak correctly?*—is that language is so intertwined with identity, power and privilege. We construct and reconstruct social reality through language. As the Jewish theologian Abraham Joshua Heschel is at-tributed with saying, "Words create worlds."

With this understanding of how language, identity, power, and privilege intersect, I hope it is clear why the central goals of CLA Pedagogy are **"self-reflection, social justice, and rhetorical agency"**: CLA Pedagogy offers opportunities, tools, and strategies for critical reflection on our ex-periences as language users, including on how our linguistic attitudes and judgments might impact others. This self-reflection helps us understand how our linguistic prejudices and practices might contribute toward or against social justice. And that understanding can in turn increase our sense of agency as language users who can make thoughtful and impactful linguistic choices. Along with that agency comes a heightened sense of responsibility, too, as we understand more deeply how language can be used to hurt and divide us, just as it can build connections and promote social healing. Below is a graphic that summarizes the three central goals of CLA Pedagogy:

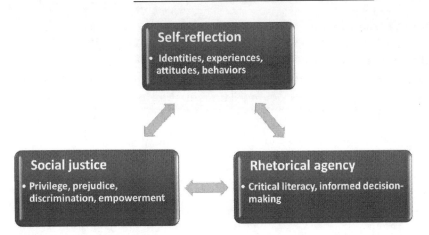

Figure 3.1 Goals for CLA Pedagogy

Unpacking Part Two

Now that we have unpacked the initial definition from Chapter 1, let's look at what was added for the extended definition, which appears at the end of the chapter:

> A CLA approach to writing instruction aims to promote a more just future, while also preparing students for the (often unjust) present. CLA Pedagogy does not ignore the power of academic norms and other linguistic standards (i.e., the status quo), but aims to demystify, critique, and—at times—resist those norms and standards.

As we began discussing in Chapter 1, scholarly conversations about English/writing instruction in the U.S. tend to perpetuate confusing and/or simplistic messages about linguistic norms and standards. It often feels we are faced with a binary choice between conformity and resistance. (And within the individualistic context of U.S. society, "conformity" is almost always heard negatively!). Many teachers feel pulled between encouraging resistance ("progressivism") and preparing students for at least some degree of conformity ("pragmatism"). CLA Pedagogy attempts to bridge this binary ideologically and pedagogically, through a "both/and" approach. If our goal is rhetorical agency, then students not only need rhetorical opportunities—i.e., decisions to be made—but also the knowledge and skills to make those decisions confidently and carry them out successfully.

Resisting linguistic norms and expectations—in small or large ways—is certainly one of the choices we can make as writers. We might, for example, insert parentheticals into scholarly writing, as a way to engage the reader on another level. (I am tempted to include a winking smiley face here—is that pushing it too far? ;-)). Or we might include a phrase from another language we know, either because an English equivalent doesn't exist, or because we want to index our identities as multilingual writers ¿Qué buena idea, no?

But there are likely situations in which we choose to conform quite closely with genre expectations, standardized language norms, or other conventions—especially when the stakes are high. In our professional lives as teachers—and as researchers, some of us—we often choose to conform with academic or professional expectations, including regarding language use. And for good reason, too, since resistance can be both exhausting and risky! (Case in point: The poet and conflict mediator John Paul Lederach noted at a public reading in 2018 that he once submitted a haiku, in lieu of a grant report, to an organization that was funding his work. The audience laughed and cheered. Then Lederach added, with some chagrin, "This strategy did not seem to translate into further funding.") The gist here is that a student's decision to conform linguistically is not a *failure* of CLA Pedagogy! The failure is if that student is unaware that they had choices to make, or if they made those choices without having the information they need to weigh the pros and cons.

The "both/and" approach of CLA Pedagogy is particularly important when it comes to working with students from linguistically minoritized backgrounds (e.g., multilingual students who use English as an additional language or multidialectal students who use Black/African American English, Chicanx[3] English or other varieties at home). CLA can help these students work through the tricky bind they are often placed in, where they are asked to choose between "standardized English"—which is itself a social construction, as we touched on in Chapter 2—and their other linguistic varieties. Many students of color are told by friends or family that they are "acting White" when they use standardized or academic language (e.g., Fordham & Ogbu, 1986). But at the same time, when teachers, employers, and others in positions of power "correct" them for using "non-standard" conventions in their speech and writing, this sends the message to students that they are "not White enough." This feeling of being linguistically—and racially—betwixt and between is an additional burden that many White teachers and students, myself included, never have to experience. And these sorts of tensions emerge in regard to other marginalized groups as well, including first-generation college students, women working in politics or and other male-dominated fields, LGBTQ+ students, and language users who are neurologically atypical.

By engaging conversations about language, identity, power, and privilege, we can help *all students* navigate the rhetorical possibilities that lie before them with confidence. They—and we—do not have to be confined to a single "voice." We can have many voices, just as we have many identities, and we can choose which of those voices to elevate in each rhetorical situation. We can even mix various codes and styles or from our idiolects ("idiolect" is the linguistics term for our "linguistic fingerprint") within a single communicative situation! Linguists use the terms **code-switching** and **code-meshing** to describe this mixing phenomenon. We will learn more about code-mixing, and see some examples from student work, in Chapters 5 and 7.

Research-based Principles and Practices for CLA Pedagogy

Now that we have unpacked our definition of CLA Pedagogy, let's look at some principles and best practices. For this section, I am drawing from the large body of scholarship on CLA Pedagogy explicitly, as well as on critical literacy and critical language studies, which have a great deal of overlap with CLA (Janks, 2010; Taylor et al., 2018).[4] The body of work that informs this section includes pedagogical accounts of CLA applications in a variety of educational contexts, as well as empirical studies of how students and teachers respond to CLA-oriented curricula. In addition to "critical literacy" (e.g., Janks et al., 2014; Vasquez et al., 2019), scholar-practitioners may use other umbrella terms for this approach, including "critical language pedagogy" (e.g., Baker-Bell, 2013; Crookes, 2017; Godley & Minnici, 2008), "pedagogical language knowledge" (e.g., Bunch, 2013; Galguera, 2011), and even "critical applied linguistics" (Pennycook, 2001). Although there are minor distinctions among all these labels, they all reference approaches that attend critically to language, identity, power, and privilege. As we touched on in Chapter 1, there is also a great deal of overlap between CLA and Students' Rights to Their Own Language (SRTOL), as well as with translingual and anti-racist orientations to writing.

For "big picture" people like me, who like seeing a map of where we are headed, below is a graphic of the six principles for CLA Pedagogy that we will be discussing.

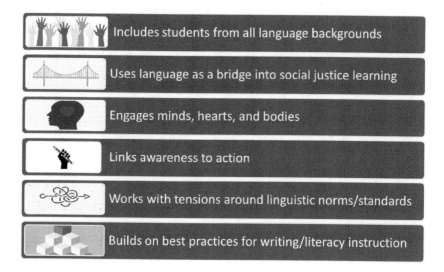

Figure 3.2 Six Principles of CLA Pedagogy

Let's now take a look at these principles one by one:

Principle #1: CLA Pedagogy Includes Students from All Language Backgrounds

It is tempting to think of CLA Pedagogy as a "special" approach for our most linguistically diverse classes. And indeed, as we have begun discussing, CLA is particularly relevant and helpful in working with multilingual and multidialectal students. However, CLA Pedagogy sees *every student* as a language user with rich knowledge and experiences that we can draw on in the classroom. Just as conversations about race need to include students from all racial backgrounds, including—especially—White students, conversations about language and power need to include all language users—even those who might think of themselves as "monolingual" (Haddix, 2008). One of the wonderful advantages of this approach, in fact, is that it allows us to tap into *everyone's* linguistic identities and resources.

Although CLA Pedagogy can be used in classes for students from a particular language background (e.g., English Learners[5]), it is most equitable when it promotes interaction and learning among students from a variety of backgrounds. A linguistically inclusive approach is also an important way to avoid exoticizing language difference and/or tokenizing particular groups. In other words, it is important that multilingual and multidialectal students not be "on display" as the only exemplars of linguistic diversity in a classroom (see Godley et al., 2006; Haddix, 2008, for more on this concern). In fact, research suggests that recognizing the variation within our *own* linguistic repertoires—no matter how many languages or language varieties we use—is an important starting point for shifting our negative attitudes toward the languaging of others (Godley et al., 2006).

This is not to say that all students will experience CLA in the same way—quite the opposite! Research shows that educators' and students' linguistic, racial, and cultural backgrounds all significantly shape their response to CLA Pedagogy (Baker-Bell, 2020a, 2020b; Devereaux & Palmer, 2019; Godley & Reaser, 2018). Thus, we *actively include* all students by incorporating multiple opportunities for them to connect CLA learning to their lived experience while also recognizing that those experiences vary widely. In the Pathways chapters, readers will find a wealth of activities and assignments that help students to make these connections and to learn from one another.

Principle #2: CLA Pedagogy Uses Language as a Bridge into Social Justice Learning

One of the concerns that gave rise to CLA, as we discussed in Chapter 2, was that "knowledge about language" (or "language study") was often taught in a way that was decoupled from—or even counter to—the aims of social justice education. Even the concept of "language awareness," as we discussed in Chapter 2, can become reductive, referring only to students' knowledge of grammatical terminology or their familiarity with the "rules" of standardized language. A CLA approach goes further than this, always keeping in mind issues of identity, power, and privilege. In other words, we cannot forget the "C" in "CLA."

And figuring out what it really means to be "critical" is no easy task. Even among practitioners who identify explicitly with CLA, there are differences in what is being critiqued, how far the critique extends, and how that critique informs curriculum and instruction. Some CLA courses focus primarily on "critical reading" of texts, using discourse analysis methods (see Chapter 6) to investigate the contextual factors shaping the author's linguistic choices (cf., Dar et al., 2010; Wallace, 1999). Other programs focus on cultivating students' appreciation for linguistic diversity, but they may not engage as much with power dynamics or social critique (cf., Reaser & Wolfram, 2007; Wheeler & Sword, 2006).

One concern raised about this more "apolitical" approach to language variation is that students may be left with the impression that all language varieties have "separate but equal" status, which, as Higgins et al. (2012) point out, does not map onto how those varieties are treated in the real world, including at school (see also Kirkland & Jackson, 2009; Reaser et al., 2017). One reason some English/literacy scholars began to use the term "code-meshing" as an alternative to "code-switching," in fact, is that they felt the latter did not go far enough in giving students' other language varieties equal status within the academic curriculum (e.g., Baker-Bell, 2020b; Young et al., 2014).

These debates about criticality are echoed in the field of multicultural education, where some scholars have critiqued the "heroes and holidays" approach for avoiding difficult conversations about equity and oppression (Lee et al., 2006). Awareness of this concern was in part what gave rise to particular iterations of CLA pedagogy that are explicitly anti-racist (e.g., Baker-Bell, 2020a; Gere et al., 2021) and/or culturally sustaining (e.g., Paris & Alim, 2017; Sembiante & Tian, 2021), which prioritize explicit social critique. As we will discuss in Chapter 10, some CLA scholar-practitioners are in fact drawing on multicultural education scholarship (e.g., Nieto, 2017) to map out developmental frameworks that can guide and assess CLA-oriented curricula (e.g., Endo, 2015; Godley & Reaser, 2018; Shi & Roldstad, 2020)

By drawing on other critical frameworks such as anti-racism and multiculturalism, we create intersections between CLA and other approaches to teaching for social justice (Gere et al., 2021; Godley et al., 2006). Thus, rather than being an "add-on" to our other work related to diversity, equity, and inclusion, CLA is a way of furthering those goals, through a more explicit focus on language. For example, a study by Ashwin (2018) found that "White teachers" who engaged the topic of "systemic linguistic discrimination against Black people" were better able to "understand covert, systemic racism," including their own role within the system (p. 206; see also Endo, 2015; Haddix, 2008). Mosley Wetzel et al. (2015) have found, similarly, that conversations about language difference and linguistic prejudice can be a strategy for "breaking silence about race" among White students and teachers (p. 29).

CLA scholars have used the topic of language and linguistic prejudice as a bridge into understanding other forms of injustice as well, including gender bias (e.g., Ho, 2020; Parsaiyan, 2019); heteronormativity and homophobia (e.g., Ho, 2020; Young, 2018), and ableism (e.g., Luna, 2003; Reagan, 2006). CLA Pedagogy can also contribute toward students' intercultural awareness and development as global citizens, as I explore in other work (Abe & Shapiro, 2021). Of course, the bridge from "language" to "social justice" does not build itself. We have to construct that bridge intentionally, as we will explore more in the chapters to come.

Principle #3: CLA Pedagogy Engages our Minds, Hearts, and Bodies

Engaging students and colleagues in critical explorations of language, identity, power, and privilege is great fun! But it is also challenging in a number of ways: First, it requires willingness to learn a shared "metalanguage" for talking about language (Bunch, 2013; Wallace, 1999). This metalanguage can be used, in turn, to validate language varieties that have traditionally been delegitimized: Students can apply CLA concepts and tools to make those varieties, or the attitudes towards those varieties, an "object of exploration" in the classroom and beyond (Higgins et al., 2012, p. 50; see also Baker-Bell et al., 2017; Reaser & Wolfram, 2007).

On top of this intense intellectual engagement, CLA Pedagogy can have a strong social and emotional impact (e.g., Britton & Lorimer Leonard, 2020; Wolfram et al., 2008). As with other social justice approaches, learning about power and social inequality means learning to recognize how we ourselves have benefited from—and/or been disadvantaged by—the status quo. It also means reflecting on how we ourselves might have contributed to inequality within our schools and communities. This sort of reflection about oppression often invokes emotions such as sadness, anger, resentment, and shame (e.g., DiAngelo, 2018; Zembylas, 2012). These emotions live not just in our heads but in our bodies (Berila, 2015; Menakem, 2017). Students need opportunities for mental and emotional processing related to this deep learning and growth. They may also need support managing social tensions that can emerge as they begin to realize how different their perspectives and lived experiences may have been from those of their peers (Cahnmann et al., 2005).

To be effective with CLA Pedagogy, we have to find ways to acknowledge and work through the intellectual, emotional, social, and even physical aspects of learning about linguistic injustice (Godley et al., 2015; Howell et al., 2020; Ohito, 2016). To this end, there is much we can learn from other anti-oppression approaches to education—in particular anti-racist education, as noted above. Some of the practices encouraged by anti-racist educators that are particularly applicable to CLA Pedagogy are:

- Use course materials, as well as activities and assignments, to make space for many voices and perspectives
- Build a "brave space" (Palfrey, 2017; Pawlowski, 2018) through community-building activities, clear norms and expectations, and explicit teaching of strategies for engaging across difference

- Offer multiple modes for dialogue (written, spoken, visual; pairs, small group, and large group; synchronous and asynchronous conversation)
- Invite—but don't force—students to share from their lived experience
- Create opportunities for mental and emotional processing through speech and writing, as well as through movement, drawing, and other modes of expression

These and other practices are discussed in greater detail in the chapters to come and at the online Hub. We can also draw strategies from the growing body of scholarship on Social and Emotional Learning (SEL), which offers insights into how we can cultivate mindfulness, empathy, compassion, perseverance, and other habits of mind—and heart!—into our classroom instruction. See Hoffman (2009) for a review of SEL research and WestEd's Center for Social and Emotional Learning[6] for a searchable list of resources created in partnership with the U.S. Department of Education (n.d.).

This is not to say that CLA Pedagogy requires that we have the skills of a therapist or social worker. But it does mean that we need to be proactive in anticipating and naming discomfort, and in supporting students through that discomfort—something many of us likely do already, as we engage difficult topics and support students through the writing process (Driscoll & Powell, 2016; Martinez et al., 2011). Chapter 9 offers some helpful strategies for building community, facilitating difficult conversations, and working with discomfort in the classroom (see also Shapiro, 2020).

Principle #4: CLA Pedagogy Always Links Awareness to Action

One of the concerns raised about social justice education in general is that the focus on "critique" can start to become an end in itself, so that students are taught to "deconstruct" an issue or problem but have few opportunities to "reconstruct"—or even research—alternatives or solutions (e.g., Delpit, 2006; Janks, 2010). As Janks (2001) explains, critical theory often frames power as "negative and productive of relations of domination" (p. 248), rather than as a force we want to be available to everyone. Along these same lines, Brown (2018)[7] has popularized a helpful distinction between "power over" and "power with/to/within," which originates in earlier work by theorists focused on the nature of power (e.g., Pantazidou, 2012). A CLA approach should engage all of these forms of power, recognizing power as connected to emancipation and agency—not just oppression.

One of the reasons that some early adopters of CLA shifted toward "critical literacy" as the dominant frame for their work, in fact, was that they liked how the latter framework was more attentive to what students can do and become as users of language (Janks, 2000, 2001; Lillis, 2003; Thesen, 1997). In one of their earliest publications introducing CLA to a wider audience, Clark et al. (1990) highlighted this concern. Truly empowering instruction, they argued, should not only:

> empower language users, in terms of developing their awareness, but should also help them on the way to emancipation by giving them the chance to challenge existing conventions and the right to offer alternatives in order to help shape new conventions.

> (p. 87)

In other words, in order to benefit students, CLA and/or critical literacy instruction must focus not just on "critique" but also on "access" to power, including through "(re)design" of texts (Janks, 2000, 2010).[8] Indeed, research into the impact of language awareness programs in general—including but not limited to CLA approaches—has found that if the program does not explicitly and consistently link awareness with pedagogical action, educators may come away with only a superficial understanding about language and language difference, with little or no impact on their teaching practice (Ashwin, 2018; Cross, 2003; Godley & Reaser, 2018; Haddix, 2008). In other words, linguistic consciousness-raising on its own may have little "trickle down" effect into teachers' actions and behaviors (Godley et al., 2015).

Clearly, then, the awareness-raising in CLA Pedagogy must include implications and opportunities for action. Some research has suggested, in fact, that the latter can facilitate the former: A study by Godley et al. (2006) found that "changes in attitude can **follow from** changes in practice" (p. 34, emphasis mine). This finding raises the exciting possibility that we do not need to wait for an "attitude shift" in order to act—or get others to act—in more just and equitable ways!

The "action" aspect of CLA Pedagogy can take many different forms. It could involve institutional activism or community advocacy, as we will explore in Chapters 7 and 10. But action can—and should—be scholarly and/or rhetorical as well. Examples of this "academic action," as we might call it, can include participating in role plays and simulations, conducting primary research, writing for audiences beyond the classroom, and even re-teaching what we have learned to peers, family, or community members. We will see in later chapters how we can incorporate these and other application activities into our curricula.

That said, action without awareness can be equally problematic. Diversity, equity, and inclusion expert Aiko Bethea (2020) has highlighted the phenomenon of **"action bias,"**[9] in which people in positions of power may look for a "quick fix" to systemic problems, resulting in poorly planned initiatives that are more symbolic than substantive. And often, such initiatives create more emotional and intellectual labor for members of marginalized groups that are supposed to be the beneficiaries of institutional change! (Gorski, 2019). A similar concern has been raised about "service learning," which is a key feature of many college writing courses (e.g., Adler-Kassner et al., 1997), and which, experts have argued, needs to include ongoing dialogue with community partners, in order to be a force for deep learning and sustainable change (e.g., Mitchell, 2008; Quan, 2020). In other words, like other critical approaches to teaching and learning, CLA Pedagogy requires a commitment to *praxis*—i.e., "reflection and action directed at the structures to be transformed" (Freire, 1970, p. 120; see also Shapiro, forthcoming).

Principle #5: CLA Pedagogy Works with the Tensions Around Linguistic Norms and Standards

The concern about awareness without action—and vice versa—also has relevance for our understanding of the tensions around academic norms and standardized language. Studies have found that writing teachers who engage in learning about language variation often struggle to channel their increased appreciation for linguistic diversity into pedagogical decision-making—particularly if they are responsible for teaching academic writing (Godley & Reaser, 2018; Lillis, 1997; Metz, 2018; Weaver, 2020). As we explored in Chapter 1, a CLA approach is committed to **both** pragmatism (i.e., making sure students have what they need to be able to write for the academy/world as it is today) **and** progressivism (i.e., making sure we are working toward a more equitable and inclusive academy/world for tomorrow). Assessment is one area where this both/and balance can seem particularly elusive (Gere et al., 2021; Wheeler, 2019). Most writing teachers want neither to penalize students unfairly nor to pretend that "anything goes" when it comes to language. As Godley and Reaser (2018) explain, we must "teach about language in a way that contributes to students' self-determination and life goals **as well as** to greater social justice in our society" (p. 166, emphasis mine).

While CLA Pedagogy does not offer an easy path through this conundrum, it does offer insights and strategies for working through these tensions *with students*. A CLA approach prioritizes transparency, contextualization, and critique around norms and standards. We can explore questions such as:

- How does academic discourse vary by discipline, genre, and cultural context?
- Who makes the rules for writing, and how are they enforced?
- Who is harmed or excluded by these rules?
- What values and assumptions are perpetuated by academic conventions?
- Where are the possibilities for resisting or changing academic norms?
- When and how might we enact this resistance or promote these changes?

We will explore creative ways to engage these questions in Chapter 5, where I reference a writing course I built around these very questions, called "English Grammar: Concepts and Controversies" (the syllabus for this and all my classes is available with the online Support Materials for this book, and at the Hub). When it comes to our practices for classroom instruction and assessment, there are a number of ways we can be both pragmatic and progressive, as we will discuss in Chapters 8, 9, and 10.

Principle #6: CLA Pedagogy Builds on What We Already Know About Best Practices for Writing/Literacy Instruction

As any U.S. writing teacher knows, and as we discussed in Chapter 2, English/literacy instruction in the U.S. is often subject to radical pendulum swings. With each swing, there is always the danger of leaving behind what was worth carrying forward—of tossing the "baby" out with the "bathwater."[10] In the case of writing instruction, there is a great deal we do *not* want to lose sight of, as we infuse CLA into our curricula and instruction. CLA Pedagogy complements and builds on research-based best practices for teaching and assessing writing. To help underscore this point, below are three pedagogical principles that are generally agreed upon by writing teachers and teacher educators at both secondary and postsecondary levels:

1 **Writing is shaped by social and rhetorical contexts:** We write primarily to connect and communicate with other people. This means that writing is inherently social, which in turn means that students need literacy instruction that engages real-world rhetorical situations. It also means that instead of trying to teach a single style of writing

or expecting students to develop a unified "voice" as writers, a state-of-the-art writing curriculum engages students in explorations of how writing varies according to purpose, discipline, genre, audience, and other contextual factors. The CLA concepts of *descriptivism* and *prescriptivism*—which we learned about in Chapter 2—provide helpful framing, in fact, for resisting overly generalized conceptions of "good writing."

2   **Student writers need to learn about writing processes as well as products:** Learning to write is a complex developmental undertaking. In order to grow in their ability to produce writing that responds effectively to a variety of rhetorical situations, students need to know about the *products* they are creating (e.g., content, organization, genre features, stylistic features, etc.) as well as the *processes* that they can engage in to create those products (how to research/read, plan, draft, revise, edit, etc.). Though there are some strategies that work for most writers, students also need to learn what works best for them personally. By focusing on both product and process, our curricula can teach habits of mind that help students to be successful as readers and writers—i.e., to experience *rhetorical agency* (see Chapter 8 for more on habits of mind in professional standards for writing/literacy instruction).

3   **Feedback on student writing should focus on growth and transfer of learning.** Responding to student writing can be both intellectually and emotionally challenging, in part because instructors have to balance a variety of roles or identities—e.g., curious reader, writing coach, evaluator—in their feedback. By thinking carefully about our timelines, modes, and strategies for responding to student work, we can tailor our feedback to our pedagogical goals and to the individual needs of the writer. We should prioritize comments and suggestions that will help students not only to improve on a single assignment, but to grow as communicators. Students also need opportunities to provide feedback to each other and to us (about our teaching, as well as about their learning). Feedback is also linked to *language ideology*, since our beliefs about language shape what we—and our students—choose to focus on when providing feedback (see Chapter 9 for more).

These principles are built into the learning sequences presented in Chapters 4–7 (the Four Pathways) and are discussed in more explicitly in Chapters 8 and 9. Readers can learn more about research-based best practices by exploring some of the pedagogical resources developed by professional organizations, such as:

- National Council of Teachers of English (NCTE) (e.g., "Understanding and Teaching Writing: Guiding Principles"[11])
- Conference for College Composition and Communication (CCCC) (e.g., "Statement on Second Language Writing and Multilingual Writers"[12])
- National Writing Project[13]
- WAC (Writing Across the Curriculum) Clearinghouse[14]

It is also important to remember, as we touched on in Chapter 1, that CLA Pedagogy shares a great deal of ground both ideologically and pedagogically with other scholarly movements in writing/literacy studies, including Students' Right to Their Own Language (e.g., Perryman-Clarke et al., 2014) and translingualism (e.g., Horner & Tetreault, 2017; Silva & Wang, 2020). Embracing CLA does *not* mean leaving behind all of the important insights from these movements! Our writing pedagogy also needs to be informed by a commitment to **accessibility**, which is why Chapter 8 includes a section on how Universal Design for Learning (e.g., Dolmage, 2015; Fornauf & Erickson, 2020) can inform our course design. In sum, CLA Pedagogy encourages us to **keep and build on** what already works well, so that our own applications of this approach are inclusive and equitable for all of the students in our writing classes.

Conclusion

In Part I (Chapters 1, 2, and 3), we have developed some foundational understanding about what CLA is, how it was developed and disseminated, and why it is still relevant to writing instruction today—particularly in a U.S. context. We have also reviewed central concepts, goals, and principles undergirding this approach to writing/literacy instruction. I hope readers will keep these foundational pieces in mind as we begin to engage more specific curricular pathways and classroom practices in Parts II and III. A solid grounding will help to adapt this approach in ways that fit best with our own pedagogical goals, needs, and contexts.

Notes

1 A number of scholars have critiqued this concept of written "voice," pointing out that it is based on certain linguistic and cultural assumptions that are not universal (e.g., Ramanathan & Atkinson, 1999; Stapleton, 2002). We'll return to this in Chapter 9, where I argue that we should focus on "choice" rather than "voice." ☺

2 The linguist Merrill Swain first coined the term "languaging" to capture the dynamic, social nature of language use, in contrast with "language," which often connotes a fixed, static phenomenon (e.g., Swain, 2006). The term has been taken up recently by many writing/composition studies scholars, but sometimes without appropriate attribution to Swain.

3 The words "Chicanx" and "Latinx" or "Latine" are alternatives to "Chicano" and "Latino," since the latter are grammatically gendered as male, and are therefore exclusive of other gender identities. The topic of labels and inclusivity is another one can engage with students in a CLA approach, by the way! There is a lot of interesting research, in fact, on which labels are preferred within particular ethnic communities (e.g., Marisol Meraji, 2020).

4 As was briefly discussed in Chapter 2, the term "critical literacy" has been heavily used in K–12 education—so much so that there is little consensus about what the "critical" descriptor actually means (Luke, 2012; Pennycook, 2010). But many approaches to critical literacy do not devote much attention to close examination of language, which is one of the reasons I have chosen to use "CLA," rather than "critical literacy," as my primary framework. "Critical language studies," in contrast, usually refers to the study of second/additional languages and/or linguistics and tends to focus less on writing/literacy (e.g., Kubota & Miller, 2017). Thus, if critical literacy and critical language studies are two ends of a continuum, CLA offers a bridge between the two.

5 Because support for English learners is another area of expertise of mine, I want to remind readers who teach EAL/ESOL that even within a newcomer or "sheltered immersion" model of instruction, there should be opportunities for interaction with other groups, through well-designed cross-classroom collaborations, and by shadowing the mainstream curriculum (e.g., Honigsfeld & Dove, 2010; Short & Boyson, 2012). CLA could be the focus for these interactions!

6 U.S. Department of Education, https://selcenter.wested.org/

7 Brown summarizes these concepts at https://brenebrown.com/wp-content/uploads/2020/10/Brene-Brown-on-Power-and-Leadership-10-26-20.pdf

8 Janks (2000, 2010) eventually began to frame CLA as one strand of critical literacy. Others, myself included, have held onto CLA as their primary frame, but have incorporated critical literacy as one of the foundational pieces of a CLA-oriented curriculum (e.g., Wallace, 1999; Weninger & Kan, 2013).

9 https://brenebrown.com/podcast/brene-with-aiko-bethea-on-inclusivity-at-work-the-heart-of-hard-conversations/

10 Analyzing these sorts of metaphors—pendulum, baby/bathwater—might in itself be a fun CLA exercise to do with teachers! Pedagogical metaphors are in fact an subfield within education scholarship (e.g., Berthoff, 1981).

11 https://ncte.org/statement/teachingcomposition/. NOTE: In Chapter 8, we will also be discussing the 2011 Framework for Success in Postsecondary Writing (FSPW), available at https://files.eric.ed.gov/fulltext/ED516360.pdf. See Chapter 8, and Gere et al. (2021), for more on a CLA approach to FSPW.

12 https://cccc.ncte.org/cccc/resources/positions/secondlangwriting

13 E.g., https://archive.nwp.org/cs/public/print/resource_topic/teaching_writing
14 E.g., https://wac.colostate.edu/resources/teaching/

References

Adler-Kassner, L., Crooks, R., & Watters, A. (1997). *Writing the community: Concepts and models for service-learning in composition*. Stylus Publishing, LLC.

Ashwin, C. M. (2018). *Beyond "talking different": White pre-service teachers' critical race talk about teaching dialect diversity* [Unpublished doctoral dissertation from the University of Pittsburgh].

Baker-Bell, A. (2013). "I never really knew the history behind African American language": Critical language pedagogy in an advanced placement English language arts class. *Equity & Excellence in Education, 46*(3), 355–370. https://doi.org/10.1080/10665684.2013.806848

Baker-Bell, A. (2020a). Dismantling anti-black linguistic racism in English language arts classrooms: Toward an anti-racist black language pedagogy. *Theory into Practice, 59*(1), 8–21. https://doi.org/10.1080/00405841.2019.1665415

Baker-Bell, A. (2020b). *Linguistic justice: Black language, literacy, identity, and pedagogy*. Routledge.

Baker-Bell, A., Paris, D., & Jackson, D. (2017). Learning Black language matters: Humanizing research as culturally sustaining pedagogy. *International Review of Qualitative Research, 10*(4), 360–377.

Berila, B. (2015). *Integrating mindfulness into anti-oppression pedagogy: Social justice in higher education*. Routledge.

Berthoff, A. E. (1981). *The making of meaning: Metaphors, models, and maxims for writing teachers*. Boynton, Cook Publishers.

Bethea, A. (2020, November 9). *Inclusivity at work: The heart of hard conversations*. Episode of "Dare to Lead" podcast with Brené Brown. https://brenebrown.com/transcript/brene-with-aiko-bethea/

Britton, E. R., & Lorimer Leonard, R. (2020). The social justice potential of critical reflection and critical language awareness pedagogies for L2 writers. *Journal of Second Language Writing, 50*, 100776.

Brown, B. (2018). *Dare to lead: Brave work. Tough conversations. Whole hearts*. Penguin Random House.

Bunch, G. C. (2013). Pedagogical language knowledge: Preparing mainstream teachers for English learners in the new standards era. *Review of Research in Education, 37*(1), 298–341. https://doi.org/10.3102/0091732X12461772

Cahnmann, M., Rymes, B., & Souto-Manning, M. (2005). Using critical discourse analysis to understand and facilitate identification processes of bilingual adults becoming teachers. *Critical Inquiry in Language Studies: An International Journal, 2*(4), 195–213.

Clark, R., Fairclough, N., Ivanič, R., & Martin-Jones, M. (1990). Critical language awareness part I: A critical review of three current approaches to language awareness. *Language and Education, 4*(4), 249–260. https://doi.org/10.1080/09500789009541291

Crenshaw, K. W. (2017). *On intersectionality: Essential writings.* The New Press.

Crookes, G. (2017). Critical language pedagogy given the English divide in Korea: A suite of practices, critique, and the role of the intellectual. *English Teaching, 72*(4), 3–21. https://doi.org/10.15858/engtea.72.4.201712.3

Cross, B. E. (2003). Learning or unlearning racism: Transferring teacher education curriculum to classroom practices. *Theory into Practice, 42*(3), 203–209.

Dar, Z. K., Shams, M. R., & Rahimi, A. (2010). Teaching reading with a critical attitude: Using critical discourse analysis (CDA) to raise EFL university students' critical language awareness (CLA). *International Journal of Criminology and Sociological Theory, 3*(2), 457–476.

Delpit, L. (2006). *Other people's children: Cultural conflict in the classroom.* The New Press.

Devereaux, M. D., & Palmer, C. C. (Eds.). (2019). *Teaching language variation in the classroom: Strategies and models from teachers and linguists.* Routledge.

DiAngelo, R. (2018). *White fragility: Why it's so hard for White people to talk about racism.* Beacon Press.

Dolmage, J. (2015). Universal design: Places to start. *Disability Studies Quarterly, 35*(2).

Doughty, P., Pearce, J., & Thornton, G. (1971). *Language in use.* Arnold.

Driscoll, D. L., & Powell, R. (2016). States, traits, and dispositions: The impact of emotion on writing development and writing transfer across college courses and beyond. *Composition Forum, 34.* https://compositionforum.com/issue/34/states-traits.php

Endo, R. (2015). From unconscious deficit views to affirmation of linguistic varieties in the classroom: White preservice teachers on building critical self-awareness about linguicism's causes and consequences. *Multicultural Perspectives, 17*(4), 207–214.

Fordham, S., & Ogbu, J. U. (1986). Black students' school success: Coping with the "burden of 'acting white'". *The Urban Review, 18*(3), 176–206.

Fornauf, B., & Erickson, J. D. (2020). Toward an inclusive pedagogy through universal design for learning in higher education: A review of the literature. *Journal of Postsecondary Education and Disability, 33*(2), 183–199.

Fowler, R., Hodge, B., Kress, G., & Trew, T. (1979/2018). *Language and control.* Routledge.

Freire, P. (1970). *Pedagogy of the oppressed* [English translation]. Bloomsbury Publishing.

Galguera, T. (2011). Participant structures as professional learning tasks and the development of pedagogical language knowledge among preservice teachers. *Teacher Education Quarterly, 38*(1), 85–106.

Gere, A., Curzan, A., Hammond, J. W., Hughes, S., Li, R., Moos, A., Smith, K., Van Zanen, K., Wheeler, K. L., & Zanders, C. J. (2021). Communal justicing: Writing assessment, disciplinary infrastructure, and the case for critical language awareness. *College Composition and Communication, 72*(3), 384–412.

Godley, A. J., & Minnici, A. (2008). Critical language pedagogy in an urban high school English class. *Urban Education, 43*(3), 319–346.

Godley, A. J., & Reaser, J. (2018). *Critical language pedagogy: Interrogating language, dialects, and power in teacher education*. Peter Lang.

Godley, A. J., Reaser, J., & Moore, K. G. (2015). Pre-service English language arts teachers' development of critical language awareness for teaching. *Linguistics and Education, 32*, 41–54. https://doi.org/10.1016/j.linged.2015.03.015

Godley, A. J., Sweetland, J., Wheeler, R. S., Minnici, A., & Carpenter, B. D. (2006). Preparing teachers for dialectally diverse classrooms. *Educational Researcher, 35*(8), 30–37. https://doi.org/10.3102/0013189X035008030

Gorski, P. C. (2019). Racial battle fatigue and activist burnout in racial justice activists of color at predominately white colleges and universities. *Race, Ethnicity and Education, 22*(1), 1–20.

Gutiérrez, K., Baquedano-López, P., & Turner, M. G. (1997). Putting language back into language arts: When the radical middle meets the third space. *Language Arts, 74*(5), 368–378.

Haddix, M. (2008). Beyond sociolinguistics: Towards a critical approach to cultural and linguistic diversity in teacher education. *Language and Education, 22*(5), 254–270.

Higgins, C., Nettell, R., Furukawa, G., & Sakoda, K. (2012). Beyond contrastive analysis and codeswitching: Student documentary filmmaking as a challenge to linguicism in Hawai'i. *Linguistics and Education, 23*(1), 49–61.

Ho, J. M. B. (2020). Queering CLIL: A critical sexual literacy curriculum for the Hong Kong context. *English Teaching & Learning, 44*(2), 193–210.

Hoffman, D. M. (2009). Reflecting on social emotional learning: A critical perspective on trends in the United States. *Review of Educational Research, 79*(2), 533–556.

Honigsfeld, A., & Dove, M. G. (2010). *Collaboration and co-teaching: Strategies for English learners*. Corwin Press.

Horner, B., & Tetreault, L. (Eds.). (2017). *Crossing divides: Exploring translingual writing pedagogies and programs*. University Press of Colorado.

Howell, N. G., Navickas, K., Shapiro, R., Shapiro, S., & Watson, M. (2020). The perpetual "but" in raciolinguistic justice work: When idealism meets practice. *Composition Forum, 44* [online, special issue]. https://compositionforum.com/issue/44/embracing.php

Janks, H. (2000). Domination, access, diversity and design: A synthesis for critical literacy education. *Educational Review, 52*(2), 175–186.

Janks, H. (2001). Critical language awareness: Curriculum 2005 meets the TRC. *Southern African Linguistics and Applied Language Studies, 19*(3–4), 241–252.

Janks, H. (2010). *Literacy and power*. Routledge.

Janks, H., Dixon, K., Ferreira, A., Granville, S., & Newfield, D. (2014). *Doing critical literacy: Texts and activities for students and teachers*. Routledge.

Kirkland, D., & Jackson, A. (2009). Beyond the silence: Instructional approaches and students' attitudes. *Affirming Students' Right to Their Own Language*, 132–150.

Kolln, M., & Hancock, C. (2005). The story of English grammar in United States schools. *English Teaching: Practice and Critique, 4*(3), 11–31.

Kubota, R., & Miller, E. R. (2017). Re-examining and re-envisioning criticality in language studies: Theories and praxis. *Critical Inquiry in Language Studies*, *14*(2–3), 129–157.

Lederach, J. P. (2018). https://onbeing.org/programs/poetry-from-the-on-being-gathering-john-paul-lederach-oct2018/

Lee, E., Menkart, D., & Okazawa-Ray, M. (2006). *Beyond heroes and holidays: A practical guide to K-12 anti-racist, multicultural education, and staff development*. Teaching for Change.

Lillis, T. (1997). New voices in academia? The regulative nature of academic writing conventions. *Language and Education*, *11*(3), 182–199. https://doi.org/10.1080/09500789708666727

Lillis, T. (2003). Student writing as academic literacies: Drawing on Bakhtin to move from critique to design. *Language and Education*, *17*(3), 192–207.

Luke, A. (2012). Critical literacy: Foundational notes. *Theory into Practice*, *51*(1), 4–11.

Luna, C. (2003). (Re)writing the discourses of schooling and of "learning disabilities": The development of critical literacy in a student action group. *Reading & Writing Quarterly*, *19*(3), 253–280. https://doi.org/10.1080/10573560308211

MacDonald, S. P. (2007). The erasure of language. *College Composition and Communication*, *58*(4), 585–625.

MarisolMerajin,S.(2020).www.npr.org/sections/codeswitch/2020/08/11/901398248/hispanic-latino-or-latinx-survey-says

Martinez, C. T., Kock, N., & Cass, J. (2011). Pain and pleasure in short essay writing: Factors predicting university students' writing anxiety and writing self-efficacy. *Journal of Adolescent & Adult Literacy*, *54*(5), 351–360.

Menakem, R. (2017). *My grandmother's hands: Racialized trauma and the pathway to mending our hearts and bodies*. Central Recovery Press.

Metz, M. (2018). Challenges of confronting dominant language ideologies in the high school English classroom. *Research in the Teaching of English*, *52*, 23.

Mitchell, T. D. (2008). Traditional vs. critical service-learning: Engaging the literature to differentiate two models. *Michigan Journal of Community Service Learning*, *14*(2), 50–65.

Mosley Wetzel, M., & Rogers, R. (2015). Constructing racial literacy through critical language awareness: A case study of a beginning literacy teacher. *Linguistics and Education*, *32*, 27–40. https://doi.org/10.1016/j.linged.2015.03.014

Nieto, S. (2017). *Language, culture, and teaching: Critical perspectives* (3rd ed.). Routledge.

Ohito, E. O. (2016). Making the emperor's new clothes visible in anti-racist teacher education: Enacting a pedagogy of discomfort with white preservice teachers. *Equity & Excellence in Education*, *49*(4), 454–467.

Palfrey, J. (2017). *Safe spaces, brave spaces: Diversity and free expression in education*. MIT Press. https://doi.org/10.2307/j.ctt1vz4994

Pantazidou, M. (2012). What next for power analysis? A review of recent experience with the powercube and related frameworks. *IDS Working Papers*, *2012*(400), 1–46.

Paris, D., & Alim, H. S. (Eds.). (2017). *Culturally sustaining pedagogies: Teaching and learning for justice in a changing world.* Teachers College Press.

Parsaiyan, S. F. (2019). "This is a food ad but it is presenting gender stereotypes!": Practicing critical language awareness in an Iranian EFL context. *Journal of English Language Teaching and Learning, 11*(24), 227–259.

Pawlowski, L. (2018). Creating a brave space classroom through writing. In S. Brookfield (Ed.), *Teaching race: How to help students unmask and challenge racism* (pp. 63–86). John Wiley & Sons. https://doi.org/10.1002/9781119548492.ch4

Pennycook, A. (2001). *Critical applied linguistics: A critical introduction.* Routledge.

Pennycook, A. (2010). Critical and alternative directions in applied linguistics. *Australian Review of Applied Linguistics, 33*(2), 16.1–16.16. https://doi.org/10.2104/aral1016

Perryman-Clarke, S., Kirkland, D., & Jackson, A. (2014). *Students' rights to their own language: A critical sourcebook.* St. Martins.

Quan, T. (2020). Critical language awareness and L2 learners of Spanish: An action-research study. *Foreign Language Annals, 53.*

Ramanathan, V., & Atkinson, D. (1999). Individualism, academic writing, and ESL writers. *Journal of Second Language Writing, 8*(1), 45–75.

Reagan, T. (2006). The explanatory power of critical language studies: Linguistics with an attitude. *Critical Inquiry in Language Studies, 3*(1), 1–22. https://doi.org/10.1207/s15427595cils0301_1

Reaser, J., Adger, C. T., Wolfram, W., & Christian, D. (2017). *Dialects at school: Educating linguistically diverse students.* Routledge.

Reaser, J., & Wolfram, W. (2007). *Voices of North Carolina dialect awareness program* [online curriculum]. https://linguistics.chass.ncsu.edu/thinkanddo/vonc.php

Richards, J. C., & Rodgers, T. (1982). Method: Approach, design, and procedure. *TESOL Quarterly, 16*(2), 153–168. https://doi.org/10.2307/3586789

Sembiante, S. F., & Tian, Z. (2021). Culturally sustaining approaches to academic languaging through systemic functional linguistics. *Language and Education, 35.*

Shapiro, S. (2020). Inclusive pedagogy in the academic writing classroom: Cultivating communities of belonging. *Journal of Academic Writing, 10*(1), 154–164. https://publications.coventry.ac.uk/index.php/joaw/article/view/607

Shapiro, S. (forthcoming). Afterword. In In B. Schreiber et al. (Eds.), *Linguistic justice on campus: Theory, pedagogy, and advocacy for multilingual writers.* Multilingual Matters.

Shi, L., & Rolstad, K. (2020). "A good start": A new approach to gauging preservice teachers' critical language awareness. *Journal of Language, Identity & Education, 35*(2), 1–15. https://doi.org/10.1080/15348458.2020.1810045

Short, D. J., & Boyson, B. A. (2012). *Helping newcomer students succeed in secondary schools and beyond* (Vol. 78). Center for Applied Linguistics.

Silva, T., & Wang, Z. (2020). *Reconciling translingualism and second language writing.* Routledge.

Stapleton, P. (2002). Critiquing voice as a viable pedagogical tool in L2 writing: Returning the spotlight to ideas. *Journal of Second Language Writing, 11*(3), 177–190.

Swain, M. (2006). Languaging, agency and collaboration in advanced second language proficiency. In H. Byrnes (Ed.), *Advanced language learning: The contribution of Halliday and Vygotsky* (pp. 95–108). Continuum.

Taylor, S. K., Despagne, C., & Faez, F. (2018). Critical language awareness. In *The TESOL encyclopedia of English language teaching* (pp. 1–14). https://doi.org/10.1002/9781118784235.eelt0660

Thesen, L. (1997). Voices, discourse, and transition: In search of new categories in EAP. *TESOL Quarterly, 31*(3), 487. https://doi.org/10.2307/3587835

U.S. Department of Education. (n.d.). *SEL center.* www.wested.org/resources/

Vasquez, V. M., Janks, H., & Comber, B. (2019). Critical literacy as a way of being and doing. *Language Arts, 96*(5), 300–311.

Wallace, C. (1999). Critical language awareness: Key principles for a course in critical reading. *Language Awareness, 8*(2), 98–110. https://doi.org/10.1080/09658419908667121

Weaver, M. M. (2020). *Critical language awareness pedagogy in first-year composition: A design-based research study* [Unpublished doctoral dissertation from Old Dominion University]. https://doi.org/10.25777/GHYT-V912

Weninger, C., & Kan, K. H. Y. (2013). (Critical) language awareness in business communication. *English for Specific Purposes, 32*(2), 59–71. https://doi.org/10.1016/j.esp.2012.09.002

Wheeler, R. S. (2019). Attitude change is not enough: Disrupting deficit grading practices to disrupt dialect prejudice. *Proceedings of the Linguistic Society of America, 4*(1), 1–10. https://doi.org/10.3765/plsa.v4i1.4505

Wheeler, R. S., & Swords, R. (2006). *Code-switching: Teaching standard English in urban classrooms.* National Council of Teachers of English.

Wolfram, W., Reaser, J., & Vaughn, C. (2008). Operationalizing linguistic gratuity: From principle to practice. *Language and Linguistics Compass, 2*(6), 1109–1134.

Young, S. L. B. (2018). From situated privilege to dis/abilities: Developing critical literacies across social issues. *Journal of Adolescent & Adult Literacy, 61*(5), 501–509. https://doi.org/10.1002/jaal.720

Young, V. A., Barrett, R., & Lovejoy, K. B. (2014). *Other people's English: Code-meshing, code-switching, and African American literacy.* Teachers College Press.

Zembylas, M. (2012). Pedagogies of strategic empathy: Navigating through the emotional complexities of anti-racism in higher education. *Teaching in Higher Education, 17*(2), 113–125.

Part II

Four Pathways for CLA Pedagogy

Part II Introduction

In the next four chapters, we will explore some of the many curricular applications of CLA Pedagogy. I have clustered these applications into thematic "Pathways," in the hopes that readers will identify one or more pathway that is the best fit for their particular teaching situation. As you explore these pathways, I encourage you to keep in mind the foundational pieces that were laid out in Part I—particularly the principles and best practices we discussed in Chapter 3.

Our three overarching goals for CLA Pedagogy, discussed on pp. 54–61, are captured in Figure 3.1,

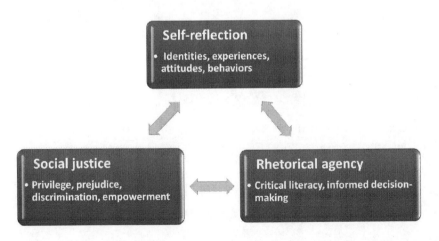

Figure 3.1 Goals for CLA Pedagogy

DOI: 10.4324/9781003171751-6

Our six principles for CLA Pedagogy, discussed on pp. 61–71 are as follows (see Figure 3.2)

1   Includes students from all language backgrounds
2   Uses language as a bridge into social justice learning
3   Engages minds, hearts, and bodies
4   Links awareness to action
5   Works with tensions around linguistic norms and standards
6   Builds on best practices for writing/literacy instruction

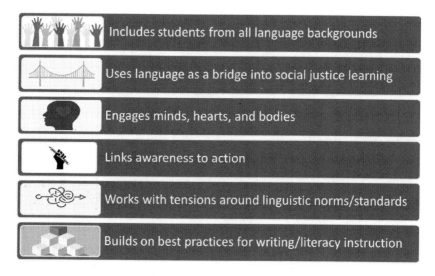

Figure 3.2 Six Principles of CLA Pedagogy

The Structure of the Pathways Chapters

The four chapters in this section all follow a similar structure, so that they are relatively easy for teachers to digest, implement, and adapt. Each chapter begins with an **Introduction,** in which we discuss questions such as:

- What does this chapter have to offer?
- What fields/disciplines does it draw on?
- For which contexts is it most viable?
- What are some general considerations to keep in mind with this pathway?

Next comes a set of **Learning Goals** for the chapter as a whole, each of which is linked to one or more of our three CLA goals (see above). I have structured these as **Essential Questions** and **Transferable Skills,** drawing on Wiggins and McTighe's (2005) "Backward Design" approach. The rationale behind Backward Design is that curricula should be centered on deep, meaningful inquiry and relevant, transferable skills (see Tinberg [2017] for more on "teaching for transfer" in writing courses). Once we have outlined our key questions and skills, we can then work backward to consider the ways that students will demonstrate their learning, and then can plan our instructional sequences to facilitate that learning. (See Mills et al. [2019] for more on the relevance of Backward Design to writing/literacy instruction.) The verbs used in the Skills list are put in bold, in order to highlight the kinds of thinking—analytical, creative, reflective, etc.—that we want students to engage in (Harris, 2004).

After the list of overall Learning Goals comes a short **Summary of Each Unit,** with the specific Essential Questions and Transferable Skills that are most relevant to each one. This is followed by an **At-a-Glance Chart** that lists central Topics/Concepts, Readings/Resources, and Activities/Assignments for each of the three units.

After all of this introductory information, I begin presenting the first unit. For each unit, there is a short **Overview,** followed by a **Learning Sequence** that includes suggestions for Tapping into Prior Knowledge and Experience, Exploring Key Topics and Questions, and Deepening and/or Personalizing Student Learning. Woven throughout the learning sequence are key concepts, reflection and discussion questions, readings/materials, and in-class activities. Each unit concludes with suggestions for **Demonstrating Learning** from that unit—usually one or two assignments, along with relevant considerations and grading criteria.

How to Navigate the Pathways Chapters

Below are some overall suggestions for engaging with these four chapters. One option, of course is to simply "jump in" and see what piques your interest. However, these chapters are chock-full of ideas and resources, and there may be readers who—like me—can begin to feel overwhelmed by all of the pedagogical possibilities. So here is how I would approach these chapters:

1   **Browse first:** After reading the introductory material for a chapter, pause to decide which unit in that chapter to engage with first. They do not need to be read in order—in fact, one reason I have included so many guideposts at the start of each chapter (e.g., Learning Goals,

Unit Summaries, At-a-Glance Chart, etc.) is to help you to make a conscious choice about which unit(s) you want to really dive into.

2   **Keep your own context and goals in mind:** As you review the introductory material for each Pathway, consider which of these goals are a good fit with your own teaching context and objectives. Let those Essential Questions and Transferable Skills—not just the topics and materials—guide your pedagogical decision-making. Note that *all of the units can be adapted to a variety of content areas, grade levels, and pedagogical goals.* Although we will discuss some ways to differentiate in Chapters 4 and 8, I trust that teachers can and will do some additional adaptation themselves. In Chapter 8, we will talk more about tailoring CLA-oriented courses and units to your own teaching context.

3   **Feel free to mix and match:** Each chapter is structured in terms of "Units" and "Learning Sequences" for readability, rather than pedagogical necessity. Some topics, activities, or assignments build on previous ones, but it is perfectly acceptable (and likely necessary!) to draw from multiple units and pathways in your own course/curriculum design. In Chapter 8, in fact, I show how and why I have done this in several of my own courses. These sequences are not lesson/unit plans, exactly— they are more like a set of ingredients you can pull together in your own way, using your own critical and creative thinking! In essence, think of each learning sequence as a **menu rather than a recipe.**

4   **Start small and build up:** As we discussed in Chapter 3, eager educators sometimes feel a pressure to re-work *everything* in light of a new framework or approach. However, we sometimes need to start small— particularly if we are trying to align our curriculum with other expectations (standards, assessments, program requirements, etc.), as we will discuss more in Chapters 8 and 9. It may be best to pilot a few topics, readings, activities, or assignments within an existing unit or course before taking on a bigger curricular transformation.

5   **Keep in mind both the "what" and the "how."** Chapter 3 also touched on the idea that CLA Pedagogy builds on—rather than replaces—best practices for teaching academic literacy. In the excitement about new curricular content (i.e., What will we read, discuss, and write about?), it can be easy to forget at the delivery of that content is *just as important* to our pedagogical effectiveness and equity in the classroom. Instructors newer to teaching writing, or to teaching in general, may want to read Chapter 9 first, as it talks about how CLA can inform our day-to-day classroom instruction. As a reminder, we also reviewed some

established best practices for writing pedagogy near the end of Chapter 3 (pp. 69–71).

6   **Stay curious!** My last bit of advice for exploring these chapters is to give yourself permission to read some of this material simply for the *sake of learning*—whether or not you think you will use it in the classroom. We can never fully shut off our teacher brains, of course, but I have found that if I let myself linger with new concepts for a while before jumping ahead to classroom applications, I stay connected to my identity as a **life-long learner**. And of course, that makes me a better teacher, too! Chapter 10 has some suggestions for how CLA might enrich our lives beyond work—in case you want to read that first, to whet your appetite! There will be other resources along these lines at the online Hub (http://clacollective.org/), which can be also found at the **Support Materials page** for this volume.

References

Harris, R. (2004). Encouraging emergent moments: The personal, critical, and rhetorical in the writing classroom. *Pedagogy, 4*(3), 401–418.

Mills, J., Wiley, C., & Williams, J. (2019). "This is what learning looks like!": Backward design and the framework in first year writing. *portal: Libraries and the Academy, 19*(1), 155–175.

Tinberg, H. (2017). Teaching for transfer: A passport for writing in new contexts. *Peer Review*. Association of American Colleges & Universities (AACU). www.aacu.org/peerreview/2017/Winter/Tinberg

Wiggins, G., & McTighe, J. (2005). *Understanding by design*. ASCD.

4
The Sociolinguistics Pathway

Introduction

Among the small but growing number of U.S.-based practitioners using CLA Pedagogy in English/writing classes, Sociolinguistics is the most common pathway. This pathway is particularly conducive to teachers who want to link CLA to **anti-racism** and other **social justice frameworks**—although, as we discussed in Chapter 3, social justice is always a core value in CLA Pedagogy, no matter what content we are working with! (NOTE: For those looking to engage social justice issues in relation to academic settings, Chapter 5 is the pathway that will take you there most directly!)

So . . . what is sociolinguistics? And why might we wish to bring it into our writing curricula?

Linguistics textbooks tend to define sociolinguistics as 1) the study of linguistic variation or 2) the study of the relationship between language and society. Although both of these definitions are accurate, I have found that neither is sufficient to excite students—or colleagues, frankly—about this rich area of study.

Here is an extended definition from the *Language and Life Project* at North Carolina State University, a resource we will be returning to later in this chapter:

> Sociolinguistics is the study of language in its social context. The term encompasses a wide range of research questions and pursuits within linguistics, including but not limited to:
>
> - How do people use language to define themselves or to set themselves apart from others?
> - How, when, and why does language change? What kinds of people start language change?

DOI: 10.4324/9781003171751-7

- What parts of speech change as people switch between different social situations? What parts stay the same? And why?
- What causes listeners to think of one type of language as "better" than another?
- How does language vary depending on the race, class, and gender of a speaker?
- How do external factors such as social tension, racism, sexism, media representation, popular entertainment, etc. affect the way people use language?

That's a bit more juicy, no?

When selling students on sociolinguistics (a fun tongue twister, by the way!), I explain that this field explores how language creates and reflects **social identities**. The theme of *identity* almost always appeals to U.S. students and teachers, as we discussed in Chapter 3. And talking about identity as "social" helps to highlight that we *construct and perform* our identities through interaction, and language is one of the tools we use most for this "identity work" (e.g., Suh & Shapiro, 2021).

I also like to tell students that sociolinguists examine how *language shapes our world*, and how *we shape language*. I like that this framing recognizes the power that language has on us, but also reminds us that we can leverage that power as language users (rhetorical agency!). One of the foundational understandings in sociolinguistics, in fact, is that humans are the drivers of linguistic variation. And this variation happens not only in speech, which has traditionally been the focal point of sociolinguistics research, but also in writing. It also occurs in what linguist John McWhorter (2013) calls "fingered speech"—the writing that takes place on digital and social media, which we will talk about more in Chapter 6. Thus, the Sociolinguistics pathway can lead to all sorts of interesting conversations related to writing, including the question: *What do we consider "writing" in the first place?*

Another thing I love about sociolinguistics is that it is adaptable to a wide range of institutional contexts, pedagogical goals, and student interests. I have explored this pathway with students in middle- and high-school settings, as well as with undergraduate and even graduate students—not to mention in professional development settings with fellow teachers! Sociolinguistics as a subfield intersects with a number of other disciplines, including anthropology, education, psychology, and sociology. Thus, it pairs well with English for Academic Purposes (EAP) curricula and Writing Across the Curriculum (WAC) programs. Moreover, as I alluded to earlier, this pathway engages issues that are socially and politically relevant, offering a bridge into conversations about systemic racism and White privilege, as well as other forms of oppression.

Sociolinguistics is also a *huge* area of study. I teach an introductory course on the topic, and we barely scratch the surface. This breadth presents an opportunity, since there is so much to explore, but also a challenge, as there is only so much we can do in a single unit or course—particularly when explicit instruction in writing is another of our pedagogical goals.

There are other challenges as well with the Sociolinguistics pathway: First, for teachers who have not done prior learning in linguistics, the new disciplinary terminology can be a bit daunting. There are short, accessible explanations of core concepts included throughout the text, to help with this. But if teachers wish to have students engage with *texts written by and for sociolinguists* (e.g., articles from scholarly journals), they may need to build up their own knowledge base first. Even in my Introduction to Sociolinguistics course, which is *not* a writing-intensive course (although we do use writing-to-learn—i.e., writing as a tool for knowledge-building, reflection, and assessment) "and assessment of content learning)", we read only a few scholarly publications beyond our textbook. We do engage with a lot of other media, however—some of which will be referenced in this chapter.

Thus, as we incorporate learning from the sociolinguistics pathway into our curricular planning, we need to think carefully about questions such as:

- To what extent is the learning of content—i.e., sociolinguistic theories and concepts—an important goal for my class? If content learning is a goal, how will I assess that learning? (We will be discussing assessment more in Chapters 8, 9, and 10.)
- How can I make the Sociolinguistics content accessible and relevant to all students? What background knowledge do students need to engage confidently with this content?
- If research—primary or secondary—is a focus of my unit/course, what background knowledge do students (and I) need to be successful with that research?

Fortunately, there are many scholar-practitioners, myself included, who have published accounts of courses or curricular units that fit within the Sociolinguistics pathway (e.g., Shapiro, 2015, 2022; Siczek & Shapiro, 2014). I will be referencing some of that scholarship below. Additional citations can be found at online at the Hub.

Before delving into the specifics of the Sociolinguistics pathway, I want to offer a few words of advice for **working with language variation** inclusively and effectively in the classroom.

1   Whenever we talk about language difference, it is helpful to **define our linguistic and geographic context(s)**. Some of my classes, such as my first-year seminar, "Language and Social Justice," which I discuss more below, focus more heavily on U.S. varieties of English. Other courses have a more global focus—in part because they are designed to appeal in particular to international students, which I will explain more in Chapter 8. It is fine to "travel around" some in exploring language variation, but I have found that students do appreciate **opportunities to linger with one place or population** for a while—either collectively or individually. To that end, this chapter includes a variety of activities and assignments that promote sustained focus on a particular variety or linguistic community.

2   It is also important to **keep inclusion in mind** when engaging language variation—something we will delve into further in Chapters 8 and 9. We want to avoid an "us vs. them" pattern, talking about U.S. English, for example, as "our language" or "our dialect"—a move that can be exclusionary to students and colleagues from other linguistic, cultural, and citizenship backgrounds. Plus, as we will explore below, there are many varieties of English used in the U.S.—so the idea of single "U.S. English" is pretty much a myth! (Lippi-Green, 2012).

3   Another piece of inclusion is **treating all language varieties with respect**. It is great fun to learn about different languages, dialects, and speaking styles—that is one of the appeals of this pathway! However, it is surprisingly easy to lapse into "othering" practices, by exoticizing, imitating, or stereotyping other language varieties. Sociolinguists such as Mary Bucholtz and Qiuana Lopez (2011) have used the term **"linguistic blackface"** to refer to the practice of appropriating and/or mimicking a minoritized dialect. As this term suggests, there are power dynamics involved in how we work with language varieties that are not our own. These are the kinds of tensions we want to talk about explicitly with students, so that they understand their own privileges, build empathy, and develop skills necessary for global citizenship (Abe & Shapiro, 2021).

4   One way to ensure that we avoid this "othering" effect is to use **audio or video clips of actual language users**, rather than attempting to "try on" unfamiliar (to us) varieties. There are many online resources we can draw on, such as linguistic atlases that contain samples of speech from different regions. One prominent and user-friendly example is the Dictionary of American Regional English, or DARE (see Abrams & Stickle, 2019 for more on pedagogical uses of DARE). We can **also provide social and political context for language varieties**, talking not

just about people and places, but also about the histories and perceptions of those varieties.

Learning Goals for the Sociolinguistics Pathway

Essential Questions

In the Introduction to Part II, I briefly explained my rationale for structuring our learning goals as "Essential Questions" and "Transferable Skills," in keeping with the principles of Backward Design (Wiggins & McTighe, 2005). Below are 10 Essential Questions that undergird much of the learning along the Sociolinguistics pathway. Next to each question, I have noted the relevant CLA goal(s): **SR** = self-reflection, **SJ** = social justice, **RA** = rhetorical agency:

1   How and why do sociolinguists study linguistic variation? (RA)
2   What role does language play in creating and reshaping communities? (SR, SJ, RA)
3   How do humans "index" their backgrounds—geographic, gender, racial/ ethnic, age, socioeconomic, etc.—in and through language? (SR, RA)
4   What attitudes do I hold about particular ways of speaking/writing? How might others judge me based on how I speak/write? (SR, SJ)
5   How do our linguistic biases influence our behaviors toward other people? (SR, SJ)
6   How does language/dialect use in literature and other media illustrate and reinforce particular attitudes and biases? (SJ, RA)
7   How do we vary our language use depending on audience, context, and purpose? (SR, RA)
8   To what extent does our language background influence how we experience the world? (SR, RA)
9   How and why do language users mix codes in their speech? (RA)
10 How can we intervene when we experience or observe instances of unfair perception or treatment based on language?

Transferable Skills

Below is a list of some of the transferable skills students can develop within this pathway. These skills are informed by Bloom's taxonomy, with the aim of promoting deep and critical thinking (e.g., Harris, 2004; Krathwohl, 2002).

Within the Sociolinguistics pathway, students will be able to (SWBAT) . . .

A   **Appreciate** the value of linguistic diversity and convey openness and empathy toward users of other language varieties
B   **Apply** sociolinguistics concepts as a lens for examining their social, academic, and civic lives
C   **Use** sociolinguistics tools and resources (e.g., dialect surveys, linguistic atlases) for primary or secondary research
D   **Interpret** findings and implications from empirical research studies in sociolinguistics and related fields
E   **Analyze** data (e.g., samples of speech/writing) etc. from a sociolinguistics perspective.
F   **Trace** linguistic attitudes and stereotypes in literature and other media
G   **Understand** the role of linguistic prejudice in perpetuating racism, sexism, and other forms of oppression
H   **Identify** ways to resist linguistic prejudice, at both micro levels (e.g., everyday interactions) and macro levels (societal structures, school policies, etc.)
I   **Connect** learning about linguistic variation to their own rhetorical choices in speech and writing

Overview of Units

Here is a short summary of the four units in this chapter, with the most relevant Essential Questions (EQs) and Transferable Skills (Skills) from the lists above:

4.1: Linguistic variation (EQs #1, 2, 3, 8, and 9; Skills A, B, C, E, and I). In this unit, students establish a foundational understanding and appreciation of linguistic variation. They learn about intersections between idiolect and social identity, including region, race/ethnicity, class, gender, etc. Assignments include a research project on a particular variety of English (or another language) and a literary analysis project focused on dialect use.

4.2: Linguistic attitudes and prejudices (EQs #2, 3, 4, 6, 8, and 10; Skills A, B, D, E, F, and I). Students explore attitudes toward linguistic varieties (in the U.S. and/or elsewhere), including reflecting on their own biases. They learn about how linguistic biases and stereotypes are perpetuated in entertainment media, and how linguistic prejudice maps onto other forms of prejudice. Assignments include an autobiographical essay and a critical analysis of television, film, or other media.

4.3: Linguistic profiling and discrimination (EQs #4, 5, 6, 7, 8, 9, and 10; Skills B, C, E, F, G, and H). Students deepen and broaden their understanding about the impact of linguistic prejudice, including how linguistic profiling contributes to discrimination in employment, housing, politics, criminal justice, and other systems and institutions. They consider ways to resist language-based discrimination in their day-to-day lives and in society more broadly.

Below is an **At-a-Glance Chart** for the three units in this chapter. I include this resource as a quick reference to locate particular points from the units. It can also serve as a "menu" for readers, helping them to identify the specific units they wish to explore.

Table 4.1 The Sociolinguistics Pathway (At-a-Glance)

	Concepts/Topics	Readings/ Resources	Activities/ Assignments
Unit 4.1: Linguistic Variation pp. 94–103	Linguistic varieties (e.g., of English) Features of a variety (e.g., lexicon, phonology, syntax, prestige/stigma) Dialect awareness/ use Value of linguistic diversity Language and thought Code-mixing	Websites (e.g., PBS's *American Tongues* [AT] and *Do You Speak American?* [DYSA]; NCSU's *Language and Life Project* [LLP]) Dialect Surveys (e.g., Cambridge) Online articles (e.g., *Psychology Today, Scientific American*, British Library, ThoughtCo)	* Media show-and tell * Peer-to-peer research * Jigsaw reading * Reading log * Dialect surveys/ quizzes * Researching a variety of English * Analyzing dialect patterns in literature
Unit 4.2: Linguistic Attitudes and Prejudice pp. 104–112	Linguistic attitudes Perceptual dialectology Linguistic insecurity Linguistic privilege Linguistic bias Accent stereotypes	Websites: AT, DYSA, LLP (see above) Podcasts (Codeswitch, Fresh Air) Artistic/ autobiographical writing	* "Four Corners" * Autobiographical essay * Analysis of sociolinguistic patterns (in film/ TV, etc.)

	Concepts/Topics	Readings/ Resources	Activities/ Assignments
	Language bias and classism, sexism, and LGBTQ+ communities	(e.g., Anzaldua, Lyiscott, Tan) News articles (e.g., BBC, Guardian, Huffington Post) Online magazines (e.g., Atlantic, Harvard Bus. Rev, New Yorker) Research studies (e.g., Dustan & Yeager; Lippi-Green)	(Also Sociolinguistics Scrapbook, below)
Unit 4.3 Linguistic Profiling and Discrimination pp. 113–123	Linguistic profiling Language as a 'proxy' (for race, gender, class, etc.) Language-based discrimination in housing, employment, politics/public sphere	Blogs (e.g., *Psychology Today,* London School of Economics) Research reports (e.g., Baugh's TEDx talk, Brookings Institute, Rickford & King) News articles (e.g., *NY Times, Harvard Bus. Review, Forbes*) Other educational resources (e.g., from Learning for Justice)	* Rating/reacting to speech samples * Critical role-play (scenarios) * Sociolinguistics Scrapbook

Unit 4.1: Linguistic Variation

Overview

Within this unit, students explore concepts, methods, and findings from studies of linguistic variation. They engage concepts such as: *language variety*, which many linguists use as an alternative to "dialect" (see explanation in Chapter 2), *linguistic community, indexicality, prestige, stigma, idiolect,* and *code-mixing/code-switching.* Engaging these concepts establishes a foundation for talking about linguistic attitudes, biases, and discrimination in the later units. Teachers who wish to progress directly to Unit 4.2 or 4.3 may want to include some of the concepts or materials from this unit.

Learning Sequence

Tapping into Prior Knowledge

We can begin our exploration of linguistic variation by engaging questions such as the following, in small or large groups—and/or in writing:

1   What kinds (varieties) of English[1] are most common at our school? In our local community? In other communities we're connected to?
2   How do I recognize varieties different from my own? What features (sounds, words, structures, norms) do I recognize as distinct or "marked"?
3   What other varieties of English am I familiar with? Where have I encountered those varieties?

Activity: Media "Show-and-Tell"

One activity that helps to generate student curiosity and engagement around language variation is a **media share,** modeled on the idea of "show and tell," which I think is an activity we should continue into secondary and postsecondary grades! Students bring to class—or post online—a short media clip or audio sample that demonstrates language variation. These can come from film/TV, music, social media, or another source. Each student introduces their clip/sample, connects it to something that has come up in class, and then shares it with the group—either small group or entire class. For online classes, the "share screen" feature works well for this activity. These speech samples be used to help students understand **idiolect** (i.e., an individual's speech style) vs. **variety** (a dialect/style used by a particu-lar group). We can also talk about **hyperperformance** (also known as **stylized speech**), which is when a speaker chooses to "play up" a par-ticular variety or speech style, as a way of **indexing** their membership in a particular linguistic community. This activity pairs nicely with the Sociolinguistics Scrapbook assignment discussed in Unit 4.3.

Topic #1: Building Dialect Awareness

After we have built some interest, we can guide students toward more sys-tematic exploration of language variation—including introducing varieties of U.S. English that may be less familiar to them. Here are some focal ques-tions and recommended resources that can help build what Wolfram (2000)[2] calls "dialect awareness":

1   What can we learn about our own idiolects from **online dialect surveys and/or quizzes** (e.g., *NYTimes*[3] and *Slate* magazine[4])? Students can dis-cuss the findings from these surveys/quizzes—or even replicate or revise them for peer-to-peer research, which we will discuss later on.

2   What factors **cause language to vary**? What **varieties of English** are used in the U.S.? (e.g., PBS's *American Tongues* and *Do You Speak American*,[5] as well as the *Language and Life Project* (LLP)[6] developed in collaboration with North Carolina State University See Figure 4.1).

3   Where can I go to learn about the **history and features of a particu-lar variety of English**? (e.g., British Library,[7] *Encyclopedia Britannica*,[8] *Washington Post*.[9] More on this in Assignment 1.)

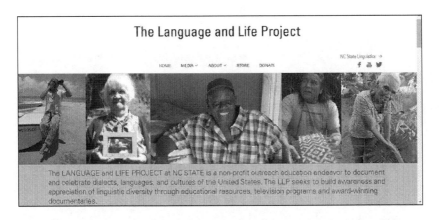

Figure 4.1 Screenshot of Homepage for the NCSU's *Language and Life Project*

4   What **tools and resources do dialectologists** (i.e., researchers who study language variation) use to document and share their findings? (e.g., the aforementioned Dictionary of American Regional English,[10] as well as lists of atlases compiled by linguists at George Mason University[11] and the University of Georgia[12]).

Activity: Jigsaw Reading

As can be seen below, there are often so many topics to explore in this unit that we may not be able to engage them all as a class. **Jigsaw reading** is one way to allow for some individualization, so students can explore a topic that they are most curious about. After doing some initial context-building and discussion around language variation (see above), we present students with a **selection of topics (usually three to five)** to choose from—each of which has one or more assigned readings/media. Their homework—or in-class assignment—is to engage with the readings/media, with the goal of **sharing highlights with their peers.**

During the share session, students first cluster with others who chose the **same topic,** in order to check for understanding, compare key points, etc. This also helps to ensure that students who struggled or forgot the assignment will still have something to share. Then students are arranged into groups with others who chose a **different topic.** Each student has a few minutes (or more, if this is a more formal assignment) to share. See below for a sampling of topics with recommended readings/media. This activity can be used with other units throughout this book as well.

Topic #2: Deepening our Understanding of Linguistic Diversity (e.g., for Jigsaw Reading)

1   What has been the impact of **English dominance** around the world?

- David Crystal[13] (2012) on how and why English became a global language
- Criticisms of linguistic imperialism (e.g., Al Jazeera[14]) and native-speakerism (e.g., NPR's Rough Translation podcast[15]); see also Chapter 5

2   To what extent does **language shape our view of the world?**

- Articles on how language variation intersects with cultural identi-
  ty—e.g., from the British Broadcasting Corporation (BBC)[16] and
  UNESCO[17]
- Studies of how language shapes thought—e.g., Lera Boroditsky's
  TED talk[18] and/or *Scientific American* article[19]; also *Smithsonian
  Magazine*,[20] which references the 2016 film *Arrival*
- Responses from members of the Linguistic Society of America[21] to
  debates about language and thought

3   Where can we find examples of **code-mixing in our day-to-day lives?**

- Articles about dialect use in literature—e.g., from Do You Speak
  American (DYSA),[22] the *Guardian*,[23] and the (U.K.'s) Royal Literary Fund[24]
- Examples of code-mixing (sometimes called *code-switching* or
  code-meshing, as we discussed in Chapter 1) in political discourse
  and popular culture—e.g., from the NPR *Codeswitch* podcast,[25]
  Babbel.com,[26] and the *Huffington Post*[27]

NOTE: Chapters 5 and 7 include examples of code-mixing in other contexts, including in both scholarly and creative writing.

Demonstrating Learning from Unit 4.1

Below are two assignments that pair well with this unit. Both involve independent research and/or analysis, but could easily be adapted into group projects.

Assignment #1: Research Project on a Particular Variety of English

With this assignment, students choose or are assigned a particular variety of
English. These can be varieties from "**inner circle**" countries such as Australia, Canada, and England, as well as the U.S. Alternatively, students can
investigate varieties of English in "**outer circle**" countries that were former
British colonies (e.g., India, Nigeria, and South Africa) or "**expanding circle**"
countries where English is a foreign language (e.g., Brazil, China, Egypt, or
France). For more explanation of inner, outer, and expanding circles, check
out the work of World Englishes scholar Braj Kachru, which is summarized
at ThoughtCo.[28]

To support students with their research, we can introduce terms such as **standardization, prestige,** and **stigma,** which we discussed in Chapter 2. We may also want to review linguistics terms for talking about features of a language, such as **lexicon** (words), **phonology** (sounds—often what we mean by "accent"), and **syntax** (grammar). The online Hub has instructions for a game I have used to help students middle and high school students learn these terms!

To learn more about their chosen variety, students usually begin with some of the resources listed above (e.g., DYSA, linguistic atlases). However, they may also need to identify additional sources, and may need support in evaluating credibility of websites. This provides an opportunity to build **information literacy skills,** which we will explore more fully in Chapter 6.

I have written about the postsecondary version of this assignment in some of my other publications (e.g., Abe & Shapiro, 2021; Shapiro, 2015; Siczek & Shapiro, 2014), but I have also adapted it for use with secondary students. The table below details how I have structured this assignment differently depending on the level.

Table 4.2 Adapting the "Variety of English" Project to Different Grade Levels

Variety of English Research Project	
Secondary	*Postsecondary*
* Students choose varieties from a given list (with occasional exceptions by request). * Research focuses on demographics, history, and linguistic features (after a review of terms such as phonology, lexicon, etc.). * Students have opportunities to work on the project in class, with support from the teacher and possibly peers. * Students present orally in groups and submit a completed note-taking grid, which could be adapted into a written report.	* Students choose a variety themselves, with feedback from instructor. * Research focuses as well on attitudes and power dynamics (e.g., prestige/stigma). Students are also expected to reference course concepts or readings. * Students do most of the research outside of class, but troubleshoot and reflect on the process in class. * Students present orally and write a paper reporting and reflecting on their findings.

When presenting this (or any) project to students, I try to provide explicit information about our *learning goals, the stages of the process, and the grading criteria.*[29] Below are lightly edited versions of the assignment handouts I use for each level.

Handout for "Varieties of English" Research Project

(7th-10th grade)

Goals: To learn about a specific variety of English, and to practice doing online research

Process:

1   Choose a variety of English to research (see list in handout for college level, below)

2   Take notes on your variety, focusing on the points in the note-taking grid; you may use recommended sources (e.g., PBS) or find additional *credible* sources

   NOTE: The "note-taking grid" is a separate handout, available at the Hub, which includes the following questions:

   a   *Where and by whom is this variety spoken?*

   b   *What historical influences have shaped this variety?*

   c   *What are some of the key features of this variety (lexical, phonological, possibly syntactic)?*

   d   *What do you find most interesting about this variety?*

   e   *What sources did you use for your information?*

   f   *What is one audio or video clip you could use in your presentation?*

3   Bring notes to next class—be prepared to share about the process

4   Continue researching next two classes (we will have 15–20 minutes each day)

5   Final product (due next week):

   a   Oral presentation (5–7 min, including one short audio or video clip)

   b   Completed note-taking grid (typed or neatly hand-written)

Handout for "Profile of a Variety of English" Research Project (College-Level—mostly first-years)

For this project, you will choose a specific country or region to focus on, to develop a linguistic profile of a variety of English spoken in that area. You will prepare a short oral presentation (five minutes plus two-minute Q/A) and write a **report and analysis paper** (approx. 4 pages), using course readings and outside sources, as necessary.

Your paper should answer the following questions:

1   What are some of the linguistic characteristics of the variety of English spoken in this region? (lexicon, syntax, phonology, pragmatics, etc.)
2   What are the particular dynamics (geographic, political, historical, social, cultural) that have shaped this variety and the attitudes toward it?
3   How does this "case study" illustrate (or complicate) themes and issues from our course readings and discussion?
4   What surprised or intrigued you most about your findings? (i.e. "So what?")

Some of the varieties of English that students have found most interesting include:

> Scottish, Irish, Welsh, Cockney, Queen's English (RP), Estuary English, Boston Brahman, Appalachian, New Zealander, Aboriginal, Jamaican, Hawaiian (and other creoles), Chinglish*, Singlish, Franglais, Denglish, S. Rusglish, Spanglish (U.S.-Mexico border), English for specific purposes (e.g. aviation, hip hop), and many more!!

*We discuss in class that some of these terms (e.g., "Chinglish") are considered derogatory by some speakers, while others embrace the term. This provides an opportunity to discuss tensions and disagreements from within linguistic communities.

Grading rubric for summary/reflection paper:

- Content (answering all four questions above) /30
- Use of evidence (secondary sources and examples) /30
- Reference to course terms and concepts /10
- Organization (structure, transitions) /20
- Clarity of writing /10

See Chapters 8 and 9 for more guidance on scaffolding and assessing CLA-oriented assignments, and visit the Hub for samples of student work.

Assignment #2: Analyzing Linguistic Variation in Literature

Since my courses are built primarily around nonfiction texts, I do not require that students analyze literature, although we do sometimes examine excerpts in class. However, a number of other CLA teacher-scholars have provided examples and guidance for how to engage students in examining language variation in literary texts. Below are four texts which are used frequently in CLA-oriented literature units and which have been written about by scholar-practitioners:

- Mark Twain's *The Adventures of Huckleberry Finn* (e.g., Devereaux, 2015; Dyches & Gale, 2019; Yu, 2017)
- Zora Neale Hurston's *Their Eyes Were Watching God*, (Arevalo, 2019; Devereaux & Wheeler, 2012; Metz, 2018)
- Sandra Cisneros's *House on Mango Street* (Devereaux, 2015; Shaffer, 2003)
- Angie Thomas's *The Hate U Give*, (Baker-Bell, 2020, Levin, 2020)

For additional text suggestions, including texts recommended within the Common Core State Standards, see Devereaux (2015). And of course, since **most fiction writing includes some sort of language variation** (e.g., different idiolects as part of character development), the steps below may be applicable to many of the texts you already teach!

Below is a recommended sequence of scaffolding steps for this assignment, including exploration, group practice, and individual analysis:

1   **Explore/observe:** We can support students' initial explorations with prompts such as:

    a   Where have you noticed differences in speaking style among the characters? (e.g., spelling, grammar, word choice)

    b   How do those patterns vary based on age, gender, place of origin, race/ethnicity, social class, personality, or other factors?

    c   Can you find examples in which a character changes their **idiolect** (i.e., individual speaking style) depending on the setting, the **interlocutor** (i.e., conversation partner), and/or the purpose for the interaction? How do these variations enrich or complicate the story?

    d   Do you have any difficulty understanding what any of the characters are saying? What makes it difficult to understand that character's idiolect?

    e   What questions or other observations do you have about language use among characters in the text?

Activity: Reading Log

One way to help students prepare to discuss the above prompts—orally and in writing—is to assign a **reading log**, also known as a "double entry diary." One such log I created and have used with both secondary and postsecondary students looks like this:

Table 4.3 Sample Reading Log

Quote or example from the text (including page #)	My connection, comment, or question (i.e., What did I find interesting, relevant, surprising, or confusing in that quote/example?)

I *enjoy* reading these logs, because they provide excellent insight into what students are thinking about as they engage with texts of all kinds (fiction or non-fiction). These can also be submitted electronically before class, to help inform our lesson planning for the next meeting. Novak et al. (1999) call this type of activity "**Just-in-Time-Teaching**," since it allows us to tailor each class session to students' emerging observations, questions, and needs.

---

2   **Guided practice:** Practice analyzing literary dialect use together as a class or small group, using the following steps:

    a   Identify a scene in which more than one language variety or speech style is used. Annotate the text, focusing on the following questions:

- Whose speech is considered **unmarked** (i.e., "normal") and whose is **marked** (i.e., "different")?
- What textual features are used to "mark" linguistic variation? (e.g., alternative spelling—i.e., **eye dialect**; word choice—i.e., **lexicon**; grammatical choices/patterns—i.e., **syntax**).
- How do those features correlate with aspects of the character or situation (history, identity, community membership, personal motivations, etc.)?
- Do you see any examples of **code/dialect-mixing**—either alternating between varieties, or "meshing" two varieties in a single sentence or utterance?

  b   After sharing above observations in groups or all together, consider what the examples of linguistic variation in this scene tell us and how they relate to our CLA concepts. From examining language variation in this text, what do we learn about the characters (identity, agency, etc.), their relationships (solidarity, competition etc.), the setting or situation (community, power, privilege), and/or the author's intent?

3   **Interpret/argue:** Begin to develop claims/arguments that can be supported by textual evidence of language variation. These arguments can be centered on:

  a.   A crucial scene in the narrative (and why that scene is so significant)
  b   A theme in the text, such as inequality, pride, courage, justice, liberation)
  c   A character's developmental trajectory across the text
  d   The broader significance of the text, as an illustration of historical or societal phenomena
  e   Alternative/critical interpretations of the text

4   **Analyze independently and/or present/share:** Students can repeat this process independently or can present the results of their group analysis in a variety of writing genres. Options include a more traditional literary analysis paper or a multimodal genre such as a poster, slide show, blog post, or zine.[30]

This sequence can be adapted for analysis of **other genres of creative writing** as well, such as plays and poetry, spoken word (e.g., Lyiscott, 2014, discussed further below) or even song lyrics.

****

Unit 4.2: Linguistic Attitudes and Prejudices

Overview

In this unit, students explore the origin and nature of linguistic attitudes and prejudices. As noted earlier, Unit 4.1 lays some important ground-work for the units that follow. Teachers who wish to progress directly to Unit 4.2 or 4.3 may wish to incorporate some of the concepts, materials, and/or activities from 4.1, so that students have some understanding of linguistic variation before they begin to explore linguistic attitudes and prejudices. This unit engages themes such as prestige, stigma, privilege, and prejudice, as they relate to language. We also learn about **language ideologies** (see Chapter 2) and research in **perceptual dialectology**, the subfield of research that maps linguistic attitudes. Some practitioners build this entire unit around one particular variety of English, such as African American Vernacular English, or AAVE (Baker-Bell, 2020; Hankerson, 2016). Others, like myself, focus on multiple varieties within the unit—in part because we have students from a variety of language backgrounds in our classes. Units like this one have been written about by scholars such as Devereaux (2015), Devereaux and Palmer (2019), Godley and Reaser (2018), and Metz (2018).

Learning Sequence

Tapping into Prior Knowledge

Some of the discussion and reflection questions can use to begin talking about linguistic attitudes include:

1   Which accents in English do you most enjoy listening to? Why?
2   Are there accents you find irritating or unappealing? Why?
3   Have you noticed any accent patterns (or other linguistic patterns) in animated films (e.g., from Disney, Pixar, etc.)? How do the villains tend to speak? How do the "sidekicks" speak? What about the heroes/ protagonists?
4   Have you ever felt insecure about the way you speak? Have you ever been made fun of for how you speak?
5   Have you ever made assumptions about someone based on their accent or style of speech?

Activity: Four Corners

To start to engage some critical questions related to linguistic attitudes, we can use kinesthetic activities such as **four corners**. With this activity, students move to a part of the room to indicate the extent to which they agree or disagree with a statement (i.e., *strongly agree, slightly agree, slightly disagree,* or *strongly disagree*). Examples of statements that work well for this activity include:

- I enjoy watching/listening to media that uses different accents of English.
- I think a British accent sounds smarter or more authoritative than a typical U.S. accent (e.g., as the voice for my smart phone).
- I associate a Southern (U.S.) twang with being less educated.
- I think it is important to speak "properly" at school (and/or in the workplace).
- It annoys me when public figures (or other authorities, such as teachers) make grammatical errors or use words incorrectly in their speech.
- It is unfair to expect everyone's speech to sound the same way.

Topic #1: Tracing Linguistic Attitudes and Prejudices

1   What are some of the most widespread **linguistic prejudices in the U.S.?**

  (e.g., PBS's 1988 documentary *American Tongues*,[31] which was the precursor to *Do You Speak American* [DYSA], discussed above. The *Language and Life Project* has also produced a number of documentary films[32]).

2   How do researchers ("perceptual dialectologists") **study language attitudes?**

  (See the DYSA companion website,[33] as well as clips from the film featuring researcher Dennis Preston at work.[34])

3   How does **entertainment media** illustrate linguistic prejudice?

  (e.g., scenes from film, literature, and/or other media, such as *My Fair Lady* [1964], *Crash* [2004], or *Sorry to Bother You* [2018]. See below for more film suggestions.)

Figure 4.2 Screenshot of *Atlantic* Article on Accent Stereotypes in Children's Media

4   How might media—especially children's animation—use accents and speech styles to reinforce **racial/ethnic stereotypes**? (*The Atlantic*[35]—see Figure 4.2; also BBC.[36])

> NOTE: There are also empirical studies on this, such as Lippi-Green (2012), who has summarized this work on her blog.[37] Faculty working with advanced undergraduates or graduate students may wish to check out recent graduate theses on these issues—e.g., Soares (2017) and Urke (2019).

5   How do users of stigmatized varieties of English experience and (at times) **push back against linguistic prejudice**? We can explore this in a number of ways, including:

a   Autobiographical writing about language and identity, such as:

- Gloria Anzaldua's (1987) "How to Tame a Wild Tongue"
- Richard Rodriguez's (1982) "Public and Private Language"
- Amy Tan's (1990) "Mother Tongue"
- Jamila Lyiscott's (2014) spoken word piece, "3 Ways to Speak English"[38]

(Other examples are included at the Hub.).

b   Other first-hand accounts—e.g., by reporters Deion Broxton (NPR's podcast *Codeswitch*[39]) and broadcaster Vanessa Ruiz (NYTimes[40]);

additional accounts can be found in Baker-Bell (2020) and on the Hub

Topic #2: Intersectionality and Linguistic Prejudice

Above we touched on some ways that language patterns are linked to racism. Below are some links between linguistic prejudice and other forms of oppression, which can be explored with the entire class or used for jigsaw reading, which we discussed in Unit 4.1.

1   How are linguistic attitudes informed by **sexism?**

- Studies on how speech patterns vary by gender—e.g., by linguist Deborah Tannen, whose work has appeared in the *Harvard Business Review*[41] and *Scientific American*[42]
- Public discussions of phenomena such as "vocal fry" or "uptalk," which are often noticed and criticized more harshly in female vs. male speakers (e.g., from the *Huffington Post*[43] and NPR's *Fresh Air*[44])

2   How is language bias leveraged against **LGBTQ+ individuals and communities?**

- Articles debunking stereotypes about "gay speech"—e.g., from the *Washington Post*[45] and *Science Magazine*[46]
- Scientific studies into what speech features *actually correlate* with sexual identity/orientation—e.g., as reported in magazines such as the *New Yorker*[47] and *Out*.[48] Also check out the (2014) film *Do I Sound Gay?*[49]

For more on this area of research, search for "Lavender Linguistics" online (e.g., Leap, 2019), including at the Hub.

3   How does language bias intersect with **classism?**

- Dunstan and Jaeger's (2015) study on linguistic prejudice against first-generation college students from Appalachia. (The *Language and Life Project*, mentioned in Unit 4.1, has additional resources on Appalachian English)

- Prejudice against "working-class accents" in the U.K.—e.g., in the *Guardian*[50]

See also the "Accentism Project,"[51] which explores intersections between language and race, class, and other criteria, and offers workshop materials for secondary-level students (see Figure 4.3).

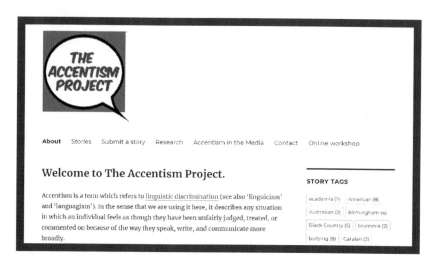

Figure 4.3 Screenshot of the U.K.-based Accentism Project

Demonstrating Learning from Unit 4.2

Assignment #1: Autobiographical Essay

In keeping with our commitment to self-reflection, I usually assign at least one piece of autobiographical writing when I teach about linguistic attitudes and prejudices, so that students have the opportunity to explore how they have **experienced and/or perpetuated** linguistic prejudice.

Guiding questions for these essays can include:

1   What linguistic attitudes and biases have I realized that I hold? Where, or from whom, might I have learned those attitudes and biases?
2   When have I judged someone based primarily on their style of speaking (i.e., idiolect)? What stereotypes and assumptions might have contributed to that judgment?

3   When and where have I experienced insecurity about my own speech or writing? What societal assumptions and attitudes might contribute to that insecurity?

4   How can we resist linguistic prejudice in our day-to-day lives? (We will explore this question further in Unit 4.3).

The focus, length, and expectations for this assignment can be adapted to the needs of the student and the pedagogical goals of the class. Sometimes I make it a daily homework assignment, graded for completion only. Other times, I make this a more formal and developed essay, scaffolding the writing process using class discussion, peer review, and revision. This assignment can also be more persuasive and/or can include **multimodal components,** as in the examples below, which is from an essay by my student Leah Metzger, who wrote about linguistic bias in newscasting.

Figure 4.4 Excerpts from Student Leah Metzger's Multimodal Writing about Linguistic Prejudice in Newscasting

Here is some additional text from Leah's essay, with a few footnotes excluded:

> So, when we hear someone speak, we're often able to infer a lot about their identity. There are some speakers, however, whose variety of English seems to reveal very little about them. These people include news anchors, radio hosts, and weather forecasters on television, and they speak in a way that many people label "neutral" and "accentless." To get a job as a newscaster, explains Amy Caples, a former news anchor and professor at the broadcasting program at Temple University, "you have to sound literally like you're from nowhere."
>
> How do these newscasters go about sounding like they are from "nowhere," their speech free of regionalisms or other markers of identity? According to linguists such as Rosina Lippi-Green and Marcos Rohena-Madrazo, the answer lies in using a dialect of English called General American English (also often referred to as Standard American English), a prestige variety based on the speech of white, upper-middle class, educated speakers from the Midwest.

In Chapter 7, we will see examples of other public-facing writing informed by students' learning about CLA.

Assignment #2: Analysis of Sociolinguistic Patterns in Entertainment Media

Another assignment I use in classes where we talk about accent stereotypes is a **critical media analysis**, in which students trace linguistic patterns in films, television shows, or other media (see also Shapiro, forthcoming). This assignment encourages students to apply their CLA learning to some of the media they engage with elsewhere in their lives. It asks them to use course concepts as an analytical lens—a skill that many of them will need for further learning in humanities and social sciences disciplines. Often, their analysis leads them to critique the media, but sometimes it highlights ways that the media resists linguistic stereotypes, giving students an opportunity to recognize what media creators are getting better at! Below is the description for this assignment, from my first-year seminar, "Language and Social Justice":

Sociolinguistic Analysis Using Theoretical Framework (4–5 pp., double-spaced)

In this paper, you will analyze a novel, film, or television show (i.e., a cultural artifact), focusing on how it illustrates or challenges key concepts related to language and social justice. You will develop an argumentative essay in which you reference <u>at least two outside sources</u> in your Intro/Rationale, explaining why this cultural artifact is worth analyzing. You will also reference <u>at least one course reading</u> as the theory/framework for your analysis. (In class, we will identify specific concepts you might use in your analysis and practice employing them.) We will learn how to find relevant secondary sources to support your analysis and how to develop a structure that best facilitates your argument, including evidence from the work you are analyzing.

Grading rubric:

Clarity and relevance of argument /25
Use of evidence (from artifact, as well as secondary sources) /30
Organization and use of transitions /25
Tone, word choice, style, mechanics, citations, honor code, etc. /20

I scaffold this assignment in the following ways:

- Students submit a proposal before writing the paper. The proposal includes what "artifact" (film, TV show, etc.) they wish to analyze and why. It also identifies some course concepts that might be useful their analysis. (One assignment that can serve as an idea incubator for this is the "Sociolinguistics Scrapbook," discussed in Unit 4.3.)
- Students share their initial findings in small groups, to help think through how they will lay out the paper. This could be adapted into a more formal oral presentation with multi-media, as I do for some other assignments.
- I provide short workshops on thesis development, use of evidence (e.g., quotes/examples from the film or TV show), and incorporating secondary sources, to support this project..
- Students give feedback to each other on early drafts (see Chapter 9 for more on peer review), and may also meet with a peer writing tutor. They then submit a revised draft to me for feedback, and a final draft along with a Writer's Memo (see p. 303) in their midterm portfolio.

Below are some of the media that recent students have analyzed for this project. (There are some samples of student work at the online Hub).

Animated films: *Aladdin* (1992), *Peter Pan* (1953), *Despicable Me 2* (2013), *The Lady and the Tramp* (1955), *The Lion King* (1994), *Planes* (2013), *Song of the South* (1946), *The Little Mermaid* (1989), *The Princess and the Frog* (2009), *Zootopia* (2016).

Other films: *GoldenEye* (1995), *Harold and Kumar Go to White Castle* (2004), *Kingsman: The Secret Service* (2014), *Legally Blonde* (2001), *Star Wars: The Phantom Menace* (1999), *The Princess Bride* (1987).

Television shows: *Dora the Explorer*, *Hannah Montana*, *Modern Family*, *Phineas and Ferb*, *The Simpsons*, *That 70s Show*, *The Fairly OddParents*.

Novels/literature: Alvarez's *How the Garcia Girls Lost Their Accents*, Shakespeare's *The Merchant of Venice*, Faulkner's *The Sound and the Fury*.

I occasionally allow students to analyze another media that involves interaction and language variation, such as **advertisements** (e.g., one student analyzed a video promoting the Berlitz language learning program), **political debates** (e.g., between Donald Trump and Hillary Clinton in 2016), or **interviews** (e.g., of athletes or other public figures). For more on how this project fits within the broader structure of my "Language and Social Justice" course, check out the syllabus, which is available at the online Hub.

****

Unit 4.3: Linguistic Profiling and Discrimination

Overview

Once students understand what linguistic prejudice is and how it is perpetuated, we can delve into how this prejudice impacts people's daily lives and can contribute to social inequality. The concept of **linguistic profiling** is particularly relevant here, as a way of highlighting that language is often a proxy for race, gender, class, etc. In other words, as Belin et al. (2004) put it, our voice is our "auditory face." And just as facial recognition software often treats White faces as the norm, we tend to treat particular linguistic varieties as **unmarked** (i.e., "the norm") and others as **marked** (i.e., "different"). This allusion to voice recognition is more than an analogy, since as we will touch on below, the design of voice recognition software is often shaped by linguistic biases.

Learning Sequence

Tapping into Prior Knowledge

There are a number of ways we can introduce the concept of linguistic profiling and help students link the concept to their own experiences. One option is to invite students to listen to samples of speech with different features (e.g., regional accents, native-like vs. non-native-like speech, higher- and lower-pitched voices) and discuss what immediately comes to mind when they hear each speaker. In a month-long unit I co-facilitated for a group of 7th–10th graders, my co-teacher Garrett Kimberly, who is also a professional dialect coach, read a passage from a play multiple times, using a different "accent" with each reading. Accents he used included Texan, Slovakian, and upper-class British (i.e., "Received Pronunciation"). Students were asked to share what images and associations they associated with that accent. The responses were illuminating! For example, student associations with a **Southern "twang"** included: *cowboy, Texas, horse, sheriff, "wanted," farmer, Western, friendly,* and *not educated.* In contrast, the list students generated after hearing the **Eastern European** accent, included: *businessman, schemer, sketchy, sleazy,* and *threat.*

A few notes on the above activity:

- Mr. Kimberly "hyper-performed" the accents, exaggerating particular phonological features. This was necessary in part because he was reading the same passage each time.

- We intentionally invited students to imagine a "character" rather than a regular person, in order to elicit stereotypes. NOTE: Because of scheduling restrictions, we had not yet engaged the topic of accents in children's media, from Unit 4.2.
- We avoided having the actor perform varieties associated with Black, Indigenous, and People of Color (BIPOC), in keeping with the points about inclusivity and sensitivity discussed in the introduction to this chapter.

There are many possible variations for this activity: As noted earlier, teachers can use speech samples from linguistic atlases or media (and probably should do so, since most of us do not have easy access to a dialect coach!). Instead of asking for "free association," we can have students rate each speech sample on criteria such as clarity, friendliness, intelligence, confidence, and trustworthiness. This is in fact an approach used in studies by many perceptual dialectologists, including two of my Middlebury colleagues, who worked with an undergraduate research assistant to investigate college students' perceptions of Spanish-accented speech in English (Baird et al., 2018).

April Baker-Bell (2013, 2020) has presented another version of this activity, which she uses in classrooms with predominantly Black/African American students, to surface perceptions about Black Language, which linguists usually refer to as African American Vernacular English, or AAVE. She gives students a table with two sets of statements: Set A is written in Black Language, while Set B is written in "standardized" English (see Figure 4.5).

Baker-Bell then asks students to describe and/or draw traits they associate with the speaker of each set of statements. For the speaker of Language A, students have used descriptors such as *African American, slang, sloppy, bad kids,* and *don't care about school.* The speaker of Language B, in contrast, was described as *proper, white, respectful, fancy,* and *knowledge*[able]. Baker-Bell then engages students in a curricular unit that examines the history, features, and varied uses of Black Language, which debunks many of the students' original assumptions. She has documented notable shifts in attitudes toward Black Language among students who complete the unit. This finding has been echoed as well in research by world/heritage language educators, who have found that curricular units on language variation, ideology, and prejudice often result in more positive attitudes toward stigmatized language varieties such as "Spanglish" (e.g., Beaudrie et al., 2019; Leeman & Serafini, 2016; Serafini, forthcoming). In Chapter 10, we will talk a bit more about assessing these kinds of outcomes.

Language A:	Language B:
• People be thinkin' teenagers don't know nothin'.	• Teenagers know more than people think they do.
• We be talking about current events all the time in our history class.	• We discuss current events in our history class on a regular basis.
• Yesterday, we was conversating with Mr. B. about the war—it was deep.	• Yesterday, we were having a conversation with our teacher about the war—it was a rich conversation.
• The teachers at South High is cool.	• The teachers at South High School are cool.
• But Ms. Nicks do be trippin' sometimes. Like that times she got really mad because Rob called her a dime piece.	
• Ms. Nicks better quit trippin' or imma drop her class like it's hot.	
• My cousin think the students at South High are all mean and stuff.	• However, my cousin thinks the students at South High are disrespectful.
• The students ain't as bad as she think though.	• I informed her that she was mistaken. Not all of the students are disrespectful.
• I told her she wrong about that.	

Figure 4.5 Contrasting Statements in Black Language vs. "Standardized" English (Baker-Bell, 2020, p. 44 e-book)

Topic #1: The Nature and Impact of Linguistic Profiling

Researchers have found evidence of linguistic profiling in many aspects of society, including the housing market, employment, and criminal justice system—not to mention in education, which we will talk about in Chapter 5. Some of this research can be difficult for newcomers to the field, but below is a sampling of questions with paired readings/media that are relatively accessible for a student audience:

1   How do researchers **define and study linguistic profiling**?

   - e.g., John Baugh's TEDx talk[52] at Emory University—see Figure 4.6. Baugh also appears in several scenes of the PBS documentary *Do You Speak American?*

2   How does linguistic profiling play out in the **U.S. court system**?

   - E.g., *The Nation*[53]; see also Rickford and King's (2016)[54] analysis of linguistic bias against Rachel Jeantel, a key witness in the trial of George Zimmerman, the man who shot and killed Trayvon Martin, an unarmed, Black teenager. Rickford also talks about this research in an interview with the *Stanford Report*.[55]

Figure 4.6 Updated Version of Fair Housing Advertisement Used in Baugh's (2019) Talk

3   How does linguistic profiling contribute to **gender discrimination**?

- In the workplace—e.g., *NYTimes*,[56] *Harvard Business Review*[57]
- In politics—e.g., from the *Washingtonian*[58] (see Sensales et al. [2016] for examples from outside the U.S.)
- In public discourse—e.g., on gendered use of the descriptor "shrill," from *Time* Magazine[59]

Topic #2: Other Intersections with Linguistic Profiling

The topics below can be explored individually or collectively:

1   **Xenophobia:** To what extent is speaking English seen as crucial to being or becoming "American"?—e.g., Pew Research study,[60] reported on by NPR[61] (see Figure 4.7); we will return to xenophobia and "native-speakerism" in Chapter 5

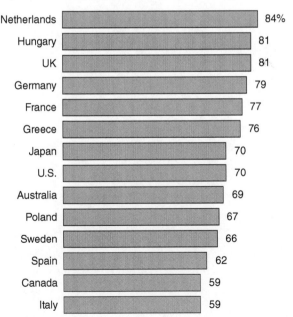

Language seen as most important requisite of nation identity

Being able to speak our national language is very important for being truly (survey country nationality)

Country	%
Netherlands	84%
Hungary	81
UK	81
Germany	79
France	77
Greece	76
Japan	70
U.S.	70
Australia	69
Poland	67
Sweden	66
Spain	62
Canada	59
Italy	59

Figure 4.7 Excerpt of Findings from Pew Research Study on National Identity

2   **Ableism:** How might linguistic profiling play a role in discrimination against people who are neurologically atypical, such as individuals on the autism spectrum?—e.g., blog post[62] from the London School of Economics

3   **Personality:** What role does personality—e.g., introvert vs. extrovert—play in our linguistic judgments and privileges? (see *Forbes*[63])

4   **Technology/Access:** How does linguistic prejudice get "built into" new technologies, and what can be done to fix the problem?—e.g., Brookings Institute[64]; *Scientific American*[65]

Demonstrating Learning from Unit 4.3

Learning about the harms caused by linguistic prejudice often evokes strong reactions in students, including anger, guilt, and sadness. As we discussed in Chapter 3, students need support in processing the discomfort that comes from recognizing patterns of privilege and oppression, as well as opportunities to channel that awareness into action (e.g., hooks, 2003; Zembylas, 2020).

As we discussed in Chapter 3, people in a more privileged position often feel a strong need to *do something* once they become aware of ways they have benefitted an inequitable system.

As teachers, we want to provide our students—and colleagues—with opportunities to channel their awareness of linguistic prejudice into action. However, we also want to promote critical reflection and self-awareness as part of that action. One activity I use to promote reflective action or praxis is what I and Lisa Leopold (Shapiro & Leopold, 2012) call **critical role play.**

Assignment #1: Critical Role-Play with Debrief

With this activity, students are given scenarios for reflection and simulation. It is important to note that students are <u>not</u> asked to try to "walk in the shoes" of someone who has experienced linguistic prejudice or discrimination. Rather, they are asked to consider their role as *witnesses and allies* who can use their words and behaviors to respond to injustice. This is an important distinction, because research on social justice education—including on anti-racist approaches—has shown that teachers sometimes use role-play in problematic ways, asking students from more privileged backgrounds to "pretend" to be someone else, in order to "understand" that person's perspective (e.g., Drake, 2008). Though well-intentioned, this strategy can perpetuate the very power dynamics we are trying to resist. It would be unrealistic—and rather arrogant—to assume that we could understand a social problem by "trying on" someone else's life experience for a day or two!

As we have seen throughout this chapter, there are plenty of more effective ways to develop empathy and understanding about the experiences of individuals and communities that are impacted by linguistic prejudice. Critical role-play, as I use it here, asks that students consider when and how they might intervene in difficult but common scenarios. Their proposed "action" becomes a starting point for further reflection, with prompts such as: *What emotions and reactions come up for me with this scenario? What emerges later, upon further reflection, and after seeing and hearing the responses of others?*

Below is a set of scenarios Mr. Kimberly and I used in our unit with 7th–10th graders.[66] We gave small groups of students about a half-hour to discuss and "perform" (if they wanted) possible responses to each scenario, and then to consider the pros and cons of each possible response. We then debriefed as a large group, emphasizing the *range of ways* we might respond when we face these sorts of situation. Because of time limitations, we did not have students **reflect in writing**, but that is another excellent way to debrief these role-plays.

Role-Play #1: Responding to Linguistic Prejudice

Scenario 1: Your class is forming groups for a project. You and your friend need two more group members. When you suggest two other people who seem not to have a group yet, your friend says: "You don't want to work with them. Their English is so hard to understand!"

Scenario 2: A friend asks you why you were laughing at a guest speaker who came to class that day. You realize it was because that speaker's accent (or speaking style) sounded strange or funny to you. What do you say to your friend? What do you say to yourself?

Scenario 3: In a conversation outside the classroom, a friend says, "I hate how people from the South sound. They're so racist and uneducated!" What might you say in response?

Scenario 4: You are having a group discussion about a project, and you notice one group member interrupting frequently and talking over others. What can you say within the group? If it becomes a persistent problem, what might you say privately to that group member?

I have also used slightly more complex scenarios with students at the postsecondary level, although in a less structured way. Below are four such scenarios, which may be suitable for some secondary-level students as well.

Role-Play #2: Responding to Linguistic Prejudice

Scenario 5: In a meeting at work (or for school), one colleague echoed a suggestion that was made by another colleague/classmate, without acknowledging the original source of the idea. How could you intervene to make sure that the appropriate person is recognized? If this happens frequently, how might you raise the issue with the group, or with the individual?

Scenario 6: A friend tells you that they think your instructor's voice/accent is "irritating," and you sense that they are planning to evaluate that instructor poorly on course evaluations. But you wonder whether this reaction might be connected to your friend's biases about the instructor's race, gender, or region of origin. What questions might you ask your friend (or yourself) to ensure fairness in evaluating this instructor?

Scenario 7: You have been asked to help select the winner of your college's first-year prize in oratory. You've noticed that while many non-native speakers of English submitted entries, the list of finalists seems to include none of those students. You wonder if linguistic bias might be playing a role. How could you raise this issue with your fellow committee members?

Scenario 8: In a social media post responding to a spoken word piece by a Black artist, one of your friends commented that the artist "sounds ghetto." What might you say (online, in person, or both!) to highlight concerns with this phrasing?

NOTE: This last scenario could be adapted for other situations—e.g., a female speaker is labeled "shrill"; a first-generation college student "sounds uneducated," etc.

Critical role-play is a useful way of **building empathy**, as well as **rhetorical agency** in responding to prejudice and injustice (Shapiro & Leopold, 2012). It can open up conversations about how to hold each other accountable in a way that is clear but also kind—what Ross (2019) frames as "calling in," rather than "calling out," which we will explore more in Chapter 9.

I also think critical role-play has much to offer to our own **professional learning as teachers**. To this end, I contributed to a recent open-access journal article (Howell et al., 2020[67]) that includes videorecorded accounts, along with written synopses, of challenging situations we have faced as instructors and administrators wanting to promote raciolinguistic justice—a topic we'll return to topic in Chapter 5. Many educational organizations use scenarios like these as part of social justice-oriented professional development. Two noteworthy examples are *EdChange*[68] and *Learning for Justice*.[69] In Chapter 10, we will discuss further implications of CLA for faculty development and institutional advocacy work.

Assignment #2: Sociolinguistics Scrapbook

Perhaps my all-time-favorite assignment for the Sociolinguistics pathway (Yes—I saved the best for last!) is a "Sociolinguistics Scrapbook." This is the assignment that my students consistently tell me is the most enjoyable and the most impactful, in terms of promoting deep learning and reflection about language variation, linguistic prejudice, and other sociolinguistic topics. The Scrapbook looks somewhat like an annotated bibliography, but instead of citations, students include URLs, images, anecdotes, or even physical objects that link to concepts from class. Here is the description of this assignment that I include in the syllabus for my Introduction to Sociolinguistics class:

> **Sociolinguistics Scrapbook:** This is a project that you will work on throughout the semester, in which you collect and reflect on **eight to ten "artifacts"** connected to our class. An artifact could be a news article (print or online), media clip or post, literary text, live event, or even an account of a conversation. Artifacts can be drawn from your other classes as well. For each artifact, you will write a paragraph reflection that explains **what** the artifact is, **why** you chose this artifact, and **how** it relates to sociolinguistics. Ideally, you will not have to look too hard to find artifacts—they will begin to "pop out" at you, as you engage with course material and connect it to your daily life. You'll also be asked to share some of your favorite entries during class and/or online.

Later in the semester, when we discuss the project in more detail, I give more detail about the three components I want to see in their annotations: *Summary, Course Connections,* and *Response/Reflection.* We also look at some sample entries, identifying where we see each element. In Figure 4.8 is a sample entry from Haruna Takeda, a Japanese international student who was studying Spanish at the time. Her annotation focuses on the linguistic practice of **mixing codes,** or **code-switching,** which is the term used more frequently among linguists. I particularly appreciate how Haruna draws on her—and her friend's—experiences as multilingual users who are also proficient in "textese." (Note: The image is a recreation of the original, which was a screenshot of an iPhone screen with a text bubble containing emojis of an ant and a cat.)

> Below is a screenshot of my friend's text message. It is a pun using emoji. What is interesting here is that there is a code-switch between Japanese and Spanish in the pun, created solely with two emoji. *Ari* means "ant(s)" in Japanese and *gato* is "a cat" in Spanish and the two emoji of an ant and a cat is supposed to be read as *Arigato*, which means "thank you" in Japanese. I see this as a case of code-switch that is only possible in texts. This fascinates me because there is so much possibilities in creating puns with emojis since one emoji can be read and interpreted in so many ways. For instance, an emoji of an ant can

not only be read as ant but can be used to mean black or small and having these possibilities in more than one language greatly increases the range of possible combinations of words and phrases that can be created only with emojis. This allows the use of icon in linguistic inter-actions which is mostly composed of symbols. This can also lead to having several layers of code-switch within a sentence if I combine this kind of emoji puns with a normal text messages (e.g., letters to emojis to text code-switch and code-switch between languages).

Figure 4.8 Sample Scrapbook Entry on "Code-Switching in Emojis"

A few final notes on this project:

- Students post their completed Scrapbooks to an online discussion, so they can explore each other's work. But I also create share sessions earlier in the process, both in class and online. This encourages them to start working on the project early, and also gives them a chance to exchange ideas.
- As noted earlier, this project can also provide a starting place for devel-oping longer assignments—e.g., autobiographical work, media analysis projects, or persuasive writing.
- I often draw on items from these scrapbooks to help update my media/pop culture examples for lecture and discussion.
- Feedback and evaluation for this assignment is focused solely on con-tent. If the writing is unclear or imprecise, however, I may give the stu-dent an opportunity to revise it.

****

Chapter Conclusion

This chapter has only scratched the surface of all there is to learn from en-gaging sociolinguistics learning in our writing classes. Although it is time to move on to other pathways for CLA Pedagogy, I want to note that we are **not** leaving the Sociolinguistics pathway behind. Chapters 5, 6, and 7 all offer additional opportunities to engage themes of language variation and linguistic prejudice. For example, we will look more closely at prescriptivism in Chapter 5, considering how prescriptivism and linguistic prejudice play out in academic settings—and how we can resist these ideologies! Chapters 6 and 7 offer some additional opportunities for exploring language variation in the classroom, in news media, and in our day-to-day interactions.

Notes

1 I am using English as the default here, but this can of course be adapted to other languages.
2 www.learningforjustice.org/magazine/fall-2000/everyone-has-an-accent
3 www.nytimes.com/interactive/2014/upshot/dialect-quiz-map.html
4 https://slate.com/human-interest/2014/07/7-best-dialect-quizzes-is-your-accent-american-british-canadian-australian.html
5 www.pbs.org/speak/
6 https://languageandlife.org/
7 www.bl.uk/british-accents-and-dialects/
8 www.britannica.com/topic/English-language/Varieties-of-English
9 www.washingtonpost.com/blogs/govbeat/wp/2013/12/02/what-dialect-to-do-you-speak-a-map-of-american-english/
10 www.daredictionary.com/
11 http://accent.gmu.edu/index.php
12 www.lap.uga.edu/
13 Crystal has written and spoken about this topic extensively. A quick internet search will identify many freely accessible talks and short articles.
14 www.aljazeera.com/program/episode/2010/10/21/linguistic-imperialism?gb=true
15 www.npr.org/2021/04/21/989477444/how-to-speak-bad-english
16 www.teachingenglish.org.uk/blogs/sandymillin/sandy-millin-accent-identity
17 www.unesco.org/new/en/indigenous-peoples/cultural-and-linguistic-diversity/
18 www.ted.com/talks/lera_boroditsky_how_language_shapes_the_way_we_think
19 www.scientificamerican.com/article/how-language-shapes-thought/
20 www.smithsonianmag.com/science-nature/does-century-old-linguistic-hypothesis-center-film-arrival-have-any-merit-180961284/
21 www.linguisticsociety.org/resource/language-and-thought also www.linguisticsociety.org/content/does-language-i-speak-influence-way-i-think
22 www.pbs.org/speak/seatosea/powerprose/hurston/
23 www.theguardian.com/books/2014/oct/03/a-difficulty-with-dialect
24 www.rlf.org.uk/showcase/in-praise-of-dialect/
25 www.npr.org/sections/codeswitch/2013/04/08/176064688/how-code-switching-explains-the-world

26 www.babbel.com/en/magazine/10-artists-who-perform-in-other-languages
27 www.huffpost.com/entry/latin-music-bilingual-crossover-songs-2017_n_5a4541
    13e4b0b0e5a7a56bb7
28 www.thoughtco.com/world-englishes-1692509
29 In Chapter 9, I discuss why my rubric for the college-level assignment uses "clarity" as a criterion, instead of "grammar," "style," or "mechanics." As you might suspect, this is an intentional choice informed by CLA!
30 A zine is a self-published magazine that often includes hand-drawn text and images. More info and examples at https://zines.barnard.edu/lesson-plans
31 www.pbs.org/pov/watch/americantongues/. NOTE: This film is outdated in a number of respects, which I tell students beforehand. One of the questions we discuss, in fact, is: *Which varieties, communities, and regions of the U.S. are underrepresented in the film?* There is also an instance early on a White man using the "N-word" to describe how "Southerners" talk. See Abe and Shapiro (2021) for more guidance on using this film. The Hub has links to the transcript and a viewer's guide.
32 https://languageandlife.org/documentaries/ has overviews and purchasing information, as well as selected clips from each film.
33 www.pbs.org/speak/speech/ and www.pbs.org/speak/speech/prejudice/attitudes/
34 www.youtube.com/watch?v=ZyJkVZ-0npI
35 www.theatlantic.com/education/archive/2018/01/why-do-cartoon-villains-speak-in-foreign-accents/549527/
36 www.bbc.com/news/world-us-canada-54566087
37 https://rosinalippi.com/weblog/shorter-works-essays/teaching-children-how-to-discriminate-what-we-learn-from-the-big-bad-wolf/
38 www.ted.com/talks/jamila_lyiscott_3_ways_to_speak_english
39 www.npr.org/2018/08/08/636442508/talk-american. I will likely be referencing other episodes of *Codeswitch* elsewhere, because language is a theme in many of their conversations (e.g., about racial/ethnic labels, about "Karen" as a trope, etc.).
40 www.nytimes.com/2015/09/04/us/latina-arizona-news-anchor-vanessa-ruiz-spanish-pronunciation.html
41 https://hbr.org/1995/09/the-power-of-talk-who-gets-heard-and-why
42 www.scientificamerican.com/article/he-said-she-said/
43 www.huffpost.com/entry/how-people-judge-womens-voices-podcasts_n_55a01a
    e9e4b0a47ac15c893c
44 www.npr.org/2015/07/23/425608745/from-upspeak-to-vocal-fry-are-we-policing-young-womens-voices
45 www.washingtonpost.com/news/wonk/wp/2015/07/28/what-it-means-to-sound-gay/
46 www.sciencemag.org/news/2015/11/where-did-gay-lisp-stereotype-come
47 www.newyorker.com/culture/culture-desk/is-there-a-gay-voice
48 www.out.com/out-exclusives/2016/8/17/lavender-linguistics-queer-way-speak
49 www.doisoundgay.com/
50 www.theguardian.com/commentisfree/2017/jul/11/prejudice-working-class-accents-mp-thick-social-media

51 https://accentism.org/

52 www.ted.com/talks/john_baugh_the_significance_of_linguistic_profiling

53 www.thenation.com/article/archive/in-the-legal-system-talking-white-is-a-pre cursor-to-justice-and-thats-wrong/

54 The 2016 article, published online by the Linguistic Society of America, is a challenging read, but some excerpts are more accessible than others, and there are helpful visuals throughout.

55 https://news.stanford.edu/news/2014/december/vernacular-trial-testi mony-120214.html

56 www.nytimes.com/2018/08/09/style/transgender-men-voice-change.html

57 https://hbr.org/2014/06/women-find-your-voice

58 www.washingtonian.com/2016/09/25/should-women-talk-like-men-to-be-tak en-seriously/

59 https://time.com/4268325/history-calling-women-shrill/

60 www.pewresearch.org/global/2017/02/01/what-it-takes-to-truly-be-one-of-us/

61 www.npr.org/sections/codeswitch/2017/02/01/512708133/to-be-american- first-speak-english-study-says

62 https://blogs.lse.ac.uk/equityDiversityInclusion/2017/08/employers-may-discrimi nate-against-autism-without-realising/

63 www.forbes.com/sites/kathycaprino/2017/12/29/im-sick-of-our-cultures-bias- against-introverts-and-im-ashamed-to-admit-i-have-one/

64 www.brookings.edu/blog/techtank/2020/12/09/voice-assistants-have-a-gender- bias-problem-what-can-we-do-about-it/

65 www.scientificamerican.com/article/speech-recognition-tech-is-yet-another-ex ample-of-bias/

66 Although we considered choosing more challenging scenarios (see second list below), we chose these as a way to ease students into discussion, particularly as some of these students did not know each other well, given that they were in four different grades.

67 https://compositionforum.com/issue/44/embracing.php

68 www.edchange.org/multicultural/activities/roleplays.html

69 www.learningforjustice.org/sites/default/files/2020-09/TT-Social-Justice-Stand ards-Anti-bias-framework-2020.pdf

References

Abe, S., & Shapiro, S. (2021). Sociolinguistics as a pathway to global citizenship: Critically observing 'self' and 'other'. *Language Awareness*, 30(4), 355–370.

Abrams, K. D., & Stickle, T. (2019). DARE (ing) language ideologies: Exploring linguistic diversity through audio data and literature in secondary language arts courses. In M. D. Devereaux & C. C. Palmer (Eds.), *Teaching language varia- tion in the classroom: Strategies and models from teachers and linguists* (pp. 84–92). Routledge.

Arevalo, S. I. (2019). Profiling, prejudice, and prestige: Language ideologies across contexts. In M. D. Devereaux & C. C. Palmer (Eds.), *Teaching language variation in the classroom: Strategies and models from teachers and linguists* (pp. 18–24). Routledge.

Baird, B. O., Rohena-Madrazo, M., & Cating, C. (2018). Perceptions of lexically specific phonology switches on Spanish-origin loanwords in American English. *American Speech*, 93(1), 79–107.

Baker-Bell, A. (2013). "I never really knew the history behind African American language": Critical language pedagogy in an advanced placement English language arts class. *Equity & Excellence in Education*, 46(3), 355–370.

Baker-Bell, A. (2020). *Linguistic justice: Black language, literacy, identity, and pedagogy*. Routledge.

Baugh, J. (2019). The significance of linguistic profiling. *TEDx Talk at Emory University*. https://www.ted.com/talks/john_baugh_the_significance_of_linguistic_profiling

Beaudrie, S., Amezcua, A., & Loza, S. (2019). Critical language awareness for the heritage context: Development and validation of a measurement questionnaire. *Language Testing*, 36(4), 573–594. https://doi.org/10.1177/0265532219844293

Belin, P., Fecteau, S., & Bedard, C. (2004). Thinking the voice: Neural correlates of voice perception. *Trends in Cognitive Sciences*, 8(3), 129–135.

Bucholtz, M., & Lopez, Q. (2011). Performing blackness, forming whiteness: Linguistic minstrelsy in Hollywood film. *Journal of Sociolinguistics*, 15(5), 680–706.

Crystal, D. (2012). *English as a global language* (2nd ed.). Cambridge University Press.

Devereaux, M. D. (2015). *Teaching about dialect variations and language in secondary English classrooms: Power, prestige, and prejudice*. Routledge.

Devereaux, M. D., & Palmer, C. C. (Eds.). (2019). *Teaching language variation in the classroom: Strategies and models from teachers and linguists*. Routledge.

Devereaux, M. D., & Wheeler, R. (2012). Code-switching and language ideologies: Exploring identity, power, and society in dialectally diverse literature. *English Journal*, 102(2), 93.

Drake, I. (2008, Spring). Classroom simulations: Proceed with caution. *Learning for Justice Magazine*, 33. www.tolerance.org/magazine/spring-2008/classroom-simulations-proceed-with-caution

Dunstan, S. B., & Jaeger, A. J. (2015). Dialect and influences on the academic experiences of college students. *The Journal of Higher Education*, 86(5), 777–803.

Dyches, J., & Gale, C. (2019). Standard English, "classic" literature: Examining canonical and linguistic ideologies in Huck Finn. In M. D. Devereaux & C. C. Palmer (Eds.), *Teaching language variation in the classroom: Strategies and models from teachers and linguists* (pp. 157–164). Routledge.

Godley, A. J., & Reaser, J. (2018). *Critical language pedagogy: Interrogating language, dialects, and power in teacher education*. Peter Lang.

Hankerson, S. D. (2016). You must learn": A critical language awareness approach to writing instruction for African American Language-speaking students in composition courses (Doctoral dissertation). Michigan State University. https://d.lib.msu.edu/islandora/object/etd:4219/datastream/OBJ/download/

Harris, R. (2004). Encouraging emergent moments: The personal, critical, and rhetorical in the writing classroom. *Pedagogy, 4*(3), 401–418.

hooks, B. (2003). *Teaching community: A pedagogy of hope.* Routledge.

Howell, N. G., Navickas, K., Shapiro, R., Shapiro, S., & Watson, M. (2020). The perpetual "but" in raciolinguistic justice work: When idealism meets practice. *Composition Forum, 44* [online, special issue]. https://compositionforum.com/issue/44/embracing.php

Krathwohl, D. R. (2002). A revision of Bloom's taxonomy: An overview. *Theory into Practice, 41*(4), 212–218.

Leap, W. (2019). This month in linguistics history: Lavender language/linguistics. *Linguistic Society of America.* www.linguisticsociety.org/content/month-linguistics-history-lavender-languagelinguistics

Leeman, J., & Serafini, E. J. (2016). Sociolinguistics for heritage language educators and students. In M. A. Fairclough & S. Beaudrie (Eds.), *Innovative strategies for heritage language teaching: A practical guide for the classroom* (pp. 56–79). Georgetown University Press.

Levin, A. (2020). Finding the "herstorical" narrative in Angie Thomas's the hate u give. *English Studies in Africa, 63*(1), 148–166.

Lippi-Green, R. (2012). *English with an accent* (2nd ed.). Routledge.

Lyiscott, J. (2014). 3 ways to speak English. *TED Talk.* https://www.ted.com/talks/jamila_lyiscott_3_ways_to_speak_english

McWhorter, J. (2013). Txting is killing language j/k. *TED Talk.* www.ted.com/talks/john_mcwhorter_txtng_is_killing_language_jk/transcript?language=en

Metz, M. (2018). Challenges of confronting dominant language ideologies in the high school English classroom. *Research in the Teaching of English, 52,* 455–477.

Novak, G. M., Patterson, E. T., Gavrin, A. D., & Christian, W. (1999). *Just in time teaching: Blending active learning with web technology.* Prentice-Hall.

Rickford, J. R. & King. S. (2016). Language and linguistics on trial: Hearing Rachel Jeantel (and other vernacular speakers) in the courtroom and beyond. *Language, 92*(4), 948–988. https://www.linguisticsociety.org/sites/default/files/Rickford_92_4.pdf

Ross, L. (2019). Speaking up without tearing down. *Learning for Justice.* www.learningforjustice.org/magazine/spring-2019/speaking-up-without-tearing-down

Sensales, G., Areni, A., & Dal Secco, A. (2016). Italian political communication and gender bias: Press representations of men/women presidents of the houses of parliament (1979, 1994, and 2013). *International Journal of Society, Culture & Language, 4*(2), 22–38.

Serafini, E. J. (forthcoming). Assessing students through a CLA framework. In S. Beaudrie & S. Loza (Eds.), *Teaching languages critically.* Routledge.

Shaffer, K. (2003). Being bilingual: A theme for an adult literacy class. *The Change Agent, 16.* [special issue on "Adult education for social justice"]. https://change-agent.nelrc.org/wp-content/uploads/2014/02/CA16.pdf

Shapiro, S. (2015). World Englishes: Academic explorations of language, culture, and identity. In M. Roberge, K. Losey, & M. Wald (Eds.), *Teaching U.S.-educated multilingual writers: Pedagogical practices from and for the classroom* (pp. 263–80). University of Michigan Press.

Shapiro, S. (2022). "Language and social justice": A (surprisingly) plurilingual first-year seminar. In G. Shuck & K. Losey (Eds.), *Plurilingual pedagogies for multilingual writing classrooms: Engaging the rich communicative repertoires of U.S. Students.* University of Michigan Press.

Shapiro, S., & Leopold, L. (2012). A critical role for role-playing pedagogy. *TESL Canada Journal, 29*(2), 121–130. https://teslcanadajournal.ca/index.php/tesl/article/view/1104

Siczek, M., & Shapiro, S. (2014). Developing writing-intensive courses for a globalized curriculum through WAC-TESOL collaborations. In M. Cox & T. Zawacki (Eds.), *WAC and second language writers: Research toward linguistically and culturally inclusive programs and practices.* Parlor Press. http://wac.colostate.edu/books/l2/chapter13.pdf

Soares, T. O., (2017). *Animated films and linguistic stereotypes: A critical discourse analysis of accent use in Disney animated films* [Master's thesis from Bridgewater State University]. https://vc.bridgew.edu/theses/53/

Suh, E., & Shapiro, S. (2021). Making sense of resistance: How adult immigrant students apply symbolic capital in the college classroom. *TESL Canada Journal, 37*(3), 27–46. https://teslcanadajournal.ca/index.php/tesl/article/view/tesl.v37i3.1343

Urke, A. B. S. (2019). *Accents in Wonderland: An attitudinal study of the use of accents in Disney's originals and remakes* [Masters thesis from the University of Bergen in Norway]. https://bora.uib.no/bora-xmlui/handle/1956/19949

Wiggins, G., & McTighe, J. (2005). *Understanding by design.* ASCD.

Wolfram, W. (2000). Linguistic diversity and the public interest. *American Speech, 75*(3), 278–280.

Yu, J. (2017). Translating "others" as "us" in Huckleberry Finn: Dialect, register and the heterogeneity of standard language. *Language and Literature, 26*(1), 54–65.

Zembylas, M. (2020). Emotions, affects, and trauma in classrooms: Moving beyond the representational genre. *Research in Education, 106*(1), 59–76.

5
The Critical Academic Literacies Pathway

Introduction

When I first began mapping out these "Pathways" chapters, I did not intend to place Critical Academic Literacies directly after Sociolinguistics. I saw the two as so different that it might give readers whiplash if they were juxtaposed! And to be sure, there are some key distinctions between the two:

- Sociolinguistics research traditionally focuses more heavily on speech, while academic literacy research focuses more on reading and writing
- Sociolinguistics is interested in language variation, while academic writing/literacy research is—at least traditionally—interested in linguistic norms and conventions
- Sociolinguists emphasize indexical functions of language, while academic writing/literacy specialists—again, *traditionally*—emphasize communicative functions

However, as you can probably sense from my over-use of the qualifier "traditionally," these two pathways are not as neatly divided as they might seem. Some sociolinguists *do* focus on writing, including writing on digital/social media—what McWhorter (2013) calls "fingered speech." We will look more closely at this in Chapter 6. Moreover, many sociolinguists care quite a lot about linguistic norms—particularly since, as we explored in Chapter 4, the expectation of conformity to those norms can disadvantage particular groups (e.g., speakers of African American Vernacular English or users of English as an additional language).

The field of writing/literacy studies, for its part, has become increasingly interested in sociolinguistic issues, in recent decades, including language variation

DOI: 10.4324/9781003171751-8

and linguistic prejudice. As we discussed in Chapter 1, movements such as Students' Rights to Their Own Language (SRTOL), translingual writing, and anti-racist pedagogy have caused many of us to question our (traditional) role as gatekeepers within the academy. This includes re-examining many of our assumptions about what academic writing is, what it could be, and how we teach and assess it. So there has never been a better time to strengthen bridges between sociolinguistics and academic writing/literacy![1]

But I also decided to make this the second curricular pathway because I know that many teachers work in programs where the curriculum focuses heavily on academic writing—e.g., English for Academic Purposes (EAP), Writing in the Disciplines (WID), or professional and technical writing. In these contexts, there is often resistance to curricular changes that broaden the scope beyond typical academic skills and genres. I know all too well how institutional cultures and structures can create hurdles to curricular innovation (e.g., Shapiro, 2011; see also Chapter 8). In such cases, the Critical Academic Literacy Pathway may be an easier "sell" to administrators, colleagues, and students.

The good news is that a critically oriented academic literacies curriculum can be just as engaging, just as relevant, and just as—dare I say it?—sexy[2] as sociolinguistics. Language, identity, power, and privilege play out in complex and important ways in academic settings. In school, to be frank, is where many of our students feel most *disempowered* as language users. We may even experience that disempowerment ourselves, at times.

Many writing teachers are aware of this concern, as we began discussing in Chapter 1, but struggle with how to respond—particularly with how to balance their commitment to both **progressivism** and **pragmatism**. We want to (re)build classrooms and institutions that are more inclusive and equitable for students from a variety of linguistic backgrounds, but we do not want to shirk our responsibility to prepare students to communicate within the academy *as it is today*. The Critical Academic Literacies Pathway offers a "both/and" response to this conundrum, demystifying the "rules" of the academic game (Casanave, 2005), while also making space for critical conversations about who is advantaged and disadvantaged by those rules—and even about how the rules could be, and are being, re-written!

A Social View of Academic Literacy

One key understanding that informs this pathway is the idea that literacy instruction plays an important role in students' academic **socialization**—i.e., their sense of connection and belonging at school (e.g., Lea & Street, 1998;

Lillis & Harrington, 2015). Becoming "literate" doesn't just mean learning to replicate writing formats and formulas, it means engaging with academic cultures and conversations. Academic literacy instruction can help academia "come alive" for students, as they study how writing genres and conventions reflect the values and priorities of different disciplines and how to analyze academic texts as **cultural artifacts**.

Here are a few considerations for this pathway: First, we need to be clear with students—and with ourselves—that our goal is *not* to survey all of the literacy practices students might need in order to communicate academically. Instead, the goal here, as with other pathways, is to teach **transferable concepts and skills,** which students can then adapt to a variety of academic situations. (The "teach someone to fish" adage seems relevant here.) Of course, the more practice we give them with applying what they have learned, the more adept they will be come.

Second, the learning in this pathway is more engaging and effective when students have **opportunities to connect with other academic programs or disciplines**. I know that many composition/writing and/or ESOL instructors teach in programs that are isolated from the rest of their departments or institutions (Shapiro, 2009, 2011). Teachers working in those situations may need to think creatively about how to build more connections to colleagues in other programs. Doing so can be valuable to us, as well as to students: As I argue in a piece with Megan Siczek (Shapiro & Siczek, 2017), cross-institutional connections can help us to redefine our own professional identities, so that we shift from **remediation**—i.e., "fixing" students' writing/language—to **mediation**, i.e., working collaboratively to support and advocate for linguistically diverse writers (see also Benesch, 1988; Shapiro, 2011).

A final reminder is that as with most of the topics in this book, **we are not reinventing the wheel**. There are many, many excellent resources for teaching critical academic literacy in both secondary and postsecondary contexts. I am simply curating some of the best ideas I have found—in particular, those that help us engage deep conversations about language, identity, power, and privilege.

Learning Goals

Essential Questions

Here are ten Essential Questions for this pathway, along with the CLA goal(s) most pertinent to each (**SR**= self-reflection, **SJ** = social justice, **RA** = rhetorical agency):

1   What does it mean to see academic disciplines as communities with distinct language/literacy practices? (SR, RA)
2   How do the language/literacy practices used in disciplinary writing embody particular cultural values and priorities? (SJ, RA)
3   What tools and strategies can we use to build our knowledge of disciplines as linguistic communities within academia? (SR, RA)
4   In what ways do academic communities perpetuate linguistic prejudice and exclusion? (SR, SJ, RA)
5   How are our assumptions about what it means to sound "educated" in writing and speech shaped by ideologies about race, class, gender, ability, and other axes of inequality? (SR, SJ, RA)
6   What does it mean to see grammar as rhetorical rather than prescriptive? (SJ, RA)
7   How can we make rhetorically informed grammar choices in our own writing? (SR, RA)
8   How does prescriptivism function in academic settings, and how does it relate to language and power? (SR, SJ, RA)
9   Where within the academy are there opportunities for linguistic creativity and rhetorical resistance? (SR, SJ, RA)
10 How can we promote more plurilingual orientations in the classroom and beyond? (SR, SJ, RA)

Transferable Skills

Students will be able to (SWBAT) . . .

A   **Apply** the concept of "linguistic community" to academic settings and situations
B   **Understand** how cultural values are embedded in particular language/literacy norms
C   **Investigate** the features, values, and linguistic practices of academic disciplines and communities
D   **Analyze** their lived experience as language users at school from a critical perspective
E   **Use** their knowledge about rhetorical grammar in academic reading and writing tasks
F   **Trace** prescriptivism or other language ideologies in everyday texts and interactions
G   **Recognize** how academic norms can perpetuate linguistic prejudice
H   **Argue** for and/or against a position on a controversial educational issue related to linguistic diversity

I   **Compose** written and spoken texts using a range of literacy practices and linguistic resources, including integrating multiple codes or styles

Overview of Units

Unit 5.1: Academic disciplines as linguistic communities (EQs #1, 2, 3, and 4; Skills A, B, C, D, and I). In this unit, students first learn how to trace the values and practices of U.S. academic culture in their schooling experience. They then explore how to read academic texts for "clues" about the values and priorities of academic disciplines. Assignments include an analysis of commonly used (and critiqued) metaphors and an academic informant project about a specific academic subfield or discipline.

Unit 5.2: Grammar concepts and controversies (EQ #3, 4, 5, 6, and 10; Skills B, C, D, E, F, H, and I). In this unit, students engage basic grammar concepts and language analysis skills, as well as controversial questions about grammatical judgment. They learn how to form a variety of grammatical structures, as well as how those structures can serve particular rhetorical purposes. Students also study the causes, impacts, and critiques of prescriptivism. Culminating assignments include critical role-play and an argument-based position paper.

Unit 5.3: Linguistic pluralism in the academy (EQs 3, 4, 5, 8, 9, and 10; Skills A, C, D, F, G, and I). This unit applies some of the concepts from Chapter 4 (e.g., linguistic prejudice) to academic settings. We engage with research documenting linguistic profiling of students from diverse linguistic and racial backgrounds and consider how we can push back against monolingual ideology in school policies and practices, as well as in our own writing. The culminating assignment involves writing for public audiences.

Table 5.1 At-a-Glance Chart for the Critical Academic Literacies Pathway

	Topics/Subtopics	Readings/ Resources	Activities/ Assignments
Unit 5.1 Academic Disciplines as Ling Communities (pp. 137–145)	Academic literacies (vs. literacy) Linguistic community Literacy narrative Contrastive Rhetoric	Websites: Digital Archive of Literacy Narratives; "Write Like a Scientist" Accounts by multilingual scholars (e.g., Shen, 1989; Villanueva, 1993)	* Peer literacy interview and debrief/report * Discussions of disciplinary norms * Linguistic sleuthing

	Topics/Subtopics	Readings/ Resources	Activities/ Assignments
	Values in U.S. academic culture (e.g., efficiency, ownership, etc.) Critiques of U.S. academic culture Changes to writing norms	Scholarly articles (e.g., Connor, 1996; Eisner & Vicinus, 2008) News articles (e.g., NPR, *NYTimes*, *The Conversation*, *The Guardian*) Public scholarship (e.g., *Aeon*, *Nature*, *The Conversation*)	* Bad academic metaphors * Becoming disciplinary cultural informants (research, presentation and/or write-up)
Unit 5.2 Grammar Concepts and Controversies (pp. 146–158)	Prescriptivism Grammar terms (e.g., parts of speech, subject/ predicate, verb tenses and types) Error analysis Grammatical ambiguity Rhetorical grammar (including rule- breaking—e.g., asyndeton) Grammar in the news Grammar and tech Offensive language	Book excerpts: Ball and Lowe (2017), Cameron (2012), Curzan (2014), Hitchings (2011), Truss (2005) Essays/talks: Fry's "Language" (video); McWhorter (2013) Websites/blogs: Buzzfeed, Lingthu- siasm, *Psychology Today* News articles (NPR, *NYTimes*) Entertainment media (pop songs, film, etc.)	* Discussion of grammar memes * Standing survey * Quizzes * Review Games * Critical Role-Play * Position Paper
Unit 5.3 Linguistic Pluralism in the Academy (pp. 159–168)	Pluralism vs. diversity Linguistic preju- dice at school Native-speakerism Accent "hallucination"	Research studies (e.g., Godsil et al., 2017; Rubin, 1992) Professional articles/ documents (e.g., *Inside Higher Ed; CCCC/NCTE* position statements)	* Linguistic moni- toring activity * Sharing (and writing about) personal experi- ences of school

(continued)

Table 5.1 (*continued*)

	Topics/Subtopics	Readings/ Resources	Activities/ Assignments
	Linguistic profiling Implicit bias (e.g., response to writing) Communicative burden Code-mixing/ meshing Translingual writing Monolingual ideology	Writing collections/ anthologies writing (e.g., Ahmad, 2007, also from U of Rochester) University websites (e.g., Norwich, Oakland)	* Reading work that mixes codes/styles * Writing Beyond the Classroom

Unit 5.1: Academic Disciplines as Linguistic Communities

Overview

It is quite common among scholars to refer to academic disciplines as "discourse communities." However, as we will discuss further in Chapter 6, students often find the concept of "discourse" difficult to define and work with. I prefer to use the term "linguistic community" instead. This unit helps students understand academic disciplines as vibrant, dynamic communities that are bound together by—and sometimes divided around—linguistic norms and literacy practices.

Learning Sequence

Tapping into Prior Knowledge

One good starting place for this unit is to have students conduct a **peer literacy interview**,[3] either in class or as homework. This can be followed by an oral debrief or a written summary/response. Below are some questions that can guide these interviews:

1   What types of reading, writing, and/or storytelling were used in your home or community growing up? What languages, dialects, and/or styles were used?
2   What are some of your most vivid memories of reading, writing, and/or storytelling?
3   Do you recall having conversations with any family or community members about literacy or language use?
4   What do you recall about learning to use technologies for reading, writing, and/or storytelling? (e.g., computers, phones, tablets)
5   What do you see as your strengths as a reader, writer, and/or storyteller?
6   What struggles have you faced as a reader, writer, and/or storyteller?

I've adapted these questions from other lists (e.g., at the Digital Archive of Literacy Narratives[4]) by including languages other than English and referencing oral storytelling, which is an important literacy practice in many Indigenous and immigrant communities (Campano, 2019).

Of course, students could answer these questions alone, in a piece of autobiographical writing. But I prefer the peer interview for a few reasons: First, having a *conversation about literacy* helps to reinforce the idea that literacy is social and cultural. Second, engaging in deep, peer-to-peer conversations helps deepen relationships among students, which in turn builds sense of community in the classroom (Shapiro, 2020; see also Chapter 9). Finally, in terms of writing, the interview report allows students to practice the literacy skills of summary, paraphrase, and quotation.

After we have debriefed the peer interviews, we can delve further into academic literacies, with questions such as:

- What does it mean to be a "good" (or "bad") academic reader or writer?
- How many types (genres) of writing have you read or written in school? Which genres are you most comfortable with? Which do you feel a need to learn or practice?
- What differences have you noticed in the writing styles of different disciplines or subject areas? (e.g., English/literature vs. history; mathematics vs. biology or chemistry)
- What differences have you observed between scholarly and public writing?

Topic #1: Academic Culture and Linguistic Norms

To explore the topic of academic disciplines as linguistic communities, I like to start with the concept of "academic culture." Many students—particularly those raised in the U.S.—have never thought about schools as subcultures. To lead into this concept, I share the following folktale, captured in Figure 5.1.

> Two young fish are swimming in a river, while an older frog looks on from the shore.
>
> The frog calls out to the fish, "How's the water today?" The fish look at each other and ask, puzzled, "What's water?"[5]

Academic culture is the "water" we are all swimming (or treading!) in at school. We may not recognize it, though, unless we are peering in from the margins. This metaphor of "margins" also helps get students thinking about issues of inclusion—something we will return to in Chapters 7 and 9. By studying some of the typical expectations for academic writing at U.S. institutions, we can begin to really "see" this water we are immersed in. One field of research that helps with this is **contrastive rhetoric**—i.e., the study of variation in academic writing across languages and cultures.

Figure 5.1 A Metaphor for Academic Culture. Original photo credit to Dalton
Caraway

Linguists in this subfield have characterized U.S. academic writing as prioritizing particular values, including *individualism, competition*, and *innovation*. For example:

1   Academic writers in the U.S. are often expected to have an **original perspective** or argument on the text/topic, rather than simply summarizing the arguments of others (Eisner & Vicinus, 2008)

2   Individual authors are presumed to have **ownership** over the words and ideas in their writing; using those words or ideas without the appropriate "borrowing practices" (i.e., citation) is seen as **stealing** (Heckler & Forde, 2015; Tomaš & Shapiro, 2021)

3   U.S. writers tend to treat academic and political arguments as **competitions** or even **battles**, in which there is a winner and loser (Lakoff & Johnson, 2008; Tannen, 1998—also interviewed on NPR[6])

4   In terms of style, U.S. teachers tend to value **efficiency** over aesthetics and **clarity** over sophistication in academic genres of writing (Atkinson, 2003; Connor, 1996)[7]

This linking of writing conventions to cultural values often resonates for students who have written in other languages. We can invite—but should not force—these students to share some of their own experiences with adjusting to writing within U.S. academic culture. The documentary *Writing Across Borders*,[8] from Oregon State University, includes clips of international students sharing these experiences. We can also read **first-hand accounts** of the adjustment process from multilingual scholars such as Min-Zhan Lu (1987), Fan Shen (1989), and Victor Villanueva (1993). Other readings/media on this topic can be found in Unit 5.3. and at the online Hub.

As we learn to link writing norms to academic culture, we can engage some **critical questions**, such as:

- **Originality**: Is it realistic to expect students to have an original perspective or argument on a text or issue—especially on a topic that is relatively new to them?
  (e.g., Haviland & Mullin, 2009[9])
- **Intellectual ownership**: How do we reconcile the concept of individual "intellectual ownership" with the realities of globalization, digitization, and collaborative learning?
  (NYTimes[10]; Lunsford, 1999)
- **Argumentation/competition**: What are the alternatives to the "war" metaphor for argumentation? (Lakoff & Johnson [2008] offer "dance" as an alternative—see Figure 5.2)
- **Efficiency**: What are the problems with prioritizing "efficiency" in academic writing?
  (e.g., from *The Guardian*[11] and *Nature*[12])

Figure 5.2 An Alternative Metaphor for Academic Debate

Topic #2: Disciplinary Subcultures and Linguistic Norms

Once we have done some general exploration—and critique—of U.S. academic culture, we can begin to examine how cultural values **manifest in different academic disciplines** (see Table 5.2).

Table 5.2 Matching Academic Cultural Values to Disciplinary Writing Conventions

Cultural Value	Common U.S. Writing Conventions
Originality/ Contribution	Presenting the thesis and/or argument in the introduction (Arts/Humanities) Establishing a "gap" in the research in the literature review (Soc. Sci/STEM)
Credibility/ Trustworthiness	Citing source material frequently, using quotations, citations, and/or footnotes (Arts/Humanities) Describing methods and findings in detail, including statistical analyses, where applicable (Soc Sci/STEM)
Objectivity/ Fairness	Addressing counter-arguments (Arts/Humanities) Discussing limitations (Soc Sci/STEM)
Clarity/ Efficiency	Providing an abstract (most disciplines) Using bolding, italics, subheadings, and transitions (Arts/Humanities)

We can also examine the **stylistic differences** among different types of writing, looking for linguistic "clues" that tell us something about academic disciplines. Here are four examples:

1   **Citation styles:** Many STEM and social sciences disciplines prefer citation styles that include the year of publication (e.g., APA), which helps to establish a narrative of past scholarship (Mueller, 2005), as opposed to MLA, which prioritizes page number over date of publication.

2   **Quotation vs. paraphrase:** Arts/humanities writers tend to include lengthier quotations from source texts than social science or STEM writers, in part because examining the language in the text is often part of the research methodology.

3   **Active vs. passive voice:** Scientists use passive voice to convey objectivity, focusing on methods and results (*what was done, what was found*) rather than on the person(s) doing the work (Ferreira, 2021). Writers in some other fields tend to see the passive as indirect or even evasive (Forbes[13]; we'll return to this in Unit 5.2).

4   **Use of hedging language:** In many disciplines, writers are expected to avoid over-stating their claims (Dudley-Evans, 1994), using hedging language such as modal verbs (*may, might, could*), linking verbs (*appear, seem,* or *suggest*), and certain adjectives (*likely, probable,* or *possible*). In business writing, however, hedging may be interpreted as indicating lack of confidence (Grammarly[14]).

These contrasts help students begin to view written texts **as a source of cultural information** about academic disciplines. There are many online resources that reinforce this idea. One example is the website "Write Like a Scientist"[15] (see below), spearheaded by my colleague Molly Costanza-Robinson, a biochemist who works on environmental issues. The site uses interactive exercises to help students become aware of the rhetorical and linguistic choices made by scientific writers.

Activity: Linguistic Sleuthing

This activity helps students to connect language choices to genre and purpose. Students analyze two passages describing the same concept, process, or study, but written for different audiences. They can examine content and organization, as well as linguistic features such as word choice, verb tense, and pronoun usage. Below is one example from the "Write Like a Scientist" website:

A   Porosity was determined using the following method: samples were dried in an oven at 40 °C; sample dimensions and dry mass were recorded; samples were blotted and weighted to obtain saturated mass.

B   Determine porosity using the following method: 1) Dry samples in an oven at 40 °C overnight. 2) Record the dimensions and the dry mass of each sample. 3) Blot each sample using MMX Oval paper. 4) Weigh each sample and record its saturated mass.

Students may notice that sentence A uses passive voice, while B uses imperative (command) verbs. They may also note that B has numbered steps, as well as additional detail (e.g., the type of paper for blotting the sample). These "clues" may help them infer that sentence A is from the **methods section of a journal article**, while B is from **lab instructions for students**. This is one of the easier examples—the site includes others from a variety of STEM disciplines. Students can bring in their own examples as well to challenge their peers' sleuthing skills!

Topic #3: Changing Academic Norms

A final question we can engage in this unit is: How are the norms of academic literacy changing? Below are some examples:

- Increased use of "informal language," such as contractions, first-person pronouns, and sentences beginning with conjunctions (*Nature*[16])
- Use of "positionality" or "reflexivity" statements, which acknowledge power/ privilege differences between researcher and human subjects (*Psychology Today*[17])
- Guidelines for inclusive language within disciplinary style guides (e.g., examples in Thomas & Hirsch, 2016[18])—we'll return to the topic of inclusive language in Chapters 7 and 9.

Demonstrating Learning for Unit 5.1

Below are two assignments that can be used to demonstrate students' learning for this unit. Each can be scaled down to be an in-class activity, or scaled up to a multiphase writing project.

Assignment #1: Bad Academic Metaphors

Many linguists (e.g., Lakoff & Johnson, 2008) have written about the power of metaphors on our thinking. And academics love to complain about "bad metaphors" that misrepresent concepts in their disciplines! This assignment gives students a window into those scholarly conversations. They work individually or collectively to research a prevalent metaphor that has been criticized by experts (see examples below). They report back orally or in writing on how the metaphor is used, why it is problematic, and—possibly—what alternative metaphors might be preferable.

For example, discussions of human reproduction often frame sperm as "aggressive" (e.g., as competitive swimmers) and the egg as "passive." This metaphor has been criticized for reinforcing gender stereotypes (*Aeon*[19]). It also can contribute to risky sexual behaviors, since people may be unaware that sperm may "hang out" in their partner's body for several days or more. This metaphor is still used in many science textbooks, although it is on the decline (Campo-Engelstein, 2014).

Here are some other "bad metaphors" that have been discussed widely online and in scholarly publications. Next to each, I have listed relevant academic disciplines:

- The human brain = computer (psychology)
- Teaching = turning on a lightbulb (education)
- Economies = engines (economics)
- The United States = melting pot (history, sociology)
- Drug policy = war (sociology, political science)
- Famine/food scarcity = war (social work, international development)
- Disease prevention/treatment = war[20] (medicine/public health)
- U.S. president = CEO (political science)
- Time = money (business, finance)
- Ideas = property (English/writing/composition)

For more on how to scaffold this type of assignment, see Montecino (1997).[21] We will return to the topic of metaphors in Chapter 6, since metaphor analysis is an important strand in Critical Discourse Analysis (CDA) scholarship.

Assignment #2: Becoming Disciplinary Cultural Informants

This assignment is my own take on a "students as researchers" approach I learned from the work of Ann Johns (1997; more at Shapiro, 2010a). The goal is to prepare students to serve as cultural informants on a particular discipline or field of study. Students gather information to deepen their rhetorical and linguistic knowledge and to share that knowledge with their peers.

Below are some questions that can guide students' investigations:

- How does this linguistic community (discipline/field of study) distinguish itself from others? What is "unique" to this disciplinary community?
- What skills and dispositions are valued among students—or researchers— in this linguistic community?

- What genres of reading and writing are used most frequently in this linguistic community? How do the conventions of those genres reflect the values of the discipline?
- What are some of the ongoing debates among members of this linguistic community? How has their discipline/field of study been changing (e.g., with a focus on access, globalization, inclusion, technology)?

"Data collection" for this assignment can include any or all of the following:

- Analyzing websites from departments and/or professional organizations (e.g., Figure 5.3)

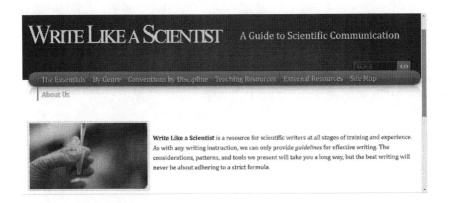

Figure 5.3 Screenshot of "Write Like a Scientist" Website

- Interviewing instructors and/or student majors in that department/program
- Gathering course documents (e.g., syllabi, writing guides, assignment prompts)
- Observing interactions in classes or co-curricular events—and/or on public message boards, listservs, social media, etc.

Students can share what they have learned in oral presentations, written reports, or multi-media projects (e.g., poster, podcast, video). I know some colleagues who actually assign the work from a previous group of students as required reading for future classes and/or as part of trainings for tutors working in writing/learning centers!

✳✳✳✳✳✳✳✳✳✳✳✳✳✳✳

Unit 5.2: Grammar Concepts and Controversies

Overview

When people find out that I teach a course called "English Grammar: Concepts and Controversies," they usually have one of two reactions: The first is to thank me for nobly fighting the "good fight" (against "bad grammar"). The other is to make a self-deprecating remark such as, "I really need a class like that. My grammar is horrible!" What strikes me in both of these responses is the emotional intensity. *Why do people care so (friggin') much about grammatical correctness?*

That question is at the heart of this unit. Part of the answer (spoiler alert!) is that conversations about grammar aren't just about grammar, really. When we judge someone's language as "good" or "bad," we are often making implicit judgments about that person's intelligence, education level, politeness, or trustworthiness. The social phenomenon underlying these judgments is **prescriptivism**, which we defined in Chapter 2. And prescriptivism, ultimately, is about power: *Who sets the rules? Who enforces them? Who benefits? Who is harmed? And how might we mitigate that harm?*

A CLA approach to grammar delves deeply into these questions. However, just because we critique the rules doesn't mean that we avoid learning them. The first portion of this unit ("Concepts") focuses on learning grammar terms and language analysis skills, so that students can make and assess writers' grammatical choices in writing. The remainder of this unit ("Controversies") engages the more critical questions, such as those above.

I encourage readers to think carefully about **the ratio of "concepts" to "controversies"** for their own classes. I lean a bit more heavily toward the "controversies," but some teachers may want or need to spend more time with the "concepts." Of course, one could design an entire course focused only on one or the other. But I think it is much funner[22] to combine them. Whatever we decide, we need to **communicate this to students** as well, so that their expectations are aligned with ours.

Learning Sequence

Tapping into Prior Knowledge

I usually begin by inviting associations with the word "grammar." This can be done as a large class discussion, in pairs or small groups, or in a jigsaw survey (p. 183). Here are some of the prompting questions I use:

- What words or phrases do you associate with "grammar"?
- What emotions come up for you when you hear the word "grammar"?
- What images come to mind? (We can even do a Google Image search together)
- Where and when do you hear people talking about "bad" grammar?
- What are your grammatical "pet peeves"—i.e., mistakes or rules that really annoy you?

Students usually have plenty to say on these questions. They often start to reference grammar memes they have seen on social media. Below (Figure 5.4) is a middle schooler's reconstruction of one such meme, from several years back. The lower half says "Use commas. Don't be a psycho!"[23]

This meme is highlighting the comical grammatical ambiguity caused by the lack of commas in the "I like" sentence. But it illustrates something else that is pervasive in public discourse: "Bad grammar" is linked to being a "bad person" (unintelligent, mentally unfit, or even immoral, in this case). The

Figure 5.4 A Student's Drawing of a Popular Grammar Meme

assumption that follows, then, is: "Good grammar = good person." Within this logic, grammatical "incorrectness" is an indicator of moral or intellectual decline—not just in an individual, but in society. This "story" about grammar goes way back: One can find quotes from public intellectuals hundreds of years ago bemoaning the "poor" speech or writing of young people as a sign of impending doom.[24]

If we continue with this logic, then "fixing" other people's grammar would be considered a means of improving society. This is the assumption behind another popular grammar meme: A police badge with the slogan "To Serve and Correct"—a riff on the motto "To Serve and Protect." The idea that we could "fix" society if we could just "fix" everyone's language was in fact part of what motivated some proponents of the "Knowledge about Language" movement, from which CLA is an outgrowth, as we discussed in Chapter 2.

We may not get to all of this in our initial class discussions for this unit. But early on, I do seek out opportunities to highlight the **"bad grammar = bad person"** equation, so that students can start noticing it in their day-to-day lives. (And they do! This often comes up in Sociolinguistics Scrapbooks, an assignment we discussed in Chapter 4). Some of the questions we want to get to eventually, especially in the "controversies" portion of the unit, are:

- What motivates us to "police" people's grammar (online, in school, etc.)?
- What are the dangers of this linguistic policing?
- What does "bad grammar" actually indicate about a person?
- How might our judgments about grammar be linked to social (in)justice?

Activity: Standing Survey

Another activity I use to surface students' beliefs and attitudes toward grammar is a **standing survey**. Similar to "Four Corners" (p. 105), students position themselves in the room to indicate their level of agreement with each statement. However, instead of having only four options, they stand along a continuum, with strong agreement on one side and strong disagreement on the other. Below are some of the statements I use for this activity:

1   I am bothered by grammar, spelling, or punctuation errors on public signs and advertisements.

2   I spend a lot of time proofreading emails to authority figures (e.g., teachers, employers, coaches).

3   I proofread my texts/social media posts before I send them.

4   I would have trouble trusting someone whose emails or texts often have grammar errors.

5   I would not want to date someone whose online profile has many errors or typos.

6   I am less likely to take a public figure seriously if their social media posts often have errors or typos.

7   If I were an employer, I would not hire someone who had errors or typos in their cover letter.

8   If I were a teacher, I would take points off for grammar errors, even if those errors don't impact clarity (use of who vs. whom, comma vs. semicolon, etc.).

Once students moved in response to a statement, I ask some of them to share their thinking. I invite others to move elsewhere on the continuum if their own thinking begins to shift. And when they do, it's quite fun to see how everyone reacts! We can revisit some of the statements later in the unit/course to see if students' attitudes have shifted. One year, students' responses for question #7 (about employment) shifted dramatically: In the first week, all but one student stood on the "agree" side. By the end of the semester, all but one had switched to "disagree."

Topic #1: Learning Grammar Concepts

When teaching the "concepts" portion, I aim for **quality more than quantity.** Below is a list of core tasks I want all students to be able to complete by the end of this portion.[25] I share a version of this list students early in the course, so they can self-assess as we go:

1   Identify the subject and predicate of a sentence.

2   Label parts of speech (noun, verb, etc.) and create sentences using the same word as a different part of speech (e.g., "water" as a noun, verb, and adjective)

3   Identify the grammatical function of phrases and clauses (e.g., adjectival, adverbial)

4   Distinguish among the following, and be able to create sentences that use them:

    a   Simple, compound, and complex sentences
    b   Action, linking, and auxiliary verbs
    c   Transitive and intransitive verbs
    d   Direct and indirect objects and subject/object complements
    e   Active and passive voice
    f   Past, present, and future tenses,
    g   Simple, perfect, and progressive aspect

To help students build these skills, I assign low-stakes homework assignments that are graded for completion only. I also facilitate in-class board work and other group activities, in which students work together to analyze and/or compose sentences.

We occasionally create "syntax trees," which are what linguists use to map sentence structure. My goal in using them is to illustrate **grammatical ambiguity**. For example, in the sentence "*She saw the room with the telescope*," the prepositional phrase "with the telescope" could answer the question, "Which room?" or the question, "How was she able to see the room?" Students can show me they understand both meanings through their placement of that phrase in the syntax tree.

Note: Syntax trees can look a bit scary to newbies! They are not essential for this unit, but for instructors who would like to learn more, Gretchen McCulloch, who co-hosts the "Lingthusiasm" podcast (more in Chapter 6), breaks down the process quite helpfully.[26] Of course, there are other ways to illustrate grammatical ambiguity, including Kellogg-Reed diagrams—the ones that start on a horizontal line, which are still used in many U.S. English/language arts classrooms. We can also get creative, inviting students to draw or act out the two meanings of a sentence.

As we learn to identify grammatical structures, it is important to consider how those structures can be used rhetorically. Some common examples of **rhetorical grammar** include:

- **Telling a story with present tense**, instead of past, to make the narrative more vivid—a strategy used by novelists, historians, and lawyers (e.g., when describing a sequence of events leading to a crime). There are some critics, of this strategy, though (e.g., *Guardian*[27]).
- **Using passive voice** to emphasize the outcome of an action rather than the "grammatical agent"—i.e., who/what did the action. Scientists use

this in the "methods" section of their reports, as noted in Unit 5.1, and journalists use this construction when reporting on a crime, accident, or crisis (e.g., "Three passengers were injured."). Politicians, however, sometimes use the passive voice as half-apology (e.g., "Mistakes were made"; more at NPR,[28] NYTimes[29]).

- **Choosing punctuation** also requires rhetorical consideration. For example, a **semicolon** invites readers to consider the link between two ideas without explicitly stating the connection (NYTimes[30]). And an **em-dash**—which happens to be my favorite punctuation mark, in case you hadn't noticed—can add emphasis and/or create a more colloquial tone in writing (NYTimes[31]).

Rhetorical grammar is a huge area of study, and I have only presented a few highlights here. To learn more, check out Kolln and Gray (2013) and Micciche (2004), and search for "rhetorical grammar" at the online Hub.

To gauge what students are learning in the "concepts" section, I often have them identify and explain **grammar errors**—i.e., unconventional grammar use that is unintentional on the part of the writer. I usually focus on common patterns that have been identified in studies of student writing (e.g., Lunsford & Lunsford, 2008).

I also assess students' learning of the "concepts" with two **quizzes**. The first, taken in-class, primarily involves labeling and sentence creation—e.g., *"Write 3 sentences using the word 'well' as a 1) noun, 2) adjective, 3) adverb."* The second is a take-home quiz, for which students must identify, explain, and correct errors in a paragraph that includes examples of patterns we have reviewed in class.

I usually avoid using timed assessments, since they can raise concerns about access and equity. But for this particular unit, they are a useful feedback tool for me and for students. Here some things I do to level the playing field, though:

- Each quiz only counts for a small percentage (5–10%) of the final grade
- We do a lot of collaborative review in class, including playing games (see an annotated list of my favorite review games on the Hub)
- Students are allowed one sheet of notes during the first quiz
- Students can have as much time as they wish to complete the quiz
- Students who do poorly can make "corrections" for partial credit, if they meet with me first

NOTE: In Chapters 9 and 10, we will discuss other assessment considerations related to CLA Pedagogy.

Topic #2: Introducing the Controversies

While we are focused on learning "concepts," I avoid assigning lengthy readings. But I do weave in bits and pieces on the "controversies" as class time allows. Here are some examples:

- **Prescriptivism on social media**: e.g., groups such as the Apostrophe Protection Society (*Guardian*[32]). We also look at Buzzfeed's annual "best of" lists of grammar memes and tweets.[33] Below are my recreations of two popular memes I like to analyze with students.
- **Prescriptivism in entertainment media**—e.g., films like My *Fair Lady* ("All Things Linguistic" blog[34]); pop songs like "Oxford Comma" by Vampire Weekend (*Vanity Fair*[35]) and "Word Crimes" by Weird Al Yankovic (*Vulture*[36]). See also *The Conversation*[37] on use of "like" in the British reality show *Love Island*
- **Prescriptivist "personalities"**—e.g., research on what kinds of personality types tend to be more critical of grammatical errors (*Huffington Post*[38]; *Psychology Today*[39])
- **High-stakes situations** where a small grammatical choice makes a big difference—e.g., court cases hinging on interpretation of punctuation/word choice in a legal document (Grammarly[40]) or debates about interpreting the second amendment to the U.S. Constitution (*Atlantic*[41])

We also look at examples of **rhetorical rule-breaking**. One of my favorites is the split infinitive "to boldly go," from *Star Trek* (*Merriam Webster*[42]). Some grammatical "violations" are so common that they are given a name, such as **asyndeton**, in which the writer intentionally creates a run-on sentence for rhetorical effect. A famous example is the opening line of Dickens's *A Tale of Two Cities*: "It was the best of times, it was the worst of times, it was the age of wisdom, it was the age of foolishness...."

Writers sometimes do the opposite as well, inserting additional conjunctions for rhetorical effect. This strategy, called **polysyndeton**, is found in a passage of Angelou's *I Know Why the Caged Bird Sings*: "Let the whitefolks have their money and power and segregation and sarcasm and big houses and schools and lawns like carpets, and books, and mostly—mostly—let them have their whiteness." We can ask students why Angelou chose to use "and" eight times in that sentence, and what would have been lost rhetorically had she deleted those "extra" conjunctions.

Talking about rhetorical grammar can also bring us back to issues of **power and privilege:** *Who is celebrated for breaking the rules? Who might be punished?* Research has found, in fact, that readers' reactions to grammatical "errors" are often shaped by racism, sexism, xenophobia, and other forms of prejudice (e.g., Godsil et al., 2017; Reeves, 2014). We will explore this more in Unit 5.3. Here is another place where we can examine the metaphor of grammatical "policing": *What communities are linguistically "policed" the most, and how might that policing harm or hold back individuals from those communities?*

Topic #3: A "Deep Dive" into Prescriptivism and Standardization

As we continue with the "controversies" section of the course, we start to unpack how standard language ideology (Lippi-Green, 2012); see also Chapter 2) and other prescriptivist attitudes shape public conversations about language. Below are some topics that can be explored as a class or within small groups—e.g., with "jigsaw reading" (p. 96).

A   How and why is **grammatical correctness linked to morality?**

- General audience books, such as Lynn Truss's (2005) best-seller *Eats, Shoots and Leaves*,[43] which often equate "proper punctuation" with politeness
- Cameron's (2012) concept of **"verbal hygiene"** (summarized at ThoughtCo[44])—also see Figure 5.5

B   How does **standardization** happen? And what makes it controversial?

- Historical accounts of English standardization as a political process (e.g., Crystal[45]; Curzan, 2014; Hitchings, 2011)
- Criticisms of the impact of standardization on users of "non-standard" varieties (ThoughtCo[46] and the readings above)
- Research on the role of technology—e.g., grammar-check and spell-check features—in reinforcing standards (e.g., Atlantic[47]; see also Curzan, 2014)

C   Where do we see **resistance to prescriptivist attitudes and language policies?**

- Essays and editorials—e.g., Steven Fry's (2008) "Don't Mind Your Language,"[48] a portion of which was made into a kinetic typography video[49]

Figure 5.5 My Recreation of Two Prescriptivist Memes from Social Media

- International movements for linguistic human rights—see summaries by the United Nations[50] and the Linguistic Society of America[51]
- Education movements informed by a "linguistic human rights" framework, such as Students' Rights to Their Own Language (SRTOL)[52] and—more recently—"Black Linguistic Justice"[53] in the U.S.

D   When might **prescriptivism be justified**?

- Historical perspectives on profanity and obscenity—e.g., Hitchings' (2011) *The Language Wars*[54]; see also documentary films, including the 2021 Netflix series *History of Swear Words*
- Studies on the impact of slurs/epithets vs. profanity—e.g., Bergen's (2019) study in *The Conversation*[55]—see Figure 5.6; also Blakemore (2015)

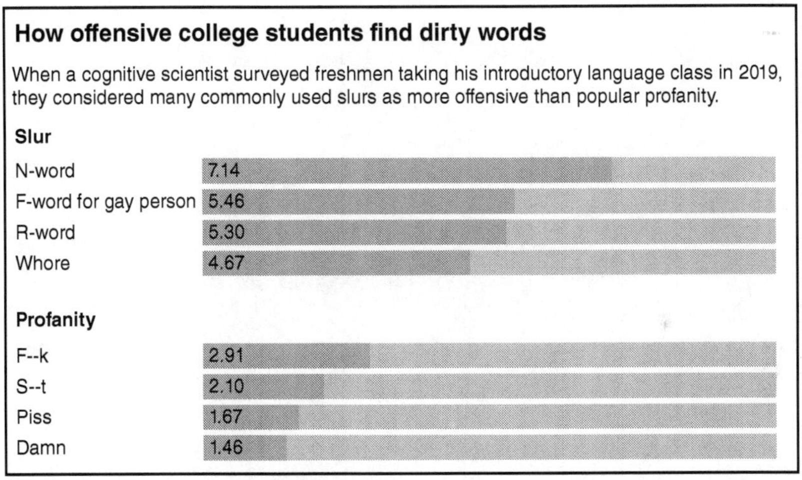

How offensive college students find dirty words

When a cognitive scientist surveyed freshmen taking his introductory language class in 2019, they considered many commonly used slurs as more offensive than popular profanity.

Slur

N-word	7.14
F-word for gay person	5.46
R-word	5.30
Whore	4.67

Profanity

F--k	2.91
S--t	2.10
Piss	1.67
Damn	1.46

Figure 5.6 Table from Bergen's Study of Students' Perceptions of Slurs vs. Profanity

Demonstrating Learning for Unit 5.2

For this unit, I like to use assignments that invite students to explore a variety of perspectives on grammar and prescriptivism.

Assignment #1: Critical Role-Play (Oral or Written)

As discussed in Chapter 4, I use critical role-play to help deepen students' understanding of complex issues, including prescriptivism. For this assignment, students form groups around a question from a given list (see text box), and each student in the group assumes a different role—either a scholar whose work we have read or a stakeholder with a particular vantage point (e.g., teacher, business owner, lawyer, etc.). Below is a sampling of questions and possible roles, although sometimes students choose a role that is not listed:

Questions for Critical Role-play (Unit 5.2)

1   Should college admissions officers take grammar into account when deciding whether to admit a particular student? (Officer, student, parent, professor)
2   Is it fair/appropriate to reject an applicant (or fire an employee) based on grammar errors or typos in their writing? (Employer, employee, HR or diversity officer)
3   Is it fair/appropriate to reject a potential roommate/tenant because of their use of grammar (e.g., in emails)? (Landlord, tenant, lawyer or other authority)
4   Is it fair to reject a potential friend—or romantic partner—based on their use of grammar? (Truss; Cameron or Curzan)
5   Should businesses (e.g., restaurants) be expected to have "error-free" English in their signage and advertising materials? (Business owners, customers)
6   Is technology use causing a "decline" in students' knowledge/use of prescriptivist grammar? (Truss; Curzan; see also the "technology" section of Ball and Loewe [2017])
7   Is it appropriate to restrict or ban certain kinds of language in the classroom? If so, how should we decide what to ban/restrict? (Psychologist, student, teacher, parent)

A few notes on this activity:

- Note that there are **more than two possible "roles"** for most questions. This is intentional, since most of these complex issues have more than two "sides."
- We want this to be a **dialogue**, not a debate! (Remember the "argument = war" metaphor from Unit 5.1). One way to promote richer conversations is to give students ample time to prepare for the conversation.

- If they are performing a role with higher social status (e.g., a scholar, teacher, or business executive), I invite students to **play with academic or professional register.** Some students really have fun with this! (Of course, we should keep in mind the earlier cautions [pp. 89-90] about *not* trying to replicate the experience—or mimic the speech—of someone from a less privileged position.)

Critical role-play can be written as well: One of the best ways to help students contrast the ideas in two texts is to invite them to **compose a dialogue between the two authors.** This can take the form of a conversation script, an email/letter exchange, or even a social media interaction. I have been fascinated to find that some students in fact become more confident using scholarly discourse when they are invited to "pretend" to be an established scholar (Shapiro, 2010b; Shapiro & Leopold, 2012). For more on bringing "playful attention to language" in writing classes, see Gegg-Harrison (forthcoming) and Chapter 7.

Assignment #2: Position Paper

Critical role-play feeds nicely into a persuasive writing assignment. Students in my "English Grammar: Concepts and Controversies" class write a Position Paper taking a stance on a topic of their choosing. Examples include:

- Should public schools in the U.S. be required to teach prescriptive approaches to grammar?
- Are grammar-checkers (or spell-checkers) more harmful than helpful to students' development as writers?
- Should departments at our school be required to have a consistent style guide or grammar marking system?
- Should offensive/derogatory language be removed from works of literature? (e.g., there is a version of the book *Adventures of Huckleberry Finn* that replaces the "N-word" with "slave"—see CBS[56])
- Should teachers/professors be responsible for ensuring use of inclusive or non-offensive language in the classroom? (We'll talk about this one more in Chapters 7 and 9)

The biggest challenge students face with this assignment is developing an **arguable thesis.** They sometimes choose a question that has a fairly obvious answer, such as: "*Does the business world promote prescriptivist attitudes toward language?* (The answer is "yes," of course, but there isn't much of a "position" to defend). In cases like these, I help re-shape the question into something arguable, such as: "*Should business owners provide grammar/copyediting support for their employees?*"

Below is the grading rubric for this assignment. I offer short "rhetorical grammar" workshops at a few points in the writing process, to help students with this aspect of the writing, noted under "Clarity and Professionalism."

Position Paper Grading Rubric:

Argument (Does the writer have a clear central question and position on that question? Are the implications for the question/topic discussed explicitly?) /25

Organization (Is there a clear overall structure to the paper, with transitions from one point/example to the next? Does the writer use paragraphs and transition words/phrases to help structure the analysis?) /25

Evidence (Does the writer give examples and cite secondary sources to support their points? Is the evidence credible and varied? Are there explicit connections between evidence and argument?) /25

Clarity and Professionalism of Writing (Is there a strong academic tone to the writing? Does the writer use a variety of "rhetorical grammar" choices? Is the paper edited/proofread?) /25

****

Unit 5.3: Linguistic Pluralism in the Academy

Overview

This unit follows nicely on Unit 5.2, but I've used it on its own as well. The focus is on how schools can become more inclusive and equitable for students from diverse linguistic backgrounds. First, though, we must explore how and why schools are often **exclusionary and inequitable** to these students. We have touched on this a few times already: In Chapter 4, we discussed how users of stigmatized varieties of English are often seen as "less intelligent" than other groups (e.g., Dunstan & Jaeger, 2015; Strickland, 2010). And in Unit 5.2, we discussed how prescriptivist attitudes can contribute to implicit judgments about people based on their grammar usage.

Underlying these prejudices is what some scholars call **monolingual ideology**—the belief that linguistic sameness is the ideal and language difference is a problem (e.g., Canagarajah, 2002; Watson & Shapiro, 2018[57]). Many school policies and practices are undergirded by an assumption that only one language variety—"standardized" English—matters (Baker-Bell, 2020; Mitchell, 2012; Weaver, 2019). A **plurilingual** (or translingual[58]) mindset, in contrast, asks: *How can we learn to see and treat language difference as an educational resource?*

Before we engage this question, two quick points of clarification: First, this unit is not just about "**celebrating diversity**." Appreciating students' linguistic and cultural backgrounds is important, but that alone will not make our classrooms or schools more equitable (Affolter, 2019; Gere et al., 2021; Shapiro et al., 2016). As DEI—diversity, equity, and inclusion—experts like to say, we can't just "count people" (or languages): We have to "make people count." In other words, it is what we *do with* diversity that makes a difference in students' lives and leads to more equitable and inclusive schools and societies.[59]

A second caveat is that there is a **huge body of other scholarship** on asset-oriented approaches to working with students from diverse language backgrounds. One challenge in engaging with that scholarship, however, is that many different terms are used. Here's just a sampling:

- Translingual approaches (e.g., Horner & Tetreault, 2017)
- Translanguaging pedagogy (e.g., García et al., 2017)
- Linguistically responsive teaching (e.g., Haan & Gallagher, 2021; Lucas et al., 2008)
- Teaching for linguistic justice (e.g., Baker-Bell, 2020; Schreiber et al., forthcoming)

There are important differences among these approaches, but all of them share a commitment to challenging monolingual ideologies. There are even more terms used frequently by our colleagues outside the U.S., one of which—**plurilingual pedagogies**—I've chosen as the frame for this chapter (Shuck & Losey, 2022; Taylor & Snoddon, 2013).

Learning Sequence

Tapping into Prior Knowledge

Often, I present material from this unit after students have already had opportunities to tap into their prior knowledge and experience. But if I engage this topic earlier in the semester, or in a one-session workshop, I often begin with questions like the following:

1   How many of you identify as "native English speakers"?
2   How many of you identify as "non-native English speakers"?
3   How many of you consider yourselves bilingual or multilingual?
4   Have you ever experienced linguistic insecurity about how you speak (in any language)?
5   Have you ever experienced linguistic insecurity about how you write?

These questions seem straightforward. However, a few complexities usually emerge: First, some students do not fit neatly into the binary of native vs. non-native speaker. (After asking questions 1 and 2, I often pause to ask whether anyone's answer is "It's complicated!"). Second, many students are unsure how to answer question 3, because they've studied another language but may not think they are "fluent" enough to answer "yes." For questions 4 and 5, many "native" English speakers will admit that they struggle with linguistic insecurity, which surprises some students. To help build understanding among students who have **not** experienced this struggle, I use the activity below.

Activity: Linguistic Monitoring

I adapted this activity from my Middlebury colleague in Education Studies Tara Affolter, an expert in anti-racist pedagogy (Affolter, 2019). The goal is to give students—particularly those from more privileged backgrounds—a reference point for understanding linguistic insecurity. Students are put into pairs and given a discussion prompt that requires some reflection but is not unduly difficult. One example I use is: *Why did you choose Middlebury College?* The "catch" is that when speaking, students can **only use words that have one or two syllables**. If the partner ("monitor") catches the "speaker" using a larger word, they signal the "mistake" using a buzzer sound or hand gesture.

After each partner has had a chance to be both "speaker" and "monitor," I ask students to describe their experience. Many say they felt "stupid" or "slow" when speaking, and that they had difficulty concentrating. They also sometimes admit that when they were in the monitor role, they were much more focused on catching "mistakes" than on listening to the speaker. Usually, a few students say that the activity was "easy" or even "refreshing," which might lead to a discussion about why some of us experience this activity more negatively than others.

Building on this activity, we can consider the forms of linguistic monitoring that occur in the classroom. Students often share comments such as:

- "Classroom discussion sometimes feels more like a competition than a conversation."
- "The pace of the discussion moves so quickly that I don't feel I can ever get a word in."
- "The fear that I will sound ignorant or might accidentally offend someone often prevents me from contributing to discussions about social justice issues."

These kinds of honest meta-conversations are themselves a useful tool for promoting inclusion in our classrooms (e.g., Shapiro, 2020). We will return to this point in Chapters 7 and 9.

Topic #1: Research on Linguistic (and Racial) Bias in Academic Settings

The above activity can be a nice bridge into exploring **native speaker bias**—also known as "native-speakerism"—since students who are "non-native speakers" of English often feel that their "monitor"[60] is on over-drive during class discussion. And for good reason! There is a lot of research documenting **implicit linguistic bias** against L2 users English: Instructors are sometimes more critical of errors by "ESL" writers than those by L1 ("native") speakers (e.g., Lindsey & Crusan, 2011). And in course evaluations, students are often more critical of instructors with "foreign" accents (e.g., Fan et al., 2019; Lee & Du, 2020).

⚠ Warning: Accent Hallucinations Ahead!

But wait—there's more! {{{Deep breath here}}} Researchers have found that students sometimes *think* they hear a "foreign accent" based solely on the teacher's **physical appearance**. Here is the set-up of the original study by Donald Rubin (1992): Two groups of students with similar demographic profiles listen to the same audio-recorded lecture. While they listen, they are shown a photo of the (supposed) speaker. Group A sees a photo of a phenotypically[61] White face. Group B sees a phenotypically Asian face. After the lecture, students rate the speaker on a variety of traits, including perceived accent and effectiveness of communication. They also take a quiz on the lecture material.[62]

Can you guess the results?

Bingo! Group B, which saw the "Asian" face, noted a more prominent "foreign accent" and gave a lower rating to the speaker's communication abilities. They also **retained less from the lecture**. Yes, that's right: The (hallucinated) accent actually interfered with students' learning. The study has been replicated and/or adapted several times, with similar results (e.g., Babel & Russell, 2015; Damron, 2003).

This same "raciolinguistic" bias (Rosa & Flores, 2017) also shapes perceptions of student writing. Teachers may notice more "errors" in writing that they think is from a student of color (e.g., Godsil et al., 2017; Johnson & Van-Brackle, 2012) than in writing from a White student. This is an issue in the workplace as well: A study by Reeves (2014) found that lawyers gave higher ratings to the "analytical skills" of a piece of writing when they thought the writer was "Caucasian." This is just a sampling of the research demonstrating that **linguistic profiling,** a concept we learned about in Chapter 4, applies just as much to writing as to speech, and has just as much to do with race as with language background.

Topic #2: Pushing Back Against Raciolinguistic Bias

I find studies like these quite upsetting—and many of my students do as well. As we discussed in Chapter 3, students need opportunities to **process their emotional responses** in small groups, in writing, or via other means (we will talk more about this in Chapter 9). Students also want to know how they can channel their awareness into action, so they can be part of the solution, rather than perpetuating the problem.

Of course, we may first want to help students think critically about their "action bias"—i.e., their tendency to want to take immediate action, in order to alleviate their own discomfort, as we discussed in Chapter 3. But there are actions they (and we) can take in our day-to-day lives to understand and resist implicit bias. For instance, students can conduct surveys or interviews with peers in order to document raciolinguistic bias, or they can do research on teachers' (or peers') beliefs about "good" writing or speaking.

Students can also resist linguistic prejudice in their daily lives. Critical role-play scenarios—e.g., the one earlier in this chapter and in Chapter 4—can help prepare them to intervene when they have the opportunity. Moreover, students in a more privileged position can learn to share the **communicative burden** (Chaparro, 2014; Lippi-Green, 2012) more equitably, by devoting additional effort toward ensuring effective communication. As one expert explained in a recent episode[63] of "Rough Translation," one of my favorite NPR podcasts, rather than expecting **accent reduction** on the part of non-native speakers, we can all strengthen our skills for **accent recognition**—i.e., comprehension of a wider range of accents and speaking styles! (See Baese-Berk [2019] for more on this[64]; also see Chapter 4 for more on dialect awareness and language variation.)

Topic #3: Promoting Linguistic Pluralism in Schools

To continue on the topic of how our awareness can be channeled into action, we can talk about what it looks like to promote plurilingualism in educational settings. Here are some questions and recommended readings/media:

1   How do writers push back against monolingual ideology and native speaker bias?

- Literary anthologies of writing in "non-standard" or minoritized varieties of English—e.g., Ahmad's (2007) *Rotten English*
- Scholarly writers who mix codes—e.g., Smitherman, 1986; Villanueva, 1993; Young, 2007; find more at the compilation by colleagues at the University of Rochester[65] and in Chapter 7

2   What can schools do to reduce linguistic prejudice and show support for linguistic diversity?

- Providing workshops and resources on resisting linguistic bias—e.g., *Inside Higher Ed*[66]; also CCCC/NCTE position statements[67]
- Highlighting linguistic diversity in co-curricular programming and public communications—e.g., by Norwich University[68] (see Figure 5.7) and Oakland University[69]

Figure 5.7 A Student's Instagram Post, Part of a Linguistic Diversity Initiative at Norwich University

In Chapter 10, we will continue this conversation, exploring other ways we can promote plurilingualism across our schools, campuses, and communities.

Demonstrating Learning for Unit 5.3

Many of the assignments we have discussed in previous units can be used here as well, including peer-to-peer research, autobiographical essays, critical role-play, and position papers. In the following section, I present one additional option that I use in several of my classes.

Assignment: "Writing Beyond the Classroom"

The goal of this assignment is for students to communicate their CLA learning with an outside audience. They choose the purpose, audience, and genre, with input from me as needed. They also determine the style and register, which may include code-mixing. Some of my students have used this as an opportunity to try out a genre or style of writing they've never done before. Hooray for rhetorical risk-taking! We'll come back to this in Chapter 7.

Engaging with these projects has been a highlight of my teaching. Some students have written beautiful **personal letters** to family members, often about the language dynamics in their homes and communities (Chapter 7 has an example). Other students write for more **public audiences**—for example:

- A brochure persuading parents of the value of bilingual or dual language programs for their children
- A school newspaper editorial about the role of linguistic bias in course evaluations
- A children's picture book explaining linguistic prejudice (see p. 244)
- Speeches or spoken word pieces about language and identity, inspired by Lyiscott's (2014) TED talk (more in Chapter 7 and Shapiro)
- Short stories, plays, poetry, and other creative writing, often with a critical introduction from the writer

In their feedback to me about this assignment, students often emphasize two points:

1   **Choice is key, as is support:** Students appreciate the opportunity to decide what they write, for whom, and in what form. But some need more guidance and direction than others, so it is important to provide

feedback and support early in the process (e.g., via written proposals and/or individual meetings).

2   **Grading should be flexible but also transparent**: Since the work for this assignment takes so many forms, I work with each student to develop a grading rubric that reflects their rhetorical priorities. I also build in a number of "process" grades (e.g., proposal, peer review, progress report). This rewards students' labor (Inoue, 2019), and also helps them stay on track in the process. We'll talk more about scaffolding assignments in Chapter 9.

To close this chapter, I want to share one of favorite iterations of this project, a collection of poetry entitled *rice burger and banana milk*, written by Ho-June (Sean) Rhee, a Korean international student who had lived in several other countries prior to college. The first poem is written entirely in English, and the other three mix English with Korean, Tagalog, and Spanish, respectively. The content and the style of each poem work together to illustrate something about Sean's relationship to each language. The poems are accompanied by his artistic commentary, as well as hand-drawn illustrations (see Figures 5.8 and 5.9). I nominated Sean's work for our first-year writing prize, and he won first place! This was the first time that a piece of creative writing using multiple languages had been selected for the top honor.

In the version of the collection that he submitted for publication to our college website, Sean added a note about what winning the award meant to him.[70] Here is an excerpt from his remarks:

> I [often] feel like a literary fraud who is imitating people's unique styles and parroting their voices. However, *rice burger and banana milk* showed me the exit to step outside of the ivory tower and roam around my inner thoughts and emotions. I didn't feel the pressure to use specific jargons and complex sentence structures to make my work sound more "sophisticated." . . . I was finally able to find my voice and share my thoughts. In a way, [this prize] was a gentle nod of recognition that the readers heard my voice and that I should be more confident. . . . To a non-native speaker of English, that simple nod goes a long way and means the world to him or her.

I saw Sean's increased confidence during the remainder of his time at Middlebury. He even became a peer writing tutor—something he said he never would have thought he was "qualified" for! To me, this example illustrates the power of plurilingual pedagogies: **We all benefit** when students from diverse linguistic backgrounds have opportunities to channel their Critical Language Awareness into writing for audiences beyond the classroom. In

rice burger and

banana milk

By Ho June (Sean) Rhee, 이호준

Figure 5.8 Cover Page from Sean Rhee's Poetry Collection

애국심 (Patriotism)	
저는 한국인입니다.	(I am Korean.)
"I am an Americanized Korean."	
한국인으로서 대한민국이 자랑스럽습니다.	(As a Korean, I am proud of South Korea.)
"I'm not really attached to Korea."	
그런데, 왜 외국인 취급을 하시나요?	(But, why do you treat me like a foreigner?)
"Please think of me as a foreigner."	
한국어는 당연히 쓸 수 있는데,	(I can obviously use Korean.)
"I hope you can understand my awkward Korean!"	
예의범절도 당연히 지킬 수 있는데,	(I can obviously be respectful.)
"I know all about the Korean respect culture."	
"It's like a rap, you basically put "yo" at the end!"	
왜 영어로 대답하시나요?	(But why do you respond in English.)
"I can understand English too!"	
왜 한국어를 잘 한다고 칭찬하시나요?	(Why do you compliment my Korean?)
"But I swear my Korean is still good!"	
"Annyeonghaseyo?"	
왜 이방인 취급을 하시나요?	(Why do you treat me like an outsider?)
"I'm pretty much a banana."	
말할나위 없이 한국인이였을 때가 그립습니다.	(I miss being Korean without suspicions)
"Am I "Korean" enough?"	
저는…진정한 한국인입니까?	(Am I a real Korean?)

Figure 5.9 Sean's Poem in Korean and English, with English Translations in Parentheses

Chapter 7, we will take a closer look at some of the linguistic choices Sean and other student writers make in these more public-facing assignments.

Notes

1 It's worth pointing out that "sociolinguistics of writing" is itself a growing area of study (e.g., Hartse, 2016; Lillis, 2013).
2 Being a good linguist, I of course did some online sleuthing to see if "sexy" is ever used in academic contexts, and it is—occasionally—in case you wondered!
3 I would like to thank my CLA reading group members for furthering my thinking on this assignment. Erika I-Tremblay and her colleagues, for example, have students write a profile of their interview partner in the style of a Wikipedia entry!
4 www.thedaln.org/
5 There are many versions of this folktale in circulation. Perhaps the most widely known is from a commencement address given by the novelist David Foster Wallace in 2005, entitled "This Is the Water." We'll talk about this a bit more in Chapter 6.
6 www.npr.org/templates/story/story.php?storyId=1006937
7 For more on general features of U.S. academic culture, see Chapter 2 of my first book (Shapiro et al., 2014).
8 https://writingcenter.oregonstate.edu/WAB
9 https://wac.colostate.edu/books/usu/owns/
10 www.nytimes.com/2010/08/02/education/02cheat.html
11 www.theguardian.com/books/2018/sep/21/how-to-write-a-great-sentence
12 www.nature.com/articles/d41586-021-00899-y
13 www.forbes.com/sites/laurambrown/2019/05/10/whats-the-big-deal-about-the-passive-voice/
14 www.grammarly.com/blog/hedging-language/
15 https://sites.middlebury.edu/middsciwriting/
16 www.nature.com/news/scientific-language-is-becoming-more-informal-1.20963
17 www.psychologytoday.com/us/blog/the-web-violence/201805/know-thyself-how-write-reflexivity-statement
18 https://s3.amazonaws.com/s3.sumofus.org/images/SUMOFUS_PROGRESSIVE-STYLEGUIDE.pdf
19 https://aeon.co/essays/the-idea-that-sperm-race-to-the-egg-is-just-another-macho-myth
20 The war metaphor is so pervasive in medicine that a group of healthcare professionals recently published an editorial urging the field to "wage war on war metaphors" (Marron et al., 2020).
21 http://mason.gmu.edu/~montecin/metaphor-97.htm
22 Did you have a strong reaction to this word? You're not alone! One of my favorite linguistics memes—one that is printed on a mask I wore early on in the COVID-19 pandemic—says: "Prescriptivism is fun, but descriptivism is funner!" According

to Merriam Webster (and other dictionaries), *funner* is a perfectly acceptable word (www.merriam-webster.com/words-at-play/are-funner-and-funnest-real-words-usage). If this irks you, keep reading!

23 Close readers will notice that the figure includes a spelling error. When I pointed this out to the student, hoping to open up a conversation about prescriptivism and irony, he simply rolled his eyes and went back to looking at his phone. I might have pointed out as well that "psycho" is ableist language—but alas, I had lost his attention by that point.

24 For more on the long history of complaints about student writing, visit https://www.chronicle.com/article/what-critics-of-student-writing-get-wrong/

25 For readers wondering about materials for this portion, I have used Kolln and Gray (2013) and Morenberg (2014). However, I hope one day to shift to—or even create—an open access workbook, similar to Brehe (2019).

26 https://allthingslinguistic.com/post/102131750573/how-to-draw-a-syntax-tree-part-8-a-step-by-step

27 www.theguardian.com/commentisfree/2014/jul/28/historic-present-tense-past-john-humphrys

28 www.npr.org/sections/thetwo-way/2013/05/14/183924858/its-true-mistakes-were-made-is-the-king-of-non-apologies

29 https://opinionator.blogs.nytimes.com/2012/04/30/the-pleasures-and-perils-of-the-passive/

30 www.nytimes.com/2021/02/09/magazine/the-case-for-semicolons.html

31 https://opinionator.blogs.nytimes.com/2012/10/22/mad-dash/ (clearly, NYT publishes a lot on rhetorical grammar! See also https://opinionator.blogs.nytimes.com/2009/09/07/what-should-colleges-teach-part-3/

32 www.theguardian.com/education/shortcuts/2019/dec/02/the-pedants-pedant-why-the-apostrophe-protection-society-has-closed-in-disgust

33 www.buzzfeednews.com/article/emersonmalone/grammar-memes-2020. One of my favorites is from @Tachyon100, who asked this tongue-in-cheek question on Twitter: *"Is it 'for fucks sake' or 'for fuck sake'? It's for a work email so has to sound professional."*

34 https://allthingslinguistic.com/post/87540892941/why-does-henry-higgins-teach-eliza-doolittle-to

35 www.vanityfair.com/news/2008/01/michael-hogan-v

36 www.vulture.com/2017/03/weird-al-on-word-crimes-his-blurred-lines-parody.html

37 https://theconversation.com/like-isnt-a-lazy-linguistic-filler-the-english-language-snobs-need-to-like-pipe-down-122056

38 www.huffpost.com/entry/grammar-police_b_10617288. This study is part of a growing body of language on the nature and impact of grammar-related judgments in the workplace, housing market, and other sectors.

39 www.psychologytoday.com/us/blog/the-red-light-district/201604/personality-traits-grammar-and-spelling-sticklers

40 www.grammarly.com/blog/how-grammar-influences-legal-interpretations/

41 www.theatlantic.com/politics/archive/2018/03/second-amendment-text-context/555101/

42 www.merriam-webster.com/words-at-play/to-boldly-split-infinitives

43 An excerpt can be found at www.nytimes.com/2005/11/15/books/chapters/eats-shoots-leaves.html?mcubz=3

44 www.thoughtco.com/verbal-hygiene-language-usage-1692580

45 www.davidcrystal.com/Files/BooksAndArticles/-4006.pdf is one of many articles on this topic at Crystal's website.

46 www.thoughtco.com/what-is-standard-english-1691016

47 www.theatlantic.com/international/archive/2012/10/a-call-for-spelling-standardization-or-is-that-standardisation/263091/

48 www.stephenfry.com/2008/11/dont-mind-your-language%E2%80%A66/

49 www.youtube.com/watch?v=J7E-aoXLZGY

50 www.ohchr.org/en/issues/minorities/srminorities/pages/languagerights.aspx

51 www.linguisticsociety.org/content/human-rights-and-linguistics

52 https://cccc.ncte.org/cccc/resources/positions/srtolsummary

53 https://cccc.ncte.org/cccc/demand-for-black-linguistic-justice

54 A version of this chapter can be found here: https://fsgworkinprogress.com/2011/11/henry-hitchings-unholy-shit/

55 https://theconversation.com/wtf-slurs-offend-young-adults-more-than-swearing-125193

56 www.cbsnews.com/news/huckleberry-finn-and-the-n-word-debate/

57 http://compositionforum.com/issue/38/monolingualism.php

58 These two frames—plurilingual and translingual—are often used interchangeably. However, the latter tends to emphasize aspects of linguistic hybridity and performance that have not always been foregrounded in discussions of plurilingualism (García & Otheguy, 2020).

59 For more information and a cool infographic on pluralism, check out: www.pluralism.ca/who-we-are/#what-is-pluralism

60 "Self-monitoring" is an actual concept in second language acquisition theory, by the way!

61 We use "phenotypically" to reference physical traits that are often associated with racial groups.

62 Did you notice my rhetorical use of present tense verbs here? We talked about this in Unit 5.2., remember?

63 www.npr.org/transcripts/989477444

64 https://qz.com/1586592/a-linguists-trick-to-perfectly-understanding-accented-speakers/

65 https://swang.digitalscholar.rochester.edu/code-meshing/

66 www.insidehighered.com/advice/2021/01/27/how-professors-can-and-should-combat-linguistic-prejudice-their-classes-opinion

67 https://cccc.ncte.org/cccc/resources/positions https://ncte.org/resources/position-statements/all/#Language/179

68 http://newsmanager.commpartners.com/tesolheis/issues/2019-05-13/3.html

69 https://oakland.edu/oumagazine/news/cas/2021/oakland-university-launches-new-initiative-to-celebrate-linguistic-diversity

70 The collection is available on the Middlebury College webpage, with a link also at the Hub.

References

Affolter, T. L. (2019). *Through the fog: Towards inclusive anti-racist teaching*. IAP.

Ahmad, D. (2007). *Rotten English: A literary anthology*. WW Norton & Company Incorporated.

Atkinson, D. (2003). Writing and culture in the post-process era. *Journal of Second Language Writing, 12*(1), 49–63.

Babel, M., & Russell, J. (2015). Expectations and speech intelligibility. *The Journal of the Acoustical Society of America, 137*(5), 2823–2833.

Baese-Berk, M. M. (2019, April 3). A linguist's trick to perfectly understanding people with different accents. *Quartz* [online magazine]. https://qz.com/1586592/a-linguists-trick-to-perfectly-understanding-accented-speakers/

Baker-Bell, A. (2020). *Linguistic justice: Black language, literacy, identity, and pedagogy*. Routledge.

Ball, C. E., & Loewe, D. M. (2017). Bad ideas about writing. *Open Access*. https://commons.erau.edu/oer-main/3/.

Benesch, S. (1988). *Ending remediation: Linking ESL and content in higher education*. Teachers of English to Speakers of Other Languages.

Bergen, B. (2019, 8 November). WTF? Slurs offend young adults more than swearing. *The Conversation*. https://theconversation.com/wtf-slurs-offend-young-adults-more-than-swearing-125193

Blakemore, D. (2015). Slurs and expletives: A case against a general account of expressive meaning. *Language Sciences, 52*, 22–35.

Brehe, S. (2019). *Brehe's grammar anatomy*. University of North Georgia Press. https://open.umn.edu/opentextbooks/textbooks/717

Cameron, D. (1995/2012). *Verbal hygiene*. Routledge, Psychology Press.

Campano, G. (2019). *Immigrant students and literacy: Reading, writing, and remembering*. Teachers College Press.

Campo-Engelstein, L., & Johnson, N. L. (2014). Revisiting "the fertilization fairytale": An analysis of gendered language used to describe fertilization in science textbooks from middle school to medical school. *Cultural Studies of Science Education, 9*(1), 201–220.

Canagarajah, A. S. (2002). *Critical academic writing and multilingual students*. University of Michigan Press.

Casanave, C. P. (2005). *Writing games: Multicultural case studies of academic literacy practices in higher education*. Routledge.

Chaparro, S. (2014). The communicative burden of making others understand: Why critical language awareness is a must in all ESL (and non-ESL) classrooms. *Working Papers in Educational Linguistics (WPEL), 29*(1), 3x.

Connor, U. (1996). *Contrastive rhetoric: Cross-cultural aspects of second language writing.* Cambridge University Press.

Curzan, A. (2014). *Fixing English: Prescriptivism and language history.* Cambridge University Press.

Damron, J. (2003). What's the problem? A new perspective on ITA communication. *Journal of Graduate Teaching Assistant Development, 9*(2), 81–88.

Dudley-Evans, T. (1994). Academic text: The importance of the use and comprehension of hedges. *ASP* [online]. http://journals.openedition.org/asp/4054; https://doi.org/10.4000/asp.4054

Dunstan, S. B., & Jaeger, A. J. (2015). Dialect and influences on the academic experiences of college students. *The Journal of Higher Education, 86*(5), 777–803.

Eisner, C., & Vicinus, M. (2008). *Originality, imitation, and plagiarism: Teaching writing in the digital age.* University of Michigan Press.

Fan, Y., Shepherd, L. J., Slavich, E., Waters, D., Stone, M., Abel, R., & Johnston, E. L. (2019). Gender and cultural bias in student evaluations: Why representation matters. *PloS One, 14*(2), e0209749.

Ferreira, F. (2021). In defense of the passive voice. *American Psychologist, 76*(1), 145–153. https://doi.org/10.1037/amp0000620

Fry, S. (2008). *Don't mind your language.* www.stephenfry.com/2008/11/dont-mind-your-language%E2%80%A6/

García, O., Johnson, S. I., Seltzer, K., & Valdés, G. (2017). *The translanguaging classroom: Leveraging student bilingualism for learning.* Caslon.

García, O., & Otheguy, R. (2020). Plurilingualism and translanguaging: Commonalities and divergences. *International Journal of Bilingual Education and Bilingualism, 23*(1), 17–35.

Gegg-Harrison, W. (forthcoming). Encouraging playful, productive curiosity about language in the writing classroom. *Journal of Teaching Writing.*

Gere, A., Curzan, A., Hammond, J. W., Hughes, S., Li, R., Moos, A., Smith, K., Van Zanen, K., Wheeler, K. L., & Zanders, C. J. (2021). Communal justicing: Writing assessment, disciplinary infrastructure, and the case for critical language awareness. *College Composition and Communication, 72*(3), 384–412.

Godsil, D., Tropp, L. R., Goff, P. A., Powell, J. A., & MacFarlane, J. (2017). *The science of equality in education: The impact of implicit bias, racial anxiety, and stereotype threat on student outcomes.* Perception Institute.

Haan, J. & Gallagher, C. (2021). (Eds.). Linguistically responsive education in higher education contexts. [special issue of TESOL Quarterly]

Hartse, J. H. (2016). Writing as language in use: On the growing engagement between sociolinguistics and writing studies. *Composition Studies, 44*(1), 169–177.

Haviland, C. P., & Mullin, J. A. (2009). *Who owns this text?: Plagiarism, authorship, and disciplinary cultures.* https://digitalcommons.usu.edu/usupress_pubs/26/

Heckler, N. C., & Forde, D. R. (2015). The role of cultural values in plagiarism in higher education. *Journal of Academic Ethics, 13*(1), 61–75.

Hitchings, H. (2011). *The language wars: A history of proper English.* Farrar, Straus and Giroux.

Horner, B., & Tetreault, L. (Eds.). (2017). *Crossing divides: Exploring translingual writing pedagogies and programs.* University Press of Colorado.

Inoue, A. B. (2019). *Labor-based grading contracts: Building equity and inclusion in the compassionate writing classroom.* WAC Clearinghouse. https://wac.colostate.edu/books/perspectives/labor/

Johns, A. (1997). *Text, role, and context: Developing academic literacies.* Cambridge University Press.

Johnson, D., & VanBrackle, L. (2012). Linguistic discrimination in writing assessment: How raters react to African American "errors," ESL errors, and standard English errors on a state-mandated writing exam. *Assessing Writing, 17*(1), 35–54.

Kolln, M., & Gray, L. S. (2013). *Rhetorical grammar: Grammatical choices, rhetorical effects* (7th ed.). Pearson Education.

Lakoff, G., & Johnson, M. (2008). *Metaphors we live by.* University of Chicago Press.

Lea, M. R., & Street, B. V. (1998). Student writing in higher education: An academic literacies approach. *Studies in Higher Education, 23*(2), 157–172.

Lee, S., & Du, Q. (2020). Quantifying native speakerism in second language (L2) writing: A study of student evaluations of teaching. *Applied Linguistics, 42.*

Lippi-Green, R. (2012). *English with an accent: Language, ideology and discrimination in the United States.* Routledge.

Lillis, T. (2013). *Sociolinguistics of writing.* Edinburgh University Press.

Lillis, T., & Harrington, K. (Eds.). (2015). *Working with academic literacies: Case studies towards transformative practice.* WAC Clearinghouse, Parlor Press. https://wac.colostate.edu/books/perspectives/lillis/

Lindsey, P., & Crusan, D. (2011). How faculty attitudes and expectations toward student nationality affect writing assessment. *Across the Disciplines, 8*(4). https://wac.colostate.edu/atd/ell/lindsey-crusan.cfm

Lu, M. Z. (1987). From silence to words: Writing as struggle. *College English, 49*(4), 437–448.

Lucas, T., Villegas, A. M., & Freedson-Gonzalez, M. (2008). Linguistically responsive teacher education: Preparing classroom teachers to teach English language learners. *Journal of Teacher Education, 59*(4), 361–373.

Lunsford, A. A. (1999). Rhetoric, feminism, and the politics of textual ownership. *College English, 61*(5), 529–544.

Lunsford, A. A., & Lunsford, K. J. (2008). "Mistakes are a fact of life": A national comparative study. *College Composition and Communication,* 781–806.

Lyiscott, J. (2014). 3 ways to speak English. TED Talk. https://www.ted.com/talks/jamila_lyiscott_3_ways_to_speak_english

Marron, J. M. et al. (2020). Waging war on war metaphors in cancer and COVID-19. *JCO Oncology Practice, 16*(10), 624–627.

McWhorter, J. (2013). Txting is killing language. JK!!!. *TED Talk.* www.ted.com/talks/john_mcwhorter_txtng_is_killing_language_jk?language=en

Micciche, L. R. (2004). Making a case for rhetorical grammar. *College Composition and Communication, 55*(4), 716–737.

Mitchell, K. (2012). English is not all that matters in the education of secondary multilingual learners and their teachers. *International Journal of Multicultural Education, 14*(1).

Montecino, V. (1997). *Writing about metaphors in your discipline.* http://mason.gmu.edu/~montecin/metaphor-97.htm

Morenberg, M. (2014). *Doing grammar* (5th ed.). Oxford University Press.

Mueller, S. (2005). Documentation style and discipline-specific values. *Writing Lab Newsletter, 29*(6), 6–9. https://wlnjournal.org/archives/v29/29.6.pdf

Reeves, A. N. (2014). *Written in black & white: Exploring confirmation bias in racialized perceptions of writing skill.* Nexions. https://nextions.com/portfolio-posts/written-in-black-and-white-yellow-paper-series/

Rosa, J., & Flores, N. (2017). Unsettling race and language: Toward a raciolinguistic perspective. *Language in Society, 46*(5), 621–647.

Rubin, D. L. (1992). Nonlanguage factors affecting undergraduates' judgments of nonnative English-speaking teaching assistants. *Research in Higher Education, 33*(4), 511–531.

Schreiber, B., Fahim, N., Johnson, E., & Lee, E. (Eds.) (forthcoming). *Linguistic justice on campus Theory, pedagogy, and advocacy for multilingual writers.* Multilingual Matters.

Shapiro, S. (2009). *From isolated mediation to collaborative mediation: Confronting institutional isolation in EAP* [Unpublished dissertation from the University of Washington].

Shapiro, S. (2010a). Two birds, one stone: Using academic experiences as content for EAP courses. In S. Barduhn & J. Nordmeyer (Eds.), *Integrating language and content* (pp. 75–87). TESOL.

Shapiro, S. (2010b). Writing-to-embody: Engaging students in written role play. In S. Kasten (Ed.), *Effective second language writing* (pp. 31–38). TESOL.

Shapiro, S. (2011). Stuck in the remedial rut: Confronting resistance to ESL curriculum reform. *Journal of Basic Writing, 30*(2), 24–52.

Shapiro, S. (2020). Inclusive pedagogy in the academic writing classroom: Cultivating communities of belonging. *Journal of Academic Writing, 10*(1), 154–164. https://publications.coventry.ac.uk/index.php/joaw/article/view/607

Shapiro, S. (2022). "Language and social justice": A (surprisingly) plurilingual first-year seminar. In G. Shuck & K. Losey (Eds.), *Plurilingual pedagogies for multilingual writing classrooms: Engaging the rich communicative repertoires of U.S. students.* Routledge.

Shapiro, S., Cox, M., Shuck, G., & Simnitt, E. (2016). Teaching for agency: From appreciating linguistic diversity to empowering student writers. *Composition Studies, 44*(1), 31–52..

Shapiro, S., Farrelly, R., & Tomaš, Z. (2014/2018). *Fostering international student success in higher education.* TESOL/NAFSA.

Shapiro, S., & Leopold, L. (2012). A critical role for role-playing pedagogy. *TESL Canada Journal, 120.*

Shapiro, S., & Siczek, M. (2017). Strategic content: How globally-oriented writing courses can bridge pedagogical and political spaces. In B. Smith & N. DeJoy (Eds.), *Cross-language communication and the academy: Re-thinking orientations.* University of Michigan Press.

Shen, F. (1989). The classroom and the wider culture: Identity as a key to learning English composition. *College Composition and Communication, 40*(4), 459–466.

Shuck, G., & Losey, K. (Eds.). (2022). *Plurilingual pedagogies for multilingual writing classrooms: Engaging the rich communicative repertoires of U.S. Students.* Routledge.

Smitherman, G. (1986). *Talkin and testifyin: The language of Black America.* Wayne State University Press.

Strickland, A. L. (2010). *"Sounding white": African-American attitudes toward "whiteness" in the speech of African-Americans.* Purdue University.

Tannen, D. (1998). *The argument culture: Moving from debate to dialogue.* Random House Incorporated.

Taylor, S. K., & Snoddon, K. (2013). Plurilingualism in TESOL: Promising controversies. *TESOL Quarterly, 439*–445.

Thomas, H., & Hirsch, A. (2016). A progressive's style guide. *Sum of Us.* https://s3.amazonaws.com/s3.sumofus.org/images/sumofus_progressive-styleguide.pdf

Tomaš, Z., & Shapiro, S. (2021). From crisis to opportunity: Turning questions about "plagiarism" into conversations about linguistically responsive pedagogy. *TESOL Quarterly.*

Truss, L. (2005). *Eats, shoots & leaves: The zero tolerance approach to punctuation.* Penguin.

Watson, M., & Shapiro, R. (2018). Clarifying the multiple dimensions of monolingualism: Keeping our sights on language politics. *Composition Forum, 38.* www.compositionforum.com/issue/38/monolingualism.php

Weaver, M. M. (2019). "I still think there's a need for proper, academic, standard English": Examining a teacher's negotiation of multiple language ideologies. *Linguistics and Education, 49,* 41–51. https://doi.org/10.1016/j.linged.2018.12.005

Villanueva, V. (1993). *Bootstraps: From an American academic of color.* National Council of Teachers of English

Young, V. A. (2007). *Your average nigga: Performing race, literacy, and masculinity.* Wayne State University Press.

6
The Media/Discourse Analysis Pathway

Introduction

Media literacy. It's hot topic these days in families and communities, as well as among educators. We have seen the important role that social media plays in our students' lives—and in our own! Many of us are concerned about the impact of filter bubbles, fake news, and cancel culture. We know that our work as teachers of literacy should include preparing students to navigate this increasingly complex media landscape. The question at the heart of this chapter, then is: *What does it look like to engage media literacy from a CLA perspective?*

First, though, we have to define what we mean by "media"—not an easy task! Students may think first of social media or entertainment media. In contrast, when I hear "media"—or "the media," more accurately—I think of news or information media. In education, we also talk about "media" in terms of modes of learning and expression (e.g., "multi-media"). All of these types of media have been the focus of linguistics research, and all can be incorporated into CLA Pedagogy. In this chapter, though, we will focus first on social and digital media (Unit 6.1) and will then turn to news/information media (Units 6.2 and 6.3). However, this does not mean we are ignoring entertainment media! In Chapter 4, we talked about patterns of language variation in literature, film, and television. And in Chapter 5, we referenced social media as a place where we can observe prescriptivist attitudes—for example, in grammar memes. Chapter 7 will return to multi-media, too, in the unit on Writing-as-(Re)design.

This chapter isn't just about media, though—it's also about *discourse*, which we defined in Chapter 2 as "language as it is used in the real world." One

DOI: 10.4324/9781003171751-9

goal of this chapter is to make discourse *come alive* for you and your students! This Pathway is informed by scholarship in many fields that study discourse, including critical linguistics (see Chapter 2), as well as media/ communication studies and rhetoric/composition (e.g., Lunsford, 2007). It also builds on work from critical literacy scholars who incorporate CLA in their work (e.g., Janks, 2010; Rogers & Mosley Wetzel, 2013; Vasquez et al., 2019). One of the key contributions of these scholars is the idea that students need to be both **critics** and **creators** of discourse—something we will explore as well in Chapter 7.

This focus on both critique and creation is a central feature as well of Critical Race Theory (CRT) scholarship. CRT was first developed by legal studies scholars as a way to understand and work against systemic racism, and has since been taken up in a number of other fields, including education (e.g., Ladson-Billings, 1998; Solórzano & Yosso, 2002). One of the central methodologies used in CRT scholarship is **critical storytelling**, which focuses on identifying societal "master narratives"—i.e., dominant stories told in history books and other culturally powerful texts, usually written by White folk—and creating for "counter-stories" that center voices and perspectives of Black, Indigenous, and People of Color (BIPOC). Critical storytelling has been taken up in other social justice approaches to scholarship as well, including within work informed by feminist and queer theory (e.g., Warhol & Lanser, 2015). (There are a lot of excellent introductions to CRT and critical storytelling online, by the way, including from the American Bar Association[1] and *Time Magazine*.[2])

Part of what I love about the Media/Discourse Analysis pathway is that it makes concepts like *discourse* and *critical theory* more tangible and accessible to students. As the writer David Foster Wallace put it in a 2005 commencement address entitled "This Is the Water," discussed briefly in Chapter 5, "the most obvious, important realities are often the ones that are hardest to see and talk about." By looking closely and critically at discourse, we begin to see the water we are swimming in—the stories and ideologies that can hinder or further the cause of social justice.

I also love that the Media/Discourse Analysis pathway is also applicable to a wide range of educational contexts. We can use Critical Discourse Analysis (CDA—see Chapter 2) to examine academic, professional, and artistic texts, as well as everyday language used in both public and private interactions. Many students tell me they had "no idea" they could do this sort of textual analysis outside of a literature class!

Learning Goals

Essential Questions

Below are ten Essential Questions that undergird much of the learning along the Media/Discourse Analysis pathway. I have noted the CLA goal(s) most pertinent to each (**SR** = self-reflection, **SJ** = social justice, **RA** = rhetorical agency).

1   How do we perform identities and relationships in computer-mediated communication (CMC)? (SR, RA)
2   What tools and strategies do linguists and other researchers use to analyze language use and variation in CMC? (SJ, RA)
3   How do we see power dynamics at work in CMC? (SR, RA, SJ)
4   What is the relationship between language and inclusion on social media and in news reporting? (SR, SJ, RA)
5   What does it mean to be an ethical digital citizen? (SR, SJ, RA)
6   How can we trace political and ideological bias in news reporting? (SJ, RA)
7   How can we recognize and fight mis/disinformation? (SR, SJ, RA)
8   How is cultural storytelling connected to power? (SR, SJ, RA)
9   What can critical analysis of news media discourse teach us about social change? (SR, SJ, RA)
10   How can we seek out and amplify counter-stories from communities that are often missing or misrepresented within the dominant discourse? (SR, SJ, RA)

Transferable Skills

Students will be able to (SWBAT) . . .

A   **Analyze** digital interactions using concepts from linguistics
B   **Identify** features of computer-mediated communication (CMC), including in their own digital idiolects (when texting, using social media, etc.)
C   **Connect** their learning about media/discourse analysis to their daily experience as users of digital and social media
D   **Understand** how power dynamics function in written discourse (e.g., inclusion/exclusion, dehumanization, dominant narratives, counter-stories)

E   **Reflect** on—and possibly **Revise**—their habits as digital citizens, including as news consumers
F   **Identify** the linguistic elements of political bias and mis/disinformation in news media and elsewhere online
G   **Apply** critical/close reading strategies to a range of textual genres
H   **Design and conduct** a research project informed by Critical Discourse Analysis (CDA)
I   **Trace** master narratives and counter-stories in a variety of media

Overview of Units

Unit 6.1: Language, Identity, and Power in Digital Spaces (EQs 1, 2, 3, 4, and 5; Skills A, B, C, D, and E). This unit considers language norms and variation in social media, texting, and other CMC. Students discuss how they perform identities, strengthen relationships, and negotiate power online. Culminating assignments include genre translation ("remediation") and peer-to-peer research projects.

Unit 6.2: Savvy and Ethical News Consumers: (EQs 3, 4, 5, 6, 7, and 8; Skills C, D, E, F, G, and H). This unit engages students in critical conversations about the role of journalism in democracy, the habits of news media consumption, and the linguistic and rhetorical features of news articles. We also learn to identify and measure political bias in news media coverage and to debunk misinformation ("fake news"). Assignments include a news consumer autobiography and a linguistic analysis of news headlines.

Unit 6.3: Critiquing Frames and Narratives (EQs 2, 3, 8, and 9; Skills C, D, H, and I). This unit builds on the learning from Unit 6.2 but focuses more broadly on cultural narratives and counter-stories. Students learn to identify and critique discursive frames (e.g., deficit vs. asset) and to trace those frames in news articles. They write letters to the editor and learn to design and undertake discourse analysis projects focused on news media coverage.

Table 6.1 The Media/Discourse Analysis Pathway (At-a-Glance)

	Concepts/Topics	Readings/Resources	Activities/ Assignments
Unit 6.1: Language, Identity,	Features of computer-mediated	Podcasts (Codeswitch, On the Media, Lingthusiasm)	* Jigsaw survey * Reading workshop

(continued)

Table 6.1 (continued)

	Concepts/Topics	Readings/Resources	Activities/ Assignments
and Power in Digital Spaces (pp. 182–190)	communication (CMC) Textese Digital idiolect Cancel culture Calling-out (vs. calling-in) Cyberbullying/ online harassment	News articles (BBC, *BuzzFeed, Forbes, Guardian, NYTimes, The Conversation*) Research/reports (NIH, Pew Research, *Psychology Today,* U.S. Dept of Health and Human Services) Educational resources (e.g., Learning for Justice)	* Study share * Interaction analysis * Genre remediation * Peer-to-peer research
Unit 6.2: Savvy and Ethical News Media Consumers (pp. 191–199).	Role of news media in democracy Ethics of journalism News media consumption habits, etc. Features of news articles Measuring news bias Identifying "fake news" Combatting mis/ disinformation	Research organizations (American Press Institute, Pew Research; University programs: Columbia, MIT, Stanford) Educational organizations/ resources (Ad Fontes Media, Common Sense Media, Literacy Now; *On the Media* podcast) Open-access journals/ textbooks (*Columbia Journalism Review;* Caulfield, 2017) News articles (*Forbes, Guardian, Reuters, Poynter*)	* Circle share * Discussions of news media habits * Media analysis practice * News media autobiography * Headline analysis paper

	Concepts/Topics	Readings/Resources	Activities/ Assignments
Unit 6.3: Critiquing Frames and Narratives (pp. 200–212)	Framing Narrative Critical Race Theory Master narrative Counter-story Sourcing (in news media) Deficit vs. asset discourse Dehumanizing language Discourse Analysis	Adichie's (2009) TED talk ("Danger of Single Story") Scholarly analyses of news coverage (Benson & Wood, 2015; Crawley et al., 2016) Online reports/ guides (e.g., *Citizen's Handbook*, On the Media, Pew Research) News and blogs (*NYTimes, PBS, Politico, Psychology Today, Wall Street Journal*)	* Watch/discuss Adichie * What's trending? * Guided CDA practice * Letter to the editor * Independent CDA projects (multi-phase)

Unit 6.1: Language, Identity, and Power in Digital Spaces

Overview

This unit engages CLA learning in relation to computer mediated communication (CMC), including texting, social media, and other online interactions. One of our goals is to help students really see the "water" they are swimming in digitally—i.e., to view their everyday CMC interactions through a critical lens. In this way, what is *familiar* to them becomes *unfamiliar*, which broadens their perspective on how language and power function in the world (Abe & Shapiro, 2021).

Learning Sequence

Tapping into Prior Knowledge

Students tend to bring a great deal of experience with CMC to the classroom: They often take this topic and run with it! However, they may not run in the direction we are intending. More than once, I have seen a thoughtful class conversation about language and power in digital spaces devolve into a "free-for-all" about technology in general. We need to provide enough **structure and direction** to keep the conversation connected to our CLA goals of self-reflection, social justice, and rhetorical agency. Here is a starter list of questions that can be used for freewriting, pair or small group conversations, or in one of my favorite in-class activities, **jigsaw survey** (explained below).

1   What communities do you connect to using social media, and on which platforms?
2   With whom do you interact most via text? How different are these "private" exchanges from the more "public" ones on social media?
3   What are some features of your social media idiolect? (i.e., how might someone recognize a text/post from you, specifically? This could include spelling, punctuation, word choice, emoji use, etc.)
4   How much do you vary your idiolect, depending on your interlocutor(s)— i.e., the person(s) you are communicating with? For example, how do your text exchanges with parents/elders differ from those with your friends?
5   How do your CMC interactions vary depending on the particular social media platform or application you're using (e.g., Twitter vs. Instagram vs. TikTok)?

6   What kinds of communication do you think texting/social media encourages? What kinds does it prevent or discourage? (i.e., What is it *not* good for?)
7   What—if any—texting/social media language has made its way into your spoken idiolect? (e.g., "brb," "sus" "LOL"). When and with whom do you use this type of language?
8   What are some of the linguistic features and strategies you could classify as "cyberbullying" or "online harassment"? How frequently do you see examples of this in your own CMC interactions?

Activity: Jigsaw Survey

Like "jigsaw reading" (see Chapter 4), this activity begins with information-gathering and ends with information-sharing. In a jigsaw survey, each student chooses (or is assigned) one of the questions in a given list. For example, if a class of 24 students is using the above list, there would be three students assigned to each question. Students have 15–20 minutes to mill about and do "micro-interviews" with as many students as possible, focused only on their single question. I provide a **note-taking sheet** (see Table 6.2), and I often put music on while they are mingling, to create the feeling of a social mixer.

I remind students to keep moving, so that they have a **range of responses** by the time they finish. Afterward, they take time to review their notes—alone or with others who had the same question—and identify some trends or highlights. I usually structure the debrief by question (e.g., those who had question 1, those who had question 2, etc.). In classes focused on building writing skills, I may ask students to write a summary/response paper as the homework for next class.

Table 6.2 Note-Taking Sheet (Top Portion) for Jigsaw Survey

Interviewer: Question:

STUDENT INTERVIEWED	RESPONSE (QUOTE OR PARAPHRASE)	MY NOTES/ COMMENTS

Topic #1: Linguistic Patterns and Practices in CMC

Here are some questions and resources we can use to explore language use in digital spaces:

1   What are typical **linguistic features of "textese" and/or other CMC?** (e.g., from Colorado Public Radio[3]; see also work by Gretchen McCulloch,[4] a specialist in internet linguistics, and co-host of the podcast, *Lingthusiasm*[5]—see Figure 6.1).

2   How has **CMC varied** over time, as well as by user and platform?[6] (e.g., *Time* article[7] about teenage girls on Instagram; the *Atlantic*[8] on the evolution of emojis; the *Guardian*'s "Twitter-speak" quiz[9])

3   How do users employ **rhetorical grammar in CMC?** (e.g., *BuzzFeed*[10] on avoidance of periods, *NYTimes*[11] on "tone indicators")

4   What issues related to **diversity and inclusion arise in relation to CMC?** (e.g., on skin color in emojis, from NPR's *Codeswitch* podcast[12]; on issues of cultural appropriation and internet slang, from *Business Insider*[13])

Students are usually eager to share examples of their own CMC exchanges illustrating some of the above issues and patterns. Of course, they first need to get permission from their interlocutor(s) and/or to "black out" any identifying information. We can use students' examples to draw additional comparisons between CMC and spoken IRL ("in real life") interactions, such as:

• **Turn-taking:** How do interlocutors signal that they are listening? How do they negotiate turn-taking to ensure that no one feels excluded or interrupted?

Figure 6.1 Logo from *Lingthusiasm* Podcast

- **Affect:** How do interlocutors convey humor, sarcasm, empathy, anger, and other emotions that are usually expressed IRL with vocal intonation and/or body language?
- **Conflict resolution:** What strategies and features of CMC do we use to work through conflict? How do they decide when to switch to real-time conversation?

Unit 7.1 delves further into power dynamics in interpersonal interaction, including concepts and strategies for analyzing conversational "power plays"— or what linguists call **asymmetrical talk** (pp. 231-232). The concepts and strategies presented there can also be applied to CMC interactions, both public and private.

Additional Topics for Unit 6.1

To deepen and/or personalize in this unit, we can engage some of the following questions, which have to do with power dynamics in CMC. These can be nice lead-ins to structured debate/role play (see examples in Chapters 4 and 5) and/or persuasive writing assignments.

1   Is social media (or "anti-social media," as critics call it) **hindering our ability to communicate IRL?** (e.g., BBC,[14] *Psychology Today*[15]).

2   How has **public opinion** about social media/CMC changed over time? (e.g., studies by the Pew Research Center [PRC][16]).

3   What, really, is "**cancel culture**"? What is it good for? What are its dangers? (e.g., *Guardian*,[17] NPR,[18] and the *On the Media* podcast,[19] which references a popular video essay[20] on cancel culture by Natalie Wynn)

4   How common is **cyber-bulling/online harassment**? How can linguistic analysis of "big data" help to combat it? (e.g., PRC[21]—see Figure 6.2; see also Golbeck et al., 2017[22]; Van Hee et al., 2018[23]).

Activity: Empirical Study Share

Many of the readings/media referenced above cite empirical research (e.g., from surveys, interviews, or corpus studies). Reading empirical studies can be quite challenging, since most articles are not written for a general (or student) audience. I sometimes offer mini-workshops on **working with difficult readings**, in which we review strategies such as the following:

- Using knowledge of genre features (e.g., abstract, section headings) to guide the reading process
- Reading selectively, and sometimes out of sequence
- Self-assessing for engagement and comprehension

Chapter 9 has additional tips for supporting students with academic reading.

Students can apply these strategies to a **"study share"** assignment, which is a version of "jigsaw reading" (p. 96). They locate a research study relevant to a topic of interest and read it with the goal of sharing highlights with peers. We can require that they include at least one graph, table, or figure from the article, so that they gain practice talking about data visualization. Students can also write about their study, either in a typical academic genre (e.g., summary/response) or can represent key findings in alternative medium, as discussed below.

Demonstrating Learning for Unit 6.1

The two assignments below work particularly well for this unit, but can be used with other units as well.

Assignment #1: Genre Remediation[24]

"Remediation" is a term that has had negative connotations in writing/literacy education (e.g., Shapiro, 2011), but it is used quite differently among experts in digital literacy (e.g., Bolter & Grusin, 2000). **Remediating a text** means translating it for another genre, medium, and/or audience. This can be an informal class activity or homework assignment, or could be scaled up to a multi-phased project. After students have engaged with the text they wish to remediate, they follow these steps:

1   Analyze—and possibly report on—the linguistic and rhetorical features of the intended genre/medium
2   Create a first draft of the "translation" and, if possible, solicit feedback from a member (or more) of the intended audience

Compared with 2017, similar share of Americans have experienced any type of online harassment – but more severe encounters have become more common

% of U.S. adults who say they have personally experienced the following behaviors online

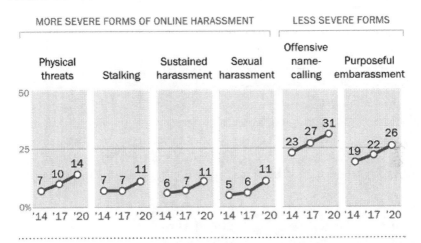

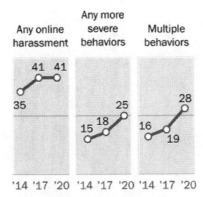

Note: Those who did not give an answer are not shown.
Source: Survey of U.S. adults conducted Sept. 8-13, 2020.
"The State of Online Harassment"

PEW RESEARCH CENTER

Figure 6.2 Findings from Pew Research Study in January 2021 on Increases in Online Harassment

3   Revise based on feedback and submit the final draft along with a Writer's Memo (see Chapter 9) explaining their rhetorical choices

Final products for this sort of assignment are often multimodal—e.g., tweets or blog posts, short video recordings (e.g., for TikTok or Youtube), or drawings/visuals (e.g., Sketchnotes[25]). Chapters 5 and 7 include other examples of writing for public audiences.

Assignment #2: Peer-to-Peer Research

One way to ensure that students continue to examine the "water" of CMC is to have them conduct their own empirical research. The final project for my English Grammar: Concepts and Controversies course (see Chapter 5), which includes a set of readings on technology and digital communication, is a primary research study with peers, instructors, or family/community members as participants. Students can work alone or with a partner, but each submits their own report. Below is an abbreviated version of the assignment description.

Independent Research Project (Five-Minute "Mini-Presentation," Plus 4–5-Page Written Report)

This project gives you an opportunity to deepen your course learning. This is **NOT** a library (secondary) research project. Rather, it requires that you **gather original data** via a survey (at least ten participants) OR set of interviews (minimum three participants). Your goal is to answer a *specific question* about grammar usage or prescriptivist attitudes about language. Some students focus their research on a particular grammar structure or common error, while others students investigate broader, sociolinguistic issues (examples of each will be shared in class). In your individual written report, you will answer the following questions:

1   What did you do for your research and why? (Rationale and Methods)
2   What did you expect to find and why? (Hypothesis)
3   What did you actually find? (Findings)
4   What makes these findings useful or noteworthy? Were there any surprises? (Implications)
5   What did you learn overall from doing this project? (Reflection)

Here is a representative sampling of research questions students have investigated for this assignment, with their chosen method. I have included several examples related to CMC, as well a few on other topics, to illustrate the range of possibilities:

- Which abbreviations do students use most frequently in texts, and with whom? (Survey)
- What expressions from texting do students use most frequently in their spoken interactions with friends? (Survey)
- What judgments do students (or instructors) make about each other based on their use of standard vs. non-standard spelling and punctuation conventions in text messages? (Survey)
- How prescriptivist are coaches in their judgments about grammatical errors in emails with athletes and recruits? (Survey)
- What do first-generation college students (and/or their family members) think it means to "sound educated"? (Interviews)
- How—if at all—do male and female students differ in their attitudes toward use of profanity in the classroom? (Interviews)

Benefits of this Assignment Include:

- Students have an opportunity to share course learning with other people in their lives.
- Students get a taste of what it is like to do empirical research.
- The write-up is fairly straightforward and does not require too much scaffolding. I do make copies of work from previous students available, though, for those who need more explicit modeling (see the online Hub for examples).

Some Additional Tips When Working with Students on This Assignment:

- Many students struggle with the difference between "primary" and "secondary" research. It helps to frame this project as **social science research with human subjects.**
- I do not require students to undergo human subjects review with an institutional review board [IRB], but that would be necessary if they wanted to present or publish their research for an outside audience.
- It is helpful—and time-saving, in the long run—to require a short, written project proposal early in the process, and/or to have a short meetings to talk through ideas.

- Students often need support in designing effective questionnaires and interview protocols.. Although I do not spend much class time on this, I do provide a few written tips, and students can submit early drafts of their questions for feedback. I also *strongly* urge students to **pilot surveys and interviews** with one or two people they trust, in order to get feedback on clarity and relevance of questions, estimated time for completion, etc. (see the Hub for more tips and resources to support student research).
- The grade for this assignment is based almost entirely on "content"—i.e., on whether students answered the five questions in the assignment description. However, if the writing is unclear, I give the student an opportunity to revise their report. (See Chapter 9 for more on "clarity" as a focus in feedback and revision.)

****

Unit 6.2: Savvy and Ethical News Consumers

Introduction

The newest course I have developed at Middlebury College is called "Narratives in the News Media," and it is by far my most "popular" in terms of student demand. It's not me, though—it's the topic! Many of our students, like us, recognize links between the news media and broader societal issues such as political polarization, misinformation, and concerns about the future of democracy.

Of course, there is no way we can address all of these issues in a single unit or two. News media literacy needs to be a sustained, cross-curricular endeavor that starts in primary grades and continues through postsecondary education and into civic/community life. There are, in fact, many organizations trying to make this happen in the U.S. (e.g., Common Sense Media[26] and Media Literacy Now[27]) and abroad (e.g., the United Kingdom's Center for Media Literacy[28]).

Critical Discourse Analysis (CDA), which we discussed above and in Chapter 2, is one of the most commonly used frameworks for analyzing news media. As Douka et al. (2017) explain, "news texts construct social reality from certain ideological perspectives" (p. 329). This unit builds on that insight, deepening students' knowledge about the functions and features of news media and their critical awareness about their news media habits. In the unit that follows (6.3), we will take a deeper dive into CDA skills and assignments, focusing not just on news media stories, but also on broader societal narratives. Both units include excerpts from student projects written for public audiences—like you!

Learning Sequence

Tapping into Prior Knowledge

On the first day of "Narratives in the News Media" course ("Narratives" for short), I facilitate a "circle share" session. **Circle sharing** is an activity used in many approaches to education and community organizing (e.g., restorative justice, anti-racism). It is sometimes referred to by other names, such as "Reflective Structured Dialogue" (Gower et al., 2020). This activity uses intentional structures and procedures to increase participation, promote deep listening, and build sense of community.[29] Every student has an opportunity to speak and a time limit (usually no more than two minutes), which helps to draw out voices that may not be heard in a typical, "popcorn style" discussion—including the voices of students from multilingual and multidialectal backgrounds (see Chapters 7 and 9 for more on this).

Activity: Circle Share

A circle share usually centers on an open-ended question—ideally one that invites a personal story, since one key tenet of dialogic approaches is, "behind every belief is a story." For my "Narratives" class, we begin with these two questions:

> *What is one social issue or community that you follow closely in the news?*
>
> *Why is this story/issue important to you?*

Here are the general steps I follow, drawing on what I have learned from experts in dialogic pedagogy (e.g., Essential Partners; Kibler et al., 2021): First, I **explain the purpose and structure** for the activity. It is particularly important to make clear that the goal is to deepen understanding rather than to change others' views. If the topic of the circle is more sensitive or controversial, we may spend some time talking about **norms or "ground rules"** for discussion (see Chapter 9 for more). Next, I give students some **processing time.** This could involve free-writing or talking in pairs or small groups. Students might even have until the next class period to prepare.

When facilitating the circle, it is important to **monitor time.** We can do this ourselves or involve students—for example, asking the person who just shared to keep an eye on time for the speaker that follows. Students always have the option to "pass"—another important feature for the activity to feel inclusive. If time allows, it can be helpful to debrief the activity, asking questions such as: *What patterns or contrasts did you observe in the responses? What have you learned overall about your peers from this activity?*

As we continue the learning in this unit, we can facilitate other circle shares on topics such as:

- What is one common misconception that people often have about a social issue or community that you follow closely in the news? What gets lost in the "master narrative"?

- What is one habit you have as a news consumer that you are proud of?
- What is one habit you would like to change? Why?

Topic #1: News Media 101

To explore our theme of savvy and ethical news consumers, we first need to build our knowledge base about some "basics" of journalism and news consumption, since students may have gaps in their understanding. Some assume, for example, that all news sources are equally biased, and they may not have learned to distinguish between quality journalism and "infotainment."

Here are some questions and resources that are useful in this exploration phase:

1   What is the role of **news media within a democracy?** (e.g., MIT Press[30])
2   What **ethical codes/standards** are professional journalists expected to adhere to? (e.g., from the Society of Professional Journalists[31])
3   What are the pros and cons of using the **metaphor of "consumption"** for our engagement with news? (e.g., *Columbia Journalism Review*[32] and Figure 6.3; a related concept useful to learn here is "attention economy"—*Forbes*[33])
4   How do typical **news media attitudes and habits** vary by age, gender, race/ethnicity, political affiliation, etc.? (American Press Institute [API][34]; PRC[35])

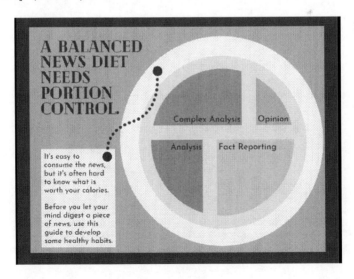

Figure 6.3 Image from Student John Schurer's "Healthy News Diets" Guide for Students

Students also begin to learn strategies for **analyzing the content of news media articles**, including:

- **Headlines:** Does the headline indicate Who, What, Why, and Where? Does it use linguistic strategies for engagement and conciseness—e.g., vivid word choice, metaphors, word play, noun stacking? (ThoughtCo[36] and WikiHow[37]—see also p. 199).
- **Structure:** Does the article use an inverted pyramid, hourglass, or other structure? (API[38])
- **Sourcing:** Are there voices of authorities and of individuals affected by the event/issue? Are multiple perspectives represented? If anonymous sources are used, is there a clear rationale? (API[39] NPR,[40] Trusting News project[41]); see also Figure 6.4)

NOTE: We will return to sourcing and other aspects of news storytelling in Unit 6.3.

Topic #2: Investigating Media Bias, Misinformation, and "Fake News"

Once students have built some a base of core knowledge and skills, we can delve further into some of the complexities within the current news media landscape. The goal here is to encourage self-reflection and rhetorical agency, so that students become more "savvy" in their use/consumption of news media.

1   How do researchers **measure political/ideological bias** in news media?

- Media bias charts (e.g., Ad Fontes Media[42]; AllSides[43]), including the methods used to create the charts and limitations of those methods (see also *Poynter*[44])
- Studies of public misconceptions about media bias and "fake news" (e.g., from API[45] and PRC[46])

2   What really is **"fake news,"** and how can we identify it?

- Explanations of **misinformation vs. disinformation**—the latter of which involves intentional deception (*Business Insider*[47] and *On the Media*[48])

- Studies of how textual analysis of big data can help detect mis/disinformation (e.g., San Francisco University[49] and the *Guardian*[50])

3   How can we contribute to a **healthier information ecosystem**?

- Tips for diversifying our news media diets (e.g., from *NYTimes*[51]; also see the John's "nutrition plate" [Figure 6.3], which includes four different types of news)
- Strategies for debunking misinformation (e.g., Caulfield's [2017] "SIFT method"[52]; see Figure 6.5)
- More on **information environmentalism** as a social and educational movement (NPR[53])

In Chapter 7, we will see other examples of student work that promotes information literacy in relation to current social issues.

Sourcing is...

where the journalist gets information or input for an article.

Sourcing can include interviews of civilians, statistics from datasets, or statements from organizations such as local police forces, NGOs, or government agencies.

When looking at how a journalist uses sources in an article, consider the following questions:

▷ Is the source an expert in their field?

▷ Is the source anonymous?

▷ What kind of information does the source provide?

Figure 6.4 Explanation of Sourcing, from Guide by Students Emily Clarkson and Brigett Weinstein

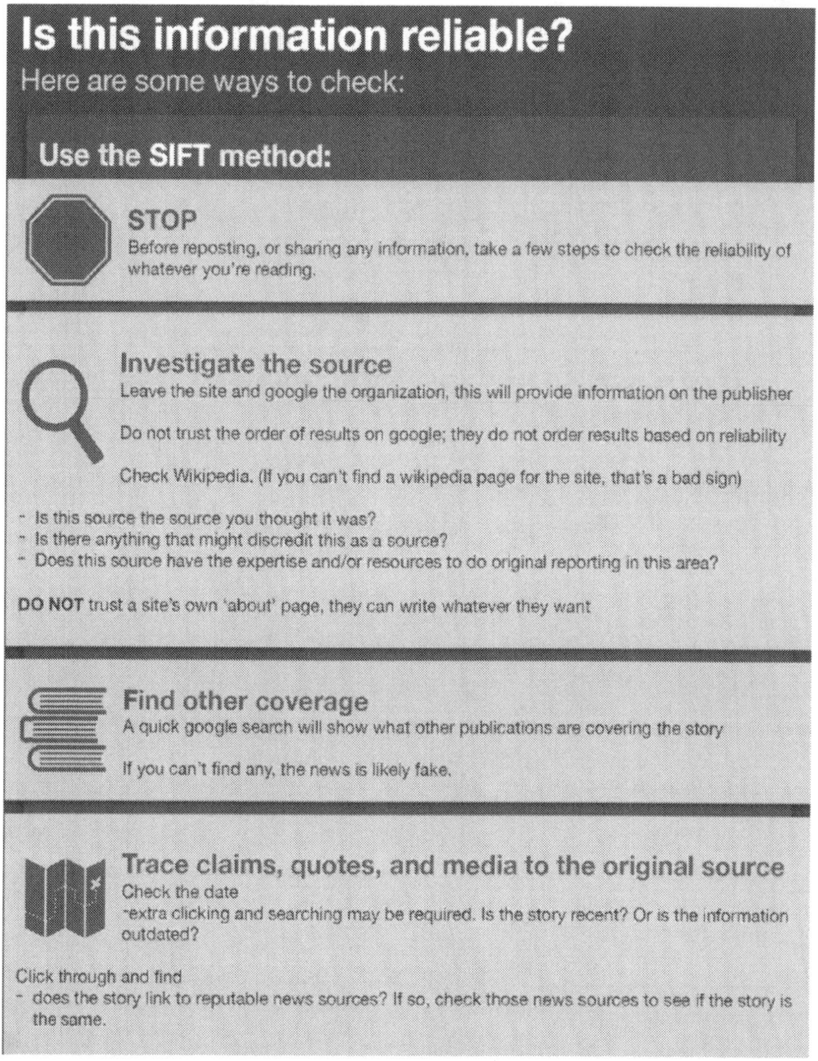

Is this information reliable?
Here are some ways to check:

Use the SIFT method:

STOP
Before reposting, or sharing any information, take a few steps to check the reliability of whatever you're reading.

Investigate the source
Leave the site and google the organization, this will provide information on the publisher

Do not trust the order of results on google; they do not order results based on reliability

Check Wikipedia. (If you can't find a wikipedia page for the site, that's a bad sign)

- Is this source the source you thought it was?
- Is there anything that might discredit this as a source?
- Does this source have the expertise and/or resources to do original reporting in this area?

DO NOT trust a site's own 'about' page, they can write whatever they want

Find other coverage
A quick google search will show what other publications are covering the story

If you can't find any, the news is likely fake.

Trace claims, quotes, and media to the original source
Check the date
extra clicking and searching may be required. Is the story recent? Or is the information outdated?

Click through and find
- does the story link to reputable news sources? If so, check those news sources to see if the story is the same.

Figure 6.5 An Infographic Created by Student Becca Clark, Explaining the SIFT Method

Demonstrating Learning for Unit 6.2

For this unit, I use assignments that demonstrate both critical reflection and the application of knowledge and skills related to news media literacy.

Assignment 1: News Media Autobiography

This assignment is similar to other autobiographical essays (e.g., from Unit 4.2) that invite students to reflect critically on their attitudes and lived experiences. In this case, students are also asked to answer the question: *Am I a 'typical' Millennial/GenZ news consumer?* In other words, they take their reflection—and their writing skills—a step further, by comparing their personal habits with findings from reports we have read and discussed for class.

Organization can be a bit of a challenge with this assignment. As with other compare/contrast-type essays, the structure that usually works best is a point-by-point comparison, in which students write about one aspect of their experience at a time, and then compare that aspect with data from secondary sources. I sometimes provide sentence scaffolds to help model these rhetorical moves, inspired by Graff and Birkenstein's (2018) *They Say, I Say.* Here are two examples:

1   "I get much of my news from ___. This is similar to student participants cited in ___."
2   "Unlike the GenZ consumers cited in ____, I do not engage much with news stories on Instagram or Facebook. Instead, I ___."

Below is the rubric I use to grade this assignment:

Depth of self-reflection: /20
Use of detail (personal examples, etc.): /20
Tie-ins to secondary sources (readings/media from class): /30
Organization and transitions (structure, etc.): /15
Clarity, tone, style, etc.: /15

Assignment 2: Headline Analysis

Our first CDA-oriented assignment in "Narratives" focuses on headlines. I have found that analyzing a collection of headlines feels less daunting to students than doing more in-depth analysis of entire articles—although that is where we are headed eventually in Unit 6.3! Here is a slightly abbreviated version of the assignment overview from my course syllabus:

Headline Analysis paper (3–4 pages, double-spaced)

You will choose one news story and compile a list of 10–20 headlines on that story. Make sure you're noting the date, type of publication, location, etc. for each headline. Also make sure the story tied to a specific point in time—not just about a general issue or event! You will then analyze those headlines, drawing on course readings and lectures. Your paper should advance a thesis about **whether and how bias is present** in the headlines about that particular story.

This assignment is relatively short, but still presents a few challenges: First, students must identify a story that is narrow enough in scope to be pinned to a particular date, so that they can compile a set of headlines that can be contrasted. I often use the phrase "apples to apples" to stress that the headlines must be **similar enough to identify meaningful differences**. If, for example, some headlines are from editorials and others from news features, students will, of course, notice differences, but those differences have more to do with the genre (editorial vs. news report) than with journalist's rhetorical and linguistic choices.

Once they have their collection of headlines—their "mini-corpus," I call it—students may also struggle with where to begin and end their analysis. I scaffold this phase in the following ways:

1   We read and discuss **published headline analysis studies** (e.g., Bleich et al., 2018[54]; see also the University of Texas's Center for Media Engagement[55]). We also look at work from previous students (see the Hub for samples).
2   We **practice headline analysis** during class and/or in online discussion. Below are some useful terms and examples:

Linguistic strategies commonly used in headlines, with examples

Alliteration: "Blizzard Stops City Cold" [also uses **cliché**] (*NY Daily News*)

Allusion: "No-mageddon: The Washington DC Snow Hole" [also uses **word play**] (*Washington Post*)

Cliché: "The Snow Must Go On" [also uses **word play**] (*Wall Street Journal*)

Metaphor: "New York Socked by Snow!" [also uses **passive voice** and **personification**] (*NY Post*)

Noun stacking: "A Few Snow Showers, but No Storm or Freeze on Horizon" (*Boston Globe*)

Word play: "The Brrrrfect Storm!" [also uses **cliché**] (*Delaware State News*)

3   When possible, I **set aside class time** for independent work, during which students can ask questions of me and of each other. A quick side note, here: I have *never* regretted building this into the process. Sometimes a bit of in-class work time, with real-time support available, is enough get students on track to continue successfully on their own.

4   Students have multiple opportunities to **talk through** the analysis and write-up, including the option of revising the final draft.

5   I provide a variety of tips and resources throughout the process, including:

- **Search tools** (Google News, Nexis, and/or Proquest Historical Newspapers)
- **Checklists** of steps and features
- **Organizational strategies** (e.g., using a spreadsheet or table for note-taking—see Figure 6.4).

Here is the grading rubric I use for this assignment:

Validity and clarity in data selection /20
Analysis/argumentation /40
Organization /20
Quality/clarity of writing /20

****

Unit 6.3: Critiquing Frames and Narratives

Introduction

This unit builds nicely on Unit 6.2, but can also stand on its own. As we touched on earlier, **discourses** are routinized ways of seeing and being in the world that are manifested in our use of language. However, these abstract definitions of discourse can be very confusing to students, who will ask questions like: "So . . . can *anything* be a discourse? What's *not* a discourse?" I'm sure that theorists have excellent answers to these questions, but from a teacher perspective, I find it more helpful to focus on "**frames**" and "**narratives**." The metaphor of framing is an accessible way of capturing how language can highlight or exclude particular elements of a story, just as a frame or cropping tool brings out certain aspects of an image. Framing "narrative" as a social and cultural phenomenon is also an accessible way to help students see how language and power are linked. This unit guides students in analyzing frames and narratives for themselves, focusing on news media or other discourse.

Figure 6.6 Framing: A Metaphor for the Functions of Language. Photo credit to Trac Vu

Learning Sequence

Opening with a Shared Experience

Although most of the units in this volume have begun with questions for reflection and discussion, I like to begin a unit on frames and narratives with a shared experience—specifically, watching author and activist Chimamanda Ngozi Adichie's TED talk, "The Danger of a Single Story." I have watched this talk dozens of times—I bet many of you have as well!—and I never tire of it. Adichie touches on a range of issues related to discourse and power, drawing examples of representations in literature, news media, and historical accounts. Though she never uses the term "discourse," Adichie provides an accessible and engaging introduction to the concept, laying the groundwork for CDA-oriented projects or other work undergirded by Critical Race Theory (CRT).

Two of my favorite quotations from the talk, which I sometimes use to center the discussion, are as follows:

- "Like our economic and political worlds, stories too are defined by *nkali* [power relations]. How they are told, who tells them, when they're told, how many stories are told, are really dependent on power. Power is the ability not just to tell the story of another person, but to make it the definitive story of that person."
- "Stories matter. Many stories matter. Stories have been used to dispossess and to malign. But stories can also be used to empower, and to humanize."

After I invite students to share their initial reactions to the talk, including to the quotes above, I guide them in applying the concept of "single story," which becomes our collective shorthand for "master narratives." We engage questions such as:

1   What "single story" might people have about you, based on your appearance, voice, or background? In what ways would this "single story" be inaccurate or incomplete?[56]
2   What—or whose—stories do you feel are overlooked in news media, literature, history books, etc.? How might giving more attention to those stories help to promote social justice?
3   How can we create more of a "balance of stories"[57] at school, in public discourse, and in our daily lives?

Activity: What's Trending?

This activity can be an in-class or homework assignment, completed individually or in pairs. Students visit the websites for two news organizations or publications at the same moment in time, to compare the "trending" stories at each. They may choose sources with different political leanings (e.g., Fox News vs. MSNBC) or from different geographic contexts (e.g., *LATimes* vs. *NYTimes*). They will often notice striking differences in which stories are trending. They may also notice that two stories about the same event or issue may emphasize very different aspects of the story. Students can share highlights orally or compose a short report or presentation on what they found.

Topic #1: Framing and Frame Analysis

The next step in this unit is to delve more deeply into what framing is and why it matters. Below are some guiding questions and recommended resources:

1   How does **framing function** psychologically and politically? (e.g., from the *Citizen's Handbook*.[58] See also the work of linguist George Lakoff[59] and media strategist Frank Luntz,[60] who have served as communications consultants to politicians on different sides of the political spectrum—more at *Business Insider*[61]).

2   How can we learn to recognize **dominant frames**—i.e., "single stories"—in news media? (e.g., from the PRC's Excellence in Journalism[62])

3   How do researchers investigate the **impact of framing strategies** within discussions of contentious political issues such as gun control (e.g., Boston Public Radio[63]) and climate change (e.g., Vox[64])?

As we explore how framing works, the goal is for students to see how the **linguistic choices** of journalists can perpetuate or resist dominant frames and narratives. It is worth noting that framing/narrative analysis can also include

paratextual elements, such as the location and appearance of the story, the choice and placement of images and other audio-visual features, and the ways that the story gets "picked up" on social media. Students can also analyze features of spoken discourse—e.g., pauses, interruptions, gestures, etc. (see Unit 7.1 for more). But for my own pedagogical purposes, including the fact that my "Narratives" course is a linguistics elective that fulfills a college writing requirement (more on this in Chapter 8), we focus primarily on textual elements.

Topic #2: Scaffolding Frame/Narrative Analysis

Eventually, I want each student to personalize their learning through an independent analysis of news coverage on a story of their choosing. But they need a lot of support and guided practice to be set up for this. I provide lists of **textual elements** they can focus on, such as *organization structure, sourcing, referencing* (e.g., use of hyperlinks), *metaphor, word choice,* and *rhetorical grammar* (e.g., use of passive voice, as discussed in Chapter 5). I also **model some of the thinking and steps** that go into a thorough analysis, using a topic I have worked with before. I usually choose a story related to immigration and/or refugee resettlement, for two reasons: First, this topic allows me to invite perspectives and experiences of international and immigrant-background students. Second, this topic provides opportunities for me to share a bit about my other research, which focuses on perceptions and treatment of refugee-background students (e.g., Shapiro, 2014, forthcoming; Shapiro et al., 2018).

We begin by **unpacking** the discourse, focusing on implicit associations with the labels "immigrant" and "refugee." Students often note, for example, that "refugee" tends to have a negative connotation and is linked to themes such as trauma, pity, and helplessness (we'll return to the idea of "unpacking discourse" in Unit 7.2). I then share with students some of the findings from my own research, informed by CRT (e.g., Shapiro, 2014; Shapiro, forthcoming), showing how this "deficit" framing gets used to justify educational inequities for refugee-background students at school. This helps students to understand the relationship between discourse, action, and power. We then discuss some of the counter-stories—i.e., alternative frames and narratives—I have collected from students themselves: stories that foreground aspiration, resilience, and other resources (see Table 6.3 and my 2018 piece in *The Conversation*[65]).

Table 6.3 Deficit vs. Asset Framing (Adapted from Shapiro & Macdonald, 2017; Shapiro, forthcoming)

Deficit	Asset
Emphasizes what individuals/families lack	Emphasizes what individuals/families bring
Oriented in the past	Oriented in the present and future
Narratives of victimization/trauma	Narratives of agency/empowerment
Surviving is the goal	Thriving is the goal
Invokes pity/sympathy	Cultivates pride/aspiration
Constructs individuals/families as recipients of help	Constructs individuals/families as willing and able to help others
Contributes to sense of alienation	Contributes to sense of belonging

We then talk about other ways that deficit framing can be seen in media coverage of immigration, including:

- **Labels** that are pejorative or othering—e.g., "resident aliens" or "illegals" (Newton, 2008; see also *NYTimes*[66])
- **Metaphors** that are dehumanizing, such as insects—e.g., "infestation," "swarm"—and natural disasters—e.g., "flood," "virus," "wave" (PBS[67]; *Psychology Today*[68])
- **Negative associations** between immigration and issues such as national security, public safety, or economic stability (Crawley et al., 2016 [see Figure 6.7]; Hogan & Haltinner, 2015)
- **Absence of immigrant/refugee voices** in news coverage of issues that impact them directly (Benson & Wood, 2015; Crawley et al., 2016)

"Deficit vs. asset" is just one of the framing contrasts we can use to analyze news media. Here are some other contrasts that have been identified by researchers:

1   **Terrorism and national security**: Who is labeled a "terrorist" vs. a "violent protestor" or "rogue shooter"? (Hint: Race and religion have a lot to do with it! This issue came up in media coverage of the insurrection at the U.S. Capitol Building in January 2021, which tended not to use the "terrorist" frame—e.g., NPR's *Codeswitch*[69]; *Psychology Today*[70])

Figure 6.7 Cover of Crawley et al.'s (2016) Report on Media Representations of Migrants in the U.K.

2   **Drug crises:** Why is opioid abuse framed as a public health issue today, while crack/cocaine abuse in the 1980s and 1990s was framed as a crime/public safety issue? (Race is a factor in this one as well—e.g., *Politico*[71]; *Wall Street Journal*[72])

3   **Criminal justice reform:** How do the labels used to talk about incarcerated people place emphasis on criminality rather than humanity? (e.g., "inmate," "felon," "offender"—more at the Marshall Project[73])

4   **Environmental protection:** What frames for climate change are used in the U.S. vs. other countries? (*Science Daily*[74]). How is climate research in the U.S. framed differently from other science? (e.g., politicians are often whether they "believe" in global warming, a verb that is not used in discussions of other scientifically documented phenomena—*New Yorker*[75])

For more on contrasts in news media framing, see Boydstun et al. (2013).

Demonstrating Learning for Unit 6.3

The culminating assignment for this unit is a multi-phrase Discourse Analysis project. Below, I describe how I set up and scaffold that project. First, though, I want to discuss a shorter assignment I use earlier in the semester.

Assignment #1: Letter to the Editor

At two points in the semester, my "Narratives" students write letters to the editor. These short pieces—usually capped at 250 words—allow students to synthesize what they are learning and to practice a style/genre of writing that is different from most of their academic papers (Hooray for rhetorical agency!). Here is how I describe this assignment in the course syllabus:

> **Writing letters to the editor** offers you the opportunity to think about how you can channel your course learning into real-world writing. Letters will respond to a recent article in the *Campus* [our student newspaper] or another publication that you engage with regularly. They should be written in a way that shows awareness of the appropriate conventions (content, style, tone, etc.) for this type of writing, including being concise, specific, and engaging.

Students craft the first letter during an in-class workshop that takes up most of our 75-minute class period. We first discuss some differences between academic writing and civic/public writing. We then discuss the purpose of letters to the editor and examine successful examples from previous students (see the Hub for samples), noting the rhetorical and linguistic strategies employed. We collectively create a list of tips/reminders that I leave on the board for the remainder of the period, as students compose their own letters. They post their finished letters, along with a link to the article they are responding to, at our online discussion board.[76]

Although I could simply make this a homework assignment, I have found several advantages to doing it together in class:

* Students appreciate the opportunity to ask questions and receive feedback in real-time.

- I can proactively check in with the students I know are likely to struggle. We can even set up a time to meet for further conversation outside of class, if needed.
- Students often like the energy of being in the same space but working independently. This is one of the reasons that "**write-ins**" have become increasingly popular on many college campuses, including mine[77]!

Two quick notes on inclusion here: First, some students find it distracting to hear the sound of everyone typing at once. I always invite students to bring earbuds/headphones to use while they work. I also try to identify a quieter space nearby where students can work apart from the larger group if desired. Second, the time-sensitive nature of this assignment can be anxiety-producing for some students, which is why they have until the end of the day—or longer, if requested—to post their letters.

Assignment #2: Discourse Analysis Project

The most challenging assignment in "Narratives" is a discourse analysis project,[78] for which students create and analyze a corpus of **ten or more articles** in order to answer a research question about news media coverage of a particular event or story. Below is a sampling of questions students have researched:

- Who was sourced—and how—in 2016 news coverage of a leaked Access Hollywood tape from 2005 (in which Donald Trump bragged about sexually assaulting women)?
- What tones—positive, critical, or mixed—are present in news media coverage of the announcement by Amazon CEO Jeff Bezos that his company is committing $10 billion to fight climate change?
- How critical, if at all, were international media in their coverage of the acquisition of special powers by Hungarian Prime Minister Viktor Orbán (in March of 2020)?
- How did the tone in national media differ from that of local/regional media in coverage of the Pacific Gas and Electric Company's guilty plea for the deadly 2018 Camp Fire?
- Was there gender bias in national news media coverage of Elizabeth Warren's decision to end her 2020 U.S. presidential bid?
- How did the publications from Native American communities vs. other state/local publications differ in their use of sourcing when covering the

U.S. Supreme Court's decision to uphold a controversial voter identification law?

We work on this project in three phases, over a span of five weeks or more.

Phase 1: Exploration and Pilot Study

For the first few weeks of this project, students develop and refine their topics. Some build on the Headline Analysis paper, while others choose a new event/story. After seeing how much students struggled the first time I facilitated this assignment, I incorporated a **3–4 page scaffolding assignment** ("Pilot Study") for which they first analyze only two or three articles. This allows them to "try out" a research question before they commit to a more extensive project. Below is a lightly edited version of the pilot study description from my syllabus:

Discourse Analysis Pilot Study

You will analyze two to three accounts of a particular news event/story, focusing on one or more of the following: *headline/lead, structure/layout, sourcing, framing, tone/attitude, word choice*, etc. Your paper should begin with an **introduction** that offers a rationale (both why you're focusing on this event and why you chose these two or three publications to analyze), as well as a **hypothesis** explaining what you expected to find. Your introduction should reference course materials/concepts that are relevant to your analysis. The body of your paper will present your **findings** and suggest **possibilities** for further research, which you can (will, I hope!) pursue for your longer discourse analysis paper.

After completing the pilot project, students can either "scale up," by expanding their corpus to ten or more articles, or switch to a different event/story. Either way, they all submit a proposal or set a meeting with me to talk through their plans for the larger project.

Phase 2: Corpus-Building

Many students find the corpus-building phase surprisingly difficult. One challenge is the **"apples to apples"** issue mentioned above (p. 198). If there is too much variation in the corpus, as noted earlier, a meaningful contrast is harder to achieve. I remind students that all of their articles must be of the same type (e.g., news reports or editorials/commentary), on the same event (tied to a specific date), and from the same type and medium of publication (e.g., tabloid or broadsheet; print or online).

A second challenge is **finding the articles** themselves. Students often use databases (e.g., Nexis, ProQuest Historical Newspapers), but some have trouble finding what they are looking for. Many decide to use Google News or simply search for their event/story within the website for each publication. Students sometimes worry that this is "cheating," as they think of a database as a more objective way to identify articles. I reassure them that as long as they are comparing like-to-like, it does not matter how they find the articles that comprise their corpus.

Another logistical issue that can take up time and energy is **getting the articles in the appropriate format** for analysis: Sometimes the versions of articles in library databases are scanned images that may need to be converted (or re-typed) so they can be highlighted, copied, and pasted. On the flip side, articles copied from websites may include additional text and images (advertisements, captions, etc.) that are not relevant to the analysis. Thus, students need to build in time to "clean their data"—a tedious but standard practice for most discourse analysis research. Teachers adapting this assignment for first-years or secondary level students may want to give students a "process grade" for having a cleaned-up corpus, ready for analysis!

A final logistical challenge students face is organizing their notes. Doing in-depth analysis of ten or more documents can be overwhelming at times! I often encourage students to **print out and annotate by hand,** because research suggests that for close or complex textual analysis, many students do better with paper vs. a screen (Singer & Alexander, 2017).

I also require that students complete a **note-taking grid**—i.e., a table or spreadsheet where they systematically note patterns and other observations (see Table 6.4). This grid provides a valuable checkpoint on how students are progressing with their analysis. Below is a sample, which I have edited lightly for readability, from the student whose project focused on media coverage of Donald Trump's public apology after the release of the 2005 Access Hollywood tape. The student's final paper did not include everything in the grid, but completing the grid helped to ensure that she analyzed the articles systematically.

Table 6.4 Sample Note-Taking Grid for Discourse Analysis Project

Article from	Political Leaning of Publication (according to Otero media bias chart)	Reliability of Publication (acc. to Otero chart)	Headline	Lede/Subheader	Key Words in Headline/Lede	Total Word Count	# Quotes from 2005 Tape	# of Sent w/ Paraphrase from tape	# Quotes from Trump Apology	# of Sent w/ Paraphrase from Trump apology	# Other Sources Quoted	# Other Direct Quotes Included	# Other Paraphrases Included	Other Observations (e.g., references to other incidents)
FOX														
CNN														
Etc.														

Perhaps the most challenging aspect of this assignment, however, is **moving from (organized) notes to an overarching finding.** The answer to the research question is, essentially, the thesis of the paper, but the research question itself often shifts as students progress through their analysis. I remind students frequently that discourse analysis research is **rarely linear.** It is normal—encouraged, even—to revise our research question(s) as we work with the data. Still, this non-linear process can be quite anxiety-producing for students, which is why I offer many opportunities for short **check-in conversations** outside of class. Here are some other ways I help students move from observations to findings:

1   I introduce a few **online tools** such as word clouds and concordances (e.g., Voyant[79]), which can help students "visualize" their data—i.e., to observe word frequencies and other linguistic patterns

2   We **use some class time** to debrief on process, troubleshoot emergent problems, and share initial findings; this helps to normalize struggles and can also reinvigorate students' excitement about their topic

3   Students have a **longer share session**—what I call a "mini-presentation" —early in the writing process, to help them organize their thoughts and refine their research questions (Chapter 9 has additional information on using oral presentations as part of the writing process)

Phase 3: Writing and Revision

As students begin drafting their papers, I provide them with the following **recommended structure,** assuming a final draft of 7–10 pages, double-spaced:

<u>Intro/Rationale</u> (approx. 2 pp): Draws on secondary sources (both concepts/theories and similar studies) to make the case for your analysis and to offer an informed hypothesis;
<u>Methods</u> (1–2 pp.): Articulates what you did and why (including how you put together your corpus, how you analyzed data, etc.);
<u>Findings and Implications</u> (3–5 pp): Includes trends and examples
<u>Limitations and Suggestions for Future Research:</u> (approx. 1p.).

Here are some final notes for this longer assignment:

- This is the **next-to-last major assignment** for the course, rather than the last, so that there is more time for feedback and revision. Students receive feedback from each other, from a peer writing tutor, and from me—sometimes multiple times—before the final draft
- Throughout the writing process, I provide **mini-workshops** on topics such as when and how to incorporate quotations and examples into their discussion of findings
- I also **upload sample student papers** to our Canvas site, often with annotations highlighting what the writer did that was effective (see the Hub for examples)
- The **grading rubric** for this assignment is quite similar to what I use for the Headline Analysis paper (see Appendix)

Doing Discourse

Although the above project focuses on discourse analysis of news media texts, it can be adapted for use with historical, literary, or political texts—as well as with multimodal texts. Before I developed my "Narratives" course, I piloted a course called "Discourse Analysis," in which students worked with texts of all kinds and in several languages! The range of projects was impressive, but there were not many of them, because only a handful of students chose to take the course. The following year, I reshaped that course into "Narratives in the News Media," and it has been full each semester! Using the frame of "narratives" rather than "discourse analysis" made a huge difference in how potential students perceived the course!

Alas, I have gone "meta" here, talking about the discourse of "discourse" and the framing of "narratives." But I do think this example illustrates that we need to be **rhetorically savvy** in how we present CLA-oriented curricula to our students. In Chapter 8, we'll talk more about how to design courses that appeal to particular groups of students. But first, in Chapter 7, we will explore the final and most wide-ranging pedagogical pathway: Communicating-Across-Difference.

****

Appendix
Grading Rubric for Discourse Analysis paper

- **Intro/Rationale** (Does the writer have a strong rationale for why they chose this event, and why they selected these particular publications? Are they comparing "apples-to-apples"? Do they draw on at least one secondary source to support their rationale?) /15
- **Methods** (Does the writer explain what/why/how when it comes to forming their corpus and analyzing the articles? Could another researcher replicate what they did?) /10
- **Findings (Analysis and Evidence)** (Did the writer arrive at one or more overall finding(s)? Do they illustrate those findings with examples?) /35
- **Implications, limitations, and possibilities for future research** (Is there a clear "so what" to the findings? REMEMBER: This is different from the "so what" of the event/issue. Does the writer note at least a couple of limitations? Is there at least one possibility for future research?) /20
- **Organization** (Is there a clear overall structure to the paper, with transitions from one point/example to the next? Does the writer use paragraphs to help structure the analysis?) /10
- **Quality of writing** (Is the writing clear, engaging, concise, and professional?) /10

Notes

1 www.americanbar.org/groups/crsj/publications/human_rights_magazine_home/ civil-rights-reimagining-policing/a-lesson-on-critical-race-theory/
2 https://time.com/5891138/critical-race-theory-explained/
3 www.cpr.org/2019/10/30/teens-arent-breaking-language-theyre-adding-to-it/
4 https://gretchenmcculloch.com/ has links to articles she has written for WIRED, the New York Times, and others
5 https://lingthusiasm.com/

6 This is a huge area for sociolinguistics research as well—e.g., Pavalanathan and Eisenstein (2015) and Strelluf (2020).

7 https://time.com/3559340/instagram-tween-girls/

8 www.theatlantic.com/technology/archive/2019/02/how-new-emoji-are-chang ing-pictorial-language/582400/

9 www.theguardian.com/science/2018/dec/17/can-you-solve-it-do-you-speak-twitter

10 www.buzzfeednews.com/article/emmyf/how-the-internet-killed-the-worlds-most-important

11 www.nytimes.com/2020/12/11/learning/lesson-of-the-day-tone-is-hard-to-grasp-online-can-tone-indicators-help.html (lesson plan that includes link to *NYTimes* article)

12 www.npr.org/sections/codeswitch/2018/03/21/425573955/white-skin-black-emojis

13 www.insider.com/internet-slang-origin-i-oop-meaning-sksk-vsco-girls-stans-2020-1

14 www.bbc.com/future/article/20180104-is-social-media-bad-for-you-the-evi dence-and-the-unknowns

15 www.psychologytoday.com/us/blog/the-moment-youth/202004/are-young-peoples-social-skills-declining

16 www.pewresearch.org/topics/social-media/

17 www.theguardian.com/lifeandstyle/2019/nov/01/call-out-culture-obama-social-media

18 www.npr.org/2021/02/10/965815679/is-cancel-culture-the-future-of-the-gop

19 www.wnycstudios.org/podcasts/otm/segments/trouble-cancel-culture

20 Transcript available at www.contrapoints.com/transcripts/canceling; video can be found on YouTube.

21 www.pewresearch.org/fact-tank/2021/01/13/qa-what-weve-learned-about-online-harassment/

22 https://dl.acm.org/doi/pdf/10.1145/3091478.3091509

23 www.ncbi.nlm.nih.gov/pmc/articles/PMC7100939/

24 This was an activity I had not used in a while, but was reminded of by Whitney Gegg-Harrison, a member of my CLA reading group who teaches at the University of Rochester.

25 Learn more about sketchnoting here: www.kqed.org/mindshift/54655/why-teachers-are-so-excited-about-the-power-of-sketchnoting

26 www.commonsense.org/education/news-media-literacy-resource-center

27 https://medialiteracynow.org/resources-for-teachers/

28 www.medialit.org/topics/how-teach-media-literacy

29 www.edutopia.org/article/building-community-restorative-circles

30 https://thereader.mitpress.mit.edu/journalism-in-a-liberal-democracy/

31 www.spj.org/ethicscode.asp

32 https://archives.cjr.org/news_literacy/you_are_what_you_read.php

33 www.forbes.com/sites/cognitiveworld/2019/11/24/sick-of-the-attention-economy-its-time-to-rebel/?sh=5bc8f66935ac

34 www.americanpressinstitute.org/publications/reports/survey-research/millennials-news/

35 www.journalism.org/

36 www.thoughtco.com/what-is-headlinese-1690921

37 www.wikihow.com/Analyze-Newspaper-Language

38 www.americanpressinstitute.org/journalism-essentials/organize-story/

39 www.americanpressinstitute.org/journalism-essentials/verification-accuracy/hierarchy-information-concentric-circles-sources/

40 https://training.npr.org/2017/09/25/the-art-and-skill-of-working-with-sources/

41 https://trustingnews.org/hownewsworks/sourcing/

42 www.adfontesmedia.com/

43 www.allsides.com/media-bias/media-bias-ratings

44 www.poynter.org/fact-checking/media-literacy/2021/should-you-trust-media-bias-charts/

45 www.americanpressinstitute.org/publications/reports/survey-research/what-americans-know-about-journalism/

46 www.pewresearch.org/fact-tank/2020/01/24/qa-how-pew-research-center-evaluated-americans-trust-in-30-news-sources/

47 www.businessinsider.com/misinformation-vs-disinformation

48 www.wnycstudios.org/podcasts/otm/segments/breaking-news-consumer-handbook-fake-news-edition There are also many fake news quizzes online—e.g., at www.buzzfeed.com/tag/fake-news-quiz

49 www.sfu.ca/big-data/stories/how-big-data-can-combat-fake-news

50 www.theguardian.com/commentisfree/2019/sep/02/language-fake-news-linguistic-research

51 www.nytimes.com/2017/02/01/us/news-media-social-media-information-overload.html

52 https://webliteracy.pressbooks.com/

53 www.wbur.org/hereandnow/2014/01/06/morozov-technology-critiques

54 www.mediaandminorities.org/about/. The lead on this project is a Middlebury colleague!

55 https://mediaengagement.org/research/the-current-state-of-news-headlines/

56 This question invokes one of my other favorite lines from Adichie's talk, which is: "The single story creates stereotypes, and the problem with stereotypes is not that they are untrue, but that they are incomplete. They make one story become the only story."

57 This another phrase from the talk, which Adichie attributes to another author, Chinua Achebe.

58 www.citizenshandbook.org/framing.pdf. There are also many video recorded presentations (e.g., TED talks) and podcasts on the topic that can be found online.

59 https://georgelakoff.com/

60 www.filuntz.com/
61 www.businessinsider.com/political-language-rhetoric-framing-messaging-lak off-luntz-2017-8
62 www.pewresearch.org/wp-content/uploads/sites/8/legacy/framingthenews.pdf
63 www.wbur.org/cognoscenti/2019/11/20/michael-siegel-gun-control-rebec ca-steinitz
64 www.vox.com/2016/3/15/11232024/reframe-climate-change
65 https://theconversation.com/how-refugee-children-make-american-education- stronger-97908
66 www.nytimes.com/2017/03/10/insider/illegal-undocumented-unauthorized- the-terms-of-immigration-reporting.html
67 www.pbs.org/wgbh/frontline/article/insects-floods-and-the-snake-what-trumps- use-of-metaphors-reveals/
68 www.psychologytoday.com/us/blog/words-matter/201807/dehumanizing-meta phors-lead-dehumanizing-policies
69 www.npr.org/sections/codeswitch/2021/01/14/956881738/what-does-it-mean-to- call-the-capitol-rioters-terrorists
70 www.psychologytoday.com/us/blog/the-first-impression/201706/media-fram ing-effects
71 www.politico.com/magazine/story/2018/06/10/opioid-crisis-crack-crisis-race- donald-trump-218602
72 www.wsj.com/articles/opioid-v-crack-congress-reconsiders-its-approach-to-drug- epidemic-1525518000
73 www.themarshallproject.org/2021/04/12/the-language-project
74 www.sciencedaily.com/releases/2019/08/190813130431.htm
75 www.newyorker.com/culture/culture-desk/how-should-the-media-talk-about-cli mate-change
76 A number of community and/or educational organizations have developed lesson plans on writing letters to the editor. One excellent example is from Learning for Justice: www.learningforjustice.org/sites/default/files/2017-07/Civil_Discourse_ in_the_Classroom_0.pdf
77 www.swarthmore.edu/writing/intlwritein. More info at www.swarthmore.edu/ writing/hosting-a-write-faq
78 I used to call it a "Critical Discourse Analysis" project, but I found that some students got a bit hung up on whether their analysis was "critical" enough.
79 https://voyant-tools.org/

References

Abe, S., & Shapiro, S. (2021). Sociolinguistics as a pathway to global citizenship: Critically observing 'self' and 'other'. *Language Awareness*, 30(4), 355–370.
Adichie, C. N. (2009). *The danger of a single story*. TED Talk.

Benson, R., & Wood, T. (2015). Who says what or nothing at all? Speakers, frames, and frameless quotes in unauthorized immigration news in the United States, Norway, and France. *American Behavioral Scientist, 59*(7), 802–821.

Bleich, E., Nisar, H., & Vazquez, C. (2018). Investigating status hierarchies with media analysis: Muslims, Jews, and Catholics in the New York times and the Guardian headlines, 1985–2014. *International Journal of Comparative Sociology, 59*(3), 239–257.

Bolter, J. D., & Grusin, R. (2000). *Remediation: Understanding new media.* MIT Press.

Boydstun, A. E., Gross, J. H., Resnik, P., & Smith, N. A. (2013, September). Identifying media frames and frame dynamics within and across policy issues. New Directions in Analyzing Text as Data [workshop handout]. https://faculty.wash ington.edu/jwilker/559/frames-2013.pdf

Caulfield, M. (2017). *Web literacy for student fact-checkers.* Open Textbooks- UMN.

Crawley, H., McMahon, S., & Jones, K. (2016). *Victims and villains: Migrant voices in the British media.* Center for Trust, Peace, and Social Relations.

Douka, A., Fterniati, A., & Archakis, A. (2017). Teaching news discourse in the Greek Lyceum: Language teaching proposals based on the multiliteracies framework. Proceedings from the University of Patras Educational Research Conference (pp. 323–331).

Golbeck, J. et al. (2017, June). A large labeled corpus for online harassment research. In *Proceedings of the 2017 ACM on web science conference* (pp. 229–233). https://dl.acm.org/doi/pdf/10.1145/3091478.3091509

Gower, K., Cornelius, L., Rawls, R., & Walker, B. B. (2020). Reflective structured dialogue: A qualitative thematic analysis. *Conflict Resolution Quarterly, 37*(3), 207–221.

Graff, G., & Birkenstein, C. (2018). *They say/I say: The moves that matter in academic writing.* WW Norton & Company.

Hogan, J., & Haltinner, K. (2015). Floods, invaders, and parasites: Immigration threat narratives and right-wing populism in the USA, UK and Australia. *Journal of Intercultural Studies, 36*(5), 520–543.

Janks, H. (2010). *Literacy and power.* Routledge.

Kibler, A., Valdés, G., & Walqui, A. (Eds.). (2021). *Reconceptualizing the role of critical dialogue in American classrooms: Promoting equity through dialogic education.* Routledge.

Ladson-Billings, G. (1998). Just what is critical race theory and what's it doing in a nice field like education? *International Journal of Qualitative Studies in Education, 11*(1), 7–24.

Lunsford, A. A. (2007). *Writing matters: Rhetoric in public and private lives* (Vol. 15). University of Georgia Press.

Newton, L. (2008). *Illegal, alien, or immigrant: The politics of immigration reform.* New York University Press.

Pavalanathan, U., & Eisenstein, J. (2015). Audience-modulated variation in online social media. *American Speech, 90*(2), 187–213.

Rogers, R., & Mosley Wetzel, M. (2013). *Designing critical literacy education through critical discourse analysis: Pedagogical and research tools for teacher-researchers.* Routledge.

Shapiro, S. (2011). Stuck in the remedial rut: Confronting resistance to ESL curriculum reform. *Journal of Basic Writing,* 24–52.

Shapiro, S. (2014). "Words that you said got bigger": English language learners' lived experiences of deficit discourse. *Research in the Teaching of English,* 48(4), 386–406.

Shapiro, S. (forthcoming). "This is about making family": Creating communities of belonging in schools serving refugee-background students. In T. Mayer & T. Tran (Eds.), *Migration, displacement, and belonging: Challenging the paradigms.* Routledge.

Shapiro, S., Farrelly, R., & Curry, M. J. (Eds.). (2018). *Educating refugee-background students: Critical issues and dynamic contexts.* Multilingual Matters.

Shapiro, S., & MacDonald, M. (2017). From deficit to asset: Locating discursive resistance in a refugee-background student's written and oral narrative. *Journal of Language, Identity & Education,* 16(2), 80–93.

Singer, L. M., & Alexander, P. A. (2017). Reading on paper and digitally: What the past decades of empirical research reveal. *Review of Educational Research,* 87(6), 1007–1041.

Solórzano, D. G., & Yosso, T. J. (2002). Critical race methodology: Counter-storytelling as an analytical framework for education research. *Qualitative Inquiry,* 8(1), 23–44.

Strelluf, C. (2020). needs+ PAST PARTICIPLE in regional Englishes on Twitter. *World Englishes,* 39(1), 119–134.

Van Hee, C., Jacobs, G., Emmery, C., Desmet, B., Lefever, E., Verhoeven, B., De Pauw, G., Daelemans, W., & Hoste, V. (2018). Automatic detection of cyberbullying in social media text. *PloS One,* 13(10), e0203794.

Vasquez, V. M., Janks, H., & Comber, B. (2019). Critical literacy as a way of being and doing. *Language Arts,* 96(5), 12.

Warhol, R., & Lanser, S. S. (2015). *Narrative theory unbound: Queer and feminist interventions.* The Ohio State University Press. https://kb.osu.edu/bitstream/handle/1811/68569/1/Warhol_Lanser_Book4CD_W.pdf

7
The Communicating-Across-Difference Pathway

Introduction

I decided to place this as the final pedagogical pathway, because it is the most wide-ranging—and the newest to me! Our focus here is on understanding and harnessing the **power of language in our day-to-day lives**. These units can be integrated with other academic content or can be used on their own, as part of academic community-building, social and emotional learning, or even civic engagement. The material in this chapter draws on linguistics, as well as psychology, anthropology, and communication studies—all disciplines in which social interaction among humans is a central focus.

I chose the frame "communicating across difference" for this chapter, because this is an aspiration many of us have for our writing classrooms as learning communities. Like a number of other scholars (e.g., Duffy, 2019; Guerra, 2016), I believe that the writing classroom holds great potential as a site for rich, meaningful engagement across difference (Shapiro, 2020). But as we've touched on already, "engaging difference" does not just mean "celebrating diversity." It means questioning our beliefs and assumptions and examining how power operates at both micro and macro levels. It also means seeing **inclusion** and **freedom of speech** as values that work hand in hand, rather than as competing priorities.[1]

Language is one of our most important tools for engaging diverse voices and perspectives, but language can also be our greatest barrier. As we learned in Chapters 4 and 5, our **linguistic biases** can cause us to lose sight of *what* someone is saying because we are so focused on *how* they are saying it—whether we are noticing accents, word choice, or styles of speech or writing. A CLA approach invites us to attend more carefully and critically to the role that language plays in our public and private conversations. We can study patterns, tensions, and power dynamics in those conversations, so that

DOI: 10.4324/9781003171751-10

we—and our students—are better prepared to participate ethically and effectively within and across diverse communities (Guerra, 2016).

Learning Goals

Essential Questions

Here are ten Essential Questions for this pathway, along with the CLA goal(s) most pertinent to each (**SR** = self-reflection, **SJ** = social justice, **RA** = rhetorical agency):

1   How does self-talk influence our thoughts, feelings, and behaviors? (SR, SJ, RA)
2   How can careful attention to language improve our relationships with friends, family, and partners? (SR, RA)
3   How can we use language to work through conflict, in both private and public interactions? (SR, SJ, RA)
4   What does deep listening look like? How can we measure and promote it? (SR, SJ, RA)
5   How can we trace power disparities (i.e., asymmetrical talk) in conversation? (SR, SJ, RA)
6   How do "free speech" and "diversity/inclusivity" work together in the classroom? (SJ, RA)
7   What makes "dialogue" different from a typical classroom discussion or political debate? (SJ, RA)
8   What is inclusive language? Why is it important? How can we learn it? (SR, SJ, RA)
9   What does it mean to think about writing as a process of "design"? (SR, RA)
10 How can writing be a way of "engaging across difference"? (SR, SJ, RA)

Transferable Skills

Students will be able to (SWBAT) . . .

A   **Explain** the power of language in relationships
B   **Reflect** on patterns in their self-talk and interpersonal interactions
C   **Utilize** linguistic strategies for deep listening and conflict resolution
D   **Understand** the complications around inclusive/"PC" language in the classroom
E   **Analyze** interaction patterns and power dynamics in classes or other group settings

F   **Distinguish** between shaming and accountability
G   **Engage** design thinking in the composing process
H   **Demonstrate** empathy, synthesis, and risk-taking in the writing process
I   **Create/compose** work that communicates effectively with public audiences

Overview of Units

Unit 7.1: The Power of Language in Personal Relationships (EQs 1, 2, 3, and 4; Skills A, B, and C). In this unit, students explore the power of language in their relationships. Drawing on research in psychology and intercultural communication, we consider how we can use language to improve our relationships with ourselves, as well as with others. Assignments include a personal essay on the power of language and an analysis of power dynamics in a real or fictional conversation.

Unit 7.2: Difficult Dialogues in the Classroom (EQs 3, 4, 5, 6, 7, and 8; Skills C, D, E, and F). This unit focuses on the dynamics of having classroom conversations about sensitive or difficult topics. Students engage with research—including some of my own work—on the nature of inclusivity and the challenges of engaging across difference. We consider features and strategies for co-creating "brave space" in the classroom. The main assignment for this unit is a "fishbowl conversation" and report.

Unit 7.3: Writing-as-(Re)Design (EQs 9 and 10; Skills G, H, and I). This unit is distinct from the others in that there are no new topics or readings. Instead, we focus on how we can craft and scaffold writing assignments that promote students' self-reflection and rhetorical agency as language users. We examine the choices of student writers in their response to a variety of assignments that involve writing for public audiences (see At-a-Glance chart for more details).

Table 7.1 The Communicating-Across-Difference Pathway (At-a-Glance)

	Concepts/Topics	Readings/Resources	Activities/Assignments
Unit 7.1: The Power of Language in Personal Relationships (pp. 224–231)	Self-talk/Positive affirmations Emotional agility Active/empathic listening	Podcasts (e.g., NPR's "Hidden Brain") Articles/blog posts	* Affirmations and body awareness * Power of Language essay

(continued)

Table 7.1 (*continued*)

	Concepts/Topics	Readings/ Resources	Activities/ Assignments
	Intercultural competence Phatic communication Turn-taking Saving/losing face Indirect speech Speech act Asymmetrical talk Codeswitching	(e.g. Gottman Institute, NYT, *Psychology Today*, TED) Conversations from film/TV/ literature (e.g., *El Norte, Slumdog Millionaire*)	* Critical Conversation Analysis (fictional or real-world)
Unit 7.2 Difficult Dialogue in the Classroom (pp. 232–236)	Inclusivity (and other terms) Dialogue (vs. debate) Active/empathic listening Shame vs. accountability (Calling out vs. calling in) Land acknowledgement statements Personal pronouns Inclusive/"PC" language Asymmetrical talk	Articles (e.g., HBR, IHE, *New Yorker*) Podcasts (e.g., NPR's Codeswitch, Unlocking Us) Guides to inclusive language (Thomas & Hirsch; Yin)	* Unpacking buzzwords * Missing voices * Fishbowl conversation and report
Unit 7.3 Writing as (Re) Design (pp. 237–250)	Design Process(es) Synthetic thinking Empathy-building Rhetorical risk-taking	*NOTE: There are no student-directed readings/media for this unit* <u>Writing Activities:</u> * Flash (short-form) writing * Imagined Interlocutors

	Concepts/Topics	Readings/ Resources	Activities/ Assignments
		Other Genres for Student Writing	

	Concepts/Topics	Readings/ Resources	Activities/ Assignments
		<u>Other Genres for Student Writing</u> * Resource guide/Infographic * Picture book * Letter home * Writing that mixes codes—see also activities/assignments in previous chapters	

Unit 7.1: The Power of Language in Personal Relationships

Overview

This unit explores how we can use language powerfully to promote social and emotional well-being. Essentially, it helps us understand the work that language does in our relationships. Of course, I am not an expert in psychology or social work, but I do love reading research from those fields—and I have discovered that much of that research focuses on language! This chapter has just a few highlights from that work. If anything, I hope it piques your interest in learning more. We will return to some of the ideas in this chapter in Chapter 10 as well, when we discuss how the applications of CLA can extend beyond our work in the classroom.

I know some of my higher education colleagues might see the title of this unit and think: "This sounds too touchy-feely to me!" And indeed, I would not want to force any teacher to engage the topics in this unit—or any other, for that matter—if they are not invested in doing so. (One of my Middlebury colleagues was teaching a course a few years back called "What is the Good Life, and How Can We Live It Together?" When I asked him how the course was going, he rolled his eyes and said that many of his class discussions "felt like group therapy." I remember thinking, "Why in the world did you choose that topic, if you didn't want students to talk about their personal lives?").

For any skeptics looking out there, here is what I would say: Deep inquiry about language, identity, power, and privilege is not just an intellectual exercise. It impacts us physically, emotionally, socially, and spiritually. Engaging the material in this unit can help our students to live "examined lives"—lives committed to reflection, learning, and growth. I can't think of a more worthwhile educational goal!

This unit may be particularly well-suited to English Learner/EAL classes, where students are still **building their academic language and literacy skills**—or even their social/communicative language proficiency—as the topics are fairly concrete and personally relevant. There are also fewer linguistics terms, though I of course had to include a few! Although all of the other units in this and other Pathways chapters can be adapted and differentiated, as we will discuss more in Chapters 8 and 9, this one might be a good starting point for teachers concerned about the amount and level of CLA content.

Learning Sequence

To **tap into students' prior knowledge and experience**, I like to begin by inviting students to reflect on the power of words/language in their lives. The questions below can be prompts for reflective writing, peer interviews, jigsaw survey (p. 183), or circle share (p. 192) activities.

- What is one of your favorite words in English or in another language? What do you love about that word? What feelings or images do you associate with that word?
- What is one of your favorite phrases or quotes from song lyrics, speeches, scripture, or another source? What resonates with you in that phrase/ quote?
- What is one word or phrase used in your family/home community that people from outside might not understand?
- What are some words of affirmation or encouragement that you have received or given to someone?
- Do you agree with the statement: "Sticks and stones may break my bones, but words will never hurt me?" Why or why not?

Topic 1: Language in Our Relationships with Ourselves

The first relationship we need to talk about is with ourselves. We can explore the power of language in our mental and emotional life by focusing on the following goals, informed by concepts from psychology:

1. Understanding the **nature and impact of self-talk** (see more in Figure 7.1)—e.g., NPR[2] and *Psychology Today*[3]; there is a great deal of empirical research on the impact of self-talk on athletes in particular—e.g., from *Verywell Fit*[4]

2. Learning to **recognize, name, and respond to different emotions**—e.g., the concepts of "Name it to tame it" (*NYT*,[5] *Psychology Today*[6]) and "emotional agility" (Harvard Business Review[7] [HBR]). These concepts are closely related to the idea of emotional triggering, which we discuss further in the following section and in Chapter 9

3. Engaging in **language/literacy practices** that have been shown to improve mental health, such as gratitude journals, letters of appreciation, and intentional goal-setting frameworks such as "WOOP"—Wish, Outcome, Obstacle, Plan (NPR's Life Kit[8] and Hidden Brain[9] podcasts)

Figure 7.1 Gratitude Journal: A Literacy Practice for Mental Well-Being. Photo credit to Gabrielle Henderson

Activity: Affirmations and Body Awareness

Research suggests that self-talk correlates closely with students' confidence and performance in the classroom, on the sports field, and in other high-stress situations (e.g., Hardy, 2006; Tod et al., 2011). This exercise helps students to explore the impact of positive linguistic "affirmations" on their minds and bodies. It is one of the activities I use in the "**mindfulness moment**" we do at the start of my class sessions, which I will share more about in Chapter 9.

After I have guided students in some grounding and breathing work, I present them with a few affirmations and ask them to spend a minute or so with each, saying the words to themselves, and noticing how they resonate physically or emotionally. As we do this, I acknowledge openly that the whole exercise can feel a bit awkward. But I remind them that the goal is to **be curious** about their own responses to language. And I also note that there is some solid research suggesting that words really do work on our hearts, minds, and bodies.

Below are some of my favorite affirmations, but there are many lists available online (e.g., https://positivepsychology.com/daily-affirmations/).

- I am kind.
- I am strong.
- I am enough.
- I belong here.
- I'm here to learn and grow.

We can channel this experience into a conversation or free-write about which affirmation resonated most for them. As a follow-up assignment, we can invite students to find or write other affirmations. Positive self-talk can also be a tool for **processing emotions** that come up when engaging difficult conversations in the classroom, as we will discuss in Unit 7.2 and in Chapter 9.

Topic 2: Exploring Language in Our Relationships with Others

One of the ways we experience the power of language most intensely is in our relationships with other people we care deeply about. All of us can likely recall something a loved one said to us—positive or negative—that we will never forget. We can also probably recall something we have said but later regretted. Research suggests that there a number of ways we can use language to strengthen our personal relationships:

1   Using empathy statements and supportive body language to show that we are **listening actively** (*Psychology Today*[10])
2   Making "I statements" and concrete requests, rather than generalizations and accusations, to **work through conflict** (e.g., from the Gottman Institute's "Love Lab"[11])
3   Offering **clear, specific, and authentic apologies** (e.g., NPR,[12] *Psychology Today*[13])
4   Recognizing how **other people's communicative needs and preferences** differ from our own (e.g., Gary Chapman's concept of "love languages"—summarized at TED[14] and in *The Atlantic*[15])

The above strategies are useful not only for face-to-face interactions, but also in computer-mediated communication (CMC), such as texting and social media exchanges, which we discussed in Chapter 6.

Students can also learn about research into how communication styles are influenced by gender, cultural background, and other factors. This **intercultural learning** is a crucial piece of preparing students for **global citizenship** (Abe & Shapiro, 2021). Here are a few examples:

- **Small talk** (i.e., "phatic communication"): How we use small talk, how much small talk is expected, and what conversational topics are considered appropriate, all vary widely across communities. Questions such as, "Are you married?" or "How much money do you make?" may be considered acceptable in some contexts, but overly intrusive in others (more at HBR[16]; *ThoughtCo*[17])
- **Interruptions/Turn-taking:** The amount of time one is expected to pause before taking a turn—i.e., to respond to what was just said—varies by language, culture, gender, and even geographical region. What is perceived as an enthusiastic reply by one interlocutor might be seen as an interruption by another (*National Geographic*,[18] PBS[19]).
- **Indirectness/Saving face:** In some communities, certain **speech acts**— i.e., genres of speaking—such as requests, criticisms, and communication of bad news are conveyed using indirect language. The goal of indirectness is to **"save face"**—i.e., to avoid awkwardness or public embarrassment—for both parties. For example, in many cultural contexts, responding to a party invitation with "maybe" is understood to be a "polite no" (HBR[20]; *Psychology Today*[21]).

In addition to the readings footnoted above, a number of best-selling memoirs include lengthy discussions and anecdotes about communicating across difference. A few examples are Maxine Hong Kingston's *The Woman Warrior*, Trevor Noah's *Born a Crime*, and Tara Westover's *Educated*.

As we discuss these linguistic patterns, it is important to keep in mind that they may or may not apply to an individual from a particular group or community. Humans are complex, as is communication. The goal of these discussions is not to be able to predict anyone's approach to communication, but rather, to **highlight difference as the norm**, and to promote reflection on how our own communication preferences might have been shaped by cultural factors and other family/community expectations.

We can bring the theme of power into this intercultural learning as well, returning to concepts such as **linguistic privilege** and **communicative burden** (p. 163). These concepts help students to recognize the "unlevel playing field" that often exists in interpersonal interactions. This understanding can then be channeled into an analysis of power plays in interactions, which are is the focus of Assignment #2.

Demonstrating Learning from Unit 7.1

The assignments below allow students to apply their critical awareness and analysis skills to everyday linguistic interactions.

Assignment #1: Power of Language Essay

This was the first major assignment in an interdisciplinary unit I co-taught for 7th–10th graders on "Language and Social Justice," discussed in Chapters 4 and 8. The prompt, which I have edited lightly for readability, is as follows:

Tell a **vivid story** of a time when you experienced the psychological power of language (good or bad) in your life. This could include words that were said to you, words you said to someone else, or words you have read, listened to, or watched, that had a strong impact on you.

Your essay should do all of the following:

- Describe the situation (Who, What, Where, When, etc.)
- Share what was said (be as specific as possible)
- Discuss how you felt, and why it was an important moment to you

Your essay will be graded on two criteria:

- Relevance of content (i.e., Did you respond fully to the prompt?)
- Use of detail in the writing

Most of the students' essays fell into one of the following categories:

- Encouraging words from teachers or coaches
- Expressions of kindness from friends or family members
- Critical comments from classmates or other friends

There was quite a range of writing abilities represented, and the unit did not include much scaffolding of the writing instruction, which is why students were graded only on relevance of content and use of detail. I have not used this assignment with students at the college level. However, students often share stories about the power of language in their Sociolinguistics Scrapbooks, an assignment we discussed in Chapter 4 (pp. 121–123). I will also be using this prompt as one of the "circle shares" (p. 192) the next time I teach my "Language and Social Justice" course for first-years.

Assignment #2: Critical Conversation Analysis

I usually facilitate this activity during class, but it can also be a homework assignment or even a multi-stage project, with the appropriate scaffolding. The goal is to examine linguistic **power plays** in a spoken interaction. The interaction could be a fictional dialogue from literature, television, or film, or it may be a real-life event, such as a political debate, a witness interrogation in court, or a confrontation with an authority figure (e.g., administrator, military personnel, or law enforcement officer). This activity can be applied as well to texting and computer mediated communication (CMC), which we focused on in Unit 6.1.

We can see evidence of power imbalances—i.e., **asymmetrical talk**—in some of the linguistic features noted above (e.g., turn-taking, interruptions, direct vs. indirect language), as well as through the use of sound quality (pitch, volume, intonation), silence, and diversion or distraction. **Code-switching**—i.e., shifting between varieties ("codes") in a single interaction—can also be used as power play, to increase connection or create distance. For more on conversation analysis as a methodology for research, check out the Lingthusiasm podcast.[22]

It is helpful to analyze a conversation together before asking students to conduct individual or small group analyses. In my "Introduction to Sociolinguistics" class, we examine scenes from the 2008 film *Slumdog Millionaire*, in which characters code-switch between English and Hindi, as well as between **standardized/prestige** and **vernacular/colloquial** varieties of English. These code-switches create solidarity in some cases (e.g., when the protagonist is making an emotional appeal to his brother) and distance in others (e.g., when a police officer is trying to intimidate the protagonist). Another example of code-switching I love is a scene from the 1983 film *El Norte* in which the main characters, a brother and a sister from Guatemala, use K'iche'(sometimes spelled Quiché), their **heritage language**, to communicate between themselves, but then use their knowledge of Mexican Spanish to persuade a U.S. border guard that they are Mexican, in order to avoid being deported all the way back to Guatemala.

A real-life example of asymmetrical talk that we have analyzed in my "Language and Social Justice" class (see Chapter 4) is a conversation involving a New York police officer, a Spanish-speaking father, and his bilingual daughter (ProPublica[23]). In the conversation, the officer makes **verbal threats** to the daughter—who was there because she had been the *victim* of a crime, by the way—and ignores the father's multiple requests for a Spanish interpreter. When a Spanish-speaking officer is eventually brought in, that officer soon switches back to English—another power move probably intended to **intimidate or exclude** the father. This footage, recorded surreptitiously by the girl's mother, who was sitting nearby but never addressed directly, was used as evidence in a successful lawsuit against that particular police department, which had a history of mistreating Latinx immigrant families.

A quick note on examples like these: It is important to warn students if they are about to watch or read a scene that could be emotionally triggering. The above conversation with police, for example, is not physically violent, but the verbal mistreatment is painful to watch—and may be even more so for students who have been the victims of police brutality or experienced other abuse at the hands of an authority figure. Watching these kinds of interactions can, however, be empowering, if students have the tools and opportunities to explore how linguistic power plays—**micro-aggressions**, really—contribute to systemic racism, xenophobia, and other forms of oppression. In Chapter 9, we will talk more about micro-aggressions, as well as **micro-affirmations**—a term proposed by Rowe (2008). We'll also discuss **trigger warnings** a bit more there as well.

****

Unit 7.2: Difficult Dialogue in the Classroom

Overview

There has been a lot of meta-conversation among educators lately about the dynamics of classroom discussion in both secondary and postsecondary settings. Many of us struggle to respond to what Warren (2000) calls "hot moments"—i.e., moments when the group tension suddenly rises in response to a provocative or ill-conceived question or comment (see also Harlap, 2014). And some of us have students who will be quite vocal in telling us whether they think we have responded appropriately. (Several times, students of mine have stayed after class to comment on how I handled something that came up in class discussion. I am always grateful for the feedback but slightly unnerved by the reminder that they are paying such close attention!).

One key finding from research on student conceptions of inclusivity—including some of my own research (e.g., Shapiro, 2019, 2020)—is that today's students want and expect us to create classroom environments in which everyone feels that their voice is valued (e.g., Oleson, 2020; Strayhorn, 2018). Many of today's students are also reporting that they want something more than intellectual **debate**: They want real **dialogue**—i.e., conversation that promotes deep learning and strengthens community ties.

A critical approach to dialogue, Kibler et al. (2020) explain, recognizes that the classroom is not a level playing field and works actively to "disrupt inequitable power dynamics inside and beyond classrooms" (p. 5). This unit invites our students to join us in co-creating classroom spaces in which robust and inclusive dialogue can take place (NOTE: This unit has some overlap with Chapter 9, which offers insights into how teachers infuse CLA into classroom instruction, including in their set up and facilitation of class discussion).

Learning Sequence

Tapping into Prior Knowledge

One excellent starting place for this unit is to unpack some of the buzzwords related to classroom dialogue.

Activity: Unpacking Our Buzzwords

As we discussed in Chapter 6, "unpacking" is a strategy informed by Critical Discourse Analysis that helps to make explicit some of our tacit assumptions and associations with particular words and phrases. Some of the "buzzwords" that can be used for this activity are: *freedom of expression, inclusivity, safe space, micro-aggression, trigger warning*, and *"cancel culture."*

Students can engage in this "unpacking" process through written reflection, pair or small group work, or as a large group discussion. Here are some prompts that can scaffold the unpacking process:

- Define "X" [the word/phrase] in your own words
- List word/image associations with "X"
- Describe what "X" looks, feels, or sounds like
- Give an example (real or imagined) of "X"
- Give a counter-example (e.g., the opposite of "X" is. . .)

Qualitative researchers sometimes use similar scaffolding strategies in interviews. For example, I trained undergraduate student research assistants unpack the concept of **inclusivity** with their peers, in order to help me understand what the concept means from a student point-of-view (Shapiro, 2019, 2020). Many of the suggestions in this book have been shaped by what I learned from those interview findings!

Topic 1: What is Dialogue? And How Do We Co-Create It?

Below are some questions and relevant readings/media that can be used to explore the topic of dialogue in the classroom. Note that we have touched on some of these topics in previous chapters as well—e.g., inclusive language in Chapter 5 and "cancel culture" in Chapter 6:

1   What are the features and functions of classroom **"dialogue,"** as compared with **discussion or debate**? (e.g., from the *Educational Leadership*[24] journal and from Essential Partners[25])

2   What does it mean to be an **active and empathic listener** in a class-room conversation? (e.g., strategies from ThoughtCo[26]; see also inter-personal strategies from Unit 7.1)

3   How can we be **clear, kind, and effective** when holding each other accountable?

- Distinguishing between public accountability and public shaming (from Brené Brown's podcast *Unlocking Us*[27])
- Aiming to "call in" rather than "call out" (Ross, 2019—see more in Chapter 9)
- Avoiding defensiveness when we have been held accountable for something we said or did—especially for White folks in discussions of race (HBR[28] and *The Body is Not an Apology*[29])

Activity: Missing Voices

I use this activity when I sense that students are holding back in dis-cussion. They may be reluctant to raise a controversial counterargu-ment or to ask a difficult question, for fear that they will be "attached" to that argument/question. This activity explicitly asks students to introduce new viewpoints into the conversation. Students are given the following prompt, along with an index card: ***"Write a question or statement that has not yet been introduced into the conversation, but which you think would be valuable to discuss."***

I tell students that someone else will be reading what they write aloud, so they should make sure it is legible and conducive to learning. I then collect and redistribute the cards. As students take turns reading what is on their cards, I note themes and patterns on the board. We then choose a few points to focus on in the next phase of our discussion.

Topic #2: Inclusive ("PC") Language in the Classroom

One way we can deepen students' learning about dialogue in the classroom is by talking about how linguistic norms and rituals in the classroom have been changing in recent years. Some questions we might explore include:

1   Why has it become common practice in many classrooms to invite students to share their **gender pronouns**?[30] What are the benefits and

potential concerns with this practice? (e.g., *Inside Higher Ed*[31]; Learning for Justice[32])

2   How has the meaning of the term **"politically correct" (PC)** changed over time? (e.g., from the Anti-Defamation League,[33] NPR's *Code-switch*[34] blog, and the *Backstory*[35] podcast)

3   Where can we learn more about using **inclusive and people-first language**? (e.g., Yin's *Conscious Style Guide* website[36]; Thomas and Hirsch's *Progressive's Style Guide*[37]) see figure 7.2 below.

Figure 7.2 Cover Image from the *Progressive's Style Guide*

Demonstrating Learning from Unit 7.2

Many of the assignments from previous chapters—such as autobiographical essays, peer interviews, and position papers—pair well with this unit, but the following is one additional assignment that promotes students' critical awareness about conversational dynamics in the classroom.

Assignment: Fishbowl Conversation and Report

A fishbowl conversation is one in which one group of students engages in a classroom conversation, while the other group observes the interaction. If possible, it is helpful to arrange students in concentric circles, with the "conversationalists" (interlocutors) in the center and the "observers" on the outside. The teacher can facilitate the discussion or allow students to moderate themselves. Throughout the conversation, the observers are invited to notice patterns in the content of the conversation, as well as in the dynamics of the interaction. Some guiding questions for the latter include:

- What strategies do the conversationalists use to manage turn-taking and interruptions?
- How do they build on or diverge from one another's contributions?
- How do they deal with tension or disagreement (if any emerges)?
- How even is the participation? Do some students dominate?
- What else do you notice about **what** was said and/or **how** it was expressed?

Observers can report back in pairs, in small groups, or with the entire class. They can also write a reflection on their experience as observers, conversationalists—or both! Whatever the mode of reporting, we can encourage ties to CLA learning, by inviting observations about language, identity, privilege, and power.

A twist on this activity is to have students observe and report back on a discussion in one of their other classes—assigning pseudonyms to participants, of course, since classmates have not given consent to be observed—or in a social grouping—e.g., sports team, student organization, etc. For a final project years ago, one of my students analyzed gender patterns in class discussion for several of her classes. She found that both the instructor and the discipline had an influence on whether there was equitable participation by gender. For more variations on "fishbowl," I recommend the teaching resources from the educational organization *Facing History and Ourselves*.[38]

Unit 7.3: Writing-as-(Re)Design

Overview

Rather than introducing new concepts, questions, or materials, this final unit delves into writing activities and assignments as a means of engaging across difference. The framework we are working with here is "design thinking," a creative approach to problem-solving used in a variety of fields, including architecture, computer science, engineering, marketing, and social entrepreneurship, (e.g., Liedtka, 2018[39]). And in many ways, problem-solving is what we are trying to do as readers, writers, and orators!

As we touched on in Chapter 6, scholars introduced the concept of "design" into discussions of critical literacy education as a way to respond to concerns that some approaches, including CLA, were too focused on critiquing the texts of others and not focused enough on students' own writing (Janks, 2010). As Janks (2001) explains, "deconstruction without reconstruction or design reduces human agency" (p. 249). One early critic[40] of CLA, in fact, joked that the acronym *actually* stood for "Cynical Language Abuse" (Yikes!).

A number of rhetoric and composition scholars (e.g., Marback, 2009; Purdy, 2014; Wible, 2020) have highlighted parallels between the design thinking process and the typical composing processes of experienced writers, including:

1   Both begin with inquiry/discovery, so as to **understand** the context and **define** the problem (i.e., the rhetorical situation, in the case of writing)
2   Both encourage empathy, collaboration, and self-awareness as we work to **ideate** and **develop** a response to the problem (i.e., planning and drafting writing)
3   Both involve **testing** and **improving** the response to the problem (i.e., review, feedback, and revision of writing)

However, as Janks (2001, 2010) reminds us, design without critique can also be problematic, leading to uniformed or hasty solutions that lack critical awareness. A CLA take on writing-as-design means that we must keep **power and privilege** foremost in our minds (Janks, 2001, 2010), and must infuse critical reflection throughout the process—particularly for multimodal work (Deroo & Ponzio, 2021) and other writing aimed at reaching audiences beyond the classroom (e.g., Cella & Restaino, 2012).

Below, I show how our writing assignments can promote students' development in four key skill areas that are central to a design thinking approach:

Thinking Synthetically, Practicing Empathy, Taking Rhetorical Risks, and *Responding to Real-World Problems.* After explaining each skill area, I discuss examples of student work that show learning in that area. Most of the examples I highlight here were in response to a "Writing Beyond the Classroom" assignment, which I introduced in Unit 5.3. I have included some excerpts from students' reflections on their work as well, in order to highlight the thought and care they invested into the design process. It is worth noting that although many of these examples are multimodal in nature, I always give students the option of choosing a more "traditional" genre, such as a persuasive essay or research paper. However, students choosing this option are still required to write for an outside audience (e.g., "other first-years" or "students majoring in STEM disciplines").

Thinking Synthetically

We tend to talk a lot in education about analytical thinking—being able to "unpack" a concept or "break down" an argument. However, just as important, particularly in terms of communicating across difference, is the skill—and art—of synthesis: *How do we* **put things back together** *in a way that makes them accessible and relevant to a broader audience?*

I have found that many students—and some faculty as well—confuse synthesis with oversimplification. They may not realize that in order to synthesize, we need to have both deep understanding and effective communication skills. Synthetic thinking is crucial to our ability to produce texts that are engaging and rhetorically effective (Lorimer Leonard, 2014; Purdy, 2014). Because it is so intellectually challenging, synthesis is ranked *higher than analysis* in Bloom's original taxonomy of higher order thinking (ThoughtCo[41])!

Genre 1: "Flash" (Short-Form) Writing

The phrase "flash writing"[42] was first used among creative writers to reference the trend toward shorter genres of fiction. However, it has been taken up among other writers as well, including among some writing teachers (Batchelor & King, 2014; Griffith, 2017). By forcing brevity, we encourage synthetic thinking, since students must really hone in on what matters most. And let's face it: Shorter assignments are often more enjoyable to read, as they focus students' attention on economizing with language rather than filling pages.

A colleague of mine in sociology, Rebecca Tiger, has replaced many of her longer paper assignments with flash writing pieces that are usually capped at three pages. She says this shift has produced writing that is clearer, more engaging, and often more useful as a measure of student learning. Professor Tiger—yes, we are all jealous of her name!—even allows some students to submit fiction pieces, as long as they demonstrate "understanding or application of course material." Students have reported to her that they find her flash writing assignments fun *and* challenging. A pedagogical win-win!

My "Letter to the Editor" assignment, discussed in Chapter 6 (pp. 206-7) is another type of flash writing: It is capped at 250 words, and students work on it primarily during class, receiving in-the-moment feedback from me. Of course, social media offers many other opportunities for short-form writing, including **micro-blogging** (e.g., on Twitter). And as we discussed in Chapter 6, having the opportunity to **translate or "re-mediate" work** from one genre of media to another can build students' rhetorical agency and connect them with public conversations happening beyond our classrooms!

Genre 2: Resource guide or Infographic

Another way to promote synthesis is to ask students to create resources that **teach something they have learned** to someone else. One of my favorite examples of this, which I referenced in Chapter 6 is a guide called "My News Diet," by John Schurer. John used the "nutrition plate" from the U.S. Department of Agriculture[43]—which has replaced the "nutrition pyramid" many of us grew up with—as a metaphor for a healthy mix of news media.

In the full project, which is available at the Hub, John devotes a page or two to each section of the plate. He likens "fact reporting" to fruits and vegetables, suggesting that it should be consumed regularly. John compares "infotainment," in contrast, to fats and sweets, which should be consumed sparingly. I found this to be a clever and memorable way for John to teach his peers about "healthy" approaches to news consumption. John's reflection on the project noted his commitment to synthesis and accessibility: "[I had to] draw on a number of sources from throughout our semester," he explained, "to provide quick tips and tidbits about these healthy habits."

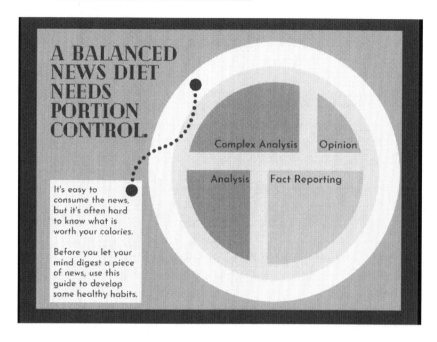

Figure 7.3 Image from Student John Schurer's "Healthy News Diets" Guide for Students

Another example we talked about in Chapter 6 is Becca Clark's infographic representing the SIFT process for identifying misinformation.

Like John, Becca thought carefully about what to include and how to portray it effectively, using her knowledge of multimodal features:

> I wanted people to have something they could check really quickly, with easy and reliable methods that worked. . . [and] that could be shared in multiple forms: a poster, put on a fridge, or posted on social media. My criteria for success was creating something that was eye catching, and to the point, so that it was really easily digestible for everyone.

As we touched on in Unit 5.1 (e.g., p. 144), students can also use synthesis to capture what they have learned about our disciplines and institutions, serving as "cultural informants" for their classmates. **Posters and oral presentations** are other excellent genres for promoting synthesis in both writing and speech (Chapter 9 has a few tips for supporting students with oral presentations, by the way!).

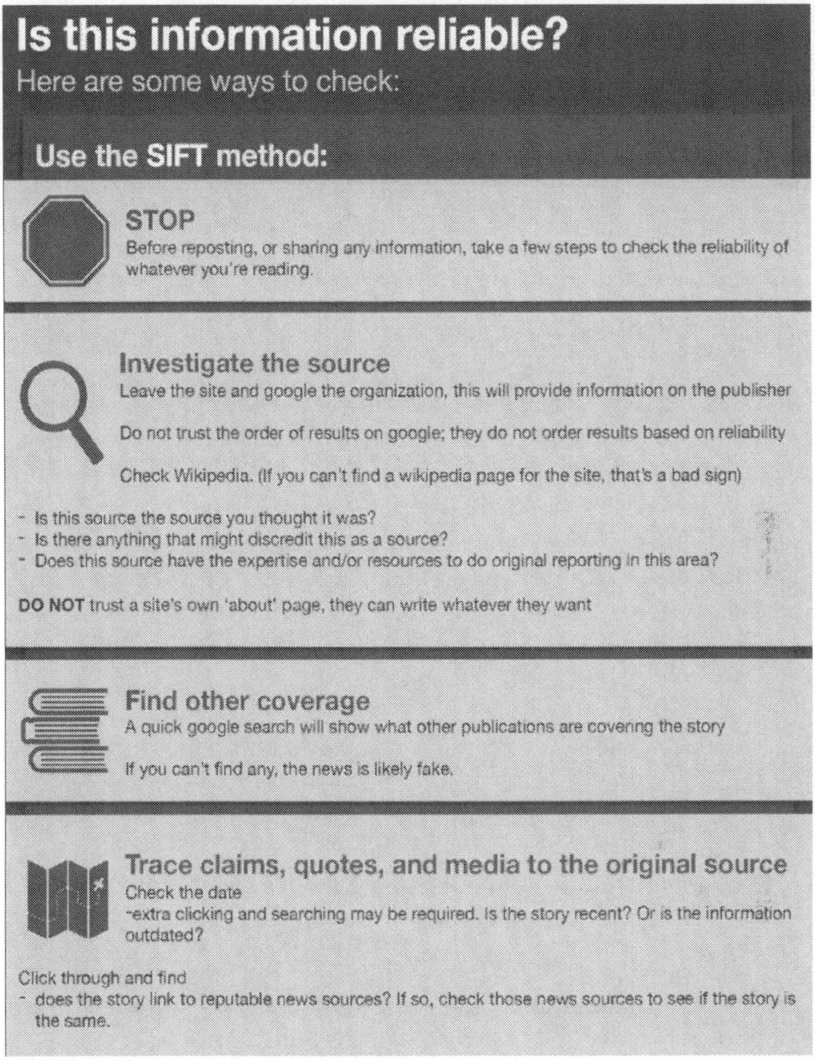

Is this information reliable?
Here are some ways to check:

Use the SIFT method:

STOP
Before reposting, or sharing any information, take a few steps to check the reliability of whatever you're reading.

Investigate the source
Leave the site and google the organization, this will provide information on the publisher

Do not trust the order of results on google; they do not order results based on reliability

Check Wikipedia. (If you can't find a wikipedia page for the site, that's a bad sign)

- Is this source the source you thought it was?
- Is there anything that might discredit this as a source?
- Does this source have the expertise and/or resources to do original reporting in this area?

DO NOT trust a site's own 'about' page, they can write whatever they want

Find other coverage
A quick google search will show what other publications are covering the story

If you can't find any, the news is likely fake.

Trace claims, quotes, and media to the original source
Check the date
- extra clicking and searching may be required. Is the story recent? Or is the information outdated?

Click through and find
- does the story link to reputable news sources? If so, check those news sources to see if the story is the same.

Figure 7.4 An Infographic Created by Student Becca Clark, Explaining the SIFT Method

Practicing Empathy

One other feature we see in the assignments above—and one that is built into the design thinking process—is empathy. As Lisa Blankenship (2019) explains, good writing requires "an act of imagination" that "consists largely in trying to inhabit the world, both interior and exterior, of an Other" (p. 4). In other words, we need both creative and critical thinking to see—and write!—beyond the confines of our own worldview. Empathic thinking and action are particularly important when we are writing as a way of engaging across difference (Blankenship, 2019; Guerra, 2016). Many iterations of design thinking, in fact, include "**empathize**" as the first step. Below are some ways we can help students build and demonstrate empathy:

Activity: "Imagined Interlocutors"

This is an activity designed to promote synthesis and rhetorical awareness, which I learned about from my colleague Carly Thomsen, a colleague in our Gender, Sexuality, and Feminist Studies Program. Professor Thomsen's students keep a reading journal, but instead of the typical "summary/response" format for each entry, they are asked to recount an imagined conversation about the text. Professor Thomsen gives a recommended interlocutor for each conversation, such as:

- A group of peers at the dining hall
- A romantic partner
- A science major who has never taken a course in gender/sexuality studies
- A family friend who sees themselves as socially liberal but fiscally conservative
- A stranger you are seated beside on a plane who sees gender/sexuality as purely biological

Students are invited to select different interlocutors if they wish. In addition to writing about these imagined conversations in their journals, students are invited to draw on them during class discussion. Recently, Professor Thomsen added one more twist to this activity: For their final journal entry, students are required to have an actual conversation with one of these interlocutors and report back on how it went.

Genre 3: Personal Letter

Some of the most empathic writing I have seen from my students comes from letters they have written to their own family members. Often, this writing is about students' relationships to **heritage languages**—i.e., languages connected to their racial, ethnic, or cultural backgrounds. In writing to loved ones about this complex topic, students have to strike a balance between two rhetorical goals: 1) Conveying something they have learned, often by asking difficult questions, such as "Why didn't you place more emphasis on learning/using our L1/heritage language at home?" and 2) Showing respect, appreciation, and understanding—for example, acknowledging the challenges that may have prevented families from emphasizing L1/heritage maintenance.[44]

It is powerful—and sometimes heartbreaking—to see how students navigate this rhetorical bind.

One of my students, Sonya Farrell, opened a letter to her grandmother ("Hasuba," in Gujarati) with the following lines:

> I know it must hurt you to hear my voice blundering your mother-tongue. The high pitched r's and your fast and rhythmic tone sounding monotone in my American accent. Your own grandchildren now sounding like the people who made fun of your accent, the people who pretended they couldn't hear you, pulled at your sari, and made fun of the "dot on your forehead." I know you faced them like the *rani* that you are, but how does it feel to hear me sounding more like them than you?
>
> I remember the day when you patiently tried to teach me Gujarati when I was five. You were so excited, and I was bored as usual. You only wanted me to be able to talk to your mother tongue, to your family, and to you. You finally wanted to be able to speak to me without rehearsing the words in your head first, but as I boredly watched the television screen instead of paying attention to you, I think you realized those dreams were long gone. The Gujarati alphabet etched on a plain piece of paper, destined to be forgotten about.

Sonya went on to reflect on her mother's experience as a bilingual speaker, and Sonya's own ambivalence, as someone who is biracial and bicultural but monolingual. Here is how Sonya closed her letter:

> Please understand the reason why I want to learn Gujarati. I want to learn about me [and] learn about you. I want to learn how to roll *rotis* round, and I want to be able to surprise the grocer and let her know that we all haven't all pretended to forget where we are from. Hasuba, I only want to know about my heritage, and I feel like I failed everyone that immigrated from India, to everyone of Indian heritage, and of course you. If you teach me this time, I promise that I'll pay attention. Your Beta, Sonya

Because some of this writing is so personal, I give students the choice of sharing about the process, reading part or all of the written product, or both. Sonya chose to read her letter aloud, and as she read, I remember feeling her pain, as well as her hope for a deeper relationship with her grandmother and stronger ties to her linguistic heritage.

Genre 4: Picture Book

Students also exercise empathy when they write for an audience whose rhetorical needs and expectations are markedly different from their own. My student Megan Mahoney demonstrated this when designing an electronic children's book about linguistic prejudice, as her final project for "Language and Social Justice"—see Chapter 4 and Shapiro (2022) for more on that course. Megan used simple vocabulary, clever rhyme schemes, and appealing visual features to give her book an inviting feel, so she could convey her message in a non-judgmental way. In her reflection, she wrote:

> I intended the book to be positive and empowering rather than critical. It is quite likely that in the reader or listener's life, they have already commented on or made assumptions based on differences in languages. So, rather than criticizing these negative behaviors, I wanted to highlight how one should embrace and respect differences in language. . . [so that] the child audience will hopefully be less overwhelmed and more likely to absorb the lessons about language discrimination.

Figure 7.5 Two Pages from Megan's Picture Book on Linguistic Prejudice

Taking Rhetorical Risks

One of the refrains I often hear in discussions of today's (GenZ) students is that they are reluctant to take emotional, social, and/or intellectual risks (e.g., Piore, 2019[45]). Although I am skeptical about generational stereotypes, I am confident that the writing classroom is an ideal site for intellectual and emotional risk-taking. Experts in design thinking often point out that experimentation, failure, and revision are all crucial parts of

innovative problem-solving. And of course, engaging across difference itself requires some risk-taking on everyone's part! (Christoph & Nystrand, 2001; Teagarden et al., 2018).

As writing teachers, we can help to set up and support students' rhetorical risk-taking as language users. One of the best ways to do so is by cultivating opportunities for **playfulness** (e.g., James & Nerantzi, 2019; Leather et al., 2020). Research in applied linguistics has found that **ludic** (playful) activities have a positive impact on students' language development (e.g., Cook, 2000; Shapiro & Leopold, 2012). A number of the activities we have discussed in these "Pathways" chapters have elements of playfulness—for example:

- Kinesthetic activities such as "Four Corners" (p. 105) and "Standing Survey" (p. 148)
- "Critical role-play" scenarios for discussion and simulation (Ch 4 pp. 119–120, Ch 5, p. 156)
- Written role-play assignments—e.g., imagined email exchange between authors—p. 157; "Imagined Interlocutors" (242)

Multimodal assignments can also encourage playfulness by inviting students to draw on skills and resources that they may have thought they had to "leave behind" at school.

Genre 5: Code-Mixed Writing

Another playful but also powerful way students can take rhetorical risks is by integrating multiple codes, styles, and/or voices into their writing. Most translingual scholars call this "code-meshing" (e.g., Lu & Horner, 2016), while scholars in applied linguistics tend to use the label "translanguaging" (García et al., 2017). This sort of writing can feel "risky" for a few reasons: First, it may not fit neatly into the genres that students are used to reading, and so the writer has to trust that readers will engage the work with openness and curiosity. Students must also trust that their instructor will "grade" the work appropriately—more on that in Chapter 9! Code-mixing is often a way of discussing emotionally difficult topics, which adds yet another element of "risk" to the mix.

In Chapter 5 (pp. 166-168), I shared a bit about the multilingual poetry collection *rice burger and banana milk*, which my student Ho-June (Sean) Rhee created for my course "The English Language in a Global Context." I referenced that project as an example of how writing "beyond the classroom" can help to promote plurilingual orientations to language.

Below, I examine more closely the poem Sean wrote in Korean and English, entitled 애국심 ("Patriotism"). This poem, which Sean says is his favorite in the collection, was crafted to "capture[ ] the concern of not knowing who I am and where I came from." Sean achieves this by contrasting public state-ments he has made in English, which downplay the importance of his Ko-rean heritage, against statements in Korean (with English translations) that are more representative of his "inner thoughts" (see table below; the full poem can be found on p. 167).

By juxtaposing these two sets of statements, Sean playfully yet powerfully conveys the tensions that he—like so many students straddling cultures and languages—experiences on a day-to-day basis. The literal "double voicing" here is a sophisticated translanguaging strategy and a clever bit of rhetorical risk-taking. In his reflection on this poem, Sean shared that writing it had "rekindled [his] pride" in his Korean heritage, and that he "hope[s] that flame never goes out again."

Table 7.2 Contrasting Lines from Sean's Poem in Korean and English

Sean's public voice (English statements about Korean identity)	Sean's private voice (English translations of statements in Korean)
"I am an Americanized Korean." "I'm not really attached to Korea." "I'm pretty much a banana."[46] "Please think of me as a foreigner."	As a Korean, I am proud of South Korea. But, why do you treat me like a foreigner? I miss being Korean without suspicions. Why do you compliment my Korean?

I have had the delight of reading many other examples of work that uses code-mixing in creative and impactful ways. Another of my favorites is from a Latino student, Roni Lezama, whose "Writing Beyond the Classroom" pro-ject was a poem addressed to the author Richard Rodriguez, whose 1982 memoir *Hunger of Memory* we read in my first-year seminar. Rodriguez is a controversial figure in many Latinx communities, in part because he has publicly criticized bilingual education programs and other multicultural ini-tiatives that in his view "ghettoize" Latinx youth.

Roni's poem, entitled *"La Guerra"* ("The War") is empathic and provoc-ative. In his introduction to the piece, Roni notes that he "wanted to ac-knowledge [Rodriguez's] arguments and pain" but also "[to] question the decisions that he made." His poem hones in on the theme of "memory," including citing a famous line by Gabriel Garcia Marquez in the first stanza:

"*La memoria del corazón/Elimina los malos recuerdos*" ("The heart's memory eliminates the bad").

Roni then proceeds to explore how "los malos" (the bad memories) that Rodriguez has experienced may have contributed to his more assimilationist stance. Yet Roni never lets the author "off the hook" completely: He concludes his poem with the question, "Did you become Richard or are you still Ricardo?" This question demonstrates genuine curiosity, as well as critical awareness about the intersections of language, identity, and power, since Rodriguez explains in his memoir that he decided early on to replace his birth name, "Ricardo," with the Anglicized "Richard" (see Shapiro [2022] for more analysis of Roni's poem).

The semester after he wrote this poem, Roni composed a spoken word piece for our first-year oratory competition. Like "La Guerra," this new piece demonstrated empathy and curiosity, but it was addressed instead to Roni's father, who had come to the U.S. as an undocumented immigrant.[47] Roni received a standing ovation for his performance—and he won the first-place prize! He has continued to employ his rhetorical repertoire in a variety of public settings, including most recently as the president of Middlebury's Student Government Association.

Genre 6: Digital Projects—with Analog Features!

A number of practitioners have pointed out that CLA can focus on many features of writing beyond the written text, including visual, multimodal, and hypertextual aspects (e.g., Deroo & Ponzio, 2021; Janks, 2010). Although multimodal writing might seem more "comfortable" than other genres to some students, I have noticed one type of rhetorical risk-taking that surprised me a bit—the inclusion of "analog" elements, such as hand-written signs or hand-drawn illustrations. In an age when savvy design templates and slick graphics are nearly ubiquitous, adding these analog features can—perhaps ironically—help to capture the viewer's attention, adding a personal or "retro" feel to the text.

Several students in my "Narratives in the News Media" class have used this rhetorical strategy in educational videos they created for their peers. In a piece teaching his peers the "basics" of online news media literacy, Anthony Turcios, a digitally savvy computer science major, chose to imitate the "scrolling screen" effect of early film genres, by putting hand-drawn images and text into a single document, and narrating while manually "scrolling" down the screen, and using screen capture software. In his reflection, he noted that this strategy was aimed at making his tutorial more "accessible" and "engaging"—check out the full video at the online Hub (tags: student work; news media literacy).

An international student from Vietnam, Linh Tranh, used a similar strategy in a parody tutorial on the topic "How to Create Fake News." In the video, Linh illustrates each "step" of the process by writing on a whiteboard and occasionally adding paper cut-outs. At one point in the video, she tosses headline after headline onto the board, helping to convey in a tongue-in-cheek way her message that fake news is ubiquitous but identifiable. In her reflection, Linh said she wanted her project to give viewers "a better understanding of each component of fake news" and that her use of "arts and crafts" made the project more "fun" and "creative."

Links to Antony and Linh's videos, and to several other multimedia projects from students, are available at the online Hub.

Responding to Real-World Problems

The student projects referenced above address important social issues in creative and engaging ways. This real-world relevance is another feature of "design" approaches to writing. As Purdy (2014) explains, "In focusing on action, design thinking reminds us and our audience that writing *does* something. And we must approach it, teach it, and research it with the care that this awareness requires" (p. 634).

To close out this chapter, I will discuss two additional examples of student work from my "Narratives in the News Media" class—both of which used design thinking to address high-stakes current issues. The first is a research project by Mariel Edokwe, who analyzed news coverage of the killing of Eric Garner, a Black man killed by asphyxiation in 2014 by a police officer who had him in a chokehold. Garner's death was one of the most prominent cases around which the #BlackLivesMatter movement gained momentum, and Mariel was interested in how initial news coverage of the Garner's death compared with retellings of the incident in 2019, when the accused officer was tried and acquitted. One of her key findings was that coverage from Fox News had become *less sympathetic* toward Garner in 2019 than it was in 2014.

The public-facing portion of Mariel's project was a slideshow about her research, in which she aimed "to be clear in explaining my methodology and findings while also being completely transparent in acknowledging my own biases." One of Mariel's last slides was a screenshot of the Google search

Figure 7.6 Image from Mariel's Presentation on News Coverage of Eric Garner Killing

suggestions completing the phrase "Eric Garner was. . . " She inserted red arrows next to three of the suggestions that were demonstrably false, yet had been circulated in some of the news media she examined for her project (see Figure 7.6).

In her reflection, Mariel said that she hoped her presentation showed how "misinformation can result in widely accepted, false narratives which can also be unethical." This issue also has professional relevance for Mariel, who currently works in a district attorney's office and plans to pursue graduate studies in criminal justice.

A final example I wish to share is from Josephine Leung, whose public project for "Narratives" was a student guide entitled "Misinformation in the Age of COVID-19." One of my favorite pages from the guide explains the difference between "inaccurate" and "incomplete" information—a distinction that often gets lost in public discourse. Josephine illustrated this point with two tweets from the Center for Disease Control (CDC; see Figure 7.7).

Josephine's analysis offered a nuanced yet accessible argument—that a governmental organization's willingness to change its guidelines in response to new scientific findings should be a cause for *confidence* rather than *distrust* among the general public. Josephine plans to pursue a career in social work, a field in which the ability to recognize and counter misinformation will be useful both to her and her clients.

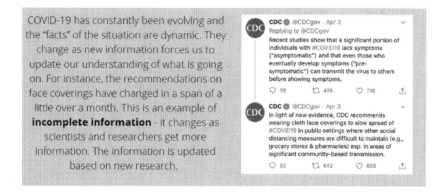

Figure 7.7 Excerpt from Josephine's Project, Explaining Incomplete vs. Inaccurate Information

Conclusion

Above are just some highlights of what students can do when given opportunities and support for designing writing projects that are socially and personally relevant, as well as rhetorically challenging. At the online Hub there are other examples of student work. There will also be a place for other teachers—like you!—to share their own activities, assignment ideas, and student work samples. I hope to see you there!

Notes

1 As one example, a Knight Foundation survey from 2019 asked students which they would choose: "protecting free speech" or "promoting an inclusive society." https://knightfoundation.org/articles/campus-speech-2020-new-survey-reveals-college-student-views-on-free-speech-and-inclusivity/ I think this is an unhelpful and overly simplistic question!
2 www.npr.org/sections/health-shots/2014/10/07/353292408/why-saying-is-believing-the-science-of-self-talk
3 www.psychologytoday.com/us/basics/self-talk
4 www.verywellfit.com/positive-self-talk-3120690
5 www.nytimes.com/2015/04/04/business/dealbook/the-importance-of-naming-your-emotions.html
6 www.psychologytoday.com/us/blog/compassion-matters/202005/three-things-do-your-mental-health-right-now
7 https://hbr.org/2013/11/emotional-agility
8 www.npr.org/2020/06/02/867905101/want-to-be-happier-evidence-based-tricks-to-get-you-there
9 www.npr.org/2016/05/10/477379965/woop-there-it-is-four-steps-to-achieve-your-goals

10 www.psychologytoday.com/us/blog/couples-thrive/201907/44-empathy-state
ments-will-make-you-great-listener

11 www.gottman.com/blog/help-your-partner-understand-your-side-of-the-conflict-
in-3-steps/. www.gottman.com/blog/gottman-relationship-recipes/

12 www.npr.org/2021/06/02/1002446748/youre-apologizing-all-wrong-heres-how-
to-say-sorry-the-right-way

13 www.psychologytoday.com/us/blog/friendship-20/201906/how-apologize-
8-tips-keep-in-mind

14 https://ideas.ted.com/whats-your-favorite-persons-love-language-heres-how-to-
tell-and-how-to-use-it/

15 www.theatlantic.com/family/archive/2019/10/how-the-five-love-languages-
gets-misinterpreted/600283/

16 https://hbr.org/2013/02/the-big-challenge-with-america

17 www.thoughtco.com/phatic-communication-1691619

18 www.nationalgeographic.com/science/article/pregnant-pauses-and-rapid-
fire-how-do-different-cultures-take-turns-to-talk

19 www.pbs.org/speak/seatosea/americanvarieties/newyorkcity/

20 https://hbr.org/2015/05/learning-the-language-of-indirectness

21 www.psychologytoday.com/us/blog/ulterior-motives/201408/saving-face-using-
ambiguous-language

22 https://lingthusiasm.com/post/189762810146/lingthusiasm-episode-39-how-
to-rebalance-a

23 www.propublica.org/article/challenged-by-long-island-lawmakers-police-will-
look-into-treatment-of-immigrant-families-who-reported-missing-children

24 www.ascd.org/publications/educational-leadership/apr15/vol72/num07/The-
Art-of-Dialogue.aspx

25 https://whatisessential.org/resources/distinguishing-debate-dialogue

26 www.thoughtco.com/active-listening-for-the-classroom-6385

27 https://brenebrown.com/podcast/brene-on-shame-and-accountability/ One useful affirmation that Brown employs to help her move through her automatic
shame responses (when she has been held accountable for something she said or
did) is: "I'm not here to be right. I'm here to get it right."

28 https://hbr.org/2020/07/youve-been-called-out-for-a-microaggression-what-do-
you-do

29 https://thebodyisnotanapology.com/magazine/dont-get-defensive/

30 I have found that this discussion is particularly helpful for international students,
as well as for those who come from more socially/politically conservative backgrounds, who may not have experienced this ritual before.

31 www.insidehighered.com/views/2018/09/19/why-asking-students-their-preferred-
pronoun-not-good-idea-opinion

32 www.learningforjustice.org/magazine/publications/best-practices-for-serving-lgbtq-
students/section-ii-classroom-culture

33 www.adl.org/education/resources/tools-and-strategies/classroom-conversations/
politically-correct-for-whom

34 www.npr.org/sections/codeswitch/2016/12/14/505324427/politically-correct-
the-phrase-has-gone-from-wisdom-to-weapon

35 www.backstoryradio.org/shows/politically-incorrect/
36 https://consciousstyleguide.com/
37 https://s3.amazonaws.com/s3.sumofus.org/images/SUMOFUS_PROGRES
SIVE-STYLEGUIDE.pdf
38 www.facinghistory.org/resource-library/teaching-strategies/fishbowl
39 https://hbr.org/2018/09/why-design-thinking-works
40 This is from Esterhuyse (1994, p. 57), cited in Janks (1996, p. 173).
41 www.thoughtco.com/blooms-taxonomy-synthesis-category-8449. I find that K-12
teachers are often more familiar with Bloom's taxonomy than higher education
folks. Although it has its critics (see Berger, 2018) I find it to be helpful as a
reference point to ensure that we are having students read and write in ways that
further their intellectual growth, as well as their language/literacy development.
Many of the "Transferrable Skills" in these Pathways chapters are informed by
my understanding of Bloom's work.
42 See https://diymfa.com/writing/short-forms-flash-nonfiction for more on flash
writing.
43 www.myplate.gov/
44 Research has found that many immigrant parents in the U.S. feel extreme pressure from schools and other forces to focus on using English in the home, even
if this means loss of other (heritage) languages (e.g., Tse, 2001). Usually the
heritage language is lost within two or three generations, which is why Rumbaut
(2009) calls the U.S. a "linguistic graveyard."
45 www.newsweek.com/2019/06/28/gen-zs-are-anxious-entrepreneurial-
determined-avoid-their-predecessors-mistakes-1443581.html
46 The word "banana" is used pejoratively in Asian and Pacific Islander communities to refer to someone who is seen as having assimilated to White or Anglo
cultural norms (Nagayama Hall, 2017). Similar analogies used by other racial/
ethnic groups are "apple," "coconut," and "Oreo."
47 Under most circumstances, I would not reveal the citizenship status of a student
or their family member, but Roni has spoken publicly about his father—including in his high school commencement address, which was picked up by the *New
York Times!* www.nytimes.com/2018/07/03/nyregion/undocumented-families-
deportation-graduation-speech.html

References

Abe, S., & Shapiro, S. (2021). Sociolinguistics as a pathway to global citizenship:
Critically observing 'self' and 'other'. *Language Awareness*, 30(4), 355–370.
Batchelor, K. E., & King, A. (2014). Freshmen and five hundred words: Investigat-
ing flash fiction as a genre for high school writing. *Journal of Adolescent & Adult
Literacy*, 58(2), 111–121.
Berger, R. (2018, March 14). Here's what's wrong with Bloom's taxonomy: A deeper
learning perspective. *EducationWeek.* www.edweek.org/education/opinion-heres-
whats-wrong-with-blooms-taxonomy-a-deeper-learning-perspective/2018/03

Blankenship, L. (2019). *Changing the subject: A theory of rhetorical empathy.* University Press of Colorado.

Cella, L. J., & Restaino, J. (Eds.). (2012). *Unsustainable: Re-imagining community literacy, public writing, service-learning, and the university.* Lexington Books.

Christoph, J. N., & Nystrand, M. (2001). Taking risks, negotiating relationships: One teacher's transition toward a dialogic classroom. *Research in the Teaching of English,* 249–286.

Cook, G. (2000). *Language play, language learning.* Oxford University Press.

Deroo, M. R., & Ponzio, C. M. (2021). Fostering pre-service teachers' critical multilingual language awareness: Use of multimodal compositions to confront hegemonic language ideologies. *Journal of Language, Identity & Education,* 1–17. https://doi.org/10.1080/15348458.2020.1863153

Duffy, J. (2019). *Provocations of virtue: Rhetoric, ethics, and the teaching of writing.* University Press of Colorado.

Esterhuyse, J. (1994). Psycholinguistic cocoon spinning and language education in a fragmenting society. *Southern African Journal of Applied Language Studies, 3*(1), 51–59.

García, O., Johnson, S. I., Seltzer, K., & Valdés, G. (2017). *The translanguaging classroom: Leveraging student bilingualism for learning.* Caslon.

Griffith, J. (2017). *From me to we: Using narrative nonfiction to broaden student perspectives.* Routledge.

Guerra, J. C. (2016). *Language, culture, identity and citizenship in college classrooms and communities.* Routledge.

Hardy, J. (2006). Speaking clearly: A critical review of the self-talk literature. *Psychology of Sport and Exercise, 7*(1), 81–97.

Harlap, Y. (2014). Preparing university educators for hot moments: Theater for educational development about difference, power, and privilege. *Teaching in Higher Education, 19*(3), 217–228.

James, A., & Nerantzi, C. (Eds.). (2019). *The power of play in higher education: Creativity in tertiary learning.* Springer.

Janks, H. (1996). Why we still need critical language awareness in South Africa. *Stellenbosch Papers in Linguistics Plus, 29,* 172–190.

Janks, H. (2001). Critical language awareness: Curriculum 2005 meets the TRC. *Southern African Linguistics and Applied Language Studies, 19*(3–4), 241–252.

Janks, H. (2010). *Literacy and power.* Routledge.

Kibler, A., Valdes, G., & Walqui, A. (2020). *Reconceptualizing the role of critical dialogue in American classrooms: Promoting equity through dialogic education.* Routledge.

Leather, M., Harper, N., & Obee, P. (2020). A pedagogy of play: Reasons to be playful in postsecondary education. *Journal of Experiential Education,* 1–19.

Liedtka. (2018). https://hbr.org/2018/09/why-design-thinking-works

Lorimer Leonard, R. L. (2014). Multilingual writing as rhetorical attunement. *College English, 76*(3), 227–247.

Lu, M. Z., & Horner, B. (2016). Introduction: Translingual work. *College English, 78*(3), 207–218.

Marback, R. (2009). Embracing wicked problems: The turn to design in composition studies. *College Composition and Communication, 61*(2), W397.

Nagayama Hall, G. (2017, April 5). Life as a banana: Asian American identity. *Psychology Today*. www.psychologytoday.com/us/blog/life-in-the-intersection/201704/life-banana

Oleson, K. C. (2020). *Promoting inclusive classroom dynamics in higher education: A research-based pedagogical guide for faculty.* Stylus Publishing, LLC.

Piore, A. (2019, June 28). Gen Zs are anxious, entrepreneurial, and determined to avoid their predecessors' mistakes. *Newsweek.* www.newsweek.com/2019/06/28/gen-zs-are-anxious-entrepreneurial-determined-avoid-their-predecessors-mistakes-1443581.html

Purdy, J. P. (2014). What can design thinking offer writing studies? *College Composition and Communication, 612–641.*

Ross, L. (2019, Spring). Speaking up without tearing down. *Learning for Justice, 61.* www.learningforjustice.org/magazine/spring-2019/speaking-up-without-tearing-down

Rowe, M. (2008). Micro-affirmations and micro-inequities. *Journal of the International Ombudsman Association, 1*(1), 45–48.

Rumbaut, R. G. (2009). A language graveyard? The evolution of language competencies, Preferences and use among young adult children of immigrants. In T. G. Wiley, J. S. Lee, & R. Rumberger (Eds.), *The education of language minority immigrants in the United States* (pp. 35–71). Multilingual Matters.

Shapiro, S. (2019, August). Why building community even through discomfort could help stressed college students. *The Conversation.* https://theconversation.com/why-building-community-even-through-discomfort-could-help-stressed-college-students-121398

Shapiro, S. (2020). Inclusive pedagogy in the academic writing classroom: Cultivating communities of belonging. *Journal of Academic Writing, 10*(1), 154–164.

Shapiro, S. (2022). "Language and social justice": A (surprisingly) plurilingual first-year seminar. In G. Shuck & K. Losey (Eds.), *Plurilingual pedagogies for multilingual writing classrooms: Engaging the rich communicative repertoires of U.S. students.* Routledge.

Shapiro, S.,& Leopold, L. (2012). A critical role for role-playing pedagogy. *TESL Canada Journal, 29*(2), 121–130. https://teslcanadajournal.ca/index.php/tesl/article/view/1104

Strayhorn, T. L. (2018). *College students' sense of belonging: A key to educational success for all students.* Routledge.

Teagarden, A., Commer, C., Cooke, A., & Mando, J. (2018). Intellectual risk in the writing classroom: Navigating tensions in educational values and classroom practice. *Composition Studies, 46*(2), 116–238.

Tod, D., Hardy, J., & Oliver, E. (2011). Effects of self-talk: A systematic review. *Journal of Sport and Exercise Psychology, 33*(5), 666–687.

Tse, L. (2001). Resisting and reversing language shift: Heritage-language resilience among US native biliterates. *Harvard Educational Review, 71*(4), 676–709.

Warren, L. (2000). Hot moments in the classroom. *NEA Higher Education Advocate, 18*(1), 5–8.

Wible, S. (2020). Using design thinking to teach creative problem solving in writing courses. *College Composition and Communication, 71*(3), 399–425.

Part III

Charting Your Own Journey with CLA Pedagogy

Introduction to Part III

Parts I and II created a foundation of understanding about what CLA Pedagogy is, why it works, and what it looks like in writing classrooms. If you decided to skip over those sections and start here, I would suggest checking out some of the figures that capture core concepts, including:

- The three goals for CLA pedagogy (graphic p.)
- The six principles for CLA Pedagogy (graphic p. 62)
- The Pathways overview chart, which lists titles for the three units in each pathway (p. 18)
- The "At-a-Glance" chart in each Pathways chapter, which lists key concepts/topics, readings/resources, and activities/assignments for that particular pathway.

Part III delves further into the **how** of this approach: How do we decide which pathways/units will work best for our teaching situation? How do we align our curriculum design and classroom instruction with the goals of CLA? How can CLA inform our work outside the classroom? I hope readers come away from these final chapters with plenty of strategies for charting their own pathways with CLA Pedagogy. Keep in mind that there are more tips and resources at the online Hub (http://clacollective.org/), as well as opportunities to connect with other practitioners!

DOI: 10.4324/9781003171751-12

8
Tailoring CLA Pedagogy to Your Teaching Context

Introduction

In the chapters of the volume thus far, we have reviewed what CLA Pedagogy is and why we might apply it in our writing classrooms. We have explored four thematic Pathways for applying CLA Pedagogy—Sociolinguistics, Critical Academic Literacies, Media/Discourse Analysis, and Communicating-Across-Difference. Each Pathway included three learning sequences from which teachers can draw topics, materials, activities, and assignments that best fit their pedagogical goals. Now that we have a sense of the many curricular possibilities for CLA Pedagogy, the question becomes: *How do we design CLA-oriented courses/units that will work well in our own teaching situations?*

Although there is no simple answer to this question, there are many strategies we can use to make informed and thoughtful curricular choices. Many of these strategies fall under the umbrella of **needs analysis**—sometimes called "needs assessment"—which I define as a process of dialogue and data-gathering aimed at deepening our understanding of curricular needs, constraints, assets, and opportunities (e.g., Flowerdew, 2018; Long, 2005[1]). Within a CLA approach, needs analysis is informed by both pragmatism and progressivism—the "both/and" approach we first discussed in Chapter 1 and unpacked more fully in Chapter 3. We want to answer the questions *How can our curricula prepare students to be successful in today's schools and societies?* And *How can our curricula promote more inclusive and equitable schools and societies for tomorrow?* (See Benesch, 1996, for more on critical approaches to needs analysis).

Below, I discuss a range of needs analysis strategies we can use to better understand our students, programs, and institutions. I then share how I applied

DOI: 10.4324/9781003171751-13

these strategies in designing four CLA-oriented writing courses that I teach regularly at Middlebury: "The English Language in a Global Context," "Language and Social Justice," "English Grammar: Concepts and Controversies," and "Narratives in the News Media." I talk about how I chose the topics, materials, and assignments in each course to respond to the needs, goals, and assets of the student population(s) I wanted to reach, and to help me achieve some of my other professional goals. I have summarized the design features of each course in a table on p. 262–263.

We then shift to exploring about how we can link CLA to national standards, since many teachers are expected to make these links explicit in their curriculum development. We consider points of overlap between our three CLA goals—self-reflection, social justice, and rhetorical agency—and the outcomes articulated in the Common Core State Standards for English/Language Arts (CCSS ELA) and the Framework for Success in Postsecondary Writing (FSPW).

The chapter concludes with some suggestions for maximizing access, equity, and inclusion in our course design. Chapter 9 continues this discussion, looking at how CLA can shape our day-to-day instructional practices.

One final note before we delve in: Some of the considerations discussed here may be more relevant to postsecondary than secondary contexts, since most of my CLA-oriented teaching has been in higher education settings. The needs analysis process may be more informal and ongoing for teachers working with middle- and high-school students (e.g., in English language arts or English Learner classrooms), whose curricula may need to respond to students' emergent needs and interests, and to ensure alignment with program, district, and/or state standards. Thus, although I am implying a linear process here for curriculum development, I want to recognize that in many cases, the process may be more complicated. Although I have not yet had an opportunity to develop an entire course at the secondary level, I did co-design and co-teach a month-long "Language and Social Justice" for 7th–10th graders (see Appendix), which I will discuss at the end of this chapter. The online Hub has citations for other examples of CLA-oriented curricula designed for secondary—and even primary—grades teachers. There are opportunities for you to share your own ideas and materials, too!

Needs Analysis: Getting (and Staying) Curious

When I first heard the phrase "needs analysis," it sounded unfamiliar and a bit daunting. Over time, though, I have realized that it is a term for something good teachers do automatically, often without knowing it has a name—or rather, two names, as noted earlier! At the heart of needs analysis is **curiosity**—about our students, our programs and departments, our institutions, and even (sometimes) our local communities. If we "stay curious" about all of these factors, we can continue to tailor our curricula to our teaching context, in both pragmatic and progressive ways.

As we engage this process from a CLA perspective, we don't just focus on student "needs." We also want to take into account their histories, goals, and assets, as well as our institutional structures and subcultures. This expansion beyond "student needs" is an important way of maintaining our commitment to viewing language difference as an asset, rather than a problem, as discussed in earlier chapters. The question we are asking is not "How can we fix students' linguistic deficiencies?" but rather "How can we create curricula and policies that are inclusive and effective with students from all language backgrounds?" (Shapiro, 2011, 2012).

The latter question is informed not only by our CLA commitment to both pragmatism and progressivism, but also by research demonstrating the value of "**appreciative inquiry** in strategic planning (e.g., Cockell et al., 2020; Kozik et al., 2009). If we begin by identifying the values, assets, opportunities, and resources we want to tap into, we recognize our existing strengths, rather than focusing only on problems we need to solve. In this way, we can avoid some of the pitfalls of deficit framing, which we discussed in Chapter 6 (e.g., p. 204).

Thus, a more holistic analysis considers questions such as:

- What are our students' goals, interests, and aspirations? Where do they want to go with their education—and beyond? What barriers are they likely to face in getting there?
- What assets do students bring to our classrooms/institutions? How might we tap into those assets more intentionally within the curriculum? What scaffolding and differentiation options can we build in so that all students are able to participate fully?
- How might our programs/institutions increase their opportunities, support, and advocacy for students from marginalized backgrounds? How might our curricula promote equity and inclusion more broadly?

Below are some strategies I have used to answer these questions at my own institution:

Data-Gathering and Analysis

- Conducting surveys, interviews, or focus groups with students (see following textbox) or with colleagues and administrators
- Examining data gathered by administration—e.g., via admissions records, institutional surveys, etc.
- Reviewing student feedback from course evaluations, department/program surveys, writing center reports, etc.
- Observing patterns in student work from other classes—e.g., What themes are students often drawn to researching and writing about? What topics do they seem eager to engage more in class discussion?

Dialogue/Observation

- Talking with faculty in other departments/entities about academic needs and curricular opportunities—e.g., by visiting department/committee meetings
- Surveying students in current courses or having them conduct peer-to-peer research, as we discussed in several of the Pathways chapters
- Noting topics/issues that come up in the school newspaper, at co-curricular events, etc.

Student Interview Questions Used for Needs—and Assets—Analysis at Middlebury College

NOTE: *This set of questions was tailored to multilingual and international college students, but could be adapted for other groups (e.g., first-generation college students) and settings (e.g., high school)*

1. What are your academic and professional goals (during and after college)?
2. Why did you choose to come to this college? What drew you here?
3. How has the adjustment to college been academically? Socially?
4. What have you enjoyed most? What are you most proud of?
5. What have been your greatest challenges or struggles?

6   What supports/resources/strategies have helped you along the way?
7   What do you wish we had more courses, workshops, or supports for? (topics, skills, etc.)
8   What do you wish faculty understood/knew about international/ multilingual students?
9   Do you have anything else to share from your perspective as a multilingual/international student?

In the following section, I discuss how these strategies informed the curriculum design for four writing courses I teach regularly at Middlebury.[2] It is important to note that for my institutional context—a small, liberal arts college with no major in writing or linguistics (yet!)—most of my courses are selected voluntarily by students, rather than being required. This means that I have to make my course descriptions **relevant to students' goals and interests** if I want the course to be successful. Table 8.1 offers a quick comparative snapshot of all four courses.

Table 8.1 Comparison of Four CLA-Oriented Courses

Course	"The English Language in a Global Context" (Writing Elective)	"Language and Social Justice " (First-Year Seminar, Fulfills First College Writing Requirement)	English Grammar: Concepts and Controversies (Linguistics Elective)	Narratives in the News Media (Linguistics Elective, Fulfills Second College Writing Requirement)
Targeted Student Population	International students (& other multilingual/L2 writers)	First-years— especially BIPOC and first-gen	All years, mix of backgrounds, interests, and goals	Sophomores and above, mix of backgrounds, interests, and goals

Key Goals	- Interdisciplinary reading and writing - Research (secondary) - Analysis and argumentation - Asset orientation to language difference - Global citizenship	- Academic reading and writing skills - Research (secondary) - Oral communication - Adjustment to Middlebury - Inclusion/connecting across difference	- Interdisciplinary reading and writing - Grammar terms - Language analysis skills - Research (primary) - Critical perspectives (prescriptivism, etc.)	- Interdisciplinary reading and writing (including empirical studies) - Research methods (primary and secondary) - Engaging across difference
CLA Units (from Ch. 4–7)	4.1, 4.2, 5.3, 6.3, 7.3	4.1, 4.2, 4.3, 5.3, 6.1, 7.2, 7.3	5.1, 5.2, 5.3, 6.1	6.1, 6.2, 6.3, 7.2, 7.3
Assignments and Assessment	Research report and oral presentation Position paper "Writing Beyond the Classroom" *Revision required for all assignments	Response paper Media criticism Research project Writing Beyond the Classroom *Revision required via portfolios (midterm and final)	Autobiographical reflection Position paper Primary research (survey or interviews) *Revision optional	Autobiographical reflection Research project (with scaffolding papers) Writing Beyond the Classroom *Revision required for all assignments

Four CLA-Oriented Courses Informed by Needs (and Assets!) Analysis

1 **The English Language in a Global Context:** This was the first new writing course I created at Middlebury, and it was intended to appeal in

particular to international students. Before settling on a course topic, I conducted a series of interviews and surveys with current students to learn more about their experiences, needs, and interests, using the questions listed above. The findings showed that:

- International students were eager for courses that included inter-disciplinary content beyond the humanities
- They were particularly interested in courses on global themes
- They wanted courses that fulfill graduation requirements—beyond counting for elective credit

In response to these findings, I chose a topic that could incorporate texts/media from a range of disciplines—in particular from social sciences—and that would fulfill our "Comparative Cultures" gradua-tion requirement. The course was cross-listed with Education Studies, to give it more visibility and to complement their elective offerings. It also became an elective option for a minor in Linguistics, which was approved a few years after I first designed the course. As I hoped, this course has drawn in many international students. However, I have also had high numbers of immigrant-background students as well, and some L1 English writers interested in linguistic diversity—so it has been a rich, multilingual, and multidialectal group. To learn more about this course, see Shapiro (2015) and Siczek and Shapiro (2014).

2   **Language and Social Justice:** In lieu of a first-year composition pro-gram, my institution has a first-year seminar program, taught by faculty across departments. Faculty in the Writing & Rhetoric Program offer first-year seminars frequently that are designed to appeal in particular to students from underrepresented groups. By the time I developed this course, I had learned more about the needs, experiences, and goals of Black, Indigenous, and People of Color (BIPOC) students on our cam-pus. I had also taken part in events and conversations with students who were "first gen"—i.e., the first in their families to attend college. Two highlights from this learning were:

- Many of our BIPOC and first-gen students are passionate about anti-racism and other social justice issues. A number of them are involved with activism on campus and in the local community.
- These students are very pragmatic in selecting courses. Graduating on time is of crucial importance, particularly since many such stu-dents are receiving needs-based financial aid.

I designed my first-year seminar with these points in mind. In addition to meeting our first-year writing requirement, this course fulfills two other graduation requirements—one for a focus on "the Americas" and the other for an emphasis on "Social Analysis." I have had strong representation of BIPOC students in that class, including both multilingual and multidialectal students. There are also many White students—in particular, students studying or already proficient in languages other than English. I've shared more about this course in Chapter 4—see also Shapiro (2022). I also co-taught a four-week adaptation of this course for 7th–10th graders (see Appendix).

3   **English Grammar: Concepts and Controversies:** This was my first opportunity to design a new linguistics elective. I designed this course taking into account several factors:

- The linguistics program needed more electives in English, to complement electives offered in other languages
- Students in my other courses often expressed an interest in learning about the applications of sociolinguistics to writing
- Students in other programs—e.g., writing center tutors, English majors, and preservice teachers—often asked about courses that would help them in their current and future work

As I shared in Chapter 5, I included both "concepts" and "controversies" in this course as a way to teach some grammar basics while also engaging critical conversations about prescriptivism and linguistic profiling. Although I could have designed this course to fulfill a College Writing requirement, I chose not to, so that I could admit a higher number of students—usually up to 22. Although I offer less explicit instruction in writing for this class, students do have some opportunities for revision, as noted in Table 8.1.

4   **Narratives in the News Media:** Although first-years are given priority in most of my other courses, this one is open to anyone, and tends to fill with sophomores and above. I designed this course in response to four observations:

- Our Writing & Rhetoric Program was receiving requests for more courses related to journalism and public communication
- The Linguistics Program wanted a "methods" course for students looking to do independent, qualitative research

- News media literacy was coming up frequently in class discussion, in students' papers and projects, at co-curricular events, and in institutional data (e.g., alumni surveys)
- I wanted to develop a course focused more intentionally on "engaging across difference"[3]—a topic that had become prominent on our campus following the 2016 U.S. presidential election, as well as a controversial speaker's visit to our campus in 2017 (Shapiro & Sanchez, 2020)

As I mentioned in Chapter 6, my first iteration of this course was called "Discourse Analysis," but I re-worked the course to focus primarily on news media. This course uses a Writing in the Disciplines (WID) model, with readings from media/communication studies and related fields, as well as Critical Discourse Analysis (CDA) theories and methods.

Table 8.1 notes additional features of each of these four courses .

I hope the backstory and details I have provided for each of these courses offers some insight into how the knowledge we build through data-gathering and dialogue can be channeled into our design of CLA-oriented courses. Below are a few additional suggestions related to the selection of course content:

- **Pilot new material in an existing class, when possible.** Before designing a new course/unit, I try out a portion of it in a class I'm already teaching, to see how students respond. I have occasionally offered a talk or workshop on a particular topic, or invited an outside speaker, in order to gauge student interest.
- **Aim for collaboration, rather than competition.** Before I propose a new course, I look at what is offered by other departments and programs, so that I can complement rather than duplicate what is currently on offer. I also seek out opportunities to connect with colleagues in other disciplines. For example, colleagues in Political Science and Digital Learning and Inquiry have become regular guest speakers in my "Narratives in the News Media" course, and I work with staff at our Center for Community Engagement to integrate community-connected learning into my "Language and Social Justice" first-year seminar (see Chapter 10).
- **Make space in class for student-generated topics.** I often leave a "topic TBD" day in my course calendar. As that day approaches, I start collecting

suggestions from students, and then we vote on one or more topics to focus on that day. I also try to include at least one assignment where students have some freedom to choose the topic—e.g., for library research or peer-to-peer research. I also sometimes have students take over as teachers and/or discussion facilitators and am often impressed with how seriously they take this peer educator role!

- **Aim for relevance *and* rigor.** Although I have emphasized here the importance of connecting with students' needs, goals, and interests, we do not want to lose sight of our CLA goals of self-reflection, social justice, and rhetorical agency—all goals that require deep intellectual and emotional engagement. This is why I centered each of the Pathways on essential questions and transferable skills. The aim is to bring together insight and intellect in students' CLA learning, and to help them express and extend that learning through rhetorically challenging activities and assignments.

CLA Pedagogy and Standards-Based Curricula

Much of what I have shared thus far in this chapter assumes teaching situations where the instructor has some flexibility and autonomy in selecting course content. But I recognize that many teachers are more constrained in what they are able to do with their curricula—either because of departmental/programmatic constraints or because they must teach to particular standards or assessments. I believe it is possible to cultivate CLA even in these more constrained situations. To help illustrate these possibilities, the table below outlines some areas of overlap between our CLA goals and two sets of **professional standards:** the Common Core State Standards (CCSS) for English Language Arts,[4] which are used in many secondary contexts in the U.S., and the Framework for Success in Postsecondary Writing (FSPW),[5] used in many U.S. higher education contexts. The points below come only from the general introduction to each set of standards.

To be clear, I do not wish to rehash the (decades-old) debate about whether standards help or hinder educational equity. The reality is that many teachers are expected to teach with and toward a set of standards, whether or not they find those standards to be useful. We have to be pragmatic and progressive in how we think about standards-based education, as with other aspects of our pedagogy. We will talk more about teaching constraints in Chapter 9.

Table 8.2 Overlap Between CLA Goals and Professional Standards

	CCSS: *"Portrait Of Students Who Meet the [ELA] Standards"*	FSPW: *"Habits of Mind Essential for Success in College Writing"*
Self-Reflection	"They demonstrate **independence.**" "They **comprehend** and **critique.**" "They value **evidence.**" (The anchor standards reference other types of reflection in relation to reading and writing.)	**"Curiosity**—the desire to know more about the world." **"Metacognition**—the ability to reflect on one's own thinking." **"Persistence**—the ability to sustain interest in and attention to short- and long-term projects."
Social Justice	"They **comprehend** as well as **critique.**" "They come to **understand other perspectives and cultures.**" (The anchor standards also include the ability to **"Respond thoughtfully to diverse perspectives."**)	**"Openness**—the willingness to consider new ways of being and thinking in the world." **"Responsibility**—the ability to take ownership of one's actions and understand the consequences of those actions for oneself and others." **"Critical thinking**—the ability to analyze a situation or text and make thoughtful decisions based on that analysis."
Rhetorical Agency	"They respond to the **varying demands of audience, task, purpose, and discipline.**" "They **use technology and digital media** strategically and capably."	**"Flexibility**—the ability to adapt to situations, expectations, or demands." **"Creativity**—the ability to use novel approaches for generating, investigating, and representing ideas." **"Rhetorical knowledge**—the ability to analyze and act on understandings of audiences, purposes, and contexts in creating and comprehending texts."

Digging deeper into each set of standards reveals other areas of overlap. For example, although "command of the conventions of standard English grammar" is a major focus throughout CCSS, suggesting a fairly prescriptivist approach, there are some inklings of descriptivism and rhetorical grammar in a few places. Within CCSS, students are expected to:

- "Compare and contrast the varieties of English (e.g., dialects, registers) used in stories, dramas, or poems." (Grade 5)
- "Recognize variations from standard English in their own and others' writing and speaking."[6] (Grade 6 and above)
- "Vary sentence patterns for meaning, reader/listener interest, and style." (Grade 6 and above)

Therefore, although the CCSS (or FSPW, for that matter–see Gere et al., 2021) are not explicitly critical of linguistic norms and standards, they at least recognize that language variation is an inherent feature of both speech and writing (it's a starting place, at least!). Moreover, at all grades, students are encouraged to "Respond thoughtfully to diverse perspectives," and one could argue that diverse perspectives *about language*—including critical conversations about norms and standards—fit nicely with this goal.

For K–12 teachers who work primarily with English Learners, by the way, the **WIDA English Language Development Standards**[7] overlap with a number of the CCSS points above. Many of the WIDA standards, particularly at the secondary level, encourage close and critical analysis of:

- Linguistic features of writing in different content areas (language arts, science, etc.)
- Rhetorical strategies authors use to accomplish their goals
- Differences between "formal" and "informal" registers of speaking and writing

See Lickenbrock (2020) for more on how CLA can be integrated into a WIDA-based curriculum.

The Framework for Success in Postsecondary Writing (FSPW) also includes several additional points that are particularly conducive to CLA Pedagogy:

- The Introduction to FSPW *discourages* the use of "[s]tandardized writing curricula or assessment instruments that emphasize formulaic writing for nonauthentic audiences."
- Under "Knowledge of Conventions," students should be encouraged to "read and analyze print and multimodal texts composed in various styles, tones, and levels of formality." (See Gere et al., 2021, for a discussion of how this section could be revised to be even more in line with CLA.)

- To cultivate "Flexibility," students should learn to "recognize that conventions (such as formal and informal rules of content, organization, style, evidence, citation, mechanics, usage, register, and dialect) are dependent on discipline and context."

To be clear, neither CCSS nor FSPW (nor WIDA) is particularly radical in its aims and scope. There is a general acceptance of standardized English as the status quo, with little or no discussion of language difference as a valued resource. However, we can certainly teach toward and with these standards as we explore language, identity, power, and privilege in our writing classes. And as we saw in Chapter 5, even within programs that are highly prescriptive in their approach to academic writing, we can make space for conversations about texts as cultural artifacts, grammar as rhetorical choice, and language difference as inherently linked to power. Moreover, if CLA becomes more widespread among writing teachers, there may be opportunities to revise the standards accordingly (Gere et al., 2021). One final note on standards: Learning for Justice—an organization devoted to supporting anti-bias education—recently published its own set of Social Justice Standards,[8] using an approach and format similar to CCSS. These are another resource we can draw on as we design and implement of CLA-oriented curricula.

Inclusive and Accessible Course Design

So far in this chapter, we have been talking primarily about course design in terms of curricular content. However, we also need to think about how to ensure that this content is inclusive and accessible for all of our students. One of the frameworks that can help us in this regard is Universal Design for Learning, or UDL (e.g., CAST, 2018[9]; Dolmage, 2015[10]). The UDL framework shares some conceptual overlap with "Backward Design," which was a feature of all of the Pathways chapters, and with "design thinking," which we learned about in Unit 7.3. At the heart of UDL is the idea that difference—neurological, cultural, linguistic, social, etc.—is the **norm, rather than the exception**. Rather than designing our courses for one type of student and then trying to retrofit for those who do not fit that mold, we can **build in access and differentiation** from the start.

Promoting access through UDL is like including an entry ramp in the design for a building. The ramp is useful for people who use wheelchairs, but it may also be helpful for those with crutches, canes, strollers, or even arms full of boxes. Some days, only a few people might need the ramp, but on others (e.g., moving day), nearly everyone benefits! The key insight here is that features that benefit a few students **all the time** might benefit other students at least **some of the time.**

UDL-oriented pedagogical strategies tend to be clustered into three categories: Engagement, Representation, and Action/Expression. Below, I briefly explain each category and outline some steps we can take in course design and delivery to maximize access and inclusion in that category.

Engagement refers to the "why" or "so what?" of learning, including students' goals, motivations, and learning processes. One way we maximize student engagement is by structuring our courses around academically, personally, culturally, and socially relevant topics and materials. Other ways we can promote engagement include:

- Being transparent about our course goals, as well as the goals for each unit and assignment
- Using warm and inviting language in syllabi and assignment handouts, rather than adopting a threatening or punitive tone (see Harnish and Bridges [2011] for more on this)
- Taking time to build community throughout the semester—not just in week one
- Adopting a broad definition of what it means to "participate" in class (more on this in Chapter 9)
- Building in opportunities for feedback to and from students throughout the course
- Making grading criteria and procedures transparent—e.g., by using rubrics. (Chapters 4–7 included a number of sample rubrics. Chapter 9 will discuss other aspects of grading/assessment)

Representation has to do with the "what" of learning, including our pedagogical objectives, concepts, and materials. Using curricular materials that are relevant to students on multiple levels, as noted earlier, is one way to expand representation. Other ways to do so include:

- Focusing course design on deep inquiry and transferable learning—not just on the topics or concepts we will "cover" (see Edutopia[11] for a critique of the "coverage" metaphor in education)
- Being selective and intentional in how we introduce new concepts and terminology—especially with students who are still building proficiency with academic English

- Offering opportunities and resources to help students build background knowledge needed to engage fully with course materials and assignments
- Thinking carefully about the type and amount of reading we assign and providing explicit instruction in reading (See Chapter 9 for more details)
- Selecting texts that are accessible (e.g., readable pdfs) and affordable (e.g., can be purchased, used, or borrowed from a library)
- Integrating other types of media, such as websites, podcasts, and video-recordings, to enhance student learning (note: Choosing audiovisual media that has **subtitles or transcripts** can increase access not just for students who are Deaf or Hard of Hearing, but also for English Learners and others who might struggle with listening comprehension—a great example of UDL principles at work!)
- Broadening the range of perspectives represented in course materials (My colleague James Chase Sanchez does a "bias assessment" of his reading list each semester, looking for ways he might bring in other perspectives. For guidance on assessing bias in course materials, check out the Comprehensive Center Network[12].)

Action/Expression involves the "how" of learning—in particular, how students demonstrate their learning. This includes both in-class and out-of-class work, as well as opportunities for students to set goals and assess their own progress. Some ways we can be more inclusive in promoting action/expression are:

- Building in formative assessment of student learning through in-class activities and low-stakes assignments (the Pathways chapters had many examples of this)
- Distributing workload across the unit/course, rather than "cramming in" major assignments at the end
- Giving students some amount of choice—for example with assigned readings (e.g., jigsaw reading, p. 96), with topics or genres for writing (e.g., in Units 5.3 and 7.3), or in whether to work alone or with a partner on an assignment or project.[13]
- Scaffolding the writing process by building in checkpoints and supports, such as:

  - A required proposal or meeting early in the process
  - Frequent progress reports, interim drafts, and/or in-class sharing sessions
  - Opportunities for feedback throughout the writing process (see Chapter 9)

- Targeted instruction or resources to address challenging aspects of each assignment

A number of other scaffolding suggestions are integrated throughout the Pathways chapters and discussed further in Chapter 9. As always, these suggestions are just the tip of the iceberg. The key takeaway from this chapter, I hope, is that **simply adding** CLA-oriented topics and materials to our syllabi *is not enough* to promote access and inclusion. To be frank, I have seen classes and units designed around very forward-thinking content but structured and delivered in a very old-school, inaccessible way. Below are a few representative examples:

- A course on global studies that includes readings so dense and theoretical that students—particularly multilingual and first-gen students—felt completely lost
- A multicultural literature unit in which students were expected to read a novel, plus several supplemental readings, every week
- A critical research methods course that required a 25-page paper due at the end, with little or no instructional scaffolding
- A unit on race and postcolonialism in which the teacher mostly lectured, offering very few opportunities for discussion or group work

If we really want to orient our courses toward social justice learning, we must think carefully about both curricular content and delivery of instruction— the latter of which is the focus of Chapter 9.

Tailoring and Differentiating CLA Content for Secondary Levels

Many of the examples I have shared in this chapter are from courses I have taught at the college level, but I want to make sure my readers in K–12 settings feel included in these discussions! To that end, below I describe some of the considerations that were taken into account in designing a "Language and Social Justice" unit for 7th–10th grade students. I created and taught the unit in collaboration with Garrett Kimberly, a teacher at the Lake Champlain Waldorf School, who just happens to be my spouse![14] (See Appendix for overview of this unit, and some additional details in Chapter 4.)

Although we would have preferred to teach only middle *or* high schoolers for this unit, scheduling constraints required that we combine them. We were a bit daunted by the idea of having four grade levels in a single class, but we decided we were up to the challenge! The plus side was that we were able to "walk the talk" of this chapter, by incorporating **differentiation by grade level**. Some of the adaptations discussed below might be useful for teachers working with students who have a variety of language backgrounds, literacy levels, and/or past educational experiences.

We designed this unit around the theme of "empathy," which is a core theme in the Waldorf curriculum. The **essential question** that guided our planning was: *How does learning about language and social justice build our empathy for others?* We opened the learning sequence with **reflection questions** such as "When have words made a difference in your life?" and "What are some specialized ways of using language within a community that you belong to outside of school?" This allowed me, as the guest teacher, to get to know the students better and helped establish the personal relevance of the topic.

As the unit progressed, students engaged with a **variety of online readings and media**, including blog posts, a podcast (with transcript), a TEDx talk (with subtitles), and a newspaper editorial. There was a bit of lecture from Mr. Kimberly on the history of language—an area he knows well—which was interspersed with **guided note-taking, comprehension checks**, and **application activities**. We were careful to recycle key terms (e.g., *idiolect, linguistic community, indexicality*) so that students were prepared to use those terms in their analysis and writing.

In terms of assignments, we provided clear goals and expectations but also gave students some amount of **choice depending on their grade level**. For example, for the "Varieties of English" project (see Unit 4.1), middle school students were urged to choose from a list we had curated in advance, while high schoolers were given more leeway. Both groups had to get final approval, however, before beginning their research. As a reminder, a table comparing features of this project for secondary vs. postsecondary levels is on p. 98.

We **differentiated** with other assignments as well. For the "Power of Language" essay discussed on p. 229, middle schoolers had a shorter length requirement than high schoolers. For a later essay on linguistic profiling, the middle school group only needed to reference one of the assigned media, while the high school students were asked to reference at least two. For the final project, the middle school group created an illustrated portfolio of their learning, while each high schooler pursued independent research on a topic of their choice, which they presented to the rest of the class during the final session. Students had opportunities to **synthesize their learning** in "carousel-style" sharing session, in which small groups of 5th-graders migrated from one presentation to the next. We also returned frequently to our theme of empathy, asking students where they saw that theme in our materials, discussions, and assignments.

Looking back, I realize that there are other ways we could have made this unit more inclusive and accessible. For example, we could have provided more **scaffolding** for the writing assignments, clearer **grading criteria** for the final projects, and more opportunities for **feedback from students** throughout the unit. I hope to co-teach this unit again in the future—and I may even seek out some additional collaborators via the Hub!

Conclusion

As we wrap up this chapter, I want to reiterate that the pedagogical applications I have described above are examples—not formulas. I have tailored my CLA-oriented units and courses to the particularities of my teaching situation(s). Now you, dear reader, get to do the same, starting with what you know—or want to know—about your students, programs, and institutions. I hope you "stay curious" about your own teaching context—and that you will visit the online discussion section of the Hub to share some of what you're learning! But as you continue to map out your own pedagogical applications, it is useful know a bit more about how this CLA can influence our day-to-day classroom instruction, which is our focus for Chapter 9. See you there!

Appendix:
Overview of "Language and Social Justice" unit for secondary-level students

Students: 7th–10th graders, mostly L1 speakers

Length: 30 hours over 3–4 weeks (~90 min sessions)

Essential Questions:

1 What power does language have in my day-to-day life?
2 What role does language play within communities?
3 How and why do languages change?
4 How does the English language vary geographically inside the U.S. and around the world?
5 How are our beliefs about language influenced by racism, classism, sexism, heteronormativity, and ableism?
6 How does linguistic profiling disadvantage particular groups and individuals?
7 How can we work against linguistic prejudice?
8 How does learning about language and social justice build our empathy for others?

Transferable Skills (Students will be able to. . .) :

A   **Explain** the power of language in their day-to-day lives
B   **Identify** linguistic communities they belong to, and name specific linguistic features/practices of those communities
C   **Take notes** from an interactive lecture
D   **Gather information** about a specific variety of language using credible online sources (see note-taking sheet in Chapter 4)
E   **Use** linguistic terminology to discuss features of a variety of English (e.g., *syntax, lexicon, phonology, prestige, stigma*) and to

DOI: 10.4324/9781003171751-

reflect on their linguistic practices and biases (e.g., *idiolect, indexicality, linguistic profiling*)

F   **Present** information about language variation to peers (both same age and younger) orally

G   **Recognize and respond** to incidents of linguistic prejudice.

Readings/Resources (Mostly from Chapter 4, the Sociolinguistics Pathway):

- Short online readings about the power of language (from Unit 7.1)
- Interactive lecture on history of English and factors contributing to language variation (Unit 4.1)
- Video clips demonstrating particular dialects and code-switching patterns (Unit 4.1)
- Codeswitch "Talk American" podcast episode about NPR reporter Deion Braxton (Unit 4.2)
- John Baugh's TEDx talk on language discrimination in the housing market (from Unit 4.3)
- McBee's (2018) editorial on gender, language, and power in NYTimes (Unit 4.3)

Major Assignments/Activities:

- Small group discussions about linguistic communities, power of language, etc.
- "Power of language" story (1–3 paragraphs—see Unit 7.1)
- "Variety of English" project: research notes and presentation (Unit 4.1)
- "Linguistic Profiling" essay referencing "Codeswitch" podcast and/or TEDx talk (Units 4.2 and 4.3)
- Critical role-play scenarios on linguistic prejudice (Unit 4.2)
- Presentation of independent learning to 5th-grade students (carousel style)

Final projects

- For 7th–8th grade: Portfolio of learning (including revisions and new illustrations)
- For 9th–10th grade: Independent research, presented to 7th/8th graders during final class session.

Notes

1 There are a number of online guides to educational needs analysis/assessment. One of my favorites is www.cde.state.co.us/sites/default/files/documents/fedpro grams/dl/consapp_na_guide.pdf

2 Course syllabi and other materials are available on my website, https://sites.mid dlebury.edu/shapiro/ and at the online Hub (clacollective.org)

3 For my most recent iteration of this course in Spring 2020, I was a faculty fellow in our grant-funded Engaged Listening Project, which helped me expand my skill set in this area. More at https://engagedlistening.middcreate.net/

4 www.corestandards.org

5 http://wpacouncil.org/aws/CWPA/pt/sd/news_article/242845/_PARENT/ layout_details/false

6 This standard admittedly prioritizes "conventional English"; however, the first part does provide an opening for some CLA-oriented conversation and analysis!

7 WIDA is the most commonly used framework and assessment model used to measure language development among English Learners. See https://wida.wisc. edu/sites/default/files/resource/WIDA-ELD-Standards-Framework-2020.pdf Note that the WIDA standards built on prior work published via TESOL International in 2006: www.tesol.org/docs/books/bk_prek-12elpstandards_frame work_318.pdf?sfvrsn=2

8 www.learningforjustice.org/sites/default/files/2020-09/TT-Social-Justice-Stand ards-Anti-bias-framework-2020.pdf. Thanks to Michelle Medved for making me aware of this resource!

9 https://udlguidelines.cast.org/

10 Links to this "workspace" with lots of ideas: http://universaldesignideas.pbworks. com/w/page/97590854/FrontPage

11 www.edutopia.org/blog/from-coverage-to-uncoverage-andrew-miller

12 www.michigan.gov/documents/mde/Tools_Guidance_Eval_Bias__ Instructional_Materials_704854_7.pdf

13 It is important to keep in mind, though, that students need rhetorical challenges in order to grow. We do not want to provide so much choice that they remain in their "comfort zones" as writers.

14 In case you wondered: Teaching with one's spouse is a rewarding but risky undertaking. I learned that compatibility with someone as a life partner does not necessarily translate to compatibility in teaching styles. I'm so glad we did it, though—I learned so much! And we continue to be happily married ♥

References

Benesch, S. (1996). Needs analysis and curriculum development in EAP: An example of a critical approach. *TESOL Quarterly*, 30(4), 723–738.

CAST. (2018). *Universal design for learning guidelines version 2.2.* http://udlguidelines. cast.org

Cockell, J., McArthur-Blair, J., & Schiller, M. (2020). *Appreciative inquiry in higher education: A transformative force*. Friesen Press.

Dolmage, J. (2015). Universal design: Places to start. *Disability Studies Quarterly, 35*(2).

Flowerdew, L. (2018). Needs analysis for the second language writing classroom. *The TESOL Encyclopedia of English Language Teaching*, 1–6.

Gere, A., Curzan, A., Hammond, J. W., Hughes, S., Li, R., Moos, A., Smith, K., Van Zanen, K., Wheeler, K. L., & Zanders, C. J. (2021). Communal justicing: Writing assessment, disciplinary infrastructure, and the case for critical language awareness. *College Composition and Communication, 72*(3), 384–412.

Harnish, R. J., & Bridges, K. R. (2011). Effect of syllabus tone: Students' perceptions of instructor and course. *Social Psychology of Education, 14*(3), 319–330.

Kozik, P. L., Cooney, B., Vinciguerra, S., Gradel, K., & Black, J. (2009). Promoting inclusion in secondary schools through appreciative inquiry. *American Secondary Education*, 77–91.

Lickenbrock, C. (2020). *Engaging middle school emergent bilinguals in language awareness: A practitioner researcher study*. Unpublished dissertation from the University of Missouri.

Long, M. (2005). *Second language needs analysis*. Cambridge University Press.

McBee, T. P. (2018 August 9). My voice got deeper. Suddenly people listened. *New York Times*. https://www.nytimes.com/2018/08/09/style/transgender-men-voice-change.html

Shapiro, S. (2011). Stuck in the remedial rut: Confronting resistance to ESL curriculum reform. *Journal of Basic Writing*, 24–52.

Shapiro, S. (2012). Citizens vs. aliens: How institutional policies construct linguistic minority students. In Y. Kanno & L. Harklau (Eds.), *Linguistic minority immigrants go to college: Preparation, access, and persistence* (pp. 238–254). Routledge.

Shapiro, S. (2015). World Englishes: Academic explorations of language, culture, and identity. In M. Roberge, K. Losey, & M. Wald (Eds.), *Teaching U.S.-educated multilingual writers: Pedagogical practices from and for the classroom* (pp. 263–280). University of Michigan Press.

Shapiro, S. (2022). "Language and social justice": A (surprisingly) plurilingual first-year seminar. In G. Shuck & K. Losey (Eds.), *Plurilingual pedagogies for multilingual writing classrooms: Engaging the rich communicative repertoires of U.S. students*. Routledge.

Shapiro, S., & Sanchez, J. C. (2020). Looking for the middle ground at Middlebury: Local exigencies, campus controversies, and the composition classroom. *Pedagogy: Critical Approaches to Teaching Literature, Language, Composition, and Culture*. https://sites.middlebury.edu/shapiro/files/2021/03/Shapiro_CV_March_2021.pdf

Siczek, M., & Shapiro, S. (2014). Developing writing-intensive courses for a globalized curriculum through WAC-TESOL collaborations. In M. Cox & T. Zawacki (Eds.), *WAC and second language writers: Research towards linguistically and culturally inclusive programs and practices* (pp. 329–346). WAC Clearinghouse. https://wac.colostate.edu/docs/books/12/chapter13.pdf

9
Infusing CLA into Classroom Instruction

Introduction

Much of our discussion thus far has been focused on the "what" of curricular content and course design. This chapter, in contrast, focuses on the "how" of our day-to-day instructional practices. We will talk about how to create **CLA moments**—opportunities to draw attention to issues of language, identity, power, and privilege—no matter what curricular content we are using. Research on critical approaches to education finds that everyday instances of "schooltalk" (Pollock, 2017), in fact, can play an important role in reinforcing our commitment to social justice (see also Quaid & Williams, 2021).

This chapter is particularly important for teachers whose control over their curriculum is quite limited and may be wondering, "Is there still a place for CLA in my classroom?" The answer is **yes—absolutely**! Below, we will discuss how CLA can shape how we talk about our programmatic and institutional constraints. We will then explore how to infuse CLA into class discussion, reading and speaking instruction, peer review, and feedback on student writing. The goal here, as always, is to build on—not replace—best practices for writing pedagogy. Readers newer to the teaching of writing may want to supplement this chapter with other readings on best practices for writing pedagogy, some of which are referenced in Chapter 3 (pp. 69-71).

Bringing CLA into Conversations about Institutional Constraints

As we touched on in Chapter 8, many writing curricula are shaped heavily by program requirements, professional standards, high-stakes assessments, and other factors. We may have to work with policies or curricular standards that we find problematic. Below, we consider the question: *How can*

DOI: 10.4324/9781003171751-14

we teach with—and talk about—these constraints in ways that reflect our commitment to CLA?

Provide Context

Students are often told about policies and curriculum requirements without being given any rationale or historical context, which may imply to students that our program or institution's way of doing things is the only way. We can "demystify" our constraints by providing some background information about who creates our policies and curricula and how. Such explicit conversations help students understand how academic institutions function—and may even illuminate some possibilities for change!

Emphasize Our Dual Commitment to Pragmatism and Progressivism

As we talk with students about our constraints, we can be transparent about our commitment to both pragmatism and progressivism. I may not use these terms with students, but I often point out that I am trying to prepare them for the world as it is today, while also promoting a more just world for tomorrow. For example, earlier in my career, I taught in an English for Academic Purposes (EAP) program that used timed writing exams for placement and course completion. Pragmatically, I had to devote a significant portion of our instructional time to teaching test performance strategies, and administering "practice tests," so that students were prepared for these high-stakes exams. This left little space in the curriculum for more authentic and engaging writing tasks, which felt like a violation of my values as a teacher.

However, I tried to weave in conversation about the ethical and pedagogical problems with using timed testing as the sole measure of writing proficiency. And I made sure the students knew that a number of instructors, myself included, were working hard to push for reform to our curriculum and policies (Shapiro, 2011, 2012). Thus, drawing on Casanave's (2005) metaphor of academic writing as a "game," I showed students how to play by the rules, but also invited them into conversations about the problems with those rules and our efforts to change them.

Make the Constraints a Focus for Analysis and Critique

Some of my fellow instructors in the EAP program referenced above had more grounding in critical approaches to EAP (e.g., Benesch, 2001, 2009;

Ruecker & Shapiro, 2020), and they took the conversations a step further: Students wrote letters describing their experiences with the program and proposing changes that could make it more equitable and effective. These letters were shared widely across the program, with student names removed, and they helped to build consensus about the need for reform—which did happen, eventually. Check out my 2011 article "Stuck in the Remedial Rut," which is available freely online, if you're curious to know more!

Thus, we may be able to give students opportunities to discuss and write about aspects of our programs that are unjust or ineffective. Possible foci can include:

- **Placement/Advising:** How did you feel about your course placement? Did you feel that you had some choice and agency in selecting courses? What information would be helpful to share with future students? (See Saenkhum [2016] for more on student-centered advising.)
- **Textbooks:** How useful, affordable, and/or accessible is our textbook? What beliefs about language and writing are evident in the book? (See Russell [2018] for more on language ideologies in writing textbooks.)
- **Grading/evaluation:** Have our course/program assessments allowed you to demonstrate your learning as a writer? Are the grading criteria clear and fair? How useful is the feedback to your growth as a writer? (See Crusan [2010] and Poe and Elliot [2019], for more on the ethics of writing assessment.)

We may be unable—or students may be unwilling—to share written critiques with decision-makers in our programs and institutions. But creating opportunities for students to voice their experiences and concerns, even if it is just within the confines of our class, can produce powerful writing with valuable insights. Moreover, it can prepare students to advocate for themselves and others as they move through our institutions and into their professional and civic lives (Benesch, 2009).

A CLA Approach to Classroom Discussion

One of the concerns I had when I first began incorporating CLA content into my writing classes was how to facilitate discussion on controversial topics. Some scholars have claimed that writing teachers should try to avoid "political" topics (e.g., Hairston, 1992; Santos, 2012), while others claim that these topics are the very ones our students need to be talking and writing about (e.g., Trimbur et al., 1993)! Instructors working in K–12 settings may face additional pressure from family or community members (or administrators) to avoid provocative or contentious issues. It is worth pointing out, however, that the definition of what is "political" or "sensitive" is very context-specific. For example, a friend of mine who works at a university affiliated with the U.S. military, has to be cautious about expressing her pacificist views. Another who works at a Jesuit-affiliated school is openly critical of U.S. military action but tends to remain quiet about the fact that she is agnostic and has no religious affiliation.

Each teacher has to decide which topics and questions have the most learning value for their students, and to weigh the benefits with the potential risks. But we must also remember that CLA Pedagogy can never be 100% "apolitical"—after all, we're talking about privilege and power! Besides, even if we choose only "safe" topics for discussion, there are bound to be instances of tension and awkwardness—what Warren (2005) calls "hot moments." CLA can help us use those moments for learning and growth. As a reminder, "difficult dialogue" was also a focus in Unit 7.2.

This section provides some insights and strategies for facilitating rich, productive discussion—no matter what the topic! It is informed by some of my other research that has examined college students' conceptions of inclusivity and their experiences engaging diverse perspectives (Shapiro, 2018[1], 2019[2], 2020[3]). One key takeaway from that research was that **inclusivity does not happen automatically.** Creating an inclusive classroom space—one in which transformative dialogue can occur—requires intentionality, preparation, and support. And as we will discuss below, CLA can be a useful resource in this process.

Distinguish Among Debate, Discussion, and Dialogue

One thing students reported to me in interviews about their experiences in the classroom is that opportunities for dialogue are rare. Often, as one student put it, "we're talking *at* people instead of *with* them." Another noted that we sometimes forget to "see the person as a person and not just a clump of ideas" (Shapiro, 2018). We can use language, then, **to frame the purpose** of our classroom conversations and to set appropriate expectations. If our goal is to lay out ideas, arguments, and evidence, we may use structured debate or another discussion format. But if we want to deepen understanding, connection, and sense of belonging, we need to craft a more **dialogic** space (Kibler et al., 2020)—perhaps something akin to what Parker (2018) calls a "gathering." The goal in this sort of dialogue is **not to persuade others** to change their views or beliefs.[4] Rather, it is to:

- Broaden our knowledge of other viewpoints
- Recognize contradictions or gaps in our own thinking
- Prepare to write about complex issues with nuance and empathy
- Strengthen community bonds

In other words, dialogue is really about what we *gain from others*—not what we want to *change in them*.

Reframe (and Prepare for) Discomfort

Another realization from my research was that many students conflate "inclusivity" with "comfort." For example, one participant described an inclusive classroom as a place where "Everyone's happy . . . There's no tension between anyone." (Um . . . reality check, please!). We need to work with students to develop a more realistic understanding of what inclusion feels like, including **reframing discomfort** as part of learning and growth, rather than as an indicator of a problem. But normalizing discomfort does not mean abandoning the idea of **safety** in the classroom. There is a "toughen up" narrative that often emerges when some teachers talk about safe spaces. Syllabi, handbooks, and letters home[5] often include statements such as:

- "You should not expect this to be a safe space."
- "I do not believe in trigger warnings."[6]
- "It is not my job to make you comfortable. In fact, I want to make you uncomfortable!"[7]

Rather than adopting this defensive posture about what we *will not* be doing, we need to tell students what we *can and will* do to help create a classroom space where everyone can learn and grow. Some experts use the frame "**brave space**" as a way of capturing this intention (e.g., Palfrey, 2017; Pawlowski, 2018). A brave space is one where students and instructors are curious,[8] respectful, and open to taking intellectual, emotional, and social risks. In this space, we expect discomfort, but we do not ignore people's physical, social, and emotional needs. Working through discomfort together, in fact, becomes one of our learning goals.

To help my students and colleagues think about managing discomfort in the classroom, I like to draw an analogy to a physically strenuous task, such as **going on a hike or playing a sport** (see Figure 9.1): We expect some inevitable discomfort, and we gear up accordingly, with supplies (clothing and shoes, water bottles, sun protection, etc.) as well as routines (warming up, stretching, taking breaks). Preparing for discomfort allows us "stay safe" (i.e., not experience injury) while pushing ourselves physically. That is the same dynamic we want in the classroom, as we prepare to take on intellectual and emotional challenges.

The question we need to ask, then, is not *How can we prevent discomfort?* but rather, *What do we need in order to prepare for uncomfortable conversations?* Being explicit about the goals of the conversation, as discussed above, is an important first step. Another is to establish clear guidelines or "ground rules," possibly crafted in collaboration with students. Some common examples include:

- Only one person should speak at a time
- Speak for yourself and not for a group
- Critique ideas—not people
- Ask curious questions rather than making accusations
  (e.g., "What in your life has influenced your views on this topic?" vs. "Can't you see how offensive that view is?")
- Be willing to "step back" or "step up" as needed, to make room for more voices

Figure 9.1 A Metaphor for Difficult Dialogue. Photo credit to Ana Essentiels

Essential Partners[9] and Facing History[10] are two of the many organizations devoted to dialogic education. Both offer lesson plans and other resources for creating discussion norms. For more information on creating brave spaces, check out the resources from Aware LA,[11] an affiliate of the national group Showing Up for Racial Justice.

Experiment with Groupings and Formats

Another strategy that can help to make our conversations more inclusive is to vary our groupings, formats, and modes of interaction. We saw many examples of this in the Pathways chapters. A more structured approach, such as a Socratic Seminar,[12] "circle share" (p. 192) or "fishbowl" (pp. 235–236) can create openings for students who might otherwise be reluctant to join the conversation, as can freewriting prior to discussion. Using pair and/or small group activities, as well as asynchronous online discussion, also helps to bring forward voices that are less likely to be heard in a "popcorn style" (i.e., voluntary) large group discussion. We can even invite students to reflect on perspectives that are missing from the conversation, using activities such as "Missing Voices" (p. 234).

Use Language to Manage Social and Emotional Dynamics

As we discussed in Chapter 7, language can be a powerful tool for understanding and processing our emotional experiences. During class discussions, we can model how to use language to **name what we are feeling** (e.g., "I'm noticing some frustrations coming up around. . . " or "I'm a little nervous to ask this question, because. . . "). We can model language for **seeking clarification** as well (e.g., "It sounds like you're saying . . . Is that accurate? Can you explain a bit more?").

Students also need instruction and support for **holding each other accountable, recognizing harm, and repairing that harm** when it occurs. As we touched on in Chapters 6 and 7, critiques of "call-out culture" (or "cancel culture") are prevalent, but the discussion rarely shifts to alternatives. Loretta Ross (2019),[13] a feminist historian and community activist, uses a "calling in" approach—one that is focused on learning rather than shaming (see examples below).

Examples of "calling in" language, from Loretta Ross's (2019) article in *Learning for Justice*

- "I need to stop you there because something you just said is not accurate."
- "I'm having a reaction to that comment. Let's go back for a minute."
- "Do you think you would say that if someone from that group was with us in the room?"
- "There's some history behind that expression you just used that you might not know about."
- "In this class, we hold each other accountable. So we need to talk about why that joke isn't funny."

We can also teach and model for students some ways to respond when we are "called in" for something we have said or done. In an excellent podcast episode about shaming vs. accountability,[14] Brené Brown describes how she uses **self-talk** (see Unit 7.1) to work through the feelings of shame that arise when she realizes she has made a mistake. One statement Brown uses is: *"You're not here to be right. You're here to get it right."* I've developed my own adaptation of that statement, which is: *"No one is perfect. You're here to learn and grow."* (Saying this aloud really helps me!) Sending these compassionate messages to ourselves—and sharing them with students, when appropriate— can help all of us develop "shame resilience" so that we respond from a place of care and curiosity, rather than defensiveness (Brown, 2018).

Another way we can use language is to **process what is happening in our bodies** when we are engaged in difficult conversations (e.g., Menakem, 2017; Taylor, 2018). I use short **mindfulness exercises** at the start of most of my class sessions, as a grounding practice. These usually include chair-based stretches (e.g., shoulder and neck roles) and guided breathing, but I occasionally incorporate body scans, visualizations, or words of affirmation (e.g., pp. 226–227). I also ask students to do body-based inquiry, with questions such as: "Where in your body are you carrying stress right now?"

I see these **mindfulness moments** as a crucial tool for building brave spaces. They offer us a connecting ritual, as well as a strategy we can use when tension rises (e.g., *"Let's all return to some deep breathing, so we can notice what we're feeling right now."*). For instructors who might be apprehensive about doing mindfulness activities with their students—I was quite nervous the first few times I did it!—it might be reassuring to know that there is research showing that most students have very positive reactions to these experiences (e.g., Bamber & Schneider, 2020; Carsley et al., 2018). One of my favorite resources for integrating mindfulness into the classroom is the "tree" of contemplative practices[15] from the Center for Contemplative Mind in Society. I hope to share and learn about other resources at the Hub!

Another contemplative activity included in the aforementioned "tree" is **reflective writing**. Sometimes the best way to respond to a difficult moment is to give students a few minutes of silence for processing through freewriting or even drawing. Some questions we can use as prompts for written processing include:

- How is the discussion landing with you thus far?
- What have you found interesting in this discussion?
- What have you found difficult or confusing?
- What questions is this conversation raising for you?

For more on working with discomfort in writing classes, also see Prebel (2016) and Stewart (2017).

Promote a Growth Mindset Toward Inclusive Language

We cannot conclude a section on CLA and class discussion without talking about **inclusive language,** which we also touched on in Unit 7.2. This is another topic where there is a great deal of finger-pointing and binary thinking. Proponents of inclusive language often accuse critics of not caring about how words can hurt, demean, or exclude. Critics accuse proponents of caring more about "policing language" than about having open and meaningful conversation (the *Psychology Today* blog[16] offers a helpful overview of the debate).

A lot of nuances get lost in these debates: First is that the most pertinent question is not *What words should we use?* but rather, *How can we create a learning environment where everyone feels respected?* In other words, inclusive language is not an end in itself; it is a tool we use to remove barriers to engagement.

Another point that often gets lost is that inclusive language has to be learned. We need to approach conversations about inclusive language from a **growth mindset** orientation (e.g., Hochanadel & Finamore, 2015)—one that assumes we all have room for improvement in our ability to use language in the most accurate and humanizing way possible. One way we can reinforce that mindset is by directing students (in our syllabi or other instructional materials) to resources that explain and teach inclusive language. Chapter 7 mentioned two resources that bear repeating here:

1   Karen Yin's *Conscious Style Guide* (see Figure 9.2)[17] which has been recommended by the Chicago Manual of Style, NASA, and the Society for Professional Journalists (see Figure 9.2), and which uses the slogan "Keep Learning"
2   Hanna Thomas and Anna Hirsch's *Progressive's Style Guide*[18]

It is also important to acknowledge that **linguistic profiling**, which we explored in Chapters 4 and 5, happens in response not only to particular accents, dialects, or speech styles, but also to politically charged language. If I use the label "pro-life" vs. "anti-abortion" or "gun rights" vs. "gun control," my interlocutor (or reader) may make assumptions about my political affiliation. They may miss out on *what I am saying* because they are so focused on the *words I am using*.

Words matter—of course they do! But students are often unaware of the political implications of their linguistic choices. For example, some of my

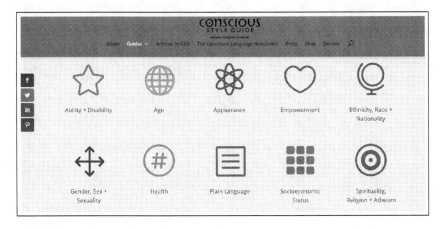

Figure 9.2 Screenshot of Yin's Conscious Style Guide

students hear the phrase "illegal immigrant" as xenophobic and/or dehumanizing, while others in the same class will tell me—usually privately—that they thought it was a politically neutral label. Those in the latter group are often open to hearing critiques of the descriptor "illegal" and to learning alternatives, such as "undocumented" or "unauthorized."

Students—and instructors, at times—sometimes also use new terms or acronyms without explaining them. One example is "BIPOC" (Black, Indigenous People of Color). Students need to know what these terms mean and why some people prefer them to the "older" terms (e.g., "People of Color"[19]). Otherwise, a conversation about inclusion might actually exclude many of the people in the room!

A CLA approach thus reminds us to **pause and focus on language**, to make sure everyone understands what our words mean and how they might be heard by different groups of people. Having honest, learning-centered conversations about inclusive language is, in fact, another way of enacting our commitment to self-reflection, social justice, and rhetorical agency. In my classes, I have begun experimenting with using Ross's (2019) "calling in" approach to talk about language. Here are a few examples:

Examples of "calling in" with attention to inclusive language

- "I noticed that you used the term/phrase X. Could you explain that, for students who are new to that term?"
- "I want to pause and make sure everyone understands what X means, and why many people prefer that to Y."
- "I heard you use the phrase X rather than Y. Was that an intentional choice?"
- "In case it's helpful, I've learned that most people in that community tend to prefer the label X, because. . . "

We can also pause to explain some of our **linguistic rituals**. For example, in many college classrooms (and an increasing number of high school ones as well), students are asked to share their personal pronouns (e.g., "she/her," "they/them") when they introduce themselves. But many students—especially international students—have never encountered this practice and may not understand the purpose. A few years ago, an international student from Russia stayed after my Sociolinguistics class one day to ask me about the ritual. Once she understood, she was excited to learn more, and eventually decided to design a survey for her final project, asking U.S. students about their pronoun-sharing practices in both academic and social settings! I now take a few moments in class to explain the practice. And as I have continued my own learning, I discovered some important critiques (e.g., from *Inside Higher Ed*[20]), which is why I now **invite** students—rather than requiring them—to share their pronouns. And if I misgender a student, I offer a sincere but brief apology, demonstrating that I continue to learn and grow as a language user.

Broaden Our Conceptions of "Participation"

A final note about CLA and class discussion: Often, participation grades can work against our goal of dialogue, putting the focus on **frequency of speaking** rather than on quality of engagement or depth of learning. We can frame participation more broadly—and grade it more equitably—by taking into account other indicators, such as:

- Using verbal and non-verbal cues to indicate empathic listening
- Connecting one's spoken contributions to those of other students (or to the text/media)
- Engaging actively in pair and small group work (e.g., helping to facilitate, take notes, report back)
- Recognizing themes and patterns from the discussion (e.g., via "fishbowl" or written reflection)
- Incorporating learning from class discussion into written work
- Participating in small group or online discussions.

See Shapiro et al., 2014/2018 (p. 81) for a longer checklist of behaviors that can be included in class participation grades.

CLA and Oral Presentations

There is a robust body of scholarship on how speaking and writing instruction enrich one another (e.g., Selfe, 2009; Siczek, forthcoming). Many schools, in fact, have shifted toward a "Communication Across the Curriculum" model for their writing programs and/or writing centers (Dannels & Housley Gaffney, 2009; Yook & Atkins-Sayre, 2012). Oral communication is not a major area of expertise for me, but I do incorporate oral presentations and other academic speaking assignments into many of my classes. Here are some pedagogical suggestions informed by CLA:

1 **Be intentional in designing and scaffolding speaking assignments**: I will admit that I have at times "added on" an oral presentation to a writing class, without thinking much about my intentions and expectations. Thanks to professional development I have received from specialists in this area, I now know that this lack of transparency **disadvantages** students who are less confident or experienced with public speaking. My "add-on" approach to speaking assignments may have worked *against* my commitment to social justice and rhetorical agency! I am now much more explicit about what I want students to do—and why—with oral presentations, just as for written assignments, answering questions such as:

   • Why are we doing oral presentations? Are they an end in themselves, a step in the writing process, or both?
   • Who is the intended audience, and how formal should the presentation be in terms of register and structure?
   • What am I looking for in a successful presentation? How much of the focus is on content vs. delivery/performance? If the latter is a major focus, what instruction or resources can I offer to level the playing field for students who have less experience with public speaking?

2 **Scaffold the process:** Just as with writing assignments, students need clear steps and supports in order to develop and deliver oral presentations. Some examples of instructional scaffolding I use include:

   • Handouts with expectations and grading criteria, tailored to the purpose and genre of the speaking assignment
   • Tips for how we can use mindfulness and body awareness to manage anxiety and build confidence
   • Workshops—in class or out of class—with oratory coaches[21]
   • Opportunities to practice and receive feedback—e.g., with coaches or classmates

3 **Recognize our assumptions and biases about "good speaking":** This point is best explained by a short anecdote: Several years back, I had a Latino student in "Language and Social Justice" who gave an excellent oral presentation on educational support for English Learners,

a topic he was passionate about. In my feedback, which was largely positive, I noted that he was pronouncing the word "ask" in a non-standard way, using a variation ("*aks*") that is common in African American Vernacular English (Baugh, 2020). I wrote something like, "I just wanted to point that out, in case you weren't aware." Although I did not use the word "error," my comments certainly implied that I saw this linguistic feature as "inappropriate" for academic settings—a stance that scholars have critiqued as complicit with systemic racism (e.g., Flores & Rosa, 2015).

The student came by my office later and explained (gently and generously) that *of course* this was intentional. Teachers had commented on it before, and he had kept it as part of his idiolect—including in academic and professional settings—because it indexed important aspects of his racial identity and political ideology. We went on to have a fascinating meta-conversation, in which I realized that I held **prescriptivist beliefs** about academic speaking that I had never questioned before. And in the years since, I have noticed other prominent figures, such as the writer Ta-Nehesi Coates, using that same phonological feature in public speaking. Although I am a bit embarrassed by this story, I am so grateful to the student for taking the time to talk with me. And retelling this anecdote gives me a chance to practice my **positive self-talk**: *I'm here to learn and grow!* For more on anti-racist approaches to academic speaking, check out Ladva (2020).

A CLA Approach to Reading

Writing teachers tend to spend a lot of time talking about the writing process, providing strategies for each phase of writing—brainstorming, drafting, revision, etc. However, when it comes to academic reading, students receive much less strategic instruction after elementary school, despite the fact that the length and complexity of assigned readings continues to grow (e.g., Alexander, 2005). We can increase students' rhetorical agency as readers by teaching reading as a **complex, dialogic interaction** (Wilkinson & Son, 2011)—i.e., a social process, rather than a solitary one.

Below are some suggestions for scaffolding each phase of the reading process. Although all of our students benefit from this explicit instruction, it is particularly helpful for students who are reading in a language, dialect, style, or genre that is less familiar to them. Many of these points apply as well to **audio (vs. print) media** (e.g., lectures, podcasts, etc.).

Before Reading: Use Linguistic Sleuthing

I often tell students that the most important part of the reading process is what we do *before we read*. Many students think that "browsing" or "looking over" a text indicates laziness or lack of focus. But quite the opposite is true: Good readers devote a lot of time to **previewing the text.** To explain why, I use the analogy of assembling a jigsaw puzzle (Figure 9.3): We start by putting together the edge pieces, because those give us an "outline" of the big picture. Previewing serves the same function, creating a mental map we can use to navigate and piece together the text.

Figure 9.3 A Metaphor for the Reading Process. Photo credit to Bianca Ackermann

As they preview, students can use their linguistic sleuthing skills (see pp. 142–143)., to infer the rhetorical context: *What type of text is this, and for whom was it written?* Noticing **textual features** such as abstracts, section headings, glossaries, and bolding or italics can help us figure out, for example, whether we are reading a journal article written for experts or a textbook chapter for students. We can also use some of these genre features (e.g., subheadings), and even the language of the text (e.g., transitional words/phrases such as "Moreover" or "Nevertheless") to help us recognize the **organizational structure** of the text or argument. For students who worry that previewing takes more time, I remind them that it **saves us time** in the long run—and it can ensure that the time we do spend reading the text is invested wisely.

While Reading: Keep Momentum Going—and Aim for 3–2–1!

Many students—particularly those reading in a less-familiar language or dialect—pause frequently while reading to highlight or look up unfamiliar words from the text. This seems like a logical strategy: Don't we need to know all of the words in the text in order to understand it? The answer, actually, is no. Good readers often **skip over words and phrases they don't know**, because stopping to write down and/or look up those items causes them to lose their grasp on the main ideas or argument of the text (Grabe & Stoller, 2019). When explaining this to students, I use the analogy of running: If we stop every few minutes to stretch or take a drink of water, we may lose our physical momentum (this is certainly the case for me, at least—I'm more of a tortoise than a hare, when it comes to exercise!).

This is not to say that students should never consult additional sources to help with reading. But they should do so **purposefully**, in ways that further their goals as readers—not out of some sense of duty or obligation. Yet part of the problem is that many students are so overwhelmed as readers that they lack a sense of purpose. To help them stay on track, I created a mnemonic I call "**3–2–1**" that my students *love*. Here it is:

When reading in preparation for class lecture or discussion, we should aim to come away with at least:

- 3 key points or concepts
- 2 connections—to *self*, to other *texts*, and/or to the *world* (Keene & Zimmerman, 1997)[22]
- 1 question or point of confusion.

Now of course, I hope that students take away more than this from their assigned readings. But having a "threshold" for reading in preparation for class can really build students' confidence and curiosity. The Hub has a worksheet that students can use to log their 3–2–1 points, which was created by peer tutors with Middlebury's Office of Learning Resources.

After Reading: Talk About It

Research tells us that metacognition—the ability to assess one's own comprehension—is a critical skill for effective reading (e.g., Dabarera et al., 2014). Yet often, students need to **talk about a text** before they know whether and what they have understood. We can make opportunities for this oral processing in class. Students can work in pairs or small groups to compare their 3–2–1 points or to read aloud passages that resonated with them. Other activities from the Pathways chapters, such as jigsaw reading (p. 96) and critical role-play (pp. 119 and 156), can also be useful for post-reading. We can encourage students to have these conversations outside of class as well, by assigning "reading buddies" or using the "Imagined Interlocutors" assignment (p. 242).

A final note: Academic reading is an area where disparities in access can become particularly prominent (e.g., Malomo & Pittaway, 2020). We should think carefully about the **quantity and type** of readings assigned and include audio and visual supplements or alternatives to print readings whenever possible. In these ways, we uphold our commitment to inclusion through Universal Design, which we discussed in Chapter 8.

Scaffolding Peer Review

Peer review is another way to encourage more intentional reading—and it of course results in better writing, too! However, peer review needs to be set up effectively; otherwise, students may be uninvested, disengaged, or unskilled in giving feedback to their peers (e.g., Brammer & Rees, 2007). There are also complex **power dynamics** that emerge around language difference, which need to be acknowledged: Students from more privileged linguistic (and racial and socioeconomic) backgrounds tend to assume more authority in peer review interactions, which can leave other students feeling that they have nothing to offer (e.g., Keating, 2019; Leverenz, 1994). Here are some ways we can make peer review more engaging and equitable:

1   **Talk openly about power and privilege:** Because power is already a central focus in CLA Pedagogy, we can transfer that learning toward a discussion of power in peer groups. One way into the conversation is to ask: *What makes peer review challenging? Why might some of us be more comfortable or confident providing feedback than others?* We can also high-light particular assets that multilingual and multidialectal writers bring to the peer review process, such as linguistic creativity and cross-cultural awareness.

2   **Provide clear goals and foci:** Students often misunderstand the role of peer review, thinking the aim is "correction" rather than "collaboration" (Brammer & Rees, 2007). When I introduce peer review, I high-light the etymology of the word **"review"** (i.e., to "look again"), to underscore that receiving feedback from other readers can help us see our work through fresh eyes. And reading others' work can open us up to new rhetorical possibilities. Studies have found, in fact, that writers learn more as *givers* of feedback than they do as *receivers* (e.g., Lund-strom & Baker, 2009).

3   **Be intentional about sequencing:** I tend to use peer review early in the writing process, when students are still working through ideas, organization, and use of details/evidence. I do this in part to discour-age students from taking on the role of "editor" or "proofreader,"[23] which is what they often default to (McGroarty & Zhu, 1997). This helps to level the playing field for multilingual and multidialectal writers, who may feel unprepared or uncomfortable offering sen-tence-level feedback. Sometimes, peer review may consist mostly of **talking through** arguments, findings, research processes, etc. When we do look at written drafts, I remind students to focus on content questions, such as: *Was this piece of writing engaging, informative, and clear to me?* (See below for more on "clarity" as an alternative to "correctness").

4   **Create checklists or guiding questions:** One way to prevent students from getting "in the weeds" is to create a tool to guide their review. Such tools should be tailored to the goals of the assignment, as well as to the phase of the writing process. Below is a lightly edited version of a checklist I have used for Position Papers (see Chapter 5, pp. 157–8). and other persuasive writing assignments. This is used with the first full draft of students' work, after they have talked through and/or pre-sented their main ideas, but before they have received feedback on a written draft.

Sample peer review checklist

- Underline what you think is the thesis or main argument of the paper
- Label (with "**E**") examples or evidence that you found persuasive
- Put a ★ next to places where the stakes or implications are coming through clearly
- Put a ? next to one point or sentence that you found confusing, or one place you got lost in the organization
- List 2 (or more) things you appreciated or learned from this paper
- List 2 (or more) suggestions or next steps for this writer

5 **Make time for guided practice:** Students are much more effective in using checklists like the above if they have a chance to practice—for example, with a paper from a previous class (with the writer's name removed, unless that student wants to be named).

6 **Invite meta-feedback.** As with other types of feedback, students need opportunities to reflect and report back on their peer review experiences. This can be done via a reflective writing assignment, in a Writer's Memo (see below), or during an in-person conference. Themes from student reflections can be channeled back into future class discussions or workshops.

Technology can also be a tremendous asset in the peer review process. If students provide comments in a shared file (e.g., via Google Docs), we can review and even respond to their feedback. We can even ask the writer to respond to each of their peer reviewer's comments, so we know whether and how they took the feedback into account. There are other tools as well that can help, such as Eli Review—a cloud-based program that provides built-in scaffolding, including a three-part feedback heuristic: "Describe-Evaluate-Suggest."[24]

Responding to Student Writing

Providing our own feedback to student writers is one of our most important responsibilities as teachers. It is also a part of our job that many of us dread. Responding to student writing requires both **mental and emotional labor:** Often, we find ourselves trying to balance a variety of roles that seem to conflict: reader, motivator, coach, critic, and—at times—evaluator (Benesch,

2017). Another challenge is deciding what to prioritize in our feedback, which can vary depending on the nature of the assignment, the point in the writing process, and the student's goals and needs. And then on top of that, we have the tensions around **norms and standards** to work through, as we discussed in Chapters 1 and 3. No wonder so many of us find this work exhausting! This is in part why there are entire journals devoted to the topic, by the way, such as the open-access *Journal of Response to Writing*[25]

There are a number of ways we can infuse CLA into our feedback policies and practices, as enumerated below. First, though, one overarching principle: **Aim for quality over quantity of feedback. Always.** Research has found that student writers often get overwhelmed by the amount of feedback they receive on their work (e.g., Anson, 1989; Harris, 2017). And let's be honest: How many of us as students loved getting work back covered in red pen? (By the way, I beseech you: Please do not use blood-colored ink to do this work. Use pencil! Or type, if your handwriting is as terrible as mine. ;-)).

In taking a **less is more** approach, we become kinder to ourselves and to our students. Here is what works for me: I allot a particular amount of time for responding to each student's work, depending on the length and complexity of the assignment, as well as my other responsibilities. I provide a few comments and suggestions per page during that allotment of time (see below for more on types of comments), leaving a few minutes at the end to write a note summarizing strengths and next steps. When I return the work to students, I remind them that I did not comment on everything. I then say: "*If you feel like you did not get enough feedback from me, please re-submit your paper, and I would be happy to add more comments and suggestions.*" Guess how many times a student has resubmitted that same draft for more feedback? Once. Just once! And that was a senior preparing to go on the job market—not my typical student.

I see my approach not as a withholding from students, but as a wise investment of time and energy. I want my students to be inspired and challenged—not overwhelmed—by my feedback. I also want my comments to be useful in the writing process, which means I need to get them to students as soon as possible. In other words, **timeliness matters more than thoroughness** of feedback (e.g., Lee, 2013). I devote much more time to feedback on midway drafts than on final versions. In fact, my feedback on the final draft is often quite minimal—it may be just a completed rubric and a few sentences recognizing what the writer has accomplished and what they should keep in mind for future assignments. I may also include a growth/reflection grade, as discussed below.

Another way to manage the workload of providing feedback is to **give students choice** in the mode and/or timing of feedback (e.g., *"Who would like written feedback before the weekend?" "Who would like to meet in person next week?"*). This gives students some agency in deciding when and how they want feedback from us, and it helps us prioritize which assignments to respond to first. I don't tend to use audio or videorecorded feedback, but that is another choice we may offer to students.

The gist here is that CLA pedagogy invites us to **give ourselves a break** when it comes to feedback—not intellectually, but logistically: We don't have to address everything. And we certainly **don't need to proofread or copyedit student work**—more on that below. In fact, research has shown that "correcting" papers results does not result in much transferable learning (e.g., Kang & Han, 2015; Lee, 2013). Below are additional strategies for providing effective feedback, informed by CLA and other scholarship.

Maximize Rhetorical Effectiveness

Sometimes we are focused so much on "getting through" student papers that we are not thinking carefully about how our feedback will be received by the writer. We may even lapse into "defensive mode," using our feedback to justify a grade or express disappointment, rather than to promote student learning. Research tells us that students learn the most from feedback that is **specific and actionable** and that they are most receptive to criticism when it is accompanied by **concrete suggestions for improvement** (e.g., Dobler & Amoriell, 1988; Hyland & Hyland, 2006). The table below provides some additional guidelines.

Table 9.1 Guidelines for Rhetorically Effective Feedback

DO	DON'T
Use feedback to increase students' understanding of their strengths and goals as writers.	Use feedback simply to "justify" the grade.
Respond to the content with "I statements." (e.g., I really enjoyed the part of your narrative where . . . I thought this was a clever way to illustrate. . .).	Ignore what the student is saying, and focus only on how it is expressed.

DO	DON'T
Offer praise on both process and product (e.g., "I can tell you have worked hard on this revision. I see a lot of improvement in the structure of the argument").	Offer only vague praise or nitpicky criticism. (e.g., "You've got some good ideas here. But you are not using commas correctly").
Tie your comments to specific points in the writing (e.g., "Here is one place where I see summary but not much analysis").	Write general comments without pointing to specific points in the text (e.g., "I would have liked to see more analysis of the text").
Provide specific critiques and suggestions (e.g., "I have highlighted in blue several places where more evidence will strengthen your argument").	Make general judgments about the writer (e.g., "You need to improve your research and citation skills").
Accompany questions with action steps (e.g., "What are some other implications of your argument? That is something I'd like you to add to your conclusion").	Disguise suggestions as questions (e.g., "Are there other implications for your argument?").

Remember the Power of Our Words

CLA also compels us to keep in mind that the particular words we say to students have real **social and emotional power** (Pollock, 2017; see also Unit 7.1). Because language is a tool we use to build identities and relationships, our comments on students' "languaging"—i.e., their uses of language—can damage the relationships we are trying to build with them. When I used to work as a professional writing tutor, I sometimes sat with students while they tried to process (often in tears) feedback from another instructor. I began to see how the harsh tone of certain comments can hinder students' learning and growth. The table below offers some representative examples:

Table 9.2 Student Interpretations of Instructor Comments

Instructor Comment	What the Student Heard	What the Instructor Probably Meant and Might Have Said Instead
"You don't seem to understand the argument in the reading."	"You are either lazy (didn't do the reading) or stupid (unable to read)."	"I think there are some points in the reading that are unclear to you. Please revisit it to clarify. Let me know if I can help!"
"Anyone hoping to learn something new from your paper would be disappointed."	"You have nothing to offer to this class. How did you even get admitted to this school?"	"This paper felt more like summary than response to me. I really want to hear what *you* have to say about the text."
"You need to visit the writing center to get help with grammar!"	"Your language is so bad that I can't even deal with you. Go get it fixed somewhere else!"	"I am having trouble understanding this piece of writing, but I don't have the skills to pinpoint the specific issues, probably because I myself have never learned an additional language."
"No." (I have seen this one word written in the margin next to entire paragraphs)	"I am so exasperated with you and your writing that I can't even complete my own sentences."	"No, that's not what the author is saying." **or** "I disagree with this claim." (But honestly, who the heck knows what that instructor meant?)

Critical feedback that does not convey a tone of **care and support** can exacerbate the "imposter syndrome" that many students already experience at school (e.g., Denny et al., 2018). This is particularly true for first-generation students, as well as for multilingual and multidialectal writers, who are often already marginalized at school, as we discussed in Chapter 5. The psychological equation goes something like this:

"Bad" writing = "Bad" student = I don't belong here.

And is it any surprise that students might arrive at this conclusion, given all we know about how people judge one another based on language? (See, for example, the rest of this book!) My point is not that we should avoid giving critical feedback. But we should assume that students can and will **read into what we say.** By focusing on **quality over quantity** of feedback, as suggested earlier, we give ourselves more time and energy to think about the impact of our words.

Create a Feedback Loop

On the positive side, we can create a feedback loop that actually strengthens our relationships with students and increases their sense of academic agency and belonging. We can be sending **micro-affirmations** (Rowe, 2008) to students throughout each phase of the writing process! Here are some ways to make feedback an ongoing and affirming dialogue:

1   **Build "check-ins" throughout the writing process.** I build in frequent "mini-meetings" and/or written updates as students are working on a complex assignment, to ensure that they stay on track. Yes, these take time, but this time is well-spent—and usually results in a better outcome down the road (Shapiro et al., 2014/2018; Tomaš & Shapiro, 2021). The Pathways chapters included a variety of scaffolding activities and assignments that can serve this "check-in" function.

2   **Require "Writer's Memos,"** or what some call "assignment wrappers," to accompany student submissions—particularly for longer assignments and/or revised work. These are short pieces of writing in which students tell us a bit about their writing process, or about their views on what they have produced. I may give them a particular question or two to answer, such as:

- How did the writing/research process go for you on this assignment?
- What was most challenging about this assignment?
- How do you feel about the draft you're submitting? What do you see as its strengths and areas for improvement?
- What would you most like feedback on and why?

Sometimes after reading a student's memo, I decide not even to read the paper, instead reaching out to them with an offer of support. For example, a student may write something like: "There are some things happening back home that are taking a lot of my time and energy, and I wasn't able to do as much as I wanted to with this paper." That student doesn't need a bunch of comments from me telling them what they already know. They need time and support to produce a draft that better reflects what they are able to do as writers!

3   **Invite feedback on our feedback.** There is nothing more frustrating than spending hours writing feedback on student work, and then wondering whether students have even read what we have written. It is worth making time in class for students to review our feedback and ask clarifying questions. We can even request some meta-feedback on questions such as:

- What is working well in your paper, as indicated in the feedback?
- What are some areas for improvement or growth?
- What surprised you in the feedback?
- What should you keep in mind for the next draft—or the next assignment?
- Were any of the comments or suggestions confusing?

This reflective writing can then be channeled back into the "Writer's Memo" with the next draft, just as those of us who write for scholarly journals might summarize feedback from reviewers when resubmitting a manuscript.

4   **Think carefully about how to sequence feedback.** As mentioned above, I provide more feedback to students midway through the process than I do at the end, but I also sequence my feedback with what students receive from peers and writing center tutors. Often, by the time I read their work, students have already received a round or two of feedback and have revised accordingly. With more difficult or complex assignments, however, I may reverse the process, giving students more of my attention early in the process, so that they have a strong start.

5   **Consider uptake of feedback when assigning grades.** When I grade the final draft of an assignment, I often provide an additional "growth/reflection grade," which I calculate based on three criteria:

- The quality and thoughtfulness of their Writer's Memo
- The amount of revision/improvement I see from the first to the final draft[26]
- The extent to which their revisions respond to the feedback they have received

One thing I like about assigning these growth/reflection grades is that the students who have struggled the most usually get the highest grades. More experienced writers, in contrast, have to work a bit harder to show me that they are challenging themselves—for example, by making revisions beyond the suggestions they received from me or their peers. Grading based on process and labor is not only in line with our CLA goals of self-reflection and rhetorical agency—it has also been proposed as a more equitable and anti-racist approach to assessment (Inoue, 2015, 2019), since it rewards effort and intentionality, meaning that every student can receive a "good grade" for the hard work they have done in our classes. Below I will discuss how I sometimes use "proxy grades" within a labor-based approach, so that students receive useful feedback on both process and product.

Providing Feedback on Language

A question I am asked frequently by colleagues in both secondary and post-secondary settings is: *When and how should I provide feedback on language issues in student writing?* This is one area in which the tensions about norms and standards can be particularly salient: Should we be "marking" student work for "errors" in grammar, style, or mechanics? If so, when and how? If not, do we simply ignore these aspects of writing? There are no easy answers to these questions, but here are some general guidelines, which I unpack further below:

Guidelines for providing feedback on language

1   Focus on choice rather than "voice"
2   Teach (and evaluate) grammar rhetorically
3   Set grammatical priorities related to the assignment
4   Focus on clarity rather than correctness
5   Distinguish between feedback and grading

Choice Over Voice

Many students I have worked with—particularly multilingual and multi-dialectal writers—have received comments from another English/writing teacher expressing concern that their "voice" was absent or underdeveloped in their writing. Comments like these usually leave students with more questions than answers, such as:

- *Where can I go to "find" or "develop" my voice?*
- *How will I know if I'm making progress?*
- *And . . . is this just another way of saying that my writing seems "fake" or plagiarized?*

Perhaps for creative writers, having a singular "voice," or what linguists would call a **written idiolect**, is a goal worth aspiring to. But when it comes to academic writing, the notion of "voice" is not particularly helpful (e.g., Ramanathan & Atkinson, 1999). It is also linguistically inaccurate, since, as we have explored in previous chapters, we all have many voices: For example, my "voice"—i.e., register or style—is a bit more colloquial in this book, compared with my articles in scholarly journals (although who knows about future publications—maybe we can start a revolution!? ;-))

Even Peter Elbow, one of the biggest proponents of "voice," has admitted that the concept is "fuzzy" and that good writers tend to draw from "an array of voices" (1994, p. 20). A CLA approach would suggest that rather than sending students on a quest for the elusive "authentic voice," we should aim to give them the knowledge and opportunities they need to make **informed linguistic choices** and to evaluate the impact of those choices (e.g., Gere et al., 2021).

A Rhetorical Approach

What I am arguing (again) is that we need to implement a **rhetorical grammar** approach, which we explored in Chapter 5 (see also Kolln & Gray, 2017; Micciche, 2004). But investigating, making, and evaluating grammatical choices is a lot of work, no? The easy way out, of course, would be either to present grammar norms as universal (e.g., *Avoid passive voice! Never use first person pronouns!*) or to avoid the topic of "language" altogether and just talk about the writer's "ideas." But if you've reached this point in the book and somehow think I would support either of those approaches, you must have missed a few things along the way!

Teaching students to grow as language users is indeed hard work—but it is fun and rewarding work as well! One way we can manage the complexity is to **set rhetorical grammar priorities in keeping with the assignment at hand**. For example, when my first-years are learning to write summary/response papers (not the most thrilling assignment, I admit, but something they need for their other classes), we talk about the pros and cons of using past tense vs. present tense verbs to capture "authorial action" (e.g., "They argue" vs. "They argued"). When students are writing up their "methods" for an empirical research report, we discuss the option of using passive voice (e.g., "The survey was distributed") or first-person ("I distributed the survey"). Chapter 5 included other examples of how grammatical patterns can vary by genre and discipline.

I even bring grammar awareness into thesis development! To help students struggling with crafting arguable thesis statements, I sometimes invite them to start their thesis with the word "Although." This sets them up for a grammatically complex sentence, resulting—sometimes, at least—in a more interesting thesis statement. I also encourage less experienced writers to explicit transitions (e.g., "However," "Nevertheless," or "In other words") to make the structure of their argument more explicit. I draw on resources such as Graff and Birkenstein's (2018) *They Say, I Say* and Kolln and Gray's (2017) *Rhetorical Grammar* to build students' knowledge of how ideas and language work hand-in-hand.

Clarity Over Correctness

When I do provide sentence-level feedback beyond what we are working on as a class, I try to focus on **clarity rather than correctness**. In the English language, lack of clarity often has to do with one of these three issues:

- Subject/verb agreement
- Word form (e.g., using a noun such as "discrimination" instead of the verb "discriminate")
- Verb tense (e.g., switching unintentionally between past tense and present tense)

And what do all three of those bullet points have in common? **VERBS**!

That's right, folks: My answer to the ubiquitous question of "Where should I start when working with students on sentence-level grammar?" is "verbs!" Well, first I give my little spiel about a rhetorical grammar approach, but eventually we end up at "verbs."

Verbs contain much of the content of sentences in English. Thus, incorrect verb usage—or rather **unconventional** usage, since the focus is on choices, and students may have a rhetorical reason for "breaking" with convention—can hinder the clarity or effectiveness of the writing. There are other grammatical elements that are much less impactful, such as use of articles (a, an, the) and prepositions (above, after, against, etc.). If I see a persistent pattern of unconventional usage with these or other structures, I may point it out. But often, the grammatical rules are so idiosyncratic that there are not many opportunities for transferable learning. Studies have shown, by the way, that students learn more when they **make edits themselves** prompted by highlighting or other marking from us than when we "correct" the writing for them (e.g., Chandler, 2003).

Feedback ≠ Grading

A final reminder—a restatement, in some ways, of what I've said thus far—is that **feedback and grading are not the same thing**. We may focus much of our feedback on a student's linguistic or stylistic choices, particularly if attending to these aspects would make the writing clearer or more rhetorically effective. But we as teachers usually get to decide how much—if at all—this is reflected in students' grades. **Grading rubrics** allow us to assign separate grades to different aspects of the writing. The Pathways chapters included a number of rubrics from my classes. Nearly all of those rubrics include a section on "language" and/or "clarity," but that section never accounts for more than 20% of the overall assignment grade.

For colleagues who are resistant to rubrics but are seeking more linguistically equitable means of evaluation, I suggest simply assigning two grades—one for **content** and the other for **clarity**—and I weight the former at least twice as much as the latter. A student who has a high "content" grade but has room for growth in "clarity" should, when possible, be allowed to keep improving the latter. I do not want to "punish" students who have had less experience or instruction with academic writing in English, but I do want to give them an incentive to keep improving as writers. The "revise for clarity" approach is my way of balancing these two commitments.

And of course, not all of my assignments follow the norms of standardized or academic English. As we discussed in Chapter 5 and 7, I also use "Writing Beyond the Classroom" assignments, in which **students decide** their purpose and audience, including the appropriate genre and language conventions. I have had students who were quite confident with writing academic papers but struggled mightily to convey the same ideas in another genre, because "academese" was the only tool in their writing toolbox. As has been highlighted several times, our goal is **not one-size-fits-all writing**. Rather, we want students to be able to use language flexibly and creatively, in keeping with their aims as writers and their understanding of rhetorical expectations.

Ungrading or Proxy Grading

There are some experts who propose **not assigning grades at all to student writing**—either as part of a labor-based approach to improve equity (e.g., Inoue, 2019) or as a means of increasing students' intrinsic (vs. extrinsic) motivation (Blum, 2020). I still assign grades to student papers, although I do take labor, growth, and reflection into account, as explained above.

However, when responding to drafts that will be revised, I assign only a **proxy grade**—i.e., an approximation of what the grade *would be* if I were grading the writing as a final draft. That way, students have a reference point that can inform their revision. Perhaps in an ideal world, students would keep working indefinitely on every piece of writing, no matter what the impact on their grade. But that is not the world I live and teach in. The proxy grade can be a useful way to address one of the concerns raised about "ungrading" (Blum, 2020) which is that students may feel they are missing out on feedback about how their work might be evaluated by future instructors.

Conclusion

I hope this chapter has helped to excite and prepare you to infuse a critical understanding of language, identity, power, and privilege into your classroom instruction. I am certain that there are topics I did not address—perhaps we can talk about them online at the Hub?! We will build on many points from this chapter in Chapter 10, which considers how CLA can inform our work outside the classroom.

Notes

1 www.insidehighered.com/views/2018/06/18/middlebury-professor-surveys-student-attitudes-about-free-speech-opinion
2 www.insidehighered.com/views/2019/05/13/exploring-student-views-inclusivity-campuses-opinion
3 https://publications.coventry.ac.uk/index.php/joaw/article/view/607
4 Research shows in fact, that intellectual debates rarely change people's minds. In fact, the presentation of new evidence or flaws in logic can sometimes lead to a "backfire effect," in which people hold even more tightly to their original beliefs (e.g., Nyhan & Reifler, 2010).
5 One prominent example is a 2016 letter sent to incoming students at the University of Chicago, which said the university did not "support so-called trigger warnings" or "condone the creation of intellectual safe spaces." Backlash led some other institutions (e.g., Bowdoin and Yale) to adopt a softer tone. More at www.insidehighered.com/news/2016/08/29/u-chicago-letter-new-students-safe-spaces-sets-intense-debate
6 For a nuanced discussion of trigger warnings, see www.theatlantic.com/health/archive/2019/03/do-trigger-warnings-work/585871/
7 One example of this one: www.insidehighered.com/blogs/just-visiting/i-want-make-students-uncomfortable
8 Fun fact: Curiosity increases dopamine in our brains! How cool is that?! Learn more, and take a quiz to determine your "curiosity type" at: https://curiosity.britannica.com/science-of-curiosity.html

9 https://whatisessential.org/resources/first-year-agreements-lesson-plan

10 www.facinghistory.org/resource-library/teaching-inspector-calls/building-class room-community

11 https://static1.squarespace.com/static/581e9e06ff7c509a5ca2fe32/t/58f25fa937 c58130853337df/1492279209799/04+AWARE-LA+Brave+Space+Guidelines+and+ History.pdf

12 www.readwritethink.org/professional-development/strategy-guides/ socratic-seminars

13 www.learningforjustice.org/magazine/spring-2019/speaking-up-without-tearing-down

14 https://brenebrown.com/podcast/brene-on-shame-and-accountability/

15 www.contemplativemind.org/practices/tree

16 www.psychologytoday.com/us/blog/speaking-in-tongues/202011/why-do-we-hate-politically-correct-language

17 https://consciousstyleguide.com/

18 https://s3.amazonaws.com/s3.sumofus.org/images/SUMOFUS_PROGRES SIVE-STYLEGUIDE.pdf

19 For a thoughtful yet accessible discussion of "BIPOC" as an alternative to "POC," check out this episode of the NPR Codeswitch podcast: www.npr.org/2020/09/29/ 918418825/is-it-time-to-say-r-i-p-to-p-o-c

20 www.insidehighered.com/views/2018/09/19/why-asking-students-their-preferred-pronoun-not-good-idea-opinion

21 We have a group called "Oratory Now" run by my colleague Dana Yeaton, who trains coaches to offer class workshops and provide one-on-one feedback and support related to oral communication. More information, as well as their "Peer Coaching Playbook," can be found at: www.oratorynow.org/

22 For more explanation of these types of text connections, check out: www. facinghistory.org/resource-library/teaching-strategies/text-text-text-self-text-world

23 My colleague Catharine Wright has a useful handout explaining the difference between revision, editing, and proofreading, which is available at the Hub, and at www.middlebury.edu/system/files/media/Revision%2C%20Editing%20and%20 Proofreading.pdf

24 https://elireview.com/2016/08/03/describe-evaluate-suggest/

25 https://scholarsarchive.byu.edu/journalrw/

26 Many teachers are unaware of the "compare drafts" feature of Microsoft Word. I use this feature as a visual starting place to see where students have made the most changes between one draft and the other. Google Docs introduced a similar "Compare Documents" feature in 2019.

References

Alexander, P. A. (2005). The path to competence: A lifespan developmental perspective on reading. *Journal of Literacy Research, 37*(4), 413–436.

Anson, C. M. (1989). Writing and response: Theory, practice, and research. *National Council of Teachers of English*. https://files.eric.ed.gov/fulltext/ED303826.pdfs

Bamber, M. D., & Schneider, J. K. (2020). College students' perceptions of mindfulness-based interventions: A narrative review of the qualitative research. *Current Psychology*, 1–14.

Baugh, J. (2020). African American languages (AAV, AAEV, Ebonics). *The International Encyclopedia of Linguistic Anthropology*, 1–6.

Benesch, S. (2001). *Critical English for academic purposes: Theory, politics, and practice*. Routledge.

Benesch, S. (2009). Theorizing and practicing critical English for academic purposes. *Journal of English for Academic Purposes*, 8(2), 81–85.

Benesch, S. (2017). *Emotions and English language teaching: Exploring teachers' emotion labor*. Routledge.

Blum, S. D. (2020). *Ungrading: Why rating students undermines learning (and what to do instead)*. West Virginia University Press.

Brammer, C., & Rees, M. (2007). Peer review from the students' perspective: Invaluable or invalid? *Composition Studies*, 35(2), 71–85.

Brown, B. (2018). *Dare to lead: Daring greatly and rising strong at work*. Random House.

Carsley, D., Khoury, B., & Heath, N. L. (2018). Effectiveness of mindfulness interventions for mental health in schools: A comprehensive meta-analysis. *Mindfulness*, 9(3), 693–707.

Casanave, C. P. (2005). *Writing games: Multicultural case studies of academic literacy practices in higher education*. Routledge.

Chandler, J. (2003). The efficacy of various kinds of error feedback for improvement in the accuracy and fluency of L2 student writing. *Journal of Second Language Writing*, 12(3), 267–296.

Crusan, D. (2010). *Assessment in the second language writing classroom*. University of Michigan Press.

Dabarera, C., Renandya, W. A., & Zhang, L. J. (2014). The impact of metacognitive scaffolding and monitoring on reading comprehension. *System*, 42, 462–473.

Dannels, D. P., & Housley Gaffney, A. L. (2009). Communication across the curriculum and in the disciplines: A call for scholarly cross-curricular advocacy. *Communication Education*, 58(1), 124–153.

Denny, H., Nordlof, J., & Salem, L. (2018). "Tell me exactly what it was that I was doing that was so bad": Understanding the needs and expectations of working-class students in writing centers. *The Writing Center Journal*, 37(1), 67–100.

Dobler, J. M., & Amoriell, W. J. (1988). Comments on writing: Features that affect student performance. *Journal of Reading*, 32(3), 214–223.

Elbow, P. (1994). What do we mean when we talk about voice in texts? In K. B. Yancey (Ed.), *Voices on voice: Perspectives, definitions, inquiry*. National Council of Teachers of English. https://cdn.ncte.org/nctefiles/resources/books/sample/56347chap01.pdf

Flores, N., & Rosa, J. (2015). Undoing appropriateness: Raciolinguistic ideologies and language diversity in education. *Harvard Educational Review*, 85(2), 149–171.

Gere, A., Curzan, A., Hammond, J. W., Hughes, S., Li, R., Moos, A., Smith, K., Van Zanen, K., Wheeler, K. L., & Zanders, C. J. (2021). Communal justicing: Writing assessment, disciplinary infrastructure, and the case for critical language awareness. *College Composition and Communication, 72*(3), 384–412.

Grabe, W., & Stoller, F. L. (2019). *Teaching and researching reading.* Routledge.

Graff, G., & Birkenstein, C. (2018). *They say I say: The moves that matter in academic writing.* W. W. Norton.

Hairston, M. (1992). Diversity, ideology, and teaching writing. *College Composition and Communication, 43*(2), 179–193.

Harris, M. (2017). When responding to student writing, more is better. In C. E. Ball & D. M. Loewe (Eds.), *Bad ideas about writing. 268 Muriel Harris* (pp. 268–272). Open Access Textbooks [West Virginia University]. https://textbooks.lib.wvu.edu/badideas/badideasaboutwriting-book.pdf

Hochanadel, A., & Finamore, D. (2015). Fixed and growth mindset in education and how grit helps students persist in the face of adversity. *Journal of International Education Research, 11*(1), 47–50.

Hyland, K., & Hyland, F. (2006). Feedback on second language students' writing. *Language Teaching, 39*(2), 83–101.

Inoue, A. B. (2015). *Antiracist writing assessment ecologies: Teaching and assessing writing for a socially just future.* WAC Clearinghouse. https://wac.colostate.edu/books/perspectives/inoue/

Inoue, A. B. (2019). *Labor-based grading contracts: Building equity and inclusion in the compassionate writing classroom.* WAC Clearinghouse. https://wac.colostate.edu/books/perspectives/labor/

Kang, E., & Han, Z. (2015). The efficacy of written corrective feedback in improving L2 written accuracy: A meta-analysis. *The Modern Language Journal, 99*(1), 1–18.

Keating, B. (2019). A good development thing: A longitudinal analysis of peer review and authority in undergraduate writing. In A. R. Gere (Ed.), *Developing writers in higher education: A longitudinal study* (pp. 56–87). University of Michigan Press. https://library.oapen.org/bitstream/handle/20.500.12657/23990/1006144.pdf?sequence=1#page=71

Keene, E., & Zimmerman, S. (1997). *Mosaic of thought.* Heinemann.

Kibler, A., Valdés, G., & Walqui, A. (Eds.). (2020). *Reconceptualizing the role of critical dialogue in American classrooms: Promoting equity through dialogic education.* Routledge.

Kolln, M., & Gray, L. (2017). *Rhetorical grammar: Grammatical choices, rhetorical effects* (8th ed.). Pearson.

Ladva, N. (2020). Is the communication center racist? An inquiry into Black linguistic justice, anti-racism, and assimilation. *Communication Center Journal, 6*(1), 3–17.

Lee, I. (2013). Research into practice: Written corrective feedback. *Language Teaching, 46*(1), 108.

Leverenz, C. S. (1994). Peer response in the multicultural composition classroom: Dissensus—a dream (deferred). *Journal of Advanced Composition,* 167–186.

Lundstrom, K., & Baker, W. (2009). To give is better than to receive: The benefits of peer review to the reviewer's own writing. *Journal of Second Language Writing, 18*(1), 30–43.

Malomo, M., & Pittaway, S. (2020). *"So you want me to read for my degree?"*: A universal design for learning approach to reading [Webinar]. https://talis.wistia.com/medias/pvzxfmrhbo

McGroarty, M., & Zhu, W. (1997). Triangulation in classroom research: A study of peer revision. *Language Learning, 47*(1), 1–43.

Menakem, R. (2017/2021). *My grandmother's hands: Racialized trauma and the pathway to mending our hearts and bodies.* Penguin.

Micciche, L. R. (2004). Making a case for rhetorical grammar. *College Composition and Communication*, 716–737.

Nyhan, B., & Reifler, J. (2010). When corrections fail: The persistence of political misperceptions. *Political Behavior, 32*(2), 303–330.

Palfrey, J. (2017). *Safe spaces, brave spaces: Diversity and free expression in education.* MIT Press.

Parker, P. (2018). *The art of gathering: How we meet and why it matters.* Riverhead Books.

Pawlowski, L. (2018). Creating a brave space classroom through writing. In S. Brookfield & Associates (Eds.), *Teaching race: How to help students unmask and challenge racism* (pp. 63–86). Wiley.

Poe, M., & Elliot, N. (2019). Evidence of fairness: Twenty-five years of research in assessing writing. *Assessing Writing, 42*, 100418.

Pollock, M. (2017). *Schooltalk: Rethinking what we say about and to students every day.* The New Press.

Prebel, J. (2016). Engaging a "pedagogy of discomfort": Emotion as critical inquiry in community-based writing courses. *Composition Forum, 34*.

Quaid, S., & Williams, H. (2021). Troubling knowledges and difficult pedagogical moments for students learning. *International Journal of Inclusive Education*, 1–19.

Ramanathan, V., & Atkinson, D. (1999). Individualism, academic writing, and ESL writers. *Journal of Second Language Writing, 8*(1), 45–75.

Ross, L. (2019). Speaking up without tearing down. *Learning for Justice.* www.learningforjustice.org/magazine/spring-2019/speaking-up-without-tearing-down

Rowe, M. (2008). Micro-affirmations and micro-inequities. *Journal of the International Ombudsman Association, 1*(1), 45–48.

Ruecker, T., & Shapiro, S. (2020). Critical pragmatism as a middle ground in discussions of linguistic diversity. In T. Silva & Z. Wang (Eds.), *Reconciling translingualism and second language writing* (pp. 139–149). Routledge.

Russell, A. L. (2018). The politics of academic language: Towards a framework for analyzing language representations in FYC textbooks. *Composition Forum, 38.* www.compositionforum.com/issue/38/language.php

Saenkhum, T. (2016). *Decisions, agency, and advising: Key issues in the placement of multilingual writers into first-year composition courses.* University Press of Colorado.

Santos, T. (2012). The place of politics in second language writing. In T. Santos & P. K. Matsuda (Eds.), *On second language writing* (pp. 173–190). Routledge.

Selfe, C. L. (2009). The movement of air, the breath of meaning: Aurality and multimodal composing. *College Composition and Communication, 60*(4), 616–663.

Shapiro, S. (2011). Stuck in the remedial rut: Confronting resistance to ESL curriculum reform. *Journal of Basic Writing, 30*(2), 24–52. https://eric.ed.gov/?id=EJ988209

Shapiro, S. (2012). Citizens vs. aliens: How institutional policies construct linguistic minority students. In Y. Kanno & L. Harklau (Eds.), *Linguistic minority immigrants go to college: Preparation, access, and persistence* (pp. 238–254). Routledge.

Shapiro, S. (2018, June). Snowflakes and free speech on college campuses. *Inside Higher Ed.* www.insidehighered.com/views/2018/06/18/middlebury-professor-surveys-student-attitudes-about-free-speech-opinion

Shapiro, S. (2019, August). Why building community even through discomfort could help stressed college students. *The Conversation.* https://theconversation.com/why-building-community-even-through-discomfort-could-help-stressed-college-students-121398

Shapiro, S. (2020). Inclusive pedagogy in the academic writing classroom: Cultivating communities of belonging. *Journal of Academic Writing, 10*(1), 154–164. https://publications.coventry.ac.uk/index.php/joaw/article/view/607

Shapiro, S., Farrelly, R., & Tomaš, Z. (2014/2018). *Fostering international student success in higher education.* TESOL, NAFSA.

Siczek, M. (Ed.). (forthcoming). *Pedagogical innovations in oral academic communication.* University of Michigan Press.

Stewart, K. D. (2017). Classrooms as "safe houses"? The ethical and emotional implications of digital storytelling in a university writing classroom. *Critical Studies in Teaching and Learning, 5*(1), 85–102.

Taylor, S. R. (2018/2021). *The body is not an apology: The power of radical self-love.* Berrett-Koehler Publishers.

Tomaš, Z., & Shapiro, S. (2021). From crisis to opportunity: Turning questions about "plagiarism" into conversations about linguistically responsive pedagogy. *TESOL Quarterly.*

Trimbur, J., Wood, R. G., Strickland, R., Thelin, W. H., Rouster, W. J., Mester, T., & Hairston, M. (1993). Responses to Maxine Hairston, "diversity, ideology, and teaching writing" and reply. *College Composition and Communication, 44*(2), 248–256.

Warren, L. (2005). Strategic action in hot moments. In M. Oullett (Ed.), *Teaching inclusively: Resources for courses, departments, & institutional change in higher education* (pp. 620–630). New Forums Press.

Wilkinson, I. A., & Son, E. H. (2011). A dialogic turn in research on learning and teaching to comprehend. In M., Kamil, P. D. Pearson, E. B. Moje, & P. Afflerbach (Eds.), *Handbook of reading research* (Vol. IV, pp. 385–413). Routledge.

Yook, E. L., & Atkins-Sayre, W. (Eds.). (2012). *Communication centers and oral communication programs in higher education: Advantages, challenges, and new directions.* Lexington Books.

10
Going Further with CLA

Introduction

In the previous chapters of this volume, we have focused on the why, what, and how of CLA Pedagogy as an approach to writing curricula and instruction. This chapter takes the conversation a step further, exploring the relevance of CLA to other aspects of our work as professionals and to our lives beyond work.

When I first started mapping out this chapter, my inner critic complained, "Isn't that going a bit too far with this CLA stuff, Shapiro?" (My inner critic is quite a curmudgeon!) But then I began noticing how CLA was making its way into my interactions with students, colleagues, and administrators—and how it was enriching my empirical research, as I discussed a bit in Chapters 7 and 9. I have my **CLA goggles** (and earbuds!) on nearly all of the time, to be honest, which is powerful and—at times—a bit exhausting.

Moreover, research tells us that the work we do in the classroom is part of the larger ecosystems of our departments, programs, and institutions (e.g., Cox et al., 2018; Enright & Gilliland, 2011; Inoue, 2015)—so it would be an oversight not to talk about the relevance of CLA to our work within those ecosystems. We may feel limited in our ability to enact programmatic and institutional change. But we can use insights from CLA to envision what those changes might look like, and to build support for that vision!

My interest in CLA goes even further than that, though. In education we talk a lot about the "whole student" but not nearly as much about the "whole teacher" (Chen & McCray, 2012; Shapiro, 2010). Research suggests that careful and critical attention to language can deepen our self-knowledge, strengthen our relationships, and improve our overall well-being—all benefits that feed back into our work as educators. These are topics I hope to

DOI: 10.4324/9781003171751-15

explore more fully in future publications. But I thought I would at least dip a toe in the water in this final chapter.

As always, a couple of caveats: First, although I have tried to be as inclusive as possible of different teaching contexts, many of the specific examples referenced here are from postsecondary settings. In the years to come—including at the online Hub—I hope to gather more examples from readers working in K-12 settings! Secondly, it is worth noting that there are entire books and sometimes entire scholarly journals devoted to each of the topics we will touch on here. This chapter is only an *amuse-bouche*, meant to whet your appetite for learning more!

Below, we first discuss some highlights from the research into how we can assess students' development of CLA beyond their reflection and growth as writers. We then look at how CLA can inform our co-curricular offerings, faculty development conversations, and institutional DEI work. We conclude with a section entitled "CLA for Life!" that talks about some ways that CLA can enrich our personal and civic lives.

CLA Assessment

There is a small but growing body of research assessing the impact of CLA-oriented curricula on students and teachers. This research is happening in English language arts classrooms and programs, as well as in other areas, such as world/heritage language instruction. CLA is also being used and assessed in professional learning for both K-12 and college teachers. Although there is not enough space to discuss this work at length, I wanted to offer a few highlights, for readers who might want to design action research (e.g., MacIntyre, 2012) or other empirical studies focused on CLA development.

Research on CLA assessment tends to look at both **content knowledge** and **shifts in beliefs and attitudes**. As we saw in the Pathways chapters, CLA-oriented curricula often teach theories and concepts from linguistics and related fields, and we can assess how students and teachers take up these concepts in class discussions and assignments (Godley et al., 2015; Gere et al., 2021; Metz, 2018). However, since CLA involves requires more than just new knowledge, researchers also consider questions such as:

- Do participants become more knowledgeable about and appreciative of language difference?
- Do participants have a more nuanced or critical understanding of prescriptivism and other language ideologies?

- Can participants articulate or demonstrate how their CLA learning might shape their behaviors toward others?

One way researchers measure these shifts is by adapting frameworks from multicultural education (e.g., Nieto, 2017) to focus on language variation. Such frameworks usually lay out a continuum of orientations to language difference, with **deficit** or **assimilationist** views on one end and **pluralist** or **critical** views on the other (see text box below).

Stages of development in English/writing teacher attitudes toward language variation

(e.g., Endo, 2015; Godley & Reaser, 2018; Shi & Rolstad, 2020)

1   A **deficit/monolingualist view**, in which language variation is seen as a problem and standardized English which is seen as superior to all other varieties
2   A **tolerance/acceptance view**, in which language variation is recognized as a societal reality but is not seen as relevant or valuable to schooling contexts
3   A **diversity/additive view**, in which language variation is seen as an asset, but not necessarily linked to power and oppression
4   A **critical/pluralist view**, in which the language variation is understood to be linked to power and oppression, and language/literacy education is linked to social justice

---

Researchers working with Spanish language classes use these sorts of frameworks to measure students' attitudes about varieties of Spanish that are usually stigmatized, such as "Spanglish" (e.g., Gasca Jiménez & Adrada-Rafael, 2021; Holguín Mendoza, 2018; Serafini, forthcoming). Scholars working in this area tend to use **pre/post surveys** that offer a quantitative, statistically validated measure of beliefs and attitudes before and after participants engage with CLA-oriented curricula (Beaudrie et al. [2019] include their questionnaire items as an Appendix; see also Serafini, forthcoming).

In contrast, researchers working in English Language Arts (ELA) settings tend to use more qualitative measures, such as:

- Individual interviews (Carpenter et al., 2015; Weaver, 2019; Woodard & Rao, 2020)

- Transcripts of class discussion (e.g., Baker-Bell, 2020; Metz, 2019)
- Asynchronous online discussion (e.g., Godley & Reaser, 2018; Metz, 2018)
- Reflective writing (Britton & Lorimer Leonard, 2020; Huang, 2013)
- Other student work, such as multimodal projects (e.g., Deroo & Ponzio, 2021)

Some scholar-practitioners are combining data sources to offer a richer account of CLA learning among preservice and/or practicing teachers in a variety of disciplines (e.g., Chang et al., 2020; Godley & Reaser, 2018; Mallinson & Hudley, 2018). At the Hub, I hope to connect with researchers who are interested in replicating and extending these lines of inquiry.

CLA-oriented Opportunities and Resources

There are a number of ways we can promote CLA learning through our co-curricular and extra-curricular offerings, both within and beyond of our own departments and programs.

Support for Academic Learning Across Languages

Schools can send a clear message about the value of multilingualism not only by offering a variety of world language courses—see the Modern Language Association[1] for reports on the status of foreign language instruction in the U.S.—but also by providing academic support in languages other than English. Many institutions already offer peer tutoring for foreign language study, and many—my own included—have shifted toward a **multilingual model** for their writing centers as well! For more on what this looks like, check out Lape's (2019) account from Dickinson College. Middlebury has also expanded support for oral communication in other languages, including through our "Oratory Now[2]" program, which I consult with regularly.

Some schools also offer **content courses in languages other than English**—outside of the world language curriculum. Middlebury occasionally offers first-year seminars in Spanish, for heritage speakers and advanced learners. A colleague in Economics offered a bilingual section of his economics course "Trade and Foreign Aid in Latin America" a few years ago, for which most of the readings and class discussions were in Spanish. Two colleagues in German and Italian, similarly, co-taught a course on "Fascism and Memory," with lectures primarily in English but discussion and some additional readings in the respective languages.

Co-Curricular and Extra-Curricular Offerings

We can also demonstrate our commitment to valuing linguistic diversity through co-curricular and extra-curricular opportunities. Below are some examples I have supported and publicized at my institution:

- **Multilingual performance and publishing opportunities**: Many of my students have performed writing that mixes languages/codes at spoken word events.[3] Some have also published their work in our student-run multilingual magazine called *Translingual*,[4] which invites student-created translations, as well as original pieces of writing in any language. Our largest student-run newspaper, the *Middlebury Campus*, has created a Translations Editor position as well, so that they can offer reporting in languages other than English.
- **Awards for multilingual and multidialectal writing:** As I mentioned in the Pathways chapters, some of my students have received prize nominations for work that uses multiple codes or styles. Even if the work does not win a prize, it is an honor for a student to be nominated, as we saw in the commentary from Sean Rhee (pp. 166–168). And an additional bonus is that the award committee members reading this work often come away with an expanded notion of what "good writing" looks and sounds like![5]
- **Linguistic diversity initiatives and events:** We have had several campus-wide symposia focused on language-related themes, including language and technology, translation/interpretation, and lavender linguistics (see pp. 107–108). My colleagues at nearby Norwich University host an annual "World Languages Fair" that usually coincides with UNESCO's International Mother Language Day.[6] They have built on this event with several student-led campaigns on social media.[7]
- **Community Engagement:** A number of universities have established school-community partnerships, such as the *Language and Life Project*[8] at North Carolina State University (p. 95) and the SKILLS program[9] at the University of California, Santa Barbara (see Figure 10.1). Both of these projects support students in conducting sociolinguistics research that is then shared with public audiences.

Although I have not yet established this level of partnership, some of my classes include community engagement: In Fall 2021, my first-year students in "Language and Social Justice" collaborated with **heritage language programs** run through my local school district in Burlington, Vermont, helping with publicity, assessment, and materials development for the program.

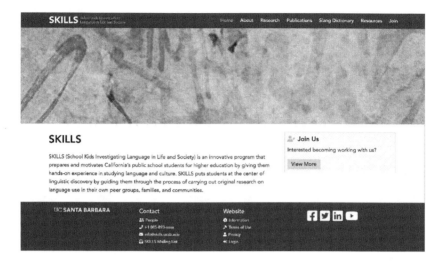

Figure 10.1 Screenshot of Homepage for UCSB's SKILLS Program

Figure 10.2 Photo from a Community Event Sponsored by Middlebury College's Language in Motion. Photo credit to Jason Duquette-Hoffman

I have also served as a faculty advisor or informal consultant for several **student-run organizations**, including: 1) Language in Motion,[10] which works with local public schools to offer global, cross-cultural, and multilingual learning opportunities (see Figure 10.2) and 2) Juntos,[11] which does education and advocacy work with Spanish-speaking migrant farmworkers.

I hope readers will visit the Hub to share their own examples of resources and opportunities that can promote and build on CLA learning!

CLA and Faculty Development

Many of us oversee or contribute to faculty development at our institutions, and conversations with colleagues often include questions about working with multilingual and/or multidialectal writers. Below are some suggestions for infusing CLA into these conversations:

Name the Tensions

Many faculty in other disciplines experience the tension between progressivism and pragmatism—one of the key issues we examine in a CLA approach—quite acutely, as reflected in representative scenarios like these:

A   A mathematics teacher is aware that many English Learners are struggling in her courses. She wants to support them but feels she has **very little room for adaptation.** Her course materials, assessments, and pacing are all predetermined. How can she support students within these curricular constraints?

B   A philosophy teacher has noticed that many of his international students are **reluctant to speak during class discussion.** He knows that there may be linguistic and cultural reasons for this, but it does not seem fair to him to give those students a "pass" on speaking in class. What is the fair thing to do?

C   A group of geography and history teachers have become increasingly concerned about **plagiarism in student writing.** They voted to adopt a "zero tolerance" policy that has resulted in harsh disciplinary action for several students—and a sharp rise in student stress levels. What other options might be available?

A starting place for talking through each of these scenarios is to **name the tensions** that are at play: Most faculty want to be student-centered in their approach, but they often worry about fairness and feasibility of any accommodations. Naming these values—and suggesting the possibility of a "both/and" approach—can be a helpful bridge into the conversation.

Ask Thoughtful Questions

Albert Einstein is reputed to have said: "If I had only one hour to save the world, I would spend 55 minutes defining the problem and five minutes solving it."[12] Sometimes the most useful thing we can do for our colleagues is to help them articulate the problem more clearly. We do this by asking **questions that are both curious and critical.** Below are some of the questions I might ask in response to each of the above scenarios, with a brief rationale:

Scenario A:

* *What patterns have you noticed among the students who struggle the most?* (This helps us to define the problem more clearly and to avoid generalizations about large groups of students.)
* *What resources/strategies have past students said they find most helpful?* (This focuses the conversation on student assets and may encourage the colleague to solicit more direct feedback from students.)
* *What activities/assignments do you use for formative assessment—i.e., prior to exams or high-stakes assignments?* (Check-ins and other formative assessments often provide more fine-grained information on student learning—and help to keep students on track.)

Scenario B:

* *How do you define "participation," and what role does it play in the learning process?* (This elicits more information on the instructor's assumptions about what counts as "participation" and may open up some additional possibilities.)
* *What have students shared with you about the barriers or challenges to participation?* (This question helps to define the program and also serves as a gentle reminder to solicit feedback directly from students, which sometimes reveals issues faculty were not aware of, such as difficulty with academic reading [pp. 293–296].)
* *Have you noticed any differences in student participation when you use smaller groupings or asynchronous online discussion?* (This helps to identify the

specific barriers to large group discussion, and also raises the possibility of other means of engagement, as discussed in Chapters 8 and 9.)

Scenario C:

- *What kinds of plagiarism have you been seeing in student writing?* (Some instances, such as copying an entire paper, are much more egregious than others, but others are less straightforward—e.g., a student's paraphrase was too similar to the original text. See Mott-Smith et al. [2017] for more on types of plagiarism.)
- *What sorts of check-ins have you built into the writing process?* (Often, including more scaffolding in the writing process results in fewer instances of plagiarism, since students are more likely to stay on track and to ask for assistance as needed.)

For more suggestions related to this third scenario, check out my (2021) article with source-use expert Zuzana Tomaš, entitled "From Crisis to Opportunity: Turning Questions about Plagiarism into Conversations about Linguistically Responsive Pedagogy."

Use Accessible and Memorable Language

One of the biggest mistakes we can make in pedagogical conversations with faculty colleagues is to use inaccessible language. Throughout this volume, I have provided examples of clear and memorable linguistic framing that resonates with colleagues who are not specialists in writing or linguistics. In Chapter 9, I used several analogies to explain particular concepts (e.g., difficult dialogue is like a strenuous hike, previewing a reading is like putting together the border pieces of a puzzle). And in the section on responding to student writing, I introduced several rules of thumb, including:

- Quality over quantity (of comments on student writing)
- Choice over voice (when talking about language issues)
- Clarity over correctness (when providing sentence-level feedback)

The language play here is intentional, because I want my words to have rhetorical staying power, particularly when it comes to high-stakes issues such as assessment. Of course, it would be impossible—and probably quite annoying—to turn all of our pedagogical suggestions into quippy mnemonics. But there are few things as gratifying as hearing a colleague say, "That line you had about . . . really stuck with me!"

Offer Multiple Modes for Engagement

Finally, just as we offer multiple modes for students to engage in course learning, as discussed in Chapter 8, we want to offer faculty a variety of opportunities for engagement around writing pedagogy. Research suggests that we need sustained, incentivized professional learning in order to create lasting curricular and pedagogical changes across our institutions (e.g., Cox et al., 2018; Phuong et al., 2018). At the online Hub, I will be sharing more about what I do to incorporate CLA into faculty development—and I hope to hear from you on this topic as well!

Linking CLA to Other DEI Work

Faculty development is just one of the ways we can support diversity, equity, and inclusion (DEI) at our institutions. Many of us are involved with other DEI work as well, such as strategic planning, policy-writing, and institutional research. Here are some ways we can bring CLA into that work:

Unpack the Buzzwords

In Chapter 7 (p. 233), we talked about the importance of unpacking our educational buzzwords. Indeed, research suggests that terms like "diversity" and "inclusion" are often conflated (e.g., Shapiro, 2020; Tienda, 2013). How can we set goals in these areas—and hold ourselves accountable for achieving those goals—if we do not even understand what we are aspiring toward?

One of the most helpful—and quippy—clarifications I have heard is that **diversity** is "counting people" while **inclusion** is "making people count."[13] In other words, it is what we *do with diversity* that makes our classrooms and campuses more inclusive (e.g., Strayhorn, 2018; Tienda, 2013). **Equity,** moreover, involves leveling the playing field—i.e., identifying and addressing the systemic barriers to success for particular groups of students (e.g., American Association of Colleges & Universities[14]).[15]

Collect Data about Linguistic Diversity

As we talked about in Unit 5.3, a pluralist orientation to language includes highlighting linguistic diversity as an asset in our schools and classrooms.

But to do this, we need to know more about our students' language backgrounds. Most K–12 schools in the U.S. collect data on students' home language(s), but this information is used more for measuring needs—such as for English Learner support—than to identify educational assets (Bailey & Kelly, 2013). And most higher education institutions collect little if any data on students' language backgrounds (Hall, 2014). We can fill in gaps in our institutional knowledge by using **language surveys** (e.g., Lorimer Leonard et al., 2021) or other data collection methods, such as interviews, which were the basis for the *Valuing Written Accents* project[16] at George Mason University. It can be useful as well to collect data on language backgrounds of faculty and staff (Hall, 2014; Ruecker et al., 2018).

Evaluate the Impact of Institutional Policies

A CLA orientation also asks that we think critically about the impact of our policies, to ensure that they are inclusive and equitable for students from all language backgrounds. Some questions we need to be asking are:

- Are multilingual (and multidialectal) students **treated fairly** when it comes to admissions, financial aid, advising/placement, and registration? If some groups are **treated differently** (e.g., required to submit test scores, placed in special classes) how can we measure the impact of that differential treatment? (e.g., Shapiro, 2012)
- How **transparent** are we with students (and families, in the case of K–12 schools) about our policies and procedures? Do they have **options** and **opportunities for feedback** when it comes to their academic decision-making? (Kanno, 2018; Saenkhum, 2016)
- Do we offer particular **resources** tailored to the needs of multilingual and/or multidialectal writers? If so, what feedback can we collect from students to ensure that these supports are effective?
- Are there ways our institutional structures and policies can more explicitly treat **language difference as an asset**? (For example, some institutions award academic credit for English Learner and/or heritage language classes—e.g., Liu et al., 2011; Melles et al., 2005).
- Are there disparities in **academic, co-curricular, or extra-curricular participation** for particular groups of students? What are the barriers to equal participation in honors classes, pre-professional programs, work/internship opportunities, community engagement, study abroad, etc.? (Im et al., 2016; Silver, 2020).[17]

Highlight Links Between CLA and Other Institutional Priorities

Many academic institutions have issued statements of purpose, strategic plans, and other institutional documents that articulate priorities such as internationalization, anti-racism, social justice, and/or decolonizing the curriculum. Yet *language* **often gets overlooked** as an important strand within these sorts of initiatives. For example, many institutions decide to increase their number of international student admits without any plan for supporting for those students' academic and social integration (Shapiro et al., 2014/2018). Or, they claim to be committed to anti-racism, but do little to promote equity and inclusion for multidialectal students from Black, Indigenous, and People of Color (BIPOC) communities.[18] A CLA approach urges us to make sure that issues of language, identity, power, and privilege are not left out of these institution-wide conversations.

For one example of how we can link writing/language support to larger institutional initiatives, check out the online teaching guide[19] coordinated by Megan Siczek, who directs the English for Academic Purposes Program at George Washington University. The guide uses the frame of "Global Diversity" as a bridge into talking about how faculty can support international and multilingual students (see Figure 10.3).

We can also bring CLA into discussions about **recruitment and retention of faculty** from diverse linguistic backgrounds. In other work (Howell et al., 2020[20]), I share how I have responded to administrators' questions about

Figure 10.3 Screenshot of GW Faculty Resource Page

whether it was appropriate to reject a job candidate because of minor grammar errors in their cover letter (the answer is NO, by the way!). Racial and linguistic biases often play a role in how students evaluate faculty on their teaching, as we explored a bit in Unit 5.3. Growing awareness of this concern has led some institutions to add implicit bias statements to course evaluation forms (Flaherty, 2019[21]). Multilingual faculty may also face additional barriers to publishing their scholarship (e.g., Politzer-Ahles et al., 2020), which suggests a need for **mentoring and logistical support**. I have no doubt that there are many other ways that CLA and DEI work intersect—another topic I hope we will explore more at the Hub!

CLA for Life!

In Chapter 3, I cited one of my favorite quotes about language, attributed to Rabbi Heschel: "Words create worlds." But there are proverbs about the power of language in virtually every community. To conclude this chapter, and this book as a whole, I want to highlight some research findings documenting this powerful role of language in our lives, in order to suggest that we can take CLA with us wherever we go!

Language and Mental Health

Research is inconclusive about the extent to which speaking a particular language shapes our thinking and behaviors (we touched on this in Chapter 4— see the Linguistic Society of America[22] for a brief overview). However, as we began talking about in Unit 7.1, psychological studies have identified a variety of linguistic strategies that can improve our mental and emotional health. For example:

1   **Naming emotions** (e.g., "anger" vs. "disappointment") can help us to understand and manage our emotional reactions; some psychologists call this effect "Name it to tame it" (e.g., Aldao, 2014[23]; Lindquist, 2009)

2   **Talking to ourselves** as if we were conversing with a friend or loved one (including using "you," rather than "I") can enhance our ability to observe and even shape our thought patterns (e.g., Kross et al., 2014; Starecheski, 2014[24])

3   **Expressing gratitude, appreciation, and awe**—including in writing— can decrease stress and increase long-term happiness (e.g., Emmons, 2007; Toepfer et al., 2012)

4   **Telling and reframing stories of difficulty** can help us to heal from trauma and/or loss (e.g., Esfahani Smith, 2021; Perry & Winfrey, 2021)—indeed, "narrative therapy"[25] is its own specialization within psychology!

Language and Physical Health

Research in other areas of healthcare has also attended more closely to language in recent years (Franz & Murphy, 2018). Here are some interesting findings:

1   **Self-talk** can be adapted in order to help manage chronic pain (Luo et al., 2020) and to increase physical endurance (e.g., Hardy et al., 2015)
2   **Linguistic framing** can harness the placebo effect by shifting patient "mindset" about disease and treatment (e.g., Crum & Zuckerman, 2017, which cites a highly publicized study with hotel housekeepers that was picked up by NPR[26] and other news venues)
3   **Use of humanizing language** can improve treatment outcomes for patients struggling with alcoholism (Kelly et al., 2016), diabetes (Dickinson et al., 2017), and other stigmatized conditions

Language in Relationships

In Chapter 7, we explored the power of language in interpersonal interactions at home and school. Indeed, research has shown that relatively small linguistic choices can help us to work through conflicts with family, friends, and co-workers (e.g., Guerrero et al., 2020; Gottman & Gottman, 2018[27]; Perel, 2020[28]). Here are a few well-documented linguistic strategies—some of which you probably use already!

• Listening to understand, rather than to criticize or give advice
• Making "I" and "we" statements rather than "you" statements
• Avoiding universals (e.g., "You always/never. . . ") and instead focusing on a specific situation or behavior
• Offering apologies that are specific, authentic, and non-defensive

There are so many wonderful podcasts and other resources talking about the role of language in relationships—I hope we can swap suggestions at the Hub!

Language and Civic Life

A final area I want to touch on here is the role that language plays—and could play—in civic life, by which I mean public conversations within communities. Research has found that strategies from family therapy and conflict mediation are often useful in civic conversations (e.g., Chasin et al., 1996). Below are a few concepts from earlier chapters that experts have suggested might be useful in navigating public life together[29]:

- *Debate* vs. *dialogue* (e.g., Hyde & Bineham, 2000)
- *Calling in* vs. *calling out* (Ross, 2019; Woods & Ruscher, 2021).
- *Shame resilience* (e.g., Burke & Brown, 2021)
- *Micro-affirmations* (Rowe, 2008)

By investing in self-reflection, social justice, and rhetorical agency in our daily lives—as well as in our classrooms and curricula—we plant seeds that may one day flourish in a more vibrant and inclusive civic life!

Building Communities of Practice

My vision—and the main reason I wanted to write this book—is to help build communities of practice around CLA Pedagogy. I am convinced that CLA can bring together teachers and students across education levels (primary, secondary, postsecondary, and community programs), disciplines (English language arts, writing/composition, ESOL, world/heritage language, and others), and geographic borders. I know it is not a pedagogical panacea—there is no such thing! But I do see great potential for CLA as a tool for building bridges across communities.

When I am feeling my most optimistic, I wonder. . .

- What if CLA could help us articulate a shared curricular vision for what we want students to know and do as language users across grade levels, from pre-K through post-graduate education?
- How could we infuse CLA into professional preparation for all teachers, administrators, and educational policy-makers?
- What if the "both/and" framing of CLA could help start to re-shape the culture of U.S. education, making it less prone to binaries, band-wagoning, and pendulum swings?

These are big questions, for sure—but I'm not the only person asking them! (e.g., Gere et al., 2021; Godley & Reaser, 2018). I envision the online Hub as a virtual gathering space where we can engage these and other essential questions related to CLA Pedagogy. I want the Hub to become a place not only for sharing materials, but also for engaging in real dialogue about our challenges and critiques. I'm curious about what works—and what doesn't—with *your* students in *your* particular context! I want to know what resources you are using, and what additional resources we might share or even create together. I also want those of us who are engaged in educational research—or who would like to be!—to connect, so that we can continue mapping out a scholarly agenda to build new knowledge about CLA and CLA Pedagogy.

Conclusion

We have arrived at the end of our journey for this book. But for me—and perhaps for you too, dear reader—it feels more like a beginning. I hope you are coming away with a fuller toolkit of concepts, strategies, and resources that will allow you to integrate CLA into your classroom, curriculum, and other work. I also hope this book has heightened your desire to learn more about how to engage in critical conversations about language, identity, privilege, and power as teachers, scholars, and community members.

Thank you for taking the time to join me in this exploration.

I can't wait to hear about what you are doing, or planning to do, with CLA Pedagogy!

Please be in touch—I look forward to learning from you!

—*Shawna*

Notes

1 www.mla.org/Resources/Research/Surveys-Reports-and-Other-Documents/Tea ching-Enrollments-and-Programs/Enrollments-in-Languages-Other-Than-English-in-United-States-Institutions-of-Higher-Education
2 www.oratorynow.org/
3 www.middlebury.edu/newsroom/archive/2018-news/node/562751
4 www.facebook.com/Translingual
5 We may need to consult with judging committees about how to evaluate this sort of work, and with the student about adding some reader-friendly features such as an introduction/rationale and an English translation or explanatory footnotes.
6 www.norwich.edu/news/2190-norwich-university-world-languages-fair-interna tional-center-modern-languages

7 http://newsmanager.commpartners.com/tesolheis/issues/2019-05-13/3.html
8 https://languageandlife.org/
9 www.skills.ucsb.edu/
10 www.middlebury.edu/office/community-engagement/programs/signature-programs/language-motion
11 https://middlebury.presence.io/organization/juntos
12 Unfortunately, no one has been able to trace this widely cited quote directly to Einstein's writing. But I still love the quote!
13 I first learned this framing from Middlebury's Director of Education for Equity and Inclusion, Renee Wells, who said it's practically a cliché among DEI folks. But it was new—and helpful—to me!
14 www.aacu.org/making-excellence-inclusive
15 For more explanation of these terms, check out this podcast conversation between Brené Brown and DEI expert Aiko Bethea: https://brenebrown.com/podcast/brene-with-aiko-bethea-on-inclusivity-at-work-the-heart-of-hard-conversations/
16 https://writtenaccents.gmu.edu/
17 One of the concerns raised by international and undocumented students at Middlebury in recent years, for example, is that many the internships we advertise to students exclude non-U.S. citizens.
18 This argument is articulated powerfully in the NCTE/CCCC statement on Black Linguistic Justice, which we have touched on in several other chapters: https://cccc.ncte.org/cccc/demand-for-black-linguistic-justice
19 http://go.gwu.edu/globaldiversity
20 Here's the URL to that section of the article: https://compositionforum.com/issue/44/embracing.php#shawna
21 www.insidehighered.com/news/2019/05/20/fighting-gender-bias-student-evaluations-teaching-and-tenures-effect-instruction
22 www.linguisticsociety.org/resource/language-and-thought
23 www.psychologytoday.com/us/blog/sweet-emotion/201408/why-labeling-emotions-matters
24 www.npr.org/sections/health-shots/2014/10/07/353292408/why-saying-is-believing-the-science-of-self-talk
25 www.psychologytoday.com/us/therapy-types/narrative-therapy
26 www.npr.org/templates/story/story.php?storyId=17792517
27 John and Julie Gottman, two of the most well-known experts on intimacy in relationships, have synthesized much of this research at their Gottman Institute website: www.gottman.com/
28 https://estherperel.com/ includes links to a variety of resources, including Perel's podcasts "Where Should We Begin" and "How's Work?", which I highly recommend!
29 One of my favorite online resources in this area is the On Being Project, led by Krista Tippett, which includes a number of initiatives and resources focused on public/civic conversations: https://onbeing.org/civil-conversations-project/

References

Aldao, A. (2014, August 8). Why labeling emotions matters: An at-home experiment on emotion labeling. *Psychology Today*. www.psychologytoday.com/us/blog/sweet-emotion/201408/why-labeling-emotions-matters

Bailey, A. L., & Kelly, K. R. (2013). Home language survey practices in the initial identification of English learners in the United States. *Educational Policy, 27*(5), 770–804.

Baker-Bell, A. (2020). *Linguistic justice: Black language, literacy, identity, and pedagogy.* Routledge.

Beaudrie, S., Amezcua, A., & Loza, S. (2019). Critical language awareness for the heritage context: Development and validation of a measurement questionnaire. *Language Testing, 36*(4), 573–594.

Britton, E. R., & Lorimer Leonard, R. (2020). The social justice potential of critical reflection and critical language awareness pedagogies for L2 writers. *Journal of Second Language Writing, 50,* 100776.

Burke, T., & Brown, B. (2021). *You are your best thing: Vulnerability, shame resilience, and the Black experience.* Penguin, Random House.

Carpenter, B. D., Achugar, M., Walter, D., & Earhart, M. (2015). Developing teachers' critical language awareness: A case study of guided participation. *Linguistics and Education, 32,* 82–97. https://doi.org/10.1016/j.linged.2015.03.016

Chang, S., Torres-Guzmán, M. E., & Waring, H. Z. (2020). Experiencing critical language awareness as a collective struggle: Methodological innovations in language awareness workshops. *The Language Learning Journal, 48*(3), 356–369. https://doi.org/10.1080/09571736.2020.1740769

Chasin, R., Herzig, M., Roth, S., Chasin, L., Becker, C., & Stains Jr, R. R. (1996). From diatribe to dialogue on divisive public issues: Approaches drawn from family therapy. *Mediation Quarterly, 13*(4), 323–344.

Chen, J. Q., & McCray, J. (2012). A conceptual framework for teacher professional development: The whole teacher approach. *NHSA Dialog, 15*(1), 8–23.

Cox, M., Galin, J., & Melzer, D. (2018). Building sustainable WAC programs: A whole systems approach. *The WAC Journal, 29,* 64–87. https://wac.colostate.edu/docs/journal/vol29/cox.pdf

Crum, A., & Zuckerman, B. (2017). Changing mindsets to enhance treatment effectiveness. *Journal of the American Medical Association, 317*(20), 2063–2064.

Deroo, M. R., & Ponzio, C. M. (2021). Fostering pre-service teachers' critical multilingual language awareness: Use of multimodal compositions to confront hegemonic language ideologies. *Journal of Language, Identity & Education,* 1–17.

Dickinson, J. K., Guzman, S. J., Maryniuk, M. D., O'Brian, C. A., Kadohiro, J. K., Jackson, R. A., D'Hondt, R., Montgomery, B, Close, K., & Funnel, M. M. (2017). The use of language in diabetes care and education. *The Diabetes Educator, 43*(6), 551–564.

Emmons, R. A. (2007). *Thanks!: How the new science of gratitude can make you happier.* Houghton Mifflin Harcourt.

Endo, R. (2015). From unconscious deficit views to affirmation of linguistic varieties in the classroom: White preservice teachers on building critical self-awareness about linguicism's causes and consequences. *Multicultural Perspectives, 17*(4), 207–214.

Enright, K. A., & Gilliland, B. (2011). Multilingual writing in an age of accountability: From policy to practice in US high school classrooms. *Journal of Second Language Writing, 20*(3), 182–195.

Esfahani Smith, E. (2021, June 24). We want to travel and party. Hold that thought. *New York Times.* https://www.nytimes.com/2021/06/24/opinion/covid-pandemic-grief.html

Flaherty, C. (2019, May 20). Teaching evals: Bias and tenure. *Inside Higher Ed.* www.insidehighered.com/news/2019/05/20/fighting-gender-bias-student-evaluations-teaching-and-tenures-effect-instruction

Franz, B., & Murphy, J. W. (2018). Reconsidering the role of language in medicine. *Philosophy, Ethics, and Humanities in Medicine, 13*(1), 1–7.

Gasca Jiménez, L., & Adrada-Rafael, S. (2021). Understanding heritage language learners' critical language awareness (CLA) in mixed language programs. *Languages, 6*(1), 37.

Gere, A., Curzan, A., Hammond, J. W., Hughes, S., Li, R., Moos, A., Smith, K., Van Zanen, K., Wheeler, K. L., & Zanders, C. J. (2021). Communal justicing: Writing assessment, disciplinary infrastructure, and the case for critical language awareness. *College Composition and Communication, 72*(3), 384–412.

Godley, A. J., & Reaser, J. (2018). *Critical language pedagogy: Interrogating language, dialects, and power in teacher education.* Peter Lang.

Godley, A. J., Reaser, J., & Moore, K. G. (2015). Pre-service English language arts teachers' development of critical language awareness for teaching. *Linguistics and Education, 32*, 41–54. https://doi.org/10.1016/j.linged.2015.03.015

Gottman, J. M., & Gottman, J. S. (2018). *The science of couples and family therapy: Behind the scenes at the "love lab".* WW Norton & Company.

Guerrero, L. K., Andersen, P. A., & Afifi, W. A. (2020). *Close encounters: Communication in relationships* (6th ed.). Sage Publications.

Hall, J. (2014). Language background and the college writing course. *Journal of Writing Assessment, 7*(1). www.journalofwritingassessment.org/article.php?article=77

Hardy, J., Begley, K., & Blanchfield, A. W. (2015). It's good but it's not right: Instructional self-talk and skilled performance. *Journal of Applied Sport Psychology, 27*(2), 132–139.

Holguín Mendoza, C. (2018). Critical language awareness (CLA) for Spanish heritage language programs: Implementing a complete curriculum. *International Multilingual Research Journal, 12*(2), 65–79.

Howell, N. G., Navickas, K., Shapiro, R., Shapiro, S., & Watson, M. (2020). Embracing the perpetual "but" in raciolinguistic justice work: When idealism meets practice. *Composition Forum, 44.* http://compositionforum.com/issue/44/embracing.php

Huang, S. Y. (2013). Revising identities as writers and readers through critical language awareness. *English Teaching: Practice & Critique, 12*(3), 65–86.

Hyde, B., & Bineham, J. L. (2000). From debate to dialogue: Toward a pedagogy of nonpolarized public discourse. *Southern Journal of Communication*, 65(2–3), 208–223.

Im, M. H., Hughes, J. N., Cao, Q., & Kwok, O. M. (2016). Effects of extracurricular participation during middle school on academic motivation and achievement at grade 9. *American Educational Research Journal*, 53(5), 1343–1375.

Inoue, A. B. (2015). *Antiracist writing assessment ecologies: Teaching and assessing writing for a socially just future*. Parlor Press. https://wac.colostate.edu/books/pers pectives/inoue/

Kanno, Y. (2018). High-performing English learners' limited access to four-year college. *Teachers College Record*, 120(4), 1–46.

Kelly, J. F., Saitz, R., & Wakeman, S. (2016). Language, substance use disorders, and policy: The need to reach consensus on an "addiction-ary". *Alcoholism Treatment Quarterly*, 34(1), 116–123.

Kross, E., Bruehlman-Senecal, E., Park, J., Aleah Burson, A., Dougherty, A., Shablack, H., Bremner, R., Jason Moser, J., & Ayduk, O. (2014). Self-talk as a regulatory mechanism: How you do it matters. *Journal of Personality and Social Psychology*, 106(2), 301–324.

Lape, N. (2019). From English-centric to multilingual: The Norman M. Eberly multilingual writing center at Dickinson college. *Composition Forum*, 41. http:// compositionforum.com/issue/41/dickinson.php

Lindquist, K. A. (2009). Language is powerful. *Emotion Review*, 1(1), 16–18.

Liu, N., Musica, A., Koscak, S., Vinogradova, P., & López, J. (2011). Challenges and needs of community-based heritage language programs and how they are addressed. *Heritage Briefs*, 1–18.

Lorimer Leonard, R., Bruce, S., & Vinyard, D. (2021). Finding complexity in language identity surveys. *Journal of Language, Identity & Education*, 1–14.

Luo, X., Liu, J., & Che, X. (2020). Investigating the influence and a potential mechanism of self-compassion on experimental pain: Evidence from a compassionate self-talk protocol and heart rate variability. *The Journal of Pain*, 21(7–8), 790–797.

Macintyre, C. (2012). *The art of action research in the classroom*. Routledge.

Mallinson, C., & Hudley, A. H. C. (2018). Balancing the communication equation: An outreach and engagement model for using sociolinguistics to enhance culturally and linguistically sustaining K—12 STEM education. *Language*, 94(3), e191–e215.

Melles, G., Millar, G., Morton, J., & Fegan, S. (2005). Credit-based discipline specific English for academic purposes programmes in higher education: Revitalizing the profession. *Arts and Humanities in Higher Education*, 4(3), 283–303.

Metz, M. (2018). Pedagogical content knowledge for teaching critical language awareness: The importance of valuing student knowledge. *Urban Education*, https://doi.org/10.0042085918756714

Metz, M. (2019). Accommodating linguistic prejudice? Examining English teachers' language ideologies. *English Teaching: Practice & Critique*, 18(1), 18–35.

Mott-Smith, J., Tomaš, Z., & Kostka, I. (2017). *Teaching effective source use: Classroom approaches that work.* University of Michigan Press.

Nieto, S. (2017). *Language, culture, and teaching: Critical perspectives* (3rd ed.). Routledge.

Perel, E. (2020). *Letters from Estel #4: Relationship dynamics in the workplace.* https://www.estherperel.com/blog/letters-from-esther-4

Perry, B., & Winfrey, O. (2021). *What happened to you? Conversations on trauma, resilience, and healing.* Macmillan.

Phuong, T. T., Cole, S. C., & Zarestky, J. (2018). A systematic literature review of faculty development for teacher educators. *Higher Education Research & Development, 37*(2), 373–389.

Politzer-Ahles, S., Girolamo, T., & Ghali, S. (2020). Preliminary evidence of linguistic bias in academic reviewing. *Journal of English for Academic Purposes, 47,* 100895.

Ross, L. (2019, Spring). Speaking up without tearing down. *Learning for Justice, 61.* www.learningforjustice.org/magazine/spring-2019/speaking-up-without-tearing-down

Rowe, M. (2008). Micro-affirmations and micro-inequities. *Journal of the International Ombudsman Association, 1*(1), 45–48.

Ruecker, T., Frazier, S., & Tseptsura, M. (2018). "Language difference can be an asset": Exploring the experiences of nonnative English-speaking teachers of writing. *College Composition and Communication, 69*(4), 612–641.

Saenkhum, T. (2016). *Decisions, agency, and advising: Key issues in the placement of multilingual writers into first-year composition courses.* University Press of Colorado.

Serafini, E. J. (forthcoming). Assessing students through a CLA framework. In S. Beaudrie & S. Loza (Eds.), *Teaching languages critically.* Routledge.

Shapiro, S. (2010). Revisiting the teachers' lounge: Reflections on emotional experience and teacher identity. *Teaching and Teacher Education, 26*(3), 616–621.

Shapiro, S. (2012). Citizens vs. aliens: How institutional policies construct linguistic minority students. In Y. Kanno & L. Harklau (Eds.), *Linguistic minority immigrants go to college: Preparation, access, and persistence* (pp. 238–254). Routledge.

Shapiro, S. (2020). Inclusive pedagogy in the academic writing classroom: Cultivating communities of belonging. *Journal of Academic Writing, 10*(1), 154–164.

Shapiro, S., Farrelly, R., & Tomaš, Z. (2014/2018). *Fostering International Student Success in Higher Education.* TESOL Press, Co-published with NAFSA.

Shi, L., & Rolstad, K. (2020). "A good start": A new approach to gauging preservice teachers' critical language awareness. *Journal of Language, Identity & Education,* 1–15.

Silver, B. R. (2020). Inequality in the extracurriculum: How class, race, and gender shape college involvement. *Sociological Forum, 35*(4), 1290–1314.

Starecheski, L. (2014, October 7). Why saying is believing: The science of self-talk. *National Public Radio.* www.npr.org/sections/health-shots/2014/10/07/353292408/why-saying-is-believing-the-science-of-self-talk

Strayhorn, T. L. (2018). *College students' sense of belonging: A key to educational success for all students.* Routledge.

Tienda, M. (2013). Diversity≠ inclusion: Promoting integration in higher education. *Educational Researcher, 42*(9), 467–475.

Toepfer, S. M., Cichy, K., & Peters, P. (2012). Letters of gratitude: Further evidence for author benefits. *Journal of Happiness Studies, 13*(1), 187–201.

Tomaš, Z., & Shapiro, S. (2021). From crisis to opportunity: Turning questions about plagiarism into conversations about pedagogy. *TESOL Quarterly.*

Weaver, M. M. (2019). "I still think there's a need for proper, academic, standard English": Examining a teacher's negotiation of multiple language ideologies. *Linguistics and Education, 49,* 41–51.

Woodard, R., & Rao, A. (2020). Tensions and possibilities in fostering critical language ideologies in elementary teacher education. *Studying Teacher Education, 16*(2), 183–203.

Woods, F. A., & Ruscher, J. B. (2021). "Calling-out" vs. "calling-in" prejudice: Confrontation style affects inferred motive and expected outcomes. *British Journal of Social Psychology, 60*(1), 50–73.

Index

Note: Page numbers in *italics* indicate a figure and page numbers in **bold** indicate a table on the corresponding page.